WHEN LAW GOES POP

Richard K. Sherwin

WHEN **LAW** GOES **POP**

The Vanishing Line between Law and Popular Culture

THE UNIVERSITY OF CHICAGO PRESS

CHICAGO AND LONDON

RICHARD K. SHERWIN is professor of law at New York Law
School.

The University of Chicago Press, Chicago 60637
The University of Chicago Press, Ltd., London
© 2000 by The University of Chicago
All rights reserved. Published 2000
Printed in the United States of America

09 08 07 06 05 04 03 02 01 00   1 2 3 4 5
ISBN: 0-226-75291-7 (cloth)

An earlier version of chapter 5 appeared in "Law Frames: Historical truth and narrative necessity in a criminal case," *Stanford
Law Review* 47 (1994): 39–83, © by the Board of Trustees of the
Leland Stanford Junior University. Some of the film analyses contained in chapter 7 have also appeared previously, in slightly different form, in my essays "Cape Fear: Law's inversion and cathartic justice," *University of San Francisco Law Review* 30 (1996):
1023–50, © 1996 University of San Francisco School of Law, and
"Framed" in John Denvir, ed., *Legal Reelism* (Urbana: University
of Illinois Press, 1996), 84–90.

Library of Congress Cataloging-in-Publication Data

Sherwin, Richard K.
    When law goes pop : the vanishing line between law and
    popular culture / Richard K. Sherwin.
      p.   cm.
    Includes bibliographical references and index.
    ISBN 0-226-75291-7 (cloth : alk. paper)
    1. Practice of law—United States. 2. Lawyers in popular
culture—United States. I. Title.

    KF300.S48   2000
    347.73'504—dc21
                                                    99-086010

∞ The paper used in this publication meets the minimum
requirements of the American National Standard for
Information Sciences—Permanence of Paper for Printed
Library Materials, ANSI Z39.48-1992.

To David and Elliana

CONTENTS

Preface   ix

Acknowledgments   xi

ONE   Introduction: Law in the Age of Images   3

TWO   Screening Reality: The Vanishing Line between Law and Popular Culture   15

THREE   Legal Storytelling: Culture's Tools for Making Meaning   41

FOUR   The Law of Desire: Cultural History and the Notorious Case   73

FIVE   The Postmodern Challenge: A Case Study   107

SIX   The Jurisprudence of Appearances: Law as Commodity   141

SEVEN   When Law Goes Pop: Strange Forces, Trauma, and Catharsis   171

EIGHT   Law's Need for Enchantment: Perils and Possibilities   205

NINE   Conclusion: Redrawing the Line between Belief and Suspicion   235

Notes   265

Index   305

PREFACE

Law in our time has entered the age of images. Legal reality can no longer be properly understood, or assessed, apart from what appears on the screen. Consider the videotaped grand jury testimony of an American president facing impeachment. Millions of TV viewers look on as the nation's chief executive struggles to define intimate sex acts and to fend off charges that he lied under oath about his conduct while alone in the company of a young White House intern. The next day the *New York Times* reports on the president's performance in a front-page article written by the paper's movie critic. In the course of her review the critic treats readers to illuminating comparisons between the videotape and filmmaker Louis Malle's *My Dinner with Andre*.

Or consider the students who, in the midst of a shootout at Columbine High School in Littleton, Colorado, use their cell phones to call a television station rather than the police to report on the violence taking place inside the school. Later we will see the same cluster of images play again and again on the screen: graphic shots of students injured or in shock, parents gripped by horror or grief. As the identical images cycle from network to network, one begins to wonder: are they meant to inform or are they, along with the victims they depict, being used to produce the sort of sensation that keeps us watching?

And what if the sensation the screen produces were to generate law—as it did in 1994, when Californians, riding a crest of outrage following the highly publicized kidnapping and murder of twelve-year-old Polly Klaas, overwhelmingly endorsed the nation's toughest crime bill ever, popularly known as "three strikes and you're out"? Only later, when the rush of retribution had eased, would the sobering consequences of their action begin to dawn. At the time the "three strikes" bill became law, California was already imprisoning a higher percentage of its citizens than any nation on earth. By June 1998, 20 percent of California's prison population had been sentenced under the new law. The juggernaut media campaign behind the law had stressed the need to keep violent felons in their cages. But the law's actual effects were far broader: as it turned out, 80 percent of the inmates subject to the law's mandatory 25-year-to-life sentencing provisions were nonviolent offenders.

Could this be what becomes of law in an age of ratings-driven images—"legal truth" and "justice" pitched to the emotional fervor of a grieving father? In such a time is it still possible to distinguish "pop law" and "pop truth" from their nonvirtual antecedents? The proliferation of electronic monitors inside the courtroom, and of strategic public relations campaigns as an adjunct to litigation in the court of public opinion, only heighten the concern. And it is unlikely to diminish anytime soon; if anything, it is likely to grow. Consider, for example, the plight of the trial judge who recently referred to a digitally constructed image as a "photograph." Surely the predicament of the jury, and of the general public, is no better. Something is up. And the old ways of thinking about law and legal practice are going to have to adapt to deal with the changes that are afoot.

In this book, I contend that it behooves us to consider with great care the legal implications of significant shifts in our storytelling practices. Such changes may betoken a collective change of mind and culture. Today the institutions of law, politics, and journalism have been radically transformed by such a change. Postmodern ideas, new communication technologies, and the unrestrained demands of the marketplace are converging with tremendous synergistic impact. Meanings are thinning out as they collapse into the popular. We see this in law as legal meanings increasingly yield to the compelling visual logic of film and TV images and by extension to the market forces that fuel their production. This is what happens when law, like politics, takes root in a culture of spectacle, when it mimics the communicative style and persuasive techniques of public relations.

As our ability to manipulate sounds and images for the sake of verisimilitude grows, a new anxiety haunts the popular imagination. What happens when the line between reality and fiction, reason and desire, fact and fantasy can no longer be drawn? What then becomes of life in the law?

In democratic societies each generation must face the task of working out anew the terms of law's legitimacy based on notions of individual dignity and respect that reflect current cultural conditions. This book represents an effort to understand those conditions a little better, and to help others meet the challenges that now lie in the path of the law.

ACKNOWLEDGMENTS

I have been unusually fortunate to have benefited from the advice and assistance of exceptional teachers, colleagues, and friends. It gives me great pleasure to acknowledge here my early mentors, Professor Mary Ann Glendon (now of Harvard Law School) and Professor Bruce Ackerman (now of Yale Law School), who inspired and encouraged my interdisciplinary approach to law; and Professors Arthur Berney and James Boyd White, who taught me to appreciate the humane spirit and culture-building force of the law. I also wish to acknowledge the exceptional collegial generosity of Professors Anthony G. Amsterdam and Jerome Bruner at the New York University Law School. I do not expect to encounter again in my lifetime the depth of learning, intellectual curiosity, and exemplary personal commitment to teaching and social involvement that they share. They taught me much, and their inspiration is enduring.

I especially want to thank Neal Feigenson for his numerous, characteristically sharp insights in response to reading these pages (and the all too many earlier versions that preceded them). I have benefited as well from conversations with, and comments by, Allan Boyer and Elayne Rapping, both of whom, in their own way, share my fascination with the culture of rhetoric. Many colleagues at New York Law School generously offered feedback on this work at various stages in its development. In particular, I wish to thank Steve Ellmann for giving me the opportunity to present an earlier version of chapter 3 at his Clinical Theory Workshop. I also wish to acknowledge the helpful comments of Robert Blecker, Michael Perlin, Rudy Peritz, and Ruti Teitel. In the face of an insipidly wide-ranging appetite for materials, Bill Mills of the New York Law School Library assisted me with an intrepid spirit and persistent good humor. I thank him for his superlative help. I also wish to acknowledge my assistant, Billie Coleman, who patiently helped me through several drafts. New York Law School provided me with generous financial assistance during several summers devoted to this project; I am most grateful for this support.

I also wish to acknowledge Charles Musser for his generous help in connection with my work on *The Thin Blue Line* and for providing me with an opportunity to share my ideas with the ever-insightful Columbia University film group. I also benefited greatly from the comments and enthusiasm of Natalie Zemon Davis and members of her "Proof and Persuasion" colloquium at Princeton University.

I owe a debt of gratitude to John Tryneski, my editor at University of Chicago Press, who discerned even before I did the broader implications of this work. It has been a pleasure working with him on this project. Two anonymous readers for the Press provided insightful readings of the manuscript and offered suggestions that improved the text. I would be remiss if I failed to express my gratitude to students in my Law and Popular Culture seminar who "test ran" a good deal of this material. They taught me many things about the new visual literacy and the challenges that attend the ancient rhetorical aspiration to combine eloquence and ethical wisdom.

Finally, I wish to thank my wife, Dr. Gilda Sherwin, whose support has extended far beyond her willingness to share the burdens, in time and effort, that accompanied the task of bringing this book to life. She also shared her deep psychoanalytic knowledge, her impeccable ear for right and wrong notes, her deeply humane spirit, her love, and at critical times her emotional strength. Words hardly suffice. I dedicate this book in the spirit of hope to my children, David and Elliana. They have been a constant source of wonder and inspiration.

WHEN LAW GOES POP

[T]he advertiser aims to stimulate, to satisfy and even to transform the tastes of his audience. . . . The truths the mathematician persuades us to accept are immutable and indubitable.

[R]hetoric starts from the assumption that there are meaningful truths "about the things which are just and unjust." . . . [It] is concerned with truths that are variable and obscure, and permanently subject to dispute, and it employs the passions as instruments of persuasion. . . .

Should we not concede that the rhetorician, mocked by the champions of both thought and power, has a respectable craft of his own, one that makes its own essential contribution to humanity?

ANTHONY T. KRONMAN,
"Rhetoric"

ONE

Introduction: Law in the Age of Images

It was by accident that I stumbled upon the path that led to this book. The journey began, simply enough, with a film, *The Thin Blue Line* (Miramax, 1988), Errol Morris's documentary account of a botched capital murder case in Dallas, Texas. As a former prosecutor and current professor of criminal procedure, I was struck by the variety of procedural errors depicted in the film. What a great review for my students at semester's end, I thought. "Spot the errors," I would tell them. It was dramatic, and the students were enthralled.

But then I began to wonder. Why was this film so convincing? After all, it wasn't just ordinary film viewers Morris managed to persuade. His film, which was based on interviews with the actual trial participants, triggered a formal reopening of the case. As a result of that review, the defendant was ultimately set free—after twelve years in prison, a good part of the time on death row. At last, the real story had emerged: a corrupt district attorney had persuaded a jury to convict an innocent man of murder and sentence him to death by electrocution. It's the story of an unlucky scapegoat, trapped in an unjust frame-up. What's left to doubt when truth and justice triumph in the end?

But not so fast. Something else is going on here, something that doesn't add up as easily as the clues in the mystery story Morris's film tells (*who framed Randall Dale Adams, and why?*). This is no simple documentary. In fact, the film is loaded with fictional devices, including simulations, dramatic reenactments, and humorous overlays of grade-B film clips—not to mention that entrancing Philip Glass soundtrack. So what's going on here? How could this Truman Capote-style narrative—a real-life crime story told with the tools of fiction—change the outcome in a real criminal case?[1]

That is the query around which this book began to take shape. For it was upon further reflection that I realized that the law is shot through with fiction. It is not simply the well-known use of legal fictions I am thinking of here, through which judges "correct" doctrinal rules to get the right result in a particular case.[2] What I have in mind is the fictional method of persuasion lawyers use to win cases, in court and out. It has always been so. Rhetoricians since the generation of Socrates taught their students as much (much to Socrates' dismay). Like contemporary postmodernists, these ancient teachers of politicians and lawyers also realized that reality was subject to de- (and re-)construction. Meanings could be shaped in ways that might incline the public or a jury to reach a desired opinion or judgment. And in the late European Renaissance, Sir Philip Sidney argued much the same thing in his defense of law's affinity with poetry and the fictional method.[3]

No, the intermingling of law and fiction, like the interpenetration of law and popular culture generally, is hardly new. But there is more to tell. For one thing, the kinds of fictions lawyers use, and the ways in which they are employed, vary from one generation to the next. Lawyers are storytellers, and the stories they tell reflect changes in the culture around them. Notorious trials are particularly useful barometers of such changes. As chapters 3 and 4 show, these are sites where deep cultural conflicts and anxieties are symbolically played out; they are enmeshed in the legal narratives we hear and (with increasing frequency these days) *see* at trial. We can tell this is so not only from the stories lawyers recount inside the courtroom, but also from the mass media's characteristic reconstructions of those stories in the court of public opinion. Notorious trials are richly overdetermined with latent meaning; we have but to attend closely. The rituals of meaning making they perform are not just for the parties concerned. These symbolic legal dramas make (as well as distort and repress) meanings that are of interest to society as a whole.

But there is more yet to be told. The legal stories we hear and see today, both in court and out, confront law and the legal process with new challenges. An unprecedented convergence is now under way among powerful cultural and economic forces. Constructivist ("postmodern") theory, communication technology, and the needs of the marketplace are coming together with tremendous synergistic impact. As a consequence of this impact we are seeing a marked destabilization in our sense of self, and in our social and legal reality. Legal meanings are flattening out as they yield to the compelling visual logic of film and TV images and the market forces that fuel their production.[4] In consequence, the customary balance within the legal system among disparate forms of knowledge, discourse, and power is under great strain, and is at risk of breaking down. For example, the virtues of the lay jury as a practical reflection of community values, expectations, and beliefs are well known.[5] So too are the virtues of judicial expertise and prudence, which operate at times as a countermajoritarian check on public opinion, particularly when the latter runs afoul of important legal principles such as due process, among other constitutional safeguards.[6] Under the influence of new modes of communication, however, these disparate forms of lay and expert knowledge, together with their respective virtues, are growing distorted. This is what we see when techniques of mass communication fold disparate meaning-making practices into the homogenous stories and images of popular culture. It is what happens when the active, offscreen dimension of lived experience and the varieties of common sense that it produces give way to the passive, self-gratification–enhancing, and image-based logic of commercial media. Then, the capacity for critical judgment—of external reality, of self and others, of truth and justice in the individual case, and of the media themselves—is significantly undercut.[7] We witness a similar institutional breakdown when the judiciary, in an effort to enhance its legitimacy, converges on the same set of images as the mass media. When that happens the courts' countermajoritarian function also breaks down. For then the courts too have internalized the image-based logic of popular culture.

In this book I will describe more fully these and other institutional distortions and the ways they affect law and the legal system generally. My conclusion is that what we are seeing today is no ordinary intermingling of law and popular culture, but a more generalized erosion of law's legitimacy. This is what happens when law goes *pop*.

We begin with the notion of culture as a symbolic order. Culture provides the signs, images, stories, characters, metaphors, and scenarios, among other familiar materials, with which we make sense of our lives and the world around us. Being part of a community means that we perceive or interpret events in overlapping ways using shared cognitive and cultural tools and materials. Law is such a community, with its own materials and preferred tools of analysis, its own practices and habits of mind. But it is also the case that law's stories and images and characters leach back into the culture at large. In this way, law is a coproducer of popular culture.[8]

Notorious trials such as those involving Bernhard Goetz, O. J. Simpson, or the Los Angeles police officers who beat Rodney King, like other notorious cases before them, tend to be absorbed into the vernacular of society. As such they often come to embody larger, sym-

bolic meanings. Will society tolerate acts of vigilante justice like Bernhard Goetz's shooting of four unarmed youths in a New York subway?
Is the legal process strong enough to resist the cult of celebrity that
attends a defendant like O. J. Simpson? Can it survive unharmed the
publicity and passions such a case arouses on top of the social and
legal questions it raises regarding racial prejudice and spousal abuse?
Can law in our time adapt to the reality-shaping power of mass-
marketed visual images without going the way of public relations and
media spin?

But this is still only part of the picture. No less significant (though
less well known) than the ways law stories leach back into the culture
at large are the various ways the materials and communicative styles
commonly found in mainstream culture leach into law.[9] Savvy trial
lawyers often tap, in order to direct strategically, the familiar meaning-
making tools and materials trial participants carry in their heads into
court. Familiar images, popular story forms, and recurring symbols,
together with a host of unconscious prejudices, impulses, and passions (including disguised or displaced feelings of rage and desire), are
all grist for the lawyer's storytelling mill. And as the dominant media
or technology of communication change, so too do the means of legal persuasion.

The proliferation of visual images[10] in contemporary society has
been accompanied by a significant cognitive shift. The linear thinking
style (or interpretive fluency) characteristic of print-based culture is
now in competition with what may be called an "associative" cognitive style, a style that is characteristic of our current image-saturated
culture. As Richard Lanham writes, today we are more inclined to
drift along the surface of electronic screens. We look *at* the signs and
symbols that flow by, rather than *through* printed words for whatever
meanings they may offer.[11] Or, as some postmodernists are fond of
saying, if meanings are there, they are all on the surface: appearing
and disappearing, being created and recreated by image-makers and
viewers alike as we gain increasing control over the flow of images we
see and the order in which we see them.

In order to be effective, legal persuasion must keep up with changing stories as well as changing storytelling styles and technologies.
Lawyers can ill afford to misjudge the thinking and speaking habits
of the audiences they face. If communication fails, how can they expect to influence the judges and jurors who determine how a particular case will come out, or the public that will construe and act upon
what it takes that outcome to mean? Thus have the methods of legal

proof always adapted to reflect the introduction of new communicative technologies, from photographic evidence to tape recordings, surveillance videos, and digital simulations.

For purposes of clarity, let me say again that I do not mean to suggest here that the interpenetration of law and popular culture is a new
phenomenon. It is not, as the historic trials discussed in chapter 4
should make clear. What *is* new, however, is the extent to which law
today is converging with the popular, and the deleterious effects of
this convergence on law's stability and continuing legitimacy in the
eyes of the public. The communication practices of law, both inside
the courtroom and in the court of public opinion, are increasingly
going the way of contemporary political discourse—law too is suc-
cumbing to the influence of public relations, mass advertising, and
fabricated media events. An increasing reliance upon public relations
campaigns in the court of public opinion as an adjunct to litigation is
part and parcel of this trend. The shift in communication practices
toward visual representations, including videos, computer-based ani-
mations, and reenactments, also reflects the growing influence of the
visual mass media on the way trial lawyers represent their clients' interests.

In these and other ways law is showing signs of postmodernization. Along the way, it is inheriting many of the problems we associate
with postmodern culture generally. Of particular concern in this respect are: the increasing conflation of truth and fiction; the image-
based manipulation of irrational desire, prejudice, and popular passions; and the concerted effort to deliberately construct preferred
versions of (and judgments about) self and social reality. These and
other meaning-making practices are displacing what, in earlier times,
one might more readily (albeit naively) have referred to as the search
for "objective" truth and "universal" justice through law. The belief
that truth and justice are "out there," just waiting to be "discovered,"
is of course only one among the numerous ideas handed down to us
from the European Enlightenment that postmodern thought has rendered problematic. Notions about the unified self, universalistic reason, and the linear logic of causation are others.[12]

In this book I maintain that the advent of postmodernism is not
without value with regard to law. Certain unrealistic aspirations and
repressive tendencies in the immoderately rationalist culture of modernity are now undergoing an important and necessary corrective.
At the same time, however, there is the danger of a new excess. Irrational forces, long repressed by mainstream culture, are breaking into

the popular imagination. They bring with them a new sense of anxiety, fear, and powerlessness. For surely the rational mind is helpless in the face of blind chance, implacable fate, surging fury, and intractable desire.

The cultural juncture we have reached has been a long time in the making. We are no doubt now reaping the harvest of modernity's decline and the surge of nihilism Nietzsche foresaw over a century ago.[13] In a more immediate sense, however, the current situation is also being affected by a strange and powerful convergence. Constructivist ("postmodern") theory, the promulgation of visual communication technology, and the insistent gratification demands of the marketplace are working in unison. Our increased theoretical and technical facility with reality construction, our ability to manipulate images and sounds for the sake of verisimilitude, reflect and feed into the market's need for and capacity to produce and absorb (and just as quickly discard) new images and new information. In conjunction with the increasing technological and market capacity to commoditize reality and *derealize* experience we continue to learn more about the contingency of meaning, the multiplicity of self and social reality, and the manifold ways of reality making. A basic and far-reaching insight is at work here: while a great deal of order may exist in the reality we experience, much of the order we perceive is there only because we put it there. Today this constructivist perspective informs such diverse fields as psychology, linguistics, sociology, anthropology, history, philosophy, law, and, of course, the study of popular culture.

Because law is both a producer and a byproduct of mainstream culture it cannot escape the forces and conflicts that play out in the culture at large. It is my contention that in law as elsewhere in the culture we are becoming increasingly enmeshed in a futile and dangerous oscillation between two extremes. I refer to them as radical disenchantment (or "skeptical postmodernism") on the one hand and a reactionary nostalgia for Enlightenment rationality and control on the other.[14] For the skeptical postmodern, the surge of the irrational is overpowering. In defense against being overwhelmed, many skeptics have retreated to a passive posture of ironic detachment. A more radical alternative, for which other skeptics have opted, is simply to leap into the flow, to nonjudgmentally merge with the irrational flux within and without. With either move, however, amoral esthetics and the appeal of immediate gratification tighten their grip upon the mind. In chapter 7 we will encounter contemporary examples of both of these strategies with regard to law and legal meaning making generally.

Faced with the equally unsavory prospects of amoral passivity and radical disorder, it is little wonder that a reactionary rationalist impulse has emerged to counter the skeptic's moves.[15] Unfortunately, however, the devoutly to be wished for certainties of the modern Enlightenment are no more likely to succeed today than they have been in the past. Indeed, current cultural conditions make it rather more likely that this nostalgic longing will not be fulfilled. That the proliferation of the visual mass media and its gratification-enhancing logic problematize in the very act of addressing the question of objectivity illustrates the difficulty we face. The more TV newscasters and film documentarians proclaim "the real," the greater our ontological anxiety becomes. A way out of the impasse between unacceptable extremes has become an imperative of our time.

In this book I contend that skeptical postmodernism is fatal to law. Ultimately, it renders judgment impossible. At the same time, however, I argue that a return to naive realism fares little better. Such a reaction to the uncertainties of skepticism fails to provide an adequate response to the immoderate repression (of chance, fate, fury, and desire) that modern rationality has long exerted. Nor can it do justice to the disappointed expectations to which modernity's unfulfilled promises have led. Simply stated, pining for the certainties of the past ignores the extent to which the failure of modernity's objectivist, rationalist, and universalistic program has helped to create postmodern conditions in the first place. Yet I believe that there is a way out of the impasse.

In what follows, I will suggest that there are signs in the culture around us of an alternative to the Hobson's choice between radical skepticism on the one hand and nostalgia for the days of the rational Enlightenment on the other. Another cultural construct is in the making, one I call tragic constructivism. It is this form of affirmative postmodernism that informs my approach to law throughout this book. In chapter 9 I attempt to flesh out what a tragic constructivist jurisprudence might be like. This effort is driven, in significant part, by the felt need to acknowledge the vicissitudes of the irrational. In seeking to eschew the immoderate repressiveness of modernity, I strive to avoid dangerous institutional and psychological forms of distortion and denial. An example of one such danger, discussed more fully in chapter 6, is repression through unconscious displacement onto others of illicit and thus highly unpalatable impulses and desires. When law goes *pop* punitive retribution against the predatory other—the "alien" among us, that perennial favorite of film and TV as well as

"real" law—becomes easy, perhaps too easy. We see this in the development of what I call the jurisprudence of appearances, a form of
legal meaning making that adopts the media's visual logic as its own.
As we will see, the ease of retribution masks significant dangers to law
and society as a whole, especially when the repressed returns—as it
inevitably does.

One of the main goals of this book is to expand the ways in which
we think and talk about law. For a long time the law has been understood in terms of written texts. Law students and scholars still spend
most of their time scrutinizing statutory rules and appellate court
opinions. The syllogism, inductive reasoning, and the analogy remain
the prime tools of legal analysis. Meanwhile, other tools of analysis
and persuasion, and other sources of legal meaning, fail to receive the
attention they deserve. The methods of legal storytelling, the strategic
uses of visual technology, and the varieties of legal discourse from
which practitioners must choose in the course of everyday lawyering
are of principal concern to attorneys; yet legal training offers no sys-
tematic account of these vital skills.[16]

In short, the historic gap between legal theory and legal practice
remains. Within the precincts of legal academia new insights concerning the role of narrative, culture, and cognition in the meaning-making
process have yet to be absorbed, much less applied to the practical
demands of effective legal persuasion. How people act in the world
on the basis of beliefs and desires, how they strive to achieve particular
goals, how they meet and overcome obstacles—all this, set in a discretely structured sequence in time, is conveyed by narrative. And it is
through narrative that they are subject to influence. Surely, then, it
makes sense to ask: What *are* the stories and storytelling tools people
typically use to organize their experience and memory of human
events? What kinds of cultural and cognitive models do they rely on
(consciously or otherwise) in their search for truth and justice in particular cases? Where do these models come from? And what kind of
truth and justice do they produce? Seeking answers to these questions
not only increases our knowledge of law and legal practice; it also
adds new meaning-making tools to the lawyer's toolkit.

Thinking about law in this way does not teach us to abandon the
study of legal texts. But it does encourage the realization that law is
not autonomous. It is not limited to the words of legislators and
judges and administrative officials alone. Law is everywhere. It is in
law offices in conversations between lawyers and clients, and between
lawyers arguing or negotiating with other lawyers. It's in the minds of

judges, clerks, bureaucrats, and jurors. And it's on the air—on television, film, and computer screens in court and out. On this view, it is not enough to do legal theory from the top down based on Kantian moral universals or utilitarian ("cost/benefit") calculations or some other comprehensive theoretical system. We also need to proceed from the bottom up. There is much to be said for unfolding law's norms from its own forms of discourse, which is to say from patterns of thought and belief within actual legal practices. This includes discursive practices inside the courtroom (at both trial and appellate levels) and elsewhere (in law offices, for example, as well as in the court of public opinion).[17]

To illustrate this more expansive view of the law's field of operation I focus in this book not only on judicial discourse, but to an even greater extent on the words and images advocates use in trial courts and in the mass media in their effort to win cases.[18] However, I also contend that we must go further still. In addition to exploring various cultural and cognitive sources and localized applications of legal meaning we must also remain open to law's implicit or hidden meanings. To do this requires a critical sensitivity to the different ways law masks meaning and power. At the same time, we must attend to the ways the irrational, subtextual, and symbolic play of rage and desire flow through law's discursive practices and strategies.[19] Meaning abounds in the unsaid as well as in written, spoken, and visual communication.

In addition to expanding the way we think and talk about law, I aim to provide an account of law's current oscillation between enchantment and disbelief and the risks that lie at either extreme. Immoderate rationality represses immoderately; but its injustice haunts us when the repressed returns. Radical skepticism, on the other hand, risks an excess of its own: left unencumbered, its embrace of irrationality leads to law's vanishing point. These are the conditions under which law goes *pop*. In responding to this situation it is incumbent upon us to open our minds to the manifold ways of legal meaning making. As filmmaker Errol Morris reminds us in *The Thin Blue Line*, there are times when law's demand for truth and justice may clash with the modernist mindset's demand for closure and certainty. Alternative narratives of justice may also clamor to be heard. But how will we hear them if we are not willing to question how a given legal narrative shapes and informs (or represses, disguises, and displaces) our needs and desires for certainty and closure, or for furious retribution, illicit gratification, or compassionate and merciful justice?

It is with this question in mind that we take up the task of confront-ing the salient cultural story lines of our time, both familiar and newly emerging. It is fitting that we do so, so that when faced with violent conflict and the prospect of law's violent response we may feel sure enough in our convictions, and in our reasonable doubts.

The plan of this book is as follows. In chapter 2, I set out more fully the conditions under which law goes *pop*. Of particular concern here is the increasingly problematic status of truth and justice within the legal system. This is what we see when legal meaning making gives way to the popular, gratification-based logic of the visual mass media. Chapter 3 takes a closer look at the role of narrative and the devices of fiction in the production of legal meaning at trial. Here we see how discrete storytelling genres, like the mystery and the heroic drama, produce particular kinds of truth and justice. Illustrations of the dif-ferent ways in which narrative constructs legal reality are drawn from cases ranging from closing arguments in the O. J. Simpson case to Gerry Spence's closing argument before the jury in behalf of Randy Weaver, who was acquitted on charges arising from the fatal shooting of a federal marshal in Ruby Ridge, Idaho.

Chapter 4 moves from the narrative construction of legal reality as a strategic matter to a symbolic one. Here we explore the richly overdetermined, often disguised symbolic meanings and unconscious forces notorious cases typically play out. Anxiety haunts the notorious case. Indeed, it is the specter of anxiety that makes these cases so strangely compelling to the public at large. Coming to grips with the invisible forces at work here is crucial if we are to understand why— and how—a particular legal controversy comes to symbolize larger social, cultural, and psychological conflicts. Deciphering the nature and effects of this symbolization process is what makes the notorious case such a useful cultural barometer.

Chapter 5 examines more closely the implications for law of post-modern storytelling by focusing on a particular case study. Here we see how antagonistic modern and postmodern narratives play out both in the capital murder case of Randall Dale Adams and in the film account by Errol Morris that helped set Adams free. In this case study we begin to see the deleterious effects on law of skeptical postmodern storytelling. At the same time, however, the analysis also points out the need for a more affirmative narrative form. Chapter 6 explores further the implications of skeptical postmodernism, specifically with respect to litigation public relations (i.e., the art of winning cases in the court of public opinion) and the jurisprudence of appearances.

Here we see the corrosive impact on law's quest for legitimacy when lawyers and judges alike converge on popular media images as a basis for public persuasion. The Supreme Court's historic decision to allow state criminal trials to be televised serves as an ironic example of the special dangers television poses for law.

Chapter 7 takes a broader look at current cultural manifestations of radical skepticism by shifting from legal to popular representations of law, justice, and the legal system in general. This popular cultural analysis ultimately points the way to law's vanishing point: the final breakdown of any coherent construction of self and of social or legal reality. In this way, it underscores the urgent need for an alternative to radical skepticism. With this need in mind, the chapter closes by examining possible cultural signs of an affirmative counterforce to disenchantment. Chapter 8 develops these suggestions further, tracing the affirmative dimension of rhetorical enchantment back to the Sophists of ancient Athens and to Sir Philip Sidney's eloquent defense, in the Elizabethan period, of law's affinity with poetry and the fictional method. Here I suggest that myth and rhetoric provide us with the tools we need to reconceptualize such core modernist notions as universal reason, the autonomous self, the objectivist ideal, and the dominance of linear causation.

Chapter 9 concludes these explorations by proffering a tragic constructivist jurisprudence. Here I attempt to unite the tragic wisdom of ancient Greek drama with the insights of traditional rhetoric and postmodern constructivism. I also seek to concretize and humanize this synthesis by seizing upon the example provided by a contemporary film: the 1996 masterpiece *Red,* the final work of Krzysztof Kieslowski and his law-trained cowriter Krzysztof Piesiewicz. This enchanting and complex account of chance encounters, surging fury, illicit desire, and the transformative power of compassion serves as a parable of law, truth, and justice in the postmodern era. I believe that it suggests an approach to law that resists systemic distortion and the leaching out of authenticity in the face of radical skepticism. Perhaps it points to a path beyond the dangers we face when law goes *pop.*

Perhaps more than any other institution, the courtroom has been put into crisis by postmodern conditions. . . . Images produce a more urgent (though necessarily more unstable) reality than events themselves.

JOHN FISKE AND FRED GLYNN,
"Trials of the Postmodern"

We live surrounded by machines that facilitate a flow of plural messages with which we as individuals can no longer keep up.

JOHANNES H. BIRRINGER,
Theatre, Theory,
Postmodernism

Everybody should be a machine.

ANDY WARHOL, in BIRRINGER,
Theatre, Theory,
Postmodernism

Screening Reality
The Vanishing Line between Law and Popular Culture

- Two women are strolling side by side. A man approaches and shoves one of them aside, then pulls out a gun and shoots the other. As she falls he shoots her again, twelve times in all. A camera crew for a local television station happens to be on the scene; they manage to capture the shooting on videotape. The next day the station broadcasts the tape. Shortly thereafter, the broadcast is picked up by a national news network. It also appears on many local newscasts around the country. The local producer whose camera crew recorded the killing explained her decision to show the tape by saying that it didn't look real. "It looks like a reenactment," she said, so she passed the tape on to the other networks.[1]
- The first criminal prosecution of Erik Menendez, 23, and Lyle Menendez, 26, the brothers accused of murdering their wealthy parents, ended in a mistrial. The state claimed that the killing was premeditated. The defendants' attorneys argued that it was self-defense: the brothers were reacting to years of sexual abuse by their father and feared for their lives at the time of the killing. The jury deadlocked; half voted for murder, half for the lesser crime of manslaughter, necessitating a new trial. In the interim between the verdict and the start of the new trial, however, CBS creates a two-night, four-hour TV miniseries about the case, while the Fox Network produces a two-hour TV docudrama. Both show reenactments of the killings. Before the two docudramas are aired, and before the brothers' second trial begins, Leslie Abramson, Erik Menendez's attorney, watches the shows in previews. She doesn't like what she sees. Apparently, neither account subscribes to the defense theory. In response, presumably to counter adverse effects on prospective jurors in the second trial, Abramson threatens to sabotage the Menendez shows by booking Erik

Menendez in the flesh from his jail cell for an interview on a rival network.[2]

- In the midst of the O. J. Simpson murder trial, with Simpson standing accused of killing his ex-wife Nicole Brown Simpson and her friend Ronald Goldman, a video production company uncovers a film of Brian "Kato" Kaelin, Simpson's former house guest and a major witness at the trial. In the video Kaelin sings a karaoke version of the Tom Jones hit "Delilah." The song refers to the stabbing of a woman by her betrayed boyfriend. The video becomes a best-seller.

- During the jury selection process in the Oklahoma City bombing trial of Terry Nichols, a prospective juror tells lawyers that she thought Nichols must be guilty because his codefendant, Timothy McVeigh, was convicted and sentenced to death. She later acknowledges that her views are based on regular viewing of the popular television drama *Law & Order.*[3]

- The day after President Bill Clinton's televised grand jury testimony arising out of the Paula Jones sexual harassment lawsuit, the president's performance is reviewed by *New York Times* film and television critic Caryn James. According to James, "the tape had an unlikely resemblance to [Louis Malle's film] *My Dinner with Andre,* with its small-scale, back-and-forth conversation and observations that seemed positively ruminative."[4] When Special Prosecutor Kenneth Starr's turn before the TV cameras arrives in the initial stages of impeachment hearings against President Clinton, another James review follows. She criticizes Starr for portraying himself along the lines of the old "just the facts, ma'am" television character Detective Joe Friday. "After all," James writes, "Joe Friday is a camp figure of fun, and choosing him as a role model reveals how out of touch the Starr approach to public relations has been." The implications at this phase of the nation's third impeachment inquiry into a president are clear: "Joe Friday's days as a television hero have passed."[5]

- At the 1996 capital murder trial of Ronnie Jack Beasley the state introduces evidence that Beasley watched Oliver Stone's film *Natural Born Killers* nineteen or twenty times and told friends that he wanted to be like "Mickey," one of the serial killers depicted in the film. After showing the film to the jury the prosecutor argues in summation that Beasley and his girlfriend did exactly what the characters in the film had done.

"It wasn't killing everybody they saw," the prosecutor tells the jury, "but they did a small time version of it."[6] For his part, Beasley's attorney has an alternative theory for why the state showed Stone's film to the jury. According to the defense, the state wanted the jurors to believe that Beasley had turned into "Mickey" because then "[the jurors] could disguise him, depersonalize him, and kill him."[7]

What happens when law becomes just like film and TV? When fact and fiction grow so confused that a trial comes to be seen as just another show and law is just another construct? What happens when law seems as if it could just as easily be otherwise? Just a flip of the channel: another case, another cast, another reality, another outcome. What of the historic "autonomy" of law? Of law as a secure refuge from media-stoked fantasies and desires, a safe haven for dispassionate reason, impartial justice, and objective truth? How are we to think about law in a society where the dominant habits of thought and perception reflect a pervasive exposure to visual mass media? What are the consequences for law when the main thrust of the popular media is to systematically suppress critical reflection? And what are we to do when the intellectual response to this situation consists of nostalgia for modernity's timeless truths and rational ideals on the one hand, and ironic detachment in the face of the mass media's spectacle of free-floating images and endlessly conflicting stories on the other?

These are the issues that inform the present situation of law in contemporary culture. It is a situation in which warring conceptions of self and social reality compete for mass cultural endorsement. To many it is as if everything were up for grabs in a relativistic universe of incommensurable norms and perspectives, as if we had entered a multicultural supermarket stocked with off-the-shelf identities and cultural norms ready to try on and take off at will. For others it is a situation in which we've lost our grip on the golden thread that will lead us back to a time when universal truths and rational norms still reigned. Yet, as culture wars rage, the technology of mass culture rolls on. And the visual mass media, particularly television, have their own models of truth and reason, law and justice, to purvey. With so pervasive a presence in our daily lives they hardly need to enter the debates. Why argue? It's enough just to stay on; the rest is academic.

In what follows, I maintain that any attempt to understand adequately the way law works in contemporary society requires that popular culture be taken into account. It is commonplace today to see the law in action: trials live on TV from inside the courtroom; talking heads of lawyers, judges, witnesses, cropped and replayed on the television news, or staged in television docudramas, made-for-TV movies, features, and weekly serials. Law stories have consistently made up a significant portion of the popular culture. For many, perhaps most, the mass media today are in fact the primary if not the exclusive source of the public's knowledge about law, lawyers, and the legal system as a whole.

Less obvious, but no less commonplace than the law's contribution to popular culture, however, is the everyday process by which popular culture contributes to the production of law. For example, ordinary expectations, shared values, and popular beliefs—what might be called the collective "folk knowledge" of the community—enter into the law directly by way of the jury in civil and criminal cases, and indirectly by way of the ballot, the process by which citizens put judges and legislators into (or out of) power. But there is more. Popular culture, especially through its chief agency, the visual mass media, also contributes to law by helping to shape the very processes of thought and perception by which jurors judge and voters vote. Put simply, it is a source of both meaning and the meaning-making tools people use to think and speak with. As legal historian Robert Ferguson notes, "speakers will use generic forms to explain themselves in a courtroom, while trial observers will impose available generic understandings on what they hear or read in order to make sense of what is happening."[8] Joseph Cotchett, an attorney who represented 23,000 bondholders in a suit against Charles H. Keating Jr. in the Lincoln Savings and Loan debacle, makes the point well:

> I give an opening statement that I hope connects with the jury, and the way you connect with the jury is using some passion and sensitivity to basic values. And you can do that with videos. Remember, your average juror spends four to six hours a day with a television in their home.[9]

Each generation learns a new set of skills for making sense of experience. These meaning-making skills make up what may be called a "communal tool kit," as cognitive psychologist Jerome Bruner likes to put it. According to Bruner, "the tool kit of any culture can be described as a set of prosthetic devices by which human beings can exceed or even redefine the 'natural limits' of human functioning." Human biology may act as a constraint on the act of making meaning, but culture, especially the cognitive tools we acquire in the search for meaning, serves as "the shaping hand." And culture even has the power to loosen biology's constraint, at least to an extent.[10] Thus the rise of a new audiovisual literacy has the concomitant effect of establishing new expectations about what a good story is like and how it should be told. With the spread of image-based communication we see a shift toward associative reasoning (i.e., using images to influence the viewer's mental associations).[11] In addition, we see a quickening of unreflective emotional impact (together with a diminishing attention span) and a confusing convergence of external reality and its image-based representation (with electronic or digital images self-referencing other mediated images).

In this view, the way we come to know self and social reality is the result of "prolonged and intricate processes of construction and negotiation deeply imbedded in the culture."[12] If this is the case it makes sense to inquire, what then are the cognitive and perceptual tools in our communal tool kit? How do we mine the information stored in our mental archives? By what mental processes, by what logic, associative or deductive, based on what sympathetic identification or aversion, what emotional affirmation or repression, do we choose from among the numerous images and stories we carry in our heads? In sum, what are the common narratives that organize our experience, and how do we use them to make sense of things in our everyday lives?

Consider in this regard what many television viewers at least subliminally recognize as the classic *Dragnet* style of televisual storytelling. It comes, as one observer put it, with "the intercutting of extreme close-ups to match precisely the monosyllabic give-and-take of the dialogue." This deliberate deromanticizing of the whodunit represents one of the chief romantic forms of twentieth-century fiction. Its dispassionate, "just the facts, ma'am" visual style suits the prosecution's frequent reliance upon history and objective truth to authorize the law's sanctions in a given case. It is, as we shall see shortly, a familiar narrative genre in court. But there are also other genres and visual styles that are useful in pursuit of other strategic purposes. Take, for example, filmmaker Oliver Stone's hyperkinetic and fragmentary style in films like *JFK, The Doors,* and *Natural Born Killers.* Here the art of the rapid cut displaces the deep-focus composition favored by an earlier generation of filmmakers, such as John Ford, Howard Hawks, and Otto Preminger.[13] With the increased speed of the cut we are taught to keep to the surface of the image. As Phillip Lopate observes:

If we are no longer invited to enter an image on the screen and dwell there inwardly for more than three seconds; if our eye is not given the time to travel from one character's face to another's and then to the objects and scenery behind or beside them; if we are being presented with too many close-ups that show us a very small amount of visual information, which make only one point per shot, if we are not encouraged to develop fidelity to a shot, then we do not make as deep a commitment to understand and interpret the material presented to us.[14]

A story's truth seduces us in accordance with the internal logic of the story itself. Riffaterre calls this the process of establishing verisimilitude.[15] The story logic at work shifts with the story. For example, within the genre of the whodunit or the mystery-exposé, we naturally expect to gather clues and reach a causally sequenced, logical conclusion. Untidy details may need to be swept aside, or overlooked, so that all may come out right in the end. But visual images may work in nonlinear fashion as well, through the logic of association. Instead of proceeding causally, in this story genre images work from moment to moment, creating intermittent meanings by juxtaposing images and the recollections, feelings, thoughts, and desires that those images trigger in the viewer's mind. As an example of this nonlinear approach, consider one of the opening scenes in Lawrence Kasdan's film *Grand Canyon* (20th Century Fox, 1991).

We see a character, a white male, driving a late-model luxury car. He makes a wrong turn and gets lost. It's nighttime and he has strayed into what the viewer is meant to perceive as a "bad" neighborhood. Shift to an image of a late-model luxury car approaching from the opposite direction. Loud music. Young blacks inside. The white driver gets the eye. They pass by. Tension in the face of the white driver. Shift again, this time to an image of the white driver's car sputtering, conking out, stopping dead. The driver gets out. He's alone on a dark street in a strange neighborhood. The same car we saw before approaches again. The black youths are parking beside the stalled car. They're getting out. . . .

It's a set-up, of course. Kasdan is working off of popular racial stereotypes and the associations, the sense of foreboding and danger, that readily come to many viewers' minds as a result of the strategic juxtaposition of these particular images. The scenario is not linear, like following the words on a page from left to right. It is associative and seemingly instantaneous. We watch reality unfold. The eye of the camera shows it all. It's happening in a constant "now," an undifferentiated present. And it is assumed that the targeted (presumably white) viewer knows how to read the images being shown, and how to fill in the gaps. The camera has but to show faces and context for the audience to grasp the significance of what is happening. In this way, even if the viewer never sees the onset of violence, he or she knows how to draw this inference from her own stock of experiences—or, more likely, from the stock of mass media representations that fit the category of events that is being evoked here. For we've seen this scenario before, enough times to know how it goes. We "know" what "inner city violence" is like. The stock images in our heads will suffice to complete the meaning Kasdan has suggestively established on the screen. And since they come from us they are that much more credible and effective.[16]

To the extent that we are all naturally inclined to keep within the bounds of our own cultural tool kits, it becomes of interest to consider what's in the kit. What stories, what recurring images and metaphors, what stock scripts and popular stereotypes help us through the day? And where do they come from?

For most people the source is not difficult to ascertain. It is the visual mass media: film, video, television, and to an increasing degree computerized imaging. This vast electronic archive provides us with the knowledge and interpretation skills we need to make sense of ordinary reality. From these familiar sources we learn the familiar plot lines, story genres, and character types out of which meanings are made. In a sense, we "see" reality the way we have been trained to watch film and TV. The camera is in our heads. We've internalized the media's logic. In the case of film and television, that logic includes a system of cues, condensations, alterations, inventions, and anachronisms that we have come to take for granted. In fact, these cognitive tools for making meaning have grown so familiar they've become invisible. Like any other element of common sense, the meanings media logic produces are "self-evident." Nothing more need be said; it's just "the way things are." In this way, the tools that help us make sense of our lives and of the world around us simply disappear from view.

Of course, before cognitive habits are formed novel frameworks for meaning tend to stand out, and may even misfire. In the early days of cinema, for example, audiences were known to duck in their seats when they saw a train speeding toward them on the screen. Today, however, the interpretive sophistication of our visual perception has become second nature. When someone moves toward a chair in one shot and is already seated in the next the meaning is clear. The viewer needn't see what went before. It is understood that the person reached the chair and sat down. This simple condensation is a common convention in the visual representation of reality. There are many such culturally acquired conventions.

Perceptual and cognitive cues in the visual mass media perform the same cognitive function as the numerous recurring social scripts and metaphors (among other common heuristics) that are at work in our everyday perceptions and thoughts. These meaning-making devices subconsciously coordinate our conduct by cueing customary expectations. Like the way we respond when the guy in the white jacket approaches our table with his pen above his pad—we know it's time to order our meal from the menu we were handed when we sat down. All of us carry around in our heads a variety of such social scripts. It is this sort of internalized social and cultural blueprint, together with a host of other equally unexamined, habituated patterns of meaning making, that accounts for our assimilation into a particular culture or subculture. We live in and through it, just as it lives in and through us.

Habits of perception and thought have a clear practical value. They allow us to respond quickly to events. They dispose of the need to pause, to interpret events afresh—something we might need to do were we to find ourselves in a strange environment where the local conventions differed from those we were used to back home. There are advantages in the economy of time and mental effort and the easing of anxiety that habituated cultural constructs of reality allow. But there are also dangers. Consider, for example, the danger associated with easily graspable, but highly distorted racial and gender-based stereotypes. There are also dangers associated with our acclimation to the increasing speed and multiplicity of images. A slower pace risks a wandering mind and an impulsive, channel-surfing hand. Attaining a sufficiently heightened level of stimulation, however, requires that meanings flatten out. The loss of depth facilitates the acceleration of image-flow across the screen.

It is as if the Cubist and Futurist vision of the instant awareness of multiple geometric planes had found a counterpart in the electronic media's fascination with visual flow. As the mass media yield to the esthetic demand for speed, and the sensation that speed creates, there is less time for words or for the pause we need for critical reflection and judgment to occur. As dialogue is condensed to fit the pace of increased visual flow, expressive language deteriorates into maxims and sound bites, mere captions for the pictures we see on the screen.

The thinning out of substantive content for the sake of heightened visual impact is not a necessary consequence of visual mass media. However, when the dominant interest is commercial and the end in view is simply to keep the viewer watching, there is a strong incentive to generate visual realities that maximize perceptual and emotional stimulation. That reality, by placing a premium on sensation as the basis for "staying tuned" while also keeping the viewer primed for the advertiser's message, leaves us cognitively diminished but emotionally charged.

The situation becomes more serious when this cognitive state carries over into other sectors of public life, such as politics and law. This has occurred in our time. A public that is not adequately trained to recognize and critically assess the play of negative stereotypes, or displaced fantasies, or the effects of other subliminal associations, is at risk when these forms of communication come to dominate political and legal discourse. James Madison famously wrote, "A popular government without popular information, or the means of acquiring it, is but a prologue to a Farce or a Tragedy, or, perhaps, both." But more recently Deanna Marcum has astutely added the following gloss on Madison's words, "In our age, when too much information can numb the mind and paralyze the will, knowledge may develop a new sort of elusiveness."[17] In short, internalizing the media's logic may well embody a contemporary mode of unwitting (self-)censorship.[18]

Becoming habituated to mediatized reality invites a peculiar sense of derealization. It is the televisual equivalent to "sentimentality" in Oscar Wilde's sense of the term: wanting an emotion without wanting to pay its price.[19] It is the state of being visually engulfed, a state in which stimulation can be enjoyed without responsibility. This kind of sensory overload or informational excess is one of the hallmarks of postmodernism. As Mark Poster writes:

> Floating signifiers, which have no relation to the product are set in play; images and words that convey desirable or undesirable states of being are portrayed in a manner that optimizes the viewer's attention without arousing critical awareness. In the hyperreal word of the TV ad, fantasies merge with banalities; the erotic with the economic.[20]

Habits of perception and cognition that reflect the commoditization of desire are habits we take with us wherever we go: from our private living rooms to public polling booths and courts of law. We should not be surprised, therefore, to find that we are habitually recreating in those public spaces political and legal realities that emulate the images, fantasies, desires, and beliefs about self and social reality that we have culled from the screen. This phenomenon may be viewed as a practical offshoot of postmodernism—it's what happens when our sense of reality rests upon images imaging images. Or, as the continental theorists say, what else should we expect when signifiers refer less to events in the world of lived experience than to the hyperreal world of free-floating signifiers?

It is the same world defense attorney Johnnie Cochran conjures when he tells the jury in the O. J. Simpson case to "do the right thing" and to "keep their eyes on the prize." These neatly packaged soundbite phrases effectively trigger mental associations to popular cultural sources that support the defense theory. According to that theory, it was up to the jurors to send a clear and plain message to a racist Los Angeles police department, and by extension to society at large: police racism will not be tolerated. And it is precisely that message that resounds within the two well-known mass media productions to which Cochran was referring—namely, Spike Lee's film *Do the Right Thing* (which narrates a story about the tribulations of contemporary urban racism and violence) and the Public Broadcasting System's well-received documentary series, *Eyes on the Prize* (which recounts the history of the American civil rights movement under the inspiring leadership of Dr. Martin Luther King Jr.). In short, this is precisely the antiracist, heroic ideal Cochran wanted the jurors to follow.

Insights regarding the constitutive role of popular culture are especially instructive for the study of law, particularly when we study the law in action. Law cases enact a battle for reality, with each side fighting to gain control over the construction of meaning. This is what trial lawyers do for a living. Like advertising executives and modern-day politicians, trial lawyers seek to tap into the popular stories and images people carry around in their heads. Cognitive studies have shown that in the course of forming a judgment about a particular legal controversy jurors seek the most comprehensive and coherent narrative that will explain what happened and why.[21] Stock characters, recognizable scenarios, and familiar plot lines, among other cognitive categories, are mined from the jurors' storehouse of common knowledge to help establish narrative patterns and to fill in gaps in the facts presented. For a lawyer's story to be compelling it must be in touch with reality. And as advertising mavens Al Ries and Jack Trout have said, the reality that counts most is the one already in the prospect's mind.[22]

Today that reality is largely acquired from mass media representations. And that is why the look and practice of law is changing. Audi-

ence expectations, both in terms of the kind of story that persuades
and the most effective way of telling it, cannot but influence trial
lawyers' discourse. Lawyers are storytellers; they are paid to affect
people's thoughts, feelings, and beliefs. It should come as no surprise
that the marathon two-day summation of Clarence Darrow's generation is all but a thing of the past. How could it be otherwise when a
generation of jurors considers a thirty-second commercial to be long?
Nor should we be surprised that for today's television-bred, visually
fluent audiences words alone may not suffice to get the attorney's message across. The power of the visual image must also be tapped.

Savvy lawyers these days are getting the message, and the medium,
right. What goes on inside the courtroom is changing. Opening and
closing statements are becoming shorter, snappier. And verbal speech
is increasingly sharing court time with visual, multimedia displays as
television and computer screens proliferate. As one attorney put it:
"Our sound-bite society has an ever decreasing attention span, requiring points to be made quickly and succinctly. . . . An eye-catching
graphic of a dramatic animation can seize the viewer/juror, with interest being the first step in understanding."[23] The new goal is to let technology do the visualizing for the jury—through computer animation,
computer graphics, and digital simulations of automobile, aviation,
and maritime accidents; bodily injury processes; structural failures;
and environmental damage patterns—even crime reenactments. In
court as elsewhere, "seeing is believing." The question is, how is the
reality we see being constructed?

Telling an effective story requires a deliberate mobilization of the
needs and expectations of the audience. As the Canadian filmmaker
Atom Egoyan put it: "What's so exciting about filmmaking [is] the
way people piece together what they need to fill in their own expectations." Persuasion and belief in this sense are often a matter of con-
firming what people already know, or of fitting new information into
patterns of meaning that are already familiar. If we've seen or heard
it before, it's easier to understand and believe when we see or hear it
again in court. Lawyers who ignore the truth of this popular cultural
reality are likely to be left talking to themselves. And for most lawyers
that is a fate tantamount to failure. Whether addressing a judge or a
juror, a legislator or a government bureaucrat, opposing counsel or
representatives of the press, the lawyer must know how to seize upon
the most compelling (legally permissible) means of persuasion available. As in politics and advertising, effective lawyering requires a familiarity and facility with commonly shared meaning-making tools as

well as commonly shared meanings. In short, lawyers must know what's in our popular cultural toolkits.

This is why the first thing a skilled trial attorney like Michael Tigar does when he takes on a case in a new city is to switch on the radio talk shows, scan the local newspapers, and watch the local TV news. Through these media sources he learns what's on (and "in") people's minds, what is the tenor of local sentiment on particular issues, and what are the words and images people use to make sense of others and events around them. In short, maximizing the effectiveness of communication often requires emulating the familiar patterns in which relevant meanings are formed and conveyed. The proliferation of visual media inside the courtroom reflects this practical need. It shows that lawyers are adjusting their storytelling and argumentation styles to reflect the modes of communication with which their audience is most familiar.

One byproduct of this development is the increased influence on law of the dominant styles of information packaging we find on the screen. Advertising in particular must be credited in this regard, for it has contributed significantly to the kinds of images we see, the expectation of easy comprehension and quick gratification that guides their selection, and the constantly accelerating pace of their flow. Advertising may be viewed as a practical site for the most advanced applications of postmodern ("constructive") theory. As Judith Williamson notes, advertising operates by selecting certain elements, things, or people from the ordinary world and then rearranging and altering them "in terms of a product's myth to create a new world." This new world is the world of the advertisement.[24]

The commercial, persuasion-driven art of creating a new world has much in common with the storytelling process in general. In order to succeed, a narrative must establish a coherent framework for meaning. And as advertisers and successful trial lawyers know, one of the chief devices for establishing order is the creation of conflict. When an event disturbs our ordinary expectations about how things happen in the world, or how people behave, or how a particular kind of story is supposed to go, we feel a strong need for resolution. Our sense of order demands that things be put right. Legal controversies in this sense are ideal sources of conflict, drama, and normalized resolution.

As it turns out, the emergence of advertising and constructivist ("postmodern") narrative expectations as popular models for communication may be connected to a more general phenomenon in contemporary society. Call it the estheticization of the real.[25] Events and individuals simultaneously appear more important and less real when they are on TV. As a result, the line between truth and fiction seems to waver, and at times vanish altogether. It is as if reality had flattened out and collapsed into its virtual representation. Consider, for example, the case of former garage owner Joey Buttafuoco. Buttafuoco was the middle-aged lover of Amy Fisher, the teenaged call girl who shot Buttafuoco's wife in the face. Buttafuoco became a minor celebrity[26] in the wake of the shooting and of the three "Amy Fisher Story" docudramas that ran on three national TV networks. In this case, the reality of Buttafuoco's unseemly character seems to have been utterly overtaken by the notoriety he won simply by being associated with such a highly mediatized case.

A strange feedback loop seems to be at work here. Persons and events selected for broadcast tend to frame the public's sense of reality. The selection process, however, is largely governed by the media's own needs. As communications scholar George Gerbner writes, "Television will create popular spectacles of great appeal but deceptive authenticity as it selects and interprets trials to fit the existing pattern of law in the world of television."[27] Nonetheless, once the media's framework has been internalized it tends to be projected back into the real world. We see what we expect to see: the familiar stories and character types, the recurring scenarios and images we've seen before. When gaps arise we are prepared to fill them in. We do so based on our expectations regarding how this kind of story or situation, with this sort of character, is supposed to go. By emulating media reality, law puts these popular expectations to practical use. Conversely, when media reality enters the law it is law's authority that helps to legitimize the media. Thus the cycle is complete.

I contend that this postmodern phenomenon is the byproduct of an unprecedented convergence of cultural, social, and economic forces. It is what happens when constructivist theory, communication technology, and the gratification demands of the marketplace combine. According to constructivist theory, language does not simply reveal the world. Words and images are not like boxcars freighting reality around; they do not simply leave the scene once their load of meaning has been dumped in our minds. The language we use, like the technological forms of communication we inherit from the culture around us, helps to create the reality we live in. And as the means of communication change so too does our sense of ourselves, others, and the world around us.

It is precisely this phenomenon that pop artist and cultural vision-

ary Andy Warhol describes in his writings and art work. The core
question is this: what happens when ideas and machines converge
in response to the market's endless demand for mass reproducible
goods? Warhol was among the first to appreciate the implications of
this convergence. Consider in this regard the way his endless silk-
screens of recycled popular images explore (and expose) the technology of mass reproduction set against the incessant gratification demands of the marketplace. These are works we remember through
commodity icons, "the soup cans and Marylin Monroes which refer
neither to Campbell or Monroe nor to Warhol, but to the commodity
system itself." As Birringer perceptively notes:

> Warhol's assimilation to the totalizing commodity system was so com-
> plete that it exemplified the disappearance of art's separate status and
> of all traditional aesthetic values of distinction. In its convergence with
> fashion, advertising, and the production of commercial culture as such,
> Pop Art's method of reproducing mass-reproduced reality—in the sur-
> faces of soup cans or the faces of stars—made it an art of disappearance
> that paradoxically both exposed the commodity character of all con-
> temporary art production and exaggerated its visual synthesizing of all
> mass-cultural forms. . . . The survival of art can be understood, in ret-
> rospect, as a logical extension of the parody of transparency and indif-
> ference posited in Warhol's factory image: the relation of art to the
> world is characterized by its own endless reproducibility.[28]

What Birringer is describing here is of critical importance in the historic emergence of what has come to be known as "postmodern"
culture. As we will see in chapter 6, it is a moment that was prefig-
ured in the rise of the American public relations movement. This is
a time when the products of the mind—whether symbols, ideas, or
metaphors—can all be turned into artifacts of mass production. In
the postmodern era, even the art work, that quintessentially unique
object, can be absorbed into and transformed by commercial mass
production. But when that commoditization process is made self-
conscious, which is the genius of Warhol's art, something else also
comes into view. This describes one of the most striking features of
postmodern culture: namely, the blurring of disparate categories, like
the categories of art and commodity and of reality and fiction.

When art goes *pop* we witness a breakdown of the traditional
boundaries that separate art from fashion or from mass-produced,
commercial commodities. The assistants in Warhol's art studio, aptly

enough dubbed "the Factory," were in fact workers on an assembly line of mass-produced art. As Warhol himself put it, "'business' was the best art. Business art is the step that comes after Art. I started as a commercial artist, and I want to finish as a business artist."[29] This mockery of the artist's exalted status as maker of objects without "use value" archly reiterates that obsessively pursued twentieth-century query, what is art? What is the difference between "reality" and artistic representation? That the subjects Warhol chose to represent were real historic figures (such as Marilyn Monroe and Mao Zedong) or actual commercial products (like Campbell's soup cans) heightens our sense of elision, of reality's slippage into a world of mass representation. Is the Warhol replica of a Campbell's soup can still a Campbell's soup can, or has it become something else? If the latter, what exactly has it become? Warhol's ambiguity in this regard leaves us with a powerfully enhanced sense of how easily the real (together with the esthetic that constitutes its reality) can be absorbed into an artifactual, commodity-based culture of mass production and mass consumption. Nothing is exempt from this all-engulfing process, Warhol tells us. Not art. And not law.

This is the estheticization of the real. It marks our entry into the strange realm of hyperreality. As Baudrillard puts it,

> What fascinates everyone is the debauchery of signs, that reality, everywhere and always, is debauched by signs. This is the interesting game, and this is what happens in media, in fashion, in publicity and more generally, in the spectacle of politics, technology, science . . . the triumph of simulation is as fascinating as catastrophe—and it is one in effect; it is a vertiginous subversion of all effects of meaning.[30]

Cultural critic Vicki Goldberg offers a substantially similar insight:

> Life today resembles a fictional paradigm more and more and sometimes even outdoes the movie version. O. J. Simpson's ride in a white Bronco might well have been an improbable episode on a television cop series; the televised Simpson and Menendez trials so convincingly melded the forms of [the popular television programs] "L.A. Law," "All My Children," and "Oprah" that talk show and soap opera ratings fell off.[31]

Consider: ours is a time when jurors and TV commentators alike react to a lawyer's performance in court with images and prototypes from Hollywood and TV. Watching O. J. Simpson defense attorney F. Lee Bailey prompts such intended praises as: "He fulfills a juror's expectation of what a defense lawyer should be. For a while there, I thought I was watching Perry Mason."[32] (And this from a respected professor of law.) Actor Marlon Brando appears on page one of the *New York Times* to comment on the performance of O. J. Simpson attorney Barry Scheck. And former Los Angeles County deputy district attorney Vincent Bugliosi explains jurors' inclination to acquit or lightly sentence defendants whom they perceive to have been "abused" as a reality effect of daytime television talk shows.[33] This conflation of fiction and reality is not confined to the media. It also can be found inside the courtroom as real cases cross over into the hyperreal.

Take, for example, *United States v. Bianco,* a complex organized crime case involving multiple defendants. To make sure the jury got the right mental image, during the trial the prosecution invoked the predatory mafia dons depicted in Francis Ford Coppola's well-known film *The Godfather.*[34] But, as defense attorney Jeremiah Donovan demonstrated, hyperreality works in more ways than one. It can be turned around. Which is precisely what Donovan did—right before the jurors' eyes he transformed his client from a malevolent gangster type into an entertaining, inoffensive cartoon character. It was like a scene out of Quentin Tarantino's popular 1993 film *Pulp Fiction.*

In Tarantino's film the characters come at us from a well-known genre. The story is built up from scenes and character types with which we are entirely familiar: the thugs, the head honcho's girl, the free-flowing drugs, the graphic violence. It's pulp, and we all recognize it as such. Indeed, everything we see in the film is experienced as if it were wrapped in the thick gauze of that well-worn story type. The fun comes when the plot and character types we know so well drift in and out of our expectations, bringing those very expectations into view. The thugs are violent, and indifferent to the pain and death they deal out, as thugs are prone to be. But they are also strangely self-aware, articulate, by turns philosophical and bizarre. These are characters who can quote scripture one moment and in the next lash out at a friend for soiling car upholstery with the blood of an innocent victim. The mix is strange and amusing. Curiously, even when they become violent they do not lose their appeal. That is because we see their violence as part of the pulp genre that has produced them. In short, everything we see passes through the lens of the genre—even as we see the lens of the genre itself. We laugh because we get it: reality is a construct. It is made up of words and images that come to us from stories and character types we know. The sense we make of what we hear and see depends on the context. Reality is a product of narrative framing.

The link to external reality has been broken. Tarantino's ironic, self-reflexive, pastiche style trains us to read visual images in terms of their relation to other visual images. Once we've been transported to this hyperreal world it becomes possible to respond to images of grotesque sadomasochistic brutality with laughter. A reality we would ordinarily regard as anything but amusing has become cartoonish, a joke. It's the same tactic the defense used in *United States v. Bianco*.[35]

Louis Failla, a relatively low-level member of a powerful organized crime family, was one of the defendants on trial in that case. Unfortunately for Failla, his car had been secretly bugged by the FBI. What is more, Failla was a man who liked to reminisce. Pages of government transcripts testified to Failla's long career in the mob, for Failla is the kind of man who, in the course of arranging a dinner date with someone, would not be content simply to say, "Let's meet at Stella's." No. Failla would say, "Let's meet at Stella's—you know, that's where so-and-so got made or, that's where we made the hit on you-know-who." As Failla's defense attorney, Jeremiah Donovan put it, "[T]he evidence was killing [him]."

Donovan's task at trial was to separate the stock ("Godfather") image of Failla-the-mobster from what Donovan preferred to think of as the "real" story, the far less incriminating one he wanted the jurors and judge to believe in. Donovan found a way to do this once he realized that the trial was becoming more and more unreal as it went on. The evidence was so shocking (so much like film reality) that, as Donovan would say, it "caused a divorcement between reality and what was portrayed in the course of the trial." For example, at one point the government introduced a board with a hundred human bones attached to it. As people filed in and out of the courtroom, nonchalantly walking past these bones that had once belonged to a living and breathing person, it dawned on Donovan that "[N]obody had any sense that these were once a man . . . they were props in a drama." Here was the key to the defense. Donovan would make his summation to the jury "into a story, something that sounded like a movie plot."

In short, once the drama inside the courtroom had entered the domain of the hyperreal, Donovan could structure his legal defense in hyperreal terms, which is to say, in terms of other familiar film images and characters. And that is precisely what he did—to great effect. His first strategy was to set the appropriate mood. Since the character he would depict for his client was a humorous, more or less innocuous "mafia-wannabe" (all bluff, no action), Donovan sprinkled his summation with humorous stories. They would capture the mood of the argument and at the same stroke the spirit of the man he was defending. Consider, for example, Donovan's allegorical tale about a man named O'Toole. Here is how Donovan describes it:

> The O'Toole story was part of my hook to the jury. You have to imagine that I have a nice jury rail here. You also need to think of a working class bar in Dublin. Everybody's sitting and having a good time. All of a sudden this big, huge fellow—I mean enormous—walks in and says, "Alright, where's O'Toole?" Everybody looks down into their beer because they don't want to be mistaken for O'Toole. Finally, way in the back, a little old guy, about seventy-five years old, weighing maybe 110 pounds, gets up and say, "I'm O'Toole. What's it to ya?" The big guy picks up O'Toole, puts him on the bar, runs him down the bar, bottles hitting him, throws him on the ground, kicks him twice, picks him up, throws him through a plate glass window, walks out the door, picks him up again, throws him back through the other plate glass window and walks off. All the patrons look at this bloody mess on the ground, worried that the man is dead. All of a sudden, the little guy lifts up his head and says, "I sure pulled a fast one on that big fella'—I'm not O'Toole at all!"[36]

That's Failla. On all those government tapes saying, "I'm gonna' be the capo for Connecticut! I've done this . . . I got the biggest this or that. . . ." But remember, "I'm not O'Toole at all!" So when you hear all those terrible things on tape, ladies and gentlemen of the jury, you have to remind yourselves, "He's not O'Toole!" The image of the befuddled old geezer and his misplaced act of impersonation, together with the amusing tone and spirit of the joke, informs, by association, the exaggeration-prone character of Louis Failla. Failla would say anything to make it seem like he was one of the big guys, a player. But he wasn't. He was just O'Toole. Everyone who knew Louis knew this. Everyone, that is, except the FBI and the prosecutors who didn't understand the context. As a result, they ended up trying to fit the wrong story frame around Louis's foolish acts of braggadocio. Failla was a braggart, not a criminal. We all know the type. The kind who plays the fool, thinks he's winning acceptance by others, but who ends up

getting hurt in the end. That, at any rate, is the stock story and character type Donovan evoked to great effect in the course of Louis Failla's
trial. By ingeniously skirting the line between fiction and reality, Donovan transformed his client into a harmless cartoon character, just like
Pulp Fiction.

The process of derealization was completed at the point in Donovan's summation when we see him propping up huge poster boards in
front of the jury. They depicted caricature-like cartoon drawings of
Louis Failla. And there above Failla's head, connected by a solid line
to Failla's mouth, are the words Failla said (as revealed by the covert
FBI tape recordings). But in a second balloon, connected to Failla's
mouth by dotted lines, the jury sees what Failla was actually thinking
while he spoke. The defense amounts to this: "Sure Failla said all these
damning things about himself, but they weren't true. He was just a
mafia wannabe trying to impress the real wiseguys." Suddenly, it's as
if we're in the middle of a Woody Allen movie. It's *Annie Hall,* and
there's Alvie and Annie having their first conversation together. As
they speak we see at the bottom of the screen subtitles telling us what
they are really thinking. Sure they're saying all these banal and embar-
rassing things to each other, but the real reality is the one silently
playing in their heads. That's Failla, he's just like Alvie in *Annie Hall.*[37]

Here, then, is the look of law when it is practiced in hyperreality:
reality by emotional association, by film esthetics, by the logic of advertising, public relations, and fabricated media events. In this domain, humor is but a tool, one effect among others, in the effort to
make a particular story or character image stick. It's like the law
teacher who starts his class by showing students a movie clip from
The Fugitive. He wants them to "associate civil procedure class with
an adrenaline rush." It's irrelevant to the subject matter, but once the
mood is set it spreads out into the material. In other words, an initial
affective response to an image can be strategically used to wash over
and inform the way we construe the image that follows. By coordinat-
ing these juxtapositions one can influence the viewer's perception and
judgment. It's what we see on television all the time. By associating a
particular image (of a beautiful and erotically charged model, say, or
an affluent and highly pleasurable lifestyle) with a specific product,
advertisers encourage consumers to purchase commodities for their
(esthetically) associated gratifications.

In a variety of ways law today is being visually projected inside the
courtroom: including day-in-the-life videos in personal injury cases,
reality-based police surveillance videos, civilian and news journalist

videos (e.g., of the police in action) and digitized reconstructions of the images they contain,[38] computer graphics, digitally reconstructed accidents and crime reenactments, and video montage (including the strategic interweaving of commercial feature film footage and evidentiary material from a case file[39]). The latter montage has even replaced an attorney's live summation before the jury.[40] These new modes of audiovisual and digitized communication are replicating within the courtroom the same mental processes and conflicts that are typically associated with the technology that produced them. As Sherry Turkle observes:

> Computers don't just do things for us, they do things to us, including to our ways of thinking about ourselves and other people. . . . We construct our technologies, and our technologies construct us and our times. Our times make us, we make our machines, our machines make our times. We become the objects we look upon but they become what we make of them. . . . The technology changes us as people, changes our relationships and sense of ourselves.[41]

Where else can one go but to the screen? It's where people look these days for reality. And it's the look of reality they get from the screen that is the object of persuasion, the look that must be captured to make the image work, for reality's sake, which is to say, for the sake of verisimilitude. In this respect, then, the function of popular culture is like that of storytelling in general. Both establish a set of norms and show how threats or disruptions ("Trouble" and "troublemakers") may be dealt with so that the established norms may be restored (or, if need be, altered or, in periods of crisis, replaced). In short, popular culture, like law, provides a source of collective understanding, social coherence, and stability. We can go on with our everyday lives because we feel secure in the knowledge that there is an underlying order and continuity to things. And when disorder breaks out the forces of order will respond. Simply stated, popular culture, like law, helps to police conventional meanings and social practices. The order we have come to know and expect and rely upon abides in the life we live and the cultural (symbolic) representations we consume. The one ensures the other.

Myths and archetypes contribute to this process. When a crime occurs, the media, and in time the lawyers for the parties involved, will struggle to come up with the most compelling means of conveying what occurred and what it means. In this way, Amy Fisher comes to be known as "the Long Island Lolita." Bernhard Goetz, who shot four unarmed youths he thought were about to rob him in a New York subway, becomes "the subway vigilante." Of course, this phenomenon is hardly new. As Andie Tucher vividly chronicles, back in 1836, when Helen Jewett, a prostitute, was viciously slain, the penny press of the era quickly assumed the task of discerning the meaning of her death. Tucher writes:

> She was an archetype, a symbol, a myth, a heroine of popular tradition; she was the latest incarnation of a painfully tragic and appallingly familiar figure, the frail, flawed female undone by sex. The spiritual sister of Helen of Troy, of Clytemnestra, of Messalina, of Guinevere, of Faust's Gretchen, of Clarissa Harbour, Jewett transcended her sordid little death. . . . She entered instead the realm of the universal and the metaphorical, giving up her life to the perennial human attempt to fathom why evil happened and who should pay for it.[42]

Catering to readers' fears and desires, the penny press was concerned less with the real details of Jewett's life than with the mythic framework that would restore a sense of control over chaotic reality. As Tucher rightly observes, "myth" in this sense works only to the extent that it illuminates an important truth in a way that is "congenial to members of the community."[43] The role of the litigator, however, unlike that of the journalist, is to come up with a narrative truth that can successfully compete against a counternarrative offered by the other side. Consider in this regard the cases of Helen Jewett and Amy Fisher. In one sense (that of the prosecution) Amy Fisher, the Long Island Lolita, like Helen Jewett, dubbed in her time "the Siren," represented threats to the established moral order. As a consequence, each would have to pay the penalty for her transgression. On the other side (that of the defense), Fisher, like Jewett, could also be framed within a counternarrative. The image of Lolita, or of the transgressive Siren, now gives way to "the poor unfortunate," the victim. In Jewett's case, the defense told a story of poverty, lack of opportunity, and class bias. In Fisher's case, it is a story of psychological disturbance and parental complacency in the face of Fisher's increasingly desperate, and futile, cries for help.

In other words, in antebellum America, as in America today, popular culture served as a rich source of sensationalism—the "hokum" or "humbug" we now call "tabloid journalism." Then as now the mass media disseminated narratives in response to the public's perceived needs and desires. Then as now these offerings were defended as harmless untruths, fictions that were presented, and meant to be taken, with a wink and a nod. As Tucher points out, an untruth that is presented as such does not deceive and thus is not a lie. And, Tucher shrewdly adds, "a truth that does not satisfy . . . is no better than a lie."[44]

Yet one wonders: what happens when fictions are presented without the wink and the nod that rob them of deceit? What happens to law when fiction merges with truth, leaving no clear sign of when the one begins and the other leaves off? When the distinction between news and tabloid entertainment, like the one between lived experience and hyperreality, blurs, the public no longer receives the signals that alerted previous generations to the presence of "humbug," such as the "hokum" or sensational (un)reality of tabloid "news."[45] On this point contemporary ad masters, political campaign managers, and postmodern scholars tend to agree: appearances and perceptions are all we are left with. But if, as the late Robert Cover reminded us, law takes place on a field of pain and death, surely confusion over standards of truth and justice is no small matter. Yet it is precisely this confusion that reigns today as law catches up with, and to some extent becomes indistinguishable from, popular culture.

It has often been said that American law exercises a profound influence on American culture. Alexis de Tocqueville famously wrote: "There is hardly a political question in the United States which does not sooner or later turn into a judicial one." Tocqueville also accurately perceived the educational role played by law in American society. "The spirit of law," he wrote, "infiltrates through society right down to the lowest ranks, till finally the whole people have contracted some of the ways and tastes of a magistrate."[46] Less well noted, however, is Tocqueville's additional insight that American lawyers serve as an important albeit generally unnoticed "brake" when the people "let themselves get intoxicated by their passions or carried away by their ideas."[47] In this capacity, law may serve as a vital check upon popular passions.

When law goes *pop* that checking function fails. It is this danger, and the circumstances that have led up to it, that I set out to describe and assess here. I do not dispute the traditional view that law plays a significant role in helping to inform and shape the public's understanding of important political and moral issues of the day. What I do claim is that Tocqueville's account of law's influence on American society tells only part of the story. I believe we can begin to fill in the gap by reversing Tocqueville's insight. Apart from law's influence on American politics and culture we must also reckon with the influence on law of American popular culture. I maintain that law cannot be and historically speaking never has been insulated from popular culture. Today, however, that influence is having a particularly pernicious effect. The proliferation of the visual image and the techniques of advertising, public relations, and the hyperreal media event inside the courtroom as well as in the court of public opinion call for close scrutiny.

In this book I maintain that law is not only collapsing into the popular, it is collapsing into an increasingly popular form of cultural postmodernism. Contemporary Italian philosopher Gianni Vattimo has noted that we are now witnessing "a giddy proliferation of communication as more and more subcultures 'have their say.'" In the face of so much possibility, so many disparate forms of reality, including realities of self, a unified sense of truth and shared values seems increasingly elusive. We see the effects upon law of this fragmentation process in law's growing pluralization and particularization. Increased contextualization, the prevalence of local truths and local knowledge over universal truths and context-transcending knowledge, and of subjective ("associative") reasoning over linear ("explanation-based") reasoning are part and parcel of what may be described as law's "postmodernization." Consistent with this development, mirroring the public's steadily increasing acceptance of multiple worlds, multiple selves, and multiple meanings, constructed from multiple cultural and cognitive perspectives, is the pervasiveness of the visual mass media.

The epistemology of constructivism, of world making in discourse and in the juxtaposition of sound and images, coincides with the technological proliferation of the dominant means of reality production. As cultural theorist John Fiske writes, "The nature, or truth, of an event is determined in part by the discourse into which it is put, and no event contains its own prescription for the correct discourse by which to know and communicate it."[48] In American society today, the parameters set by film and television increasingly serve as the measure of reality as most people know it. What we think about and the tools we think with lie, in large measure, within the province of the visual mass media.

If reality today is increasingly being perceived as the effect of the sign, if images have come to be seen as more real than the real, then that is what we should expect to see in advertising, in politics, and in law. It is the play of signs relating to signs and of images invoking other images that we should expect to see when lawyers reconstruct

events in the courtroom in the best interests of their clients. And it is
this same phenomenon that we should expect to see as part of the
process by which we come to understand what truth, law, and justice
mean in the court of public opinion.

In this book I seek to show that these expectations are well
founded. Today savvy lawyers know and are putting to use what advertisers and politicians have known and practiced for some time: how
to get the message out, how to tailor content to medium, how to spin
the image, edit the bite, and quickly seize the moment on the screen
and in the mind of the viewer. Lawyers too know that effective persuasion requires gaining control over reality, and that the reality that
counts most in this context is the one the prospect (the would-be consumer) carries around in his or her head. The persuader therefore must
know what's there: what stock stories and character types, what familiar plot lines and scenarios, what storytelling genres and conventions. With this cultural knowledge in hand the persuader gains the
leverage she needs to mobilize and strategically apply the constituents
of reality making.

It is not the end of the modern (print-based, explanatory, linear-
causal, proof-driven) storytelling style. But that style's monopoly on
truth and law and justice is over. Once this realization sinks in, the
way law is practiced and taught, how it is understood and analyzed,
cannot remain the same. It is my contention that heightened self-
consciousness about what counts as truth inside the courtroom (as an
evidentiary matter) and what makes for a compelling legal story (for
the sake of reaching a just and legally binding verdict) should be studied as it is being practiced.

The hope that drives this work is that studying the postmodernization of law (as a matter of theory and practice combined) will prompt
reconsideration of a variety of issues, including traditional legal fictions (such as the fiction of logical closure and objective truth) with
which law has kept the unruly complexities of lived experience at bay.
This includes the taboo realm of unruly emotions, hidden fantasies,
and prohibited desires. This expansion of law's domain to include the
complexities and multilevel ambiguities of everyday life must be accompanied, however, by enhanced vigilance toward new dangers. The
latter include the consequences of transforming legal into televisual
or cinematic reality, a process that involves sensationalization, sub-
jectification, and the fragmentation of authority. It is as a result of this
development that law is being transformed into a mosaic of increasingly plural, particular, and context-dependent signs.

This development in law may be viewed as a valuable corrective with respect to certain modernist distortions concerning law's unitary, objectivist, and acontextual authority. Taken too far, however, such a corrective threatens to erode law's authority, delegitimize its power, and further the breakdown in shared norms for social conduct and belief that is now well under way in society at large. In short, the ways in which law goes *pop* coincide with a broader pattern of cultural change. In seeking a better understanding of the growing convergence of law and popular culture this book seeks to join a larger project addressing contemporary conflicts in culture and politics. Crucial to that project is the effort to recognize and satisfy the felt need for a flourishing sense of shared identity and common fate in society. One of the pivotal questions underlying this effort is: How shall we re-imagine in the era of postmodernity the rudiments of liberal democracy, one of which surely is the rule of law?

The proliferation of mass culture, particularly through the visual mass media of film and television, can be viewed as a powerful tool of cultural postmodernization. The force of that tool is now coming to bear upon law. Reckoning with the consequences of that influence is one of the most formidable challenges before us. Mining popular culture for signs of change in shared values, beliefs, and expectations helps us to locate and anticipate changes in law itself. In short, it helps us to better understand and legitimize—which is to say, collectively affirm—law's constructions of truth and justice. Without a broadly shared "reality principle" to legitimize its power, law's authority is bound to falter.

It is with these critical issues in mind that we now turn to specific sites on the law's field of action. For the most part these will be sites involving crimes—real, alleged, or fictional. We will find that as a practical matter law is shaped and informed both by its own specialized culture, its own technical way of seeing, thinking, and talking about reality, and by the mass culture of contemporary life. Once we realize this is so, it becomes incumbent upon us to examine more carefully how law's factual and symbolic truths and higher legal principles intermingle with the realities we find on television, movie, and computer screens across the land.

But a fact is like a sack which won't stand up when it is empty. In order that it may stand up, one has to put into it the reason and sentiment which have caused it to exist.

LUIGI PIRANDELLO,
Six Characters in Search of an Author

[W]hile we have an "innate" and primitive disposition to narrative organization . . . the culture soon equips us with new powers of narration through its tool kit. . . .

JEROME BRUNER,
Acts of Meaning

THREE

Legal Storytelling
Culture's Tools for Making Meaning

When Prince Hamlet sought proof for the claim that his father, the king of Denmark, had died an unnatural death at the hands of Claudius, the king's brother, he resorted to a play. Or better, a play within a play. Hamlet contrived a scene in which a Duke, mad with ambition, murders his brother in order to reign in his place. This would be the thing to catch the conscience of the king. By a theatrical ruse Hamlet and his friend Horatio expected to learn the truth about the new king's ascension to the throne. They called it the mousetrap. The play's impact on the accused would tell all.

How strange, to prove the truth of a claim based on the effect that a story has upon another. But not at all—it is how the law proceeds every day. There is, in fact, no other way. Reality must be reconstructed at trial. The crime and the motive, the personal injury and the negligent act that allegedly caused it, the broken promise and the lost profits that resulted—none of this exists, as a matter of law, until it has been proven. Which is to say, until the decision maker, whether judge or jury, believes it to be so. That is what the testimony of witnesses, the admission of physical evidence, and the persuasiveness of trial lawyers are for: to get the story out.

Not just any story, of course. The best trial lawyers seek highly compelling images and story plots to advance their cause. They depict witnesses as the most (and least) believable sorts of characters. They work hard to weave together the most (and most favorable) factual details their story can bear. And they fight to get it all past the evidentiary censor, the trial judge who decides, based on formal rules of evidence, what the jury may hear and see and just how far an advocate may go in his or her efforts to make a particular reality come to life inside the courtroom. As one seasoned litigator put it, "I see what I do as playing into certain standard accepted stories that flow through society. What I do is take my client's story and fit it into one of those narrative paths that make people go, 'Okay. Yeah.'"[1]

As a practical matter, then, familiarity with traditional forms of legal argumentation, based on inductive and deductive logic, the syllogism, the analogy, and the contrasting case, will not suffice. Story-based thinking must also be reckoned with. It bears noting that argumentation and storytelling represent two distinct forms of reasoning. The one is utterly irreducible to the other.[2] For example, in appellate arguments attorneys will typically claim: "Our case is like case *x; case x* required result *y;* therefore, result *y* must apply here." Or at trial we might hear an attorney argue: "If you find fact *x,* you must conclude result *y,* for that is what the rule that applies in this case demands."

Story-based thinking is different. The critical question now becomes, what does the story require? In place of deductive and inductive logic, narrative necessity takes over. Gripped by the drama of a well-told story, we are often moved to think and feel in particular ways. We recognize a familiar plot line, we sympathize with certain characters, we develop antipathies toward others, and in the process we come to desire a particular narrative outcome. When we think with stories we make use of a variety of mental habits (or cognitive heuristics) that serve as tools for organizing experience. Here, unlike in the domain of formal logic, contradiction avails not—not when common sense rules. For common sense is no science. Rather, it is a haphazard compilation of the familiar cognitive and cultural constructs that make up our ordinary world knowledge. In a legal setting these common narrative responses may incline the decision maker toward a particular judgment about truth and justice in a specific case.

Lawyers need to be aware of the specific virtues and limitations of these two different modes of reasoning. They must know how to argue logically from rules of law to particular facts to a particular verdict category. And they must also know how to construct stories that "cry out" for a particular narrative resolution. In this sense, while story-based reasoning and logical analysis are irreducible, they are not incompatible. One form may readily complement the other. This is in fact what we see when persuasive storytelling combines with formal argumentation in support of a particular legal outcome. For example, when a plausible narrative is shown to comport with the specific legal elements of a given verdict—whether it is premeditated murder (matching up a story of death with deliberate, cold-blooded killing) or manslaughter (matching up an account of killing with extreme emotional disturbance or reckless disregard of human life) or acquittal (matching the act of killing with a justified use of lethal force)—

when, in short, the best possible match between story and verdict category has been made, then and only then will justice have been officially served and truth legally attained.

We know a good deal about the logical method. By contrast, much less is known about what makes for a compelling story. However, advances are being made. For example, we are learning more about the different ways in which particular story genres, character types, and images cognitively "cue up" certain descriptive as well as emotional and normative responses. If we're in the grip of a melodrama, say, we know there'll be good guys and bad guys and that the good guys will win out in the end. If it's a mystery story we know we'll be given all the clues we need to figure out "whodunit." If it's a heroic romance we know that we'll be called upon to go beyond ordinary expectations, that we'll have to overcome great obstacles in order to accomplish a very special task, to "do the right thing." There'll be enemies to battle along the way and a prize to bring home in the end—if we have the courage to do justice and send the right message to the bad guys who want to see us fail.

Trouble may come in a variety of ways, stories tell us. The important thing is that whatever the nature of the disturbance it is ultimately amenable to correction. Someone (the good guy) will be called upon to set things right. The ensuing effort to repair the damage that trouble has caused, and thus restore the original (normal) state of affairs, may or may not succeed. In the end, either things will get back to normal or a new sense of normality (a transformed state) will take the place of the old. The specific outcome depends upon the kind of story being told.

Narrative necessity may come from a particular kind of order that is internal to the story itself. But it is also we, the audience, who actively help it to reach an appropriate resolution on its own terms. For example, when we recognize the good guy and offer to fill in his character with details taken from our own stock of world knowledge, when we give him emotional life by rooting for his triumph over his adversary, when we feel gratified by the wrongdoer's ultimate defeat—these acts of identification and antipathy make us participants in and even cocreators of the story being told. But by making the story our own we also enhance its believability. It fits with what we know and expect concerning how things go and what people are like in the world around us. Thus the decision maker is able to say in the end, "This is the way things should have gone. And so things would have turned out if not for the actor's deviant conduct. In any event, now that his deviance has been accounted for, and appropriately judged, things can go back to normal again." In so saying, we feel it is so. It is a feeling that shores up confidence in both our descriptive and our normative expectations. What we know works. Our judgments are true. They confirm the order of things. We may continue to feel at home in the world.

Of course, inviting story-based simplifications carries a price. Sometimes they cause us to get things wrong. Messy details that don't fit the script or the image we may have in mind for such things may get left out. We may find it easier to blame someone for who they appear to be rather than for what they may or may not have done. If it's easier to perceive an alleged wrongdoer's or victim's conduct as being somehow "deviant," in violation of our ordinary expectations, it may prove easier to blame him for what happened even if his deviance had nothing at all to do with what really caused the injury.[3] We may end up ignoring multiple causes of an injury or a crime if it all gets too hard to keep straight. Under such circumstances it may be easier to latch onto a single cause, especially when it's easy to grasp, when it fits what we already know. In short, there are numerous ways in which we may be fooled by appearances or otherwise misled by an overbearing need to simplify by relying upon inappropriate images, scenarios, and character types.

From what has been said so far, it would seem that Hamlet and Horatio got it right. When it comes to the perception of truth and judgments about wrongdoing, "the play's the thing." Trials, like novels and theater, are (to borrow a phrase from novelist Don DeLillo) "all about reliving things." Except, of course, that unlike literature, trial outcomes are backed by the full force of the state. At trial, life itself may hang on what a judge or jury believes to be "true" and "just" in the particular case. For trial lawyers, then, capturing belief is the essence of the matter. Let us take a closer look at how it is done, and how it fails.

Consider in this regard the prosecution's closing arguments in the recent O. J. Simpson double murder case. Prosecutors Marcia Clark and Christopher Darden combined legal argumentation with a classic, logic-driven mystery narrative. Theirs was a plea for "calm and reason."[4] They implored the jury not to make any "quantum leaps in logic." And they frequently contrasted the "fiery rhetoric" of the defense with their own reliance upon logic and reason.[5] For the prosecutors emotion was considered a distraction, anathema to the "objective" judgment they were seeking from the jury.[6] Logic was their watchword throughout the closing argument. And the image with which they ended their address to the jury offers as fine an emblem of the logic-driven detective story as one is likely to find. It is the image of a jigsaw puzzle. There before the jury, projected on an oversized television screen, are the pieces of the puzzle clicking into place. Each piece coincides with an element of the state's case: Simpson's opportunity to kill (click), his motive (click), the blood trail he left at the scene of the crime (click), the victim's blood on his socks and glove (click), the victim's fibers on his knit cap (click), the actual glove he wore during the murders (click), the personal style of the killing (click). Until, finally, all the evidentiary pieces are in place, and there on the screen looms the completed picture: it is the face of O. J. Simpson.

For the prosecution, the Simpson jurors' task was obvious. Like detectives in a mystery story, all they needed to do was add up the pieces in an evidentiary puzzle. As prosecutor Christopher Darden would say, "This case really is a simple case when you get down to the bottom line." Simple because deductive and inductive logic in the face of objective reality dictate the result. Once the factual truth has emerged the jurors have no choice but to comply with the law's demands. Within this narrative scheme, factual and legal imperatives keep the jury's role under strict control. No wonder the prosecutors were so anxious to place rhetoric and feelings out of bounds—they might disrupt the linear march of the state's mystery-solving logic.

Of course, jurors may also be led to reject the classically passive role in which prosecutors often seek to cast them. Rather than being ruled by fixity (being bound by manifest reality) and closure (following the law's mandate), they may instead be induced to enter a symbolic world characterized by dramatic possibility and openness. The O. J. Simpson criminal trial also provides a vivid example of how this kind of symbolic truth may be used. We see it unfold in defense lawyer Johnnie Cochran's closing argument. In sharp contrast to the prosecution's narrative scheme, here the jury's task is no longer a simple matter of passive fact detection, a matter of casting an objective eye back into the past. Indeed, within the symbolic story genre of the defense the jurors' task is neither simple nor ordinary. They will now be cast as the main protagonists in an extraordinary drama. It is a story about justice, but not of the backward-looking kind. The defense story is happening here and now—in real time inside the courtroom.[7] The jurors, as Cochran repeatedly tells them, are now embarked on "a journey toward justice"[8]—a journey whose ultimate destination the jurors alone can tell.

As it turns out this is no ordinary voyage. It is a heroic quest. As the defense notes, there have been others who have joined on similar quests in the past. Those like Frederick Douglass, who fought as a former slave more than a hundred years ago against the evils of slavery and racism in America.[9] These are the jurors' forebears and comrades in the heroic struggle against what Cochran repeatedly refers to as "genocidal racism"—a phrase Cochran finds especially apt in describing the views of the state's star witness, Los Angeles police officer Mark Fuhrman. Fuhrman's overtly racist views toward blacks and mixed-race couples were an important part of the defense's evidentiary record at trial. Indeed, for the defense Fuhrman became a symbol of the official corruption and abuse of power that caused O. J. Simpson to be wrongfully targeted by the police in the first place.

From this gallery of rogues and heroes the jurors are to measure their own character and moral worth in the struggle taking place in court—and in the nation at large. For as the defense repeatedly reminds them, these jurors, and perhaps they alone, are empowered to change the current state of affairs in the country. It is up to them to undo the injustices stemming from state racism and abuse of power—if the jurors have the courage and the fortitude to realize their ideals and principles. As Cochran exhorts them during his final argument:

> If you don't stop it [i.e., the state's cover-up] then who? Do you think the police department is going to stop it? Do you think we can stop it by ourselves? It has to be stopped by you. . . . You police the police through your verdict. . . . You are the ones in war, you are the ones who are on the front line. . . . You are empowered to say we are not going to take [police abuse of power and racism] anymore. . . . You have the authority. . . . Please don't compromise your principles . . . don't rush to judgment. Don't compound what [the state has] already done in this case.[10]

In short, it is up to the jury, by their judgment, to set justice straight—not just here, in this particular case, but in the nation at large. The state's abuses—their reliance upon racist police officers like Mark Fuhrman and their proffering of tainted evidence in court—can only be checked by the jurors' heroic action. The jurors must ask themselves: "Was I naive? Was I timid? Or was I courageous? Did I believe in the Constitution? Did I believe in justice? Did I do my part for integrity and honesty?" Only a verdict of acquittal, the defense urges, will allow the jurors to realize the heroic identity the defense holds out for them. Passivity will not do. As Cochran puts it: "In a society where many people are apathetic," it is up to the jurors to act.

In the Simpson defense team's heroic narrative the mystery surrounding the deaths of Nicole Brown and Ron Goldman may remain in the end, which is to say factual truth may not have been detected after all. But in the defense view this is no cause for regret. For there is, they suggest, an even greater prize to be won than factual truth: the prize of justice. In this respect, the defense comes close to inviting the jury to nullify (or, more accurately, to disobey under these specific circumstances) the law's command. For to do otherwise here, to convict O. J. Simpson of murder, might be to collude in the state's own corruption. As for the uncertainty a verdict of acquittal leaves with respect to factual truth (who done it?), the defense counters with an alternative sense of closure. It is the closure that comes with the heroic affirmation of a compelling symbolic truth—"doing the right thing," acting for a greater good, perhaps even in the face of factual truths to the contrary.

From what has been said so far, three general observations may be offered. First, there can be little doubt that fictional methods are in common use within the courtroom. Second, for each kind of truth that an advocate might choose to elicit at trial—be it factual, legal, or symbolic—there is a distinct mode of reasoning couched in a discrete narrative and discursive form. Plainly, truth is not a unitary thing, something simply waiting "out there" to be discovered. In the course of its being constructed at trial truth may assume a number of different forms, each of which may serve a distinct strategic purpose.

There is a third observation to be made. What we commonly regard as "truth" is not easily divorced from fiction. Indeed, it often resides there.[11] As media theorist Timothy Murray has said, "fictional models permeate factual discourse."[12] To illustrate this point, consider the reality-effect of the popular film *Jaws*. It is generally well known that the risk of being attacked by a shark in the ocean near a beach is about as remote as that of being struck by lightning. Yet, notwithstanding such common knowledge, it was widely reported that after viewing the film's gripping scenes of a giant shark's violent attacks upon bathers, people avoided the ocean in droves.

The simple truth is that we want to believe. And even when we know why we shouldn't, we find ways to stick with fiction-prompted ideas. In fact, even after the fictional story has been discarded the emotionally charged associations it may have triggered can remain vivid. In other words, we can always "verify" a fictional account by projecting into it nonfictional details from our own life. As cognitive psychologist Richard Gerrig writes, "[W]hat appears to determine the extent to which the information will affect real-world judgments is the strength of the association between the story concepts and the preexisting world-knowledge concepts."[13]

Consider the following example. A popular actor, well known for his sympathetic portrayal of a beloved family doctor, appears in a television commercial for a certain cold medication. "I'm not a physician," he says with a warm smile. "But I play one on TV." He then goes on to extoll the virtues of the product he is selling. Clearly, this actor's endorsement carries no medical authority. Yet our awareness of his fictional identity has a distinct reality effect. The warm feelings of amiability and trust the viewer associates with his fictional character survive the actor's opening caveat. Indeed, it is precisely this association the advertisers are banking on.

Similar confusions of fiction and reality are not uncommon at trial. This is particularly apparent during jury deliberations. For example, in every jury trial, following the lawyers' presentation of evidence and closing arguments, judges will instruct the jury on the applicable categories of law. The jurors are told that their verdict must be based upon these categories. However, studies have shown that jurors often have trouble following the law's dry and often complex requirements. As a result, in the course of their deliberations jurors (unwittingly) end up conforming obscure legal categories to the more familiar representations of ordinary common sense.

Take robbery. The law says robbery is a crime that involves the taking of property from someone by force or threat of force. The law does not require that the property be valuable or that the robber be armed or that the robbery occur in someone's home. Yet there is a more typical (what cognitive psychologists call a "prototypical") scenario that readily springs to mind when people think of a robbery. According to that more familiar scenario, robbery occurs when something of value is taken and when the robber is armed.[14] Now if a juror mistakenly substitutes these "prototypical" features of robbery for legal ones, the absence of a prototypical feature will lead the juror (erroneously) to conclude that a robbery has not occurred. Inadvertently, the juror's everyday world knowledge, based in all likelihood on popular representations in the mass media, has done the work of law. In the words of social psychologist Vicki Smith, "[I]t appears that people construct prototype representations of crime categories similar to the way other social categories are organized, but contrary to the way the categories are organized under law." [15]

Trial lawyers, like their counterparts in advertising, may exploit various kinds of confusions, including the confusion of truth and fiction. Consider the case of *Maxis Corp. v. Kidder, Peabody Co.*[16] This was an insider trading case that pitted a popular Texas gas company against Kidder, Peabody, a high-powered investment banking firm based in New York. Since the case was being tried in Dallas, Texas, the stage for an "us" versus "them" strategy was clearly set. To exploit this theme, enhancing the jury's sympathetic identification with Maxis and their antipathy toward Kidder Peabody, the Maxis legal team drew their inspiration from a popular salsa commercial that had been playing on television at the time of trial. The commercial featured a cook who tried to feed his cowboys salsa made in New York instead of a local (i.e., more authentic) brand. The cowboys became enraged and shouted: "New York City! Get the rope!" The commercial's final image is of the hapless cook tied up near the campfire.

Exploiting this popular anti-New York animus, the Maxis legal team devised a trial graphic consisting of a map that prominently displayed a Texas flag (indicating the location of Texas). The jury then saw flying out of New York State an organizational chart featuring the faces of highly placed Kidder, Peabody executives. The Texas flag looked like it was about to lasso the entire state. These images not only pegged the defendants as prototypical "outsiders"; their associative logic also invited a familiar sentiment: "Get the rope!" As the creators of the graphic observed, "[V]isual communication has both a substantive and a stylistic component." At the Kidder trial they proved to be masters of both.[17]

People crave enchantment. But the kind of truth that we affirm may depend upon the kind of story that's being told. More specifically, in regard to legal storytelling I submit that there are at least three kinds of truth to choose from:

- factual truth,
- higher (or "legal") truth, and
- symbolic truth.

Factual truth tells us what happened as a matter of historical accuracy. Whose testimony can be believed, what the physical evidence shows, how the elements of proof add up in the course of establishing who is to blame—these are typical elements in the factual truth script at trial. Legal truth, however, tells us something else. It says that there are times when general concepts and abstract principles of law may be more important than particular facts. We see this, for example, when the defense urges a jury to acquit a criminal defendant because the prosecution has failed to meet its burden of proof, a burden that requires not just some evidence of guilt but evidence that proves guilt beyond a reasonable doubt. We see it as well when an attorney tries to exclude a defendant's confession from the evidence the jury will consider, not because it is false but because it was unlawfully obtained, in violation of due process, through the use of excessive force or coercion by the authorities. This kind of legal truth rests upon underlying concepts of human dignity and the danger of allowing the government or its agents unlimited power to obtain facts at all costs. Notably, to the extent law's higher truths may at times be deemed to trump factual truth (the factual basis for wrongdoing), the courts have ruled that this is not a matter ordinary lay jurors can reasonably be expected to determine for themselves. In short, the courts have acknowledged the limits of ordinary common sense in the application of higher legal principle.[18]

Symbolic truth is fundamentally different from legal and factual truth, although it shares certain similarities with both. Symbolic truth has the power to transcend particular facts and even particular laws. In this way, like legal truth, symbolic truth may ask a decision maker to sacrifice particular facts for the sake of something larger. But like factual truth it also seeks to root the truth not in some counterintuitive generality but in a specific human reality—albeit a higher human reality than ordinary facts typically allow. It is that higher reality that the symbolic truth script gives us. In doing so, it activates our deepest cultural beliefs, values, and aspirations. It tells us the good we may achieve, the evil we may conquer, the kind of ideal self and community we may create, and the means for doing so.

To enact a symbolic legal drama successfully requires the active, real-time participation of the jury. But it also requires more. For this is no ordinary event, and the present it evokes is no ordinary time. Symbolic legal dramas demarcate a space and time set apart, when the trial seems to open onto a realm akin to the sacred. At such times, ordinary conventions drop away together with the ingrained habits of thought, feeling, and belief that maintain them. In their absence, deeper norms, accompanied by intensified feelings and beliefs, come to be experienced as if for the first time. At such moments even self-transformation may seem possible. Spurred by heroic belief, a hero may come into being.

Just because we may have lost the words to describe certain events within secular society does not mean they no longer occur. What I am suggesting is that when symbolic legal drama operates at its most intense level it succeeds in casting jurors into mythic time. Indeed, it may well take that much to dislodge them from their conventional (habituated) modes of perception and thought. In the course of everyday life higher values are rarely so charged with vitality. In the mythic time of trial, however, jurors may experience what William James has referred to as "the simplest rudiment of mystical experience." It is, at heart, an experience of deepened significance, the kind of encounter after which one might say, "I've heard that said (or seen that sight or felt that touch) all my life, but I never realized its full meaning until now." [19] To experience an original meaning—that is the hallmark of myth.

Of course, a stigma still clings to the word "myth," just as it clings to the word "rhetoric." It is part of a long cultural heritage—the European Enlightenment, the modern age of scientific reason, of logical positivism and objective truth—that has us pit rhetoric against truth and myth against reality. While the grip of Descartes's rationalist dogma has loosened considerably in more recent times, his objectivist spirit has not altogether disappeared. It is for this reason that in seeking to evoke the deeper meaning of myth, scholars like Mircea Eliade have felt obliged to note at the outset the positivist clichés that tell us to discard myth as mere untruth. Like Freud, who labored hard to convey the symbolic power of dream-work in the unconscious, Eliade struggled to communicate the reality myth narrates *in illo tempore*—in "the Great Time," the sacred time, of the beginning. [20]

Notably, in Eliade's view myth stands apart from, not opposed to, ordinary or profane reality. According to Eliade, through the sacred history that myth relates it is possible to detach oneself from profane time and to "magically re-enter" "the holy time of the beginning." It is in the time of the beginning that a deeper truth or value emerges in its most pristine form. Eliade writes, "Being *real* and *sacred,* the myth becomes exemplary, and consequently *repeatable,* for it serves as a model, and by the same token as a justification, for all human actions." In this way myth provides "the pattern for human behavior."

In other words, by "imitating the exemplary acts of a god or of a mythic hero," or "simply by recounting their adventures," we may experience an originary truth or exemplary meaning that may then be carried forth into the secular time of everyday life.[21] Anthropologist Victor Turner has described this heightened reality as *communitas,* that storehouse of core values that undergird social and cultural life.[22] These values ordinarily lie dormant, coming into plain view only when conventional social structures have been temporarily suspended. It is this revelatory experience that the rituals Turner studied in tribal societies seek to bring about. It may also be akin to what the ancient Greeks experienced, assembled en masse, in the great, open-air amphitheaters in which the works of Sophocles, Aeschylus, and Euripides were enacted. It is this kind of collective transport that religious rituals and even some theater performances today still induce, albeit on a much smaller scale. It is an experience that also occurs inside the courtroom.

But can we really say in our day that the secular time of the trial can give way to the sacred time of mythic reality? Can modern jurors be lured out of their mundane lives, called to transform themselves, and perhaps even the social world around them, into something closer to an originary ideal? Can a modern jury be challenged to imitate some exemplary heroic action? Consider the following criminal case.

It is June 15, 1993. Gerry Spence is about to make his closing argument before a jury in federal district court in Boise, Idaho. He is defending Randy Weaver, a man accused of criminal charges arising from the murder of a federal marshal during a shootout on Weaver's property. The facts of the case may be summarized as follows.

In October 1989, Randy Weaver sold illegal firearms—two sawed-off shotguns—to a confidential informant who was working for the Bureau of Alcohol, Tobacco, and Firearms (BATF). The agent knew Weaver from a meeting they had both attended of the Aryan Nations, a neo-Nazi, white separatist organization. Eight months later, agents of the BATF let Weaver know he was subject to arrest for the illegal sale. The agents then invited Weaver to serve as a BATF informant, but he refused.

In December 1990, Randy Weaver was indicted for manufacturing, possessing, and selling illegal firearms. He was arrested on January 17, 1991. His trial was initially set for February 19, 1991, but that date was subsequently changed to February 20. It is not clear whether Weaver ever received correct information about the actual trial date, but he had no intention of appearing in any event. Following Weaver's failure to appear for trial, a bench warrant was issued for his arrest.

Weaver fled with his family—wife Vicki, 16-year-old Sara, 14-year-old Sammy, 10-year-old Rachel, and 10-month-old Elisheba—to a cabin they owned on Ruby Ridge, a remote, heavily wooded mountaintop in northern Idaho. Randy and Vicki Weaver claimed they had moved their family there from Iowa more than a decade before seeking refuge from a government they mistrusted and in order to practice, free from interference, religious beliefs that included belief in the separation of the white and black races. Over the years Randy Weaver had attended several Aryan Nation meetings that were held not far from his home on Ruby Ridge.

Federal marshals subsequently learned of Weaver's whereabouts in Idaho. They also knew that the Weavers were sharing their cabin with a family friend named Kevin Harris. On August 21, 1992, six deputy U.S. marshals went onto the Weavers' property as part of a plan to place Randy Weaver under arrest. Three agents approached the Weavers' cabin and threw some stones in order to attract the attention of the Weavers' dogs. The family's yellow Labrador, Striker, began to follow the agents. Together with his 14-year-old son Sammy and Kevin Harris, Randy Weaver took up after the dog.

One of the agents then spotted Weaver and ordered him to stop. Weaver yelled at Kevin and Sammy to head back to the cabin and fired a couple of shots in the air. The agents then fired two shots at the dog, killing it. In response, Sammy fired two shots from his Mini-14 rifle in the marshals' direction. The marshals shot Sammy in the arm and in the back, killing him. Harris returned fire. It was his shot, he later concedes, that killed deputy marshal Billy Degan. Harris and the marshals then retreated.

Soon after this exchange of gunfire and the casualties it led to, the Marshals Service called the FBI in Washington for help. Faced with one marshal killed and the prospect of escalating violence, Larry Potts, head of the FBI's criminal division, ordered the FBI's elite Hostage Rescue Team (HRT), commanded by Richard Rogers, to go to Ruby Ridge. Rogers, apparently out of concern for the safety of his men, drafted new rules of engagement. FBI snipers were instructed that they "can and should" shoot any armed adult, whether or not their lives or the lives of others are in imminent danger.

The next day, August 22, 1992, numerous state police, federal marshals, and FBI agents converged on Ruby Ridge. Nine HRT snipers, having been briefed on the new rules of engagement, were positioned around the Weavers' cabin. At approximately 6 P.M., HRT sniper Lon Horiuchi spotted Randy Weaver outside the cabin and fired a shot, hitting Weaver in the arm. Kevin Harris and Sara Weaver, who were also outside, ran toward the cabin for cover as Vicki Weaver called to them. Vicki held the door open with one arm, and held 10-month-old Elisheba with the other. As Sara, Kevin, and Randy pushed through the cabin door, Horiuchi fired a second shot. It passed through the window in the door and struck Vicki in the head, killing her almost instantly. Kevin Harris was wounded by the same bullet.

Harris remained inside the cabin for eight days before surrendering to authorities. Randy Weaver surrendered two days later.

Harris was subsequently indicted for first degree murder and six other charges, including assault and firearms violations. The charges subsequently brought against Randy Weaver included aiding and abetting murder, assault on a federal officer, conspiracy to provoke a violent confrontation, and sale and possession of illegal firearms.

With this factual background in mind, let us now return to Gerry Spence's closing argument before the jury in behalf of Randy Weaver. Spence will skillfully tailor the facts of the case into a powerful and moving narrative. Ultimately, he will transform the story of Randy Weaver into a tale of mythic proportions. It will become a symbolic legal drama in which the jurors will be called upon to play a very special role. They may not realize it yet, but they are about to be summoned to a hero's quest—a journey that will transport them to the realm of mythic reality.

Spence begins his address:

> And I should tell you that since my argument starts with me, that maybe I ought to tell you how I feel. I think to myself, can I do what I need to do. I feel afraid. I feel inadequate. I wish, instead of doing this for 40 years I had done it a lot more, and was a much better lawyer than I am right now. I need to be the best lawyer I can be in the next two hours and 35 minutes.

Here, then, is Gerry Spence. Renowned defense attorney, an impeccable record of victory in court, expressing doubt, inadequacy, fear. He feels afraid. He confesses as much to the jury as he stands alone before them. It seems a simple stance. Its complexity will become clear only once we allow his dramatic themes and characters to develop.

Yet even here at the outset, the key note has already been sounded. Spence is afraid. What does it mean? Let us consider the possibilities:

(1) Spence is afraid because he should be afraid. Anyone would be if they but realized the danger at hand: a federal government that has run amok, promoting carnage and terror, suppressing freedom, intimidating and demonizing plain family folk at will. Anyone who knew would be afraid. Only the uninitiated, the naive, could claim otherwise. ("I'm not afraid to learn," Luke Skywalker assures his mentor at the beginning of his apprenticeship into Jedi knighthood. "You will be," his master replies.)

(2) Spence is afraid because Randy Weaver was afraid and it is his job as Weaver's attorney to embody Weaver's fear, to make it real for the jury. The client will not testify in this case, the jury will not have a chance to hear his voice or test his candor. It will be up to Spence to fill in the silence. He must assume Weaver's voice, Weaver's truth. And so he stands before the jury, and he is afraid.

(3) Spence is afraid because he might fail. Spence might not do his client justice. He might not be able to show well enough why Weaver was afraid, why anyone would be afraid, why the jury should be afraid, in the face of the kind of power-hungry, death-dealing, inhuman force they are up against in the form of the federal government.

(4) Spence is afraid because he, too, is up against the same power, the same federal government. Right now, here in the courtroom, he too is standing up to the federal bigwigs—the head of the FBI and its sister enforcement division, the Bureau of Alcohol, Tobacco, and Firearms. Agencies under the thumb of the prosecution. Spence must pit himself against them, here and now, and he knows their power. So he is afraid.

(5) Spence is afraid, and says so, because in this way he becomes real to the jury. He is who he is, and who the jury may perhaps become. He is there to show them how, to show what it takes to succeed in adversity, to exemplify a counterforce to corruption, the power that inheres in what is good and right. Spence is himself, in real time, and he is afraid. If he hid his fear how could he be trusted? How can he hide when he must embody what is true and real?

It is the last time Gerry Spence will be allowed to address the jury. And so he speaks with honesty and openness, in painful self-revelation, so that a bond of trust may be consummated between him and the jurors, and so that all the rest of what he has to say may be heard aright. It is as if to say, "This is who I am. I am willing to open myself up to you, to expose my innermost feelings along with what I know. And in this moment of vulnerability you see that I am willing to place myself in your hands, subject to your judgment, and to do the same for my client." Showing trust often begets trust in return. Here, by placing himself and his client in the hands of the jury, Spence has demonstrated confidence in the jurors' judgment, their ability to do what is right, to recognize the truth, and to act with justice.

In this way, Spence may come to be seen by the jury not only as an honest man (provided he can show that the basis for his fear is legitimate); he may also come to be seen as an exemplar, a guide, a mentor. To achieve the latter role, however, he must be able to demonstrate in his own person, in both words and actions, the proper response to overreaching power. Yet in the end it is not Spence's protest that really matters, he tells the jury. He may sound a call to action, but it is up to the jurors to respond—or not. The choice is theirs. Will they succumb to fear in the face of the state's tyrannical threat? Or will they find the heroic impulse within, will they be able to transform themselves in a way they may not previously have thought possible, or even thought about at all? Spence's task will not be easy; he must call the jurors to themselves, to their higher selves, if they will but heed what he has to say.

Thus we arrive at the first stage of the hero's journey: the call to adventure. The jury will now have to decide whether they are willing to leave the ordinary world behind. They have been summoned, and it will be no ordinary journey. How do we know? Spence tells them:

> You may be the most important jury that has come along for many a decade. It is an experience that you will never forget and your efforts and your determination and your thoughts may change the history of this country.
>
> This is a watershed case. . . . [Y]our purpose here isn't just to find who wins the case. It seems to me that you have a larger function here, a more noble function.[23]

But are the jurors up to such a challenge? After all, who are these ordinary citizens, selected by chance from the community at large, to undertake such a heroic task? Spence knows this too, that doubt and resistance to the call are part of the story. In the great tales of adventure the summons is almost always greeted at first with skepticism and reluctance. (Didn't Luke at first resist Obi-Wan Kenobi's invitation to follow in his father's footsteps? Only when it was too late, when the Enemy had killed his aunt and uncle, when Luke had nowhere else to go, did he join Obi-Wan on the path to adventure. Like Dorothy, before her ascension to Oz. She too had tried to escape the call, to remain at home. But for her as well it was too late. The cellar doors could no longer be opened, and the cyclonic forces of the adventure had advanced too far to be stopped. They would soon propel her far from the ordinary life she had known.) The jury too will resist the call. Spence knows this is so. They will do as anyone would in their place. Which is why Spence must spur them on:

> I want you to realize that few of us, me included, ever really know how important we are or where we stand in history. Go back to 1775 and the Continental Congress, and we see old George sitting there—I guess he wasn't there, but Jefferson was there, Adams was there. Do you think they thought they were important? They were just local guys doing their job, like you are local people doing your job, but as we look back on history they did something permanent and magnificent and lasting, and that is what you will do with your verdict in this case, something permanent, magnificent and lasting.[24]

They're just plain folks, like good old Tom and George. They too could hardly see at the time that they were making history, that they had become irrevocably caught up in the cyclonic forces of fate. They too were just plain folks, just doing their jobs as they saw fit. And what job was that? What was Tom Jefferson's mission? To protect freedom. The same mission, as it turns out, as these very jurors, here, inside this Idaho courtroom. Spence will use Jefferson's own words: "Now, one of those fellows, Tom, named Thomas, called him Tom, made a statement. He said, 'Eternal vigilance is the price of liberty.'" Soon the jurors will learn that these are not idle words. For somehow their fate and the fate of a heroic figure like Jefferson have crossed. And Jefferson's words, heard and appreciated as never before, must now become the jurors' words as well.

Thus even as he addresses the jury's understandable skepticism, their resistance to the call, Spence is also sounding the deepest theme of his case. Why have these jurors, these ordinary men and women, been singled out for so high a purpose? Who knows? All we know is that, as with Tom and George, it just happened. And like those early American heroes, these jurors too must face a similar call, to stand up to power, to resist in their own time tyranny's threat to freedom. And like those before them these jurors too will be armed from the same arsenal of true and heroic ideas: "Eternal vigilance is the price of liberty."

"But why me?" Spence hears the words still echoing in the jurors' minds. And so he responds again, assuaging the doubts that remain. No one can ever say for sure "where we stand in history":

> So I have to ask you, and you must ask yourselves, why are we here? Why were we chosen? How did I get chosen for this job? There were many other jurors there. Why was I left? Why? And the question is, is there something more here than simply finding the answer to some charges that have been leveled by the Government?[25]

There must be something more, Spence suggests. We may not be able to explain it, some mysterious force may be operating. But for whatever reason, it is these jurors' fate to leave their ordinary lives behind. They have been seized by History, called upon to do something permanent, magnificent, and lasting. In short, they are on a hero's journey. And the stakes could hardly be higher. For surely they must realize that what happened to Randy Weaver and his family could happen to anyone. It is exactly what happens when government forces are out of control. Which is why the need to stand up to the federal government's abuse of power, to actualize the hero's task here and now by voting to acquit Randy Weaver of murder, is so vital. It is a matter of the most basic principle. Ours is a system of laws, not men, Spence explains. This is the axiomatic truth on which the rule of law is founded. It is, Spence tells them, that "basic proposition" upon which we all can agree:

> Government agents are bound by the law the same as we. They're bound by morals and by justice and by decency the same as we. And that Government agents can't lie and say it's right because they're officers. And they can't come into court and play hide and seek with the facts and say that's all right because they are federal employees. . . . And they can't persecute people and they can't entrap people, and state the wrong law. . . . [T]hey can't attack us because of our religious or our political beliefs simply because they have the power. . . .[26]

"They" can't attack "us." "They can't come into Idaho from Washington, D.C., and claim that Idaho law is null and void." That is what is at stake. "They" are threatening "us." Our local laws, our local communities, our homes, our very lives. The intrusive, threatening Other must be held at bay. But to do that, local folk are going to have to band together, to stay strong, to protect their own from the Federal Interlopers:

> We have a task here of defending Randy Weaver in eight counts with a bunch of subcounts contained in the murder charge. My goal is to, when we leave here, for us all to walk out together. This is what I am trying to do, this is the purpose of my final argument, to ask you to free Randy Weaver and to free that boy, and let us all walk out together in this case. . . . I want him to walk out and be free with his little children. I want you to—stand up, please. This is Sarah and this is Rachel. . . .[27]

To walk out together. All of us. With our community intact, determined, united. Right here in Boise, Idaho. A town of good folk, not perfect, not incapable of misjudgment, but good folk, family people, Bible-believing people. Like Randy Weaver and his young children. And if folk like Randy and his family can be put through all this, on trial for aiding and abetting the murder of a federal marshal after his own young son and wife were shot dead, with Randy himself wounded, even the family dog killed by federal sharpshooters just waiting for the chance to open fire, who wouldn't be afraid? No, Randy Weaver's fear, like Spence's, makes sense.

Then, in an effort to tighten further the protective bond of community around his client, himself, and the jurors, Spence says straight out,

> I will tell you what Randy is guilty of. Randy you are guilty of being one stubborn mother. I will tell you that. You are guilty of being afraid. And aren't we all guilty of that? Aren't we all afraid? Wouldn't all of you, under the circumstances that existed in this case be afraid?[28]

In this way, Spence draws the jurors further into the world of his client. It is their world too. But this move alone will not suffice. There must be more. The jurors' identification with Randy Weaver's plight may open up the possibility of empathy. This is surely one reason why Spence seeks to create a sense of familiarity, of shared identity, of "us" against "them." It is why Randy's and Spence's fear may come to be seen as an entirely natural response to the federal government's violence and lies. And if Randy occasionally showed poor judgment, like that time when he briefly associated with an Aryan Nation group, well, that cannot be helped. Poor judgment is inescapable; it's a natural part of being human. Even Spence can't avoid it, as he demonstrates in court, calling on his wife, Imaging, to stand up for the jury to see. "We've been married a long time," Spence says. "Why shouldn't I be proud of her? When I get home, she's going to say to me, you used poor judgment. You shouldn't have had me stand up like that." See? Everyone, even Spence, is capable of exercising poor judgment from time to time. But as Spence quickly adds, poor judgment is no reason to make a man guilty of a crime.

Empathy is good, but the jurors must now be moved toward making a choice. They can either help the federal government "cover up their crimes by finding [Randy Weaver] guilty of something," they can "join that conspiracy," join in the state's attempt to "demonize" Randy Weaver because of his beliefs. Or they can set him free and walk out of court together, they can return with Randy and his family to their community, to their homes and loved ones. The jurors' identification with Randy's plight helps, but it will take more than empathy to activate the jurors' core values, to stir not just pity, but also their fear and outrage and heroic solidarity, so that their fear may be overcome and their outrage may be properly channeled.

To reach the next stage of their journey the jurors will have to feel themselves drawn into real battle. This is not simply a matter of re-experiencing, in historic time, the battle Randy Weaver was forced to wage when federal sharpshooters confronted him and his family up on Ruby Ridge. They must now battle against the same danger, and the same foe, in real time, right there inside the courtroom. Just as Gerry Spence is being forced to do battle against deceitful federal prosecutors in open court. In real time, yes. But this is no longer ordinary time. The jurors will now be drawn into a time set apart, the intensified moment of mythic reality. Within this strange, transient but unforgettable moment, the jurors' habituated feelings and beliefs will give way to something far stronger. They will now encounter feelings and beliefs as if for the first time, *in illo tempore,* in the Great Time, the time of the beginning. The experience may be unfamiliar. No doubt it is ill-described in our time, if we still have words for it at all. Even so, in the intensified moment originary meanings will be revealed.

There is a threshold the jurors will now have to cross. The ordeal must be brought home, faced live. There is a battle that remains for the jurors to wage. (For the house has landed and they are no longer in Kansas; the Wicked Witch waits in the wings. Jedi knighthood may be conferred, but not before the evil father, Darth Vader, has been confronted.) The jurors themselves must now walk a road of trials. They too must meet the enemy. They too will have to be tested, as Randy Weaver was. Fear may now become more real as they recognize who the enemy is and who the ally, and what must be done. For as it turns out the foe is closer and more dangerous than they might have thought:

> Big Brother has come. The worst of our fears are here, and thank God, I'm in a courtroom where I can say this with protection. I can point my finger at a government agent in America and say, this man and that agency are the new gestapo in this country. . . .
>
> Now something is very horrid that's happening here and I want you to hear this. I told you that this is a watershed case and I want you to hear this. What is happening in America when the government begins to point, not to criminals who are joining conspiracies like dope dealers who join up and bankers who do behind-the-scene conspiracies and cheat old ladies out of their savings, but families. The new low in American jurisprudence is to attack the American family and to say that they the American family now can be guilty of a conspiracy by virtue of the fact that they are a family.[29]

The enemy is real and the danger is close at hand. No longer is this simply a case about an isolated incident, a single violent confrontation up on Ruby Ridge where federal marshals ran amok. This is about federal agents who "can bring in their airplanes and they can bring in their helicopters, and they can bring in their snipers and their assaulters, and they can have themselves a big war up in northern Idaho. In August. Get out of that hot Washington, D.C. and have themselves a ball" (18). That is the force we are dealing with here—a force that can break out suddenly, in anyone's backyard. And it's worse than that. Because after their "orgy of violence," instead of admitting the wrong they had done these federal marshals-run-amok came back to wield their power again, in court, to cover up and distort the truth. And it's Randy Weaver who must now be demonized for his beliefs, to cover up for the government's wrongs. As if that would make the government's outrageous violence easier to take. "You know, we're starting to get at it now," Spence explains with mounting vigor. "Power, power, power, power."

But even if the danger we all face is real and present, for all their power and subtlety Spence also lets it be known that this tyrannical force can be successfully resisted. Spence, guide and mentor, shows the way. He shows the jurors first by telling them of their power, more power than they may have realized:

> Somebody has to say no . . . [that] you cannot do this, Federal Government, to one of our citizens, because a jury in the final analysis—do you understand your power? Stop and think about it. You have more power than anybody, and that's the way it's supposed to be. Because you're the only ones who can say no. You've got more power than His Honor. . . . You've got a lot more power than [the federal prosecutors]. You've got a lot more power than the Federal Bureau of Investigation and the ATF, you've got more power than the marshals. You've got more power than anybody because you can say no . . . and that is the end of it.[30]

But Spence goes further. He not only tells the jurors of the power that is theirs, but he also models for them the very act of resistance he wants them to perform. Right there, inside the courtroom, Spence stands up to power, shows the jury the way it's done:

> MR. SPENCE: By the way, Mr. Lindquist, I understand you don't have the chart anymore, is that right?
> U.S. ATTORNEY LINDQUIST: I have it.
> SPENCE: You have it?
> LINDQUIST: I do.
> SPENCE: May I have it, please?
> LINDQUIST: I'm going to use it when I rebut this, as you well know.
> SPENCE: I have a right to use the chart to rebut. . . . I have a right to see the chart, and I would like to have you bring it up here so that I can answer that.
> THE COURT: The chart should be produced. . . .
> SPENCE: May I have it, please?
> LINDQUIST: Sure. (11)

Well now, what do we see? Stand up to their power and guess what? They cave. ("May I have it, please?" "Sure.")

We are ready now for the climactic moment, ready to face the supreme ordeal on the hero's journey. The jurors now know of the urgency of the moment and what it takes to stand up to federal power. Next they will have to see what happens when the moment is lost, what happens when they forget to be vigilant in the face of "the new storm troopers." Fail to resist here and now, Spence warns, and who knows whose beliefs, whose actions, whose homes and personal freedom will be subject to federal scrutiny and control next time? Just consider Randy Weaver, as Spence tells the jury:

> We've got a man here who was curious about what was going on, was looking for the religious truth. I commend him for that. I've spent a lifetime wondering and wondering, and looking and looking. Why can't a citizen look, hear and wonder and go and inquire? Why can't he do that?

Isn't it clear? Those who are on their own special journey, those who may be seeking a different sort of knowledge, a deeper truth perhaps, a spiritual truth, people like Randy Weaver, like Gerry Spence, and like the jurors themselves, here and now inside the courtroom, these are the very people who are at special risk. For these are the people the federal government is most inclined to target and demonize for their personal beliefs, beliefs that may set them apart.[31]

Fail to stand up to that threat and our most precious possessions— freedom, privacy, religious belief—may be lost. That is the test the jurors must face. Will they stand up for who they are, and what they most believe in? One thing is certain: if they fail the cost will be great. But if they succeed so too will be their reward. For then their most precious ideals may be made real and brought home to be shared with loved ones for generations to come:

> We are going to teach something. We are going to tell the whole world something here by our verdict here of justice. . . . [T]his is a watershed case . . . a case that kids in law school are going to read about and your grandchildren and your great-grandchildren are going to be a part of.[32]

But first "somebody has to say no." "I can't do it," Spence tells them. "The only thing I can do is ask you to do it." It is the jurors alone who have the power, if they but have the courage to fulfill the heroic quest. It is by their verdict of acquittal that the jurors can consummate their heroic journey. Only then may they complete the transformative process, in mythic time, by which the hero within may be

realized, the hero who wields the force of justice to defeat lies, treach-
ery, and unconscionable violence. For it is by their verdict that the
jurors may bring the elixir of freedom back to their community and,
by their heroic example, to the nation as a whole. "This government
is our servant, not our master." "Doesn't [your] verdict want to say
no to this kind of conduct across the nation? . . . These are the top
government people that your verdict is going to talk to, and it's going
to say either yes, or no." "Doesn't this terror and this horror have to
end sometime? Shouldn't it end with you and shouldn't it end without
compromise? Shouldn't this jury have the courage to stand up and say,
no, they over-exercised their power?"

It is here, at the climactic moment of choice, near the end of his
argument, that Spence shifts to his most graphic, visual storytelling
style. His searing images will leave the jurors moved, infused (just as
the ancient rhetoricians taught) with the "right" emotions in the face
of what has happened, is happening, but may be stopped from happening again. These are the purified and heightened emotions of fear,
pity, and outrage.[33] It is the key moment in the historic event that has
brought them together. A fury of bullets is about to be unleashed.
How did it start? Randy's son Sammy is outside the house, walking
with his dog, "Old Yeller" Spence calls him. It is the dog who is shot
first. Spence then takes the narrative forward from there:

> Sammy lets fly a couple of rounds at [federal marshal] Roderick, in his
> own self-defense. I mean, if you're going to shoot my dog and he's yelp-
> ing can you hear that dog yelping? Can you see that little kid watching
> his dog yelp and he thinks he's going to get shot himself by people
> who've got masks on? And they never said anything about you're under
> arrest to anybody. To anybody ever . . . and they shot the dog. With no
> cause. Old Yeller who wouldn't hurt anybody. . . . Sammy is running,
> can you see him stop and turn his back and saying, "Kevin, come on,"
> because Kevin is behind him, he gets shot in the arm, maybe two
> shots. . . . Then after his arm is shot off either before or after, I don't
> know which. All I can see is his little arm shot off, running home and
> [federal marshals] Cooper and Degan open up on his back. . . .[34]

Fear, pity, outrage. Only after they too have "seen" the ordeal and
felt for themselves the threat, and the suffering, for loved ones suddenly and horribly taken, can the jurors find their way out of the
woods and back onto the road home. Only once they have sensed their
own terrible vulnerability, and the awful price to be paid for forgoing

vigilance. Christopher Vogler writes: "The hero is transformed by these moments of death-and-rebirth, and is able to return to ordinary life reborn as a new being with new insights."[35] Here then is the next-to-last stage of the hero's journey, the stage of resurrection: to have encountered death and survived. Only then may the final stage be achieved:

> The hero Returns to the Ordinary World, but the journey is meaning-less unless she brings back some Elixir, some treasure, or lesson from the Special World. . . . It may be a great treasure like the Grail that magically heals the wounded land, or it simply might be knowledge or experience that could be useful to the community someday.[36]

And so in the end we return to the beginning, recalling once more Tom Jefferson's words: "Eternal vigilance is the price of liberty." For it is liberty that is the "treasure," the curative grail, that the jurors will bring home with them.

The story will now end, the hero's quest all but fulfilled. There is only one more step to be taken—the verdict. It is up to the jurors, here and now, to complete the drama, to make it real and give it force. But what will they do? Spence's final words again model the jury's power and the need for wisdom in the way they use it:

> I want to tell you a story. I want to tell you a story of the times. It's one of my favorite stories. It's a story about an old man and a smart-aleck little boy. The smart-aleck boy had decided he was going to show the old man up, show him what a fool he was. The smart-aleck boy caught a little bird on the porch and his plan was to go up to the old man and say, old man, what have I got in my hand? What have I got in my hand? And he figured the old man would say, well, you've got a bird. And the smart-aleck boy's plan was to say, well, old man, is the bird alive or is it dead? And if the old man said, the bird is dead, then the smart-aleck boy would open his hands and the little bird would fly off into the forest. Or if the old man said, the bird is alive, then the smart-aleck boy would crush it and crush it, crush it, crush it. And say, see, it's dead. So he went up to the old man, the kid did, and he said, old man, what do I have in my hand? And the old man said, you have a bird my son. He said, old man, is the bird alive or is it dead? The old man said, the bird is in your hands my son. And justice, truth, and the future, but not only of this country, but this family is in your hands.[37]

Will the bird die, or fly to freedom? Arriving at the right answer is no game, not a trick for the sake of a fool's triumph (the legalistic ploy of a smart-aleck prosecutor?[38]). A life, a family, a nation are at stake. Freedom or death? Justice and truth, or tyranny and deceit? It is in the jury's hands. Their decision will complete the journey that they have been on and that must now draw to a close. They alone hold the key. Old man Spence, silver-haired mentor and companion along the way, has shown them how truth and justice might triumph in this case. But only the jury's verdict can transform that possibility into reality.[39]

In this exemplary closing argument for the defense I believe we witness, among other things, the obscure but ongoing power of mythic reality. It is a reality that, in the words of anthropologist Bronislaw Malinowski, "expresses, enhances and codifies belief; it safeguards and enforces morality; it vouches for the efficiency of ritual and contains practical rules for the guidance of man. Myth is thus a vital ingredient of human civilization; it is not an idle tale, but a hard-worked active force."[40] It is this power to intensify the moment's possibility, a moment laden with the latent force of belief and heroic self-transformation, that Gerry Spence taps in his summation. The power operating here is the power to clarify and intensify basic values, the power to make meanings appear as if for the first time.

Here we see ordinary time transcended. Here, in mythic time, heroic figures like Washington, Adams, and Jefferson become living models, simultaneously familiar and exemplary to the jurors who are called upon to follow in their footsteps. They are knowable, unblemished by time's passing, as are the ideas they embody: freedom, courage, vigilance. They too are released from the ravages of time, untouched by interpretive difficulties of any kind. It is as if the jurors may now drink from the same fount of faith and moral wisdom as those great Americans who went before. The source is pure as it flows across time. And even as we see the boundaries of ordinary time being transcended, so too are the boundaries of the ordinary self.

The psychologist Abraham Maslow recounts such an experience during an academic procession in which he participated. "I became a symbol," Maslow recalls. "I stood for something outside my skin. I was not exactly an individual. I was also a 'role' of the eternal teacher."[41] In this time-transcendent moment, past and future merged. The same appeal is at work in Spence's oration. For just as Maslow felt he could personally engage such historic figures as "Spinoza, Abraham Lincoln, Jefferson, William James, Whitehead, etc., as if they still lived,"[42] so too were the jurors called to walk with Washington, Adams, and Jefferson. And just as Maslow was able to sense that he was "working hard for not yet born great-grandchildren or other successors," so too are the jurors reminded that this is a case that their "grandchildren and [their] great-grandchildren are going to be a part of."[43] In short, time avails not as past and future merge in the transcendent "now." It is the same sentiment Walt Whitman expressed in "Crossing Brooklyn Ferry," describing a trip across the East River between Manhattan and Brooklyn:

> The similitudes of the past, and those of the future;
> The glories strung like beads on my smallest sights and hearings . . .
> The others that are to follow me, the ties between me and them;
> The certainty of others—the life, love, sight, hearing of others.
> It avails not, neither time nor place—distance avails not.
> I am with you, you men and women of a generation, or ever so many
>   generations hence; . . .
> Just as you feel when you look on the river and sky, so I felt. . . .

In the transcendent moment ordinary boundaries of time and self drop away, allowing core values and exemplary ideals to be powerfully felt and concurrently enacted. Perhaps it is the exemplary ideal rising up from the past, from the mythic time of the beginning, fusing with a profound sense of union with and obligation to future generations, that makes the call to heroic action so compelling.

It is this time-transcending moment, conjured by Gerry Spence before the Weaver jury, that Eliade and others have described as the emergence in sacred time of the original model, the exemplar. But mysticism, conjured at trial—toward what end? "Toward an end of the most practical kind," comes the reply. As that great American pragmatist William James observed:

> When we commune with [the mystical region], work is actually done upon our finite personality, for we are turned into new men, and consequences in the way of conduct follow in the natural world upon our regenerative change. But that which produces effects within another reality must be termed a reality itself, so I feel as if we had no philosophic excuse for calling the unseen or mystical world unreal.[44]

It is the purpose of public spectacles—whether in the form of divinatory ritual, theater, special media events, or the spectacular criminal trial—to clarify and, in so doing, strengthen (or in some cases help to alter) deep cultural values. As Roland Barthes notes in his analysis of wrestling, in the spectacle each sign is "endowed with an absolute clarity, since one must understand everything on the spot. . . . As in theater, each physical type expresses to excess the part that has been assigned to the contestant."[45] The ignoble traitor, the heroic avenger, the suffering victim. This is, Barthes writes, "a real Human Comedy, where the most socially-inspired nuances of passion (conceit, rightfulness, refined cruelty, a sense of 'paying one's debts') always felicitously find the clearest sign which can received them, express them and triumphantly carry them to the confines of the hall."[46]

Here then we are not dealing with spectacle in the popular postmodern sense of the "hyperreal," Jean Baudrillard's term for degraded, image-saturated reality. To the contrary, in Barthes's sense the spectacle is a significant cultural event in which deeply shared values, beliefs, and emotions, in conjunction with familiar genre and character type expectations, may be publicly played out. In the process notions of self and community are strengthened as deeper than usual meanings are compellingly encountered and actively assimilated in the course of the event. This is, in short, a public forum for purer forms of cultural expression. As Barthes puts it:

> What is thus displayed for the public is the great spectacle of Suffering, Defeat, and Justice. Wrestling presents man's suffering with all the amplification of tragic masks. The wrestler who suffers in a hold which is reputedly cruel (an arm-lock, a twisted leg) offers an excessive portrayal of Suffering; like a primitive Pieta, he exhibits for all to see his face, exaggeratedly contorted by an intolerable affliction.

It is the extreme that conveys the pure form of the sign or value that has come into play. Barthes's religious allusions in this context are far from incidental. They comport with the kind of intensified reality, the encounter with original meanings, that Eliade locates within mythic reality, the exemplary reality that emerges in sacred time (*in illo tempore*). In this sense then it is not surprising to find in the spectacle of wrestling signs not just of defeat, but of "total defeat," what Barthes calls "the exemplary debasement of the vanquished" that "takes up the ancient myths of public Suffering and Humiliations: the cross and the pillory." It is what the public senses as well, as can readily be discerned when one fan says of a prostrate wrestler: "'He is dead, little Jesus, there, on the cross.'" This is not mere irony.

As Barthes comments, these words reveal "the hidden roots of spectacle which enacts the exact gestures of the most ancient purifications."[47]

The courtroom, too, is an arena in which purification of deep cultural meanings may occur. Here too, as I have tried to suggest in my analysis of Gerry Spence's "exemplary" summation, known character and story types may serve as vehicles for shared beliefs and expectations: the felt need to make the villain pay, the capacity for indignation, revengeful fury, righteous justice, and even compassion, a gentler mercy in the face of some fateful reversal of fortune that may be individually and collectively realized inside the courtroom. In court, as in the wrestling ring, one may encounter a certain "moral beauty"—a sense of truth and justice that comports with appropriate narrative forms of expression. As Barthes insightfully observes: "[I]t is from the fact that there is a Law that the spectacle of the passions which infringe it derives its value."[48] The Law—the archetype, the originary model—experienced in sacred time at the site of mythic reality, teaches us anew the proper patterns for belief, for feeling, and for social behavior generally. Here lies the originary fount for cultural and characterological normalization. Here is a site where transgression of newly appreciated cultural and social norms may be appropriately assessed and resolved—with the aid of refreshed cultural forms: legendary or mythic themes, popular genres, familiar plots and character types through which the drama of trial is enacted. In this way the trial assures us of the intelligibility of reality. The heightened understanding it allows lifts us, at least for a while, above the "constitutive ambiguity" of everyday life.[49] And in the transcendent euphoria it brings comes the moral beauty, and persuasive payoff, of a well-played narrative truth.

On this analysis, then, it may be possible to grasp more readily the phenomenon of the trial as public spectacle. For the trial offers a unique public site in which previously un- or ill-articulated norms or normative clashes may be publicly enacted. It is here that breaches in conventional norms are addressed. And in the process of reparation order and stability are at least symbolically restored—both within and without. For not only will a particular deviation from social norms have been adjudicated in the specific case at bar, but more generally so too will the norms that people expect and desire to see confirmed. In this sense order itself, and the norms that uphold it, are on trial.

It is also possible, however, that the familiar narratives that ordinarily fulfill this social norm-maintenance function may come under unusually intense internal and external pressure. Change may be in the wings. New narrative forms together with the new normative expectations they bring may be struggling to be born. At such times, the clash at trial may go far beyond the particular parties involved. For they may then become symbolic agents of larger social and cultural forces swirling around them.

This symbolic function is particularly notable in the notorious case. There are times when, by virtue of some fortuitous overdetermination of meaning that has come to be associated with a particular legal conflict, public fascination, perhaps crossing over to obsession, focuses upon a particular legal drama. The "larger-than-life" quality of this sort of spectacular trial is most likely attributable to the deep values or normative conflicts it has managed to activate. Ordinary domestic or societal disruptions may then be transformed into allegories of social and cultural strife and transformation.

Singular trials of this sort enter mainstream culture as hallmark events in which deep normative conflicts of the time may either be resolved in a particularly powerful way or left open. To be sure, these are traumatic events for society in either case. In the latter case, however, it is a trauma that is bound to recur. For the special power these dramas tap stems from the felt need shared by many to clarify certain core values that are in some way threatened—whether by conflict with other values, by a general weakening in their power to compel belief, or by some other means. The spectacular trial's overdetermined meaning, its symbolic quality, may be largely unconscious at the outset. Yet like an inarticulate buzz it is likely to resonate in some strangely compelling fashion on the surface of the trial—suggesting the untapped depths below. That unarticulated charge may even remain when the spectacle concludes. But such a conclusion forebodes some future reenactment—just as any unconscious symptom, if inadequately worked through, inevitably returns to haunt the psyche anew. This is what Freud called the return of the repressed. It is a phenomenon that attends legal conflicts as well as those of the intrapsychic kind.

That, at any rate, is the thesis presented in the next chapter. We turn now to historic trials that for one reason or another became freighted with unusually intense public interest and emotion. Clearly these trials are about far more than the stories of the particular parties or legal issues before the court. Only by examining their historic and cultural context can we begin to unravel the various meanings being played out inside the courtroom and beyond—in the court of public opinion. These are trials that have been transformed—together perhaps with the persons and issues they involve—into symbols. But symbols of what sort? And to what end?

[T]here is in all of us a persistent pressure to deny reality, to not renounce gratification. . . . Reality and perception are never free of the impact of wishful thinking and defensive functioning.

HAROLD P. BLUM, *Fantasy, Myth, and Reality*

It's like you're in a movie all the time. That's how you think about it—like you're a character in a movie.

A STUDENT, describing life on the streets in Oakland, California; quoted in WENDY LESSER, *Pictures at an Execution*

FOUR

The Law of Desire
Cultural History and the Notorious Case

A terrible urgency in the way of belief is a powerful engine for historical untruth. If a belief is urgent enough, facts that stand in its way
may need to yield. Disagreeable details may be conveniently forgotten,
repressed, or changed into something else. The change gives us insight
into the nature of the urge behind it. Consider, for example, the urge
to identify with a heroic act. In order to succeed, the act's depiction
as heroic requires supportive details. This helps to explain why more
than a decade after Bernhard Goetz shot four black teenagers on a
New York subway, news reports still repeated the false claim that the
"victims" had been armed with sharpened screwdrivers. The popular
urge at the time to support Goetz's violent act needed details to enhance its appeal. Shooting armed rather than unarmed antagonists is
an effective transformation.

Expectations are a product of belief. They are an offshoot of what
we already know. But they may also give rise to phantom realities
wherein belief outstrips what we know. In the face of a particularly
urgent belief, reality often conforms—shaped and reshaped by the
stories we hear and tell. From harmless fantasy to paralyzing para-
noia, psychological needs alter the reality of self, others, and the world
around us. External and internal realities are inextricably linked. The
visible is haunted by the invisible. Potent but hidden forces by turns
impel and impede human action and the felt need for judgment. The
same may be said of the forces that lie hidden within the popular
imagination; they, too, impel and impede judgment in the concrete
and symbolic search for truth and justice through law. And in the
quest for "proof"—a quest that lies close to law's heart—this link
between the manifest and the hidden should not be forgotten.

Among legal conflicts, notorious cases are the most haunted. They
are sites of law where the deepest, most intractable social and cultural
conflicts of the day play out. Vastly overdetermined, operating on several levels of meaning at once, these trials for one reason or another

infuse the particular facts of a specific legal controversy with larger meanings. The trial is no longer about factual truths only; its truths have become symbolic. And because in the midst of such cases we cannot always be sure on what level a particular fact may be operating, or because we may be unwilling to face directly the symbolic truth that is at play, like Hamlet we feel caught in a net of ambiguity. There is a charge of anxiety in the air, tinged with excitement. It is a peculiar emotional brew, like the one that draws us to forbidden fruits yet repels us at the same time. It is precisely this tension, this complex, overdetermined ambiguity that gives the notorious trial its spectral quality, its edge, and its seemingly inexhaustible fascination. In the surplus meaning it supplies lie the thrill and the fear that so often accompany impermissible violence and illicit desire. It is the proximity of these forbidden impulses that raises the specter of anxiety—and the urge to defend against it. As we shall see, fantasy is the fountainhead of such defense.

Notorious legal cases are social dramas that take place on a field of embattled discourse where contested stories, metaphors, and character types vie for dominance in the culture at large. They are, as Richard Wightman Fox has written, both "culture-disclosing" and "culture-shaping" events.[1] And as Janna Malamud Smith has noted, "The nation uses these events for addressing psychological and social agendas on a large scale."[2] Of course, to say as much does not mean that whatever deep conflicts are at play necessarily will be worked out. Trial outcomes vary. They are as apt to produce evasions or intensified denials of difficult truths pressing to be heard as to address them head on. However, when such evasions occur—usually in the form of some intensely compelling, collectively shared fantasy—the result tends to be unstable. The underlying urgency that has been dodged will not be kept under wraps for long. Assuming that a more radical intervention, such as outbursts of violence or economic crisis, does not render them moot, future trials will be needed. And even when a particular trial succeeds in generating a more lasting resolution, one that is well received within society as a whole, new urgencies await. The nature of the cultural conflict to which they pertain, the kind of anxiety they bring, and the sort of fantasy that will serve as a defense against forbidden or unacceptable knowledge, will be known in due course by notorious trials to come.

When disparate stories or narrative genres battle for supremacy in courts of law, discrete worlds of meaning, perhaps embodying competing ways of life, may hang in the balance. Yet precisely because the stakes are so high there is a strong temptation to dodge the hard choices these conflicts present. The notorious trials this chapter describes illustrate specific cultural conflicts and evasions that have occurred at critical junctures in our history. The analysis specifically brings into view the peculiar acts of denial and distortion of factual reality that notorious trials often express. One way to approach the notorious trial is to focus on its response or failure to respond to a specific kind of cultural anxiety.

Anxiety is often experienced when deep-seated truths are threatened or when unacceptable feelings of aggression or desire come too close to the surface of consciousness. It is then that the need for a fiction, often in the form of a protective fantasy, is most pressing— more pressing than the reality it seeks to avoid. Notorious trials generate such fictions in the form of publicly shared fantasies as a way of avoiding highly undesirable truths or destabilizing anxieties. These communal myths take shape in the form of discrete narrative fictions. Studying the genesis, transformation, or demise of such fictions provides a key to understanding the most profound cultural anxieties of our time. In this respect, notorious trials may be viewed as cultural riddles. They pose complex questions, such as:

- How is the desire for justice to be rendered at the cheapest possible cost in terms of conventional beliefs, active commitment, social change, and personal suffering?
- Against what account must we borrow the moral or legal capital needed to cover the debt to reality a particular fantasy creates?
- And how is that debt to be settled?

All of these questions share a common concern about the cause and consequences of using fantasy as a means of repelling a discrete and intensely pressing cultural anxiety.

The notorious cases described in this chapter point to three discrete kinds of cultural anxiety. First, we will encounter the moral anxiety that pervades the famous trial of John Brown in 1859. Brown's conviction and execution for murder, treason, and conspiracy arose out of his raid on Harper's Ferry in a failed effort to trigger a large-scale slave rebellion. Brown's bold (if foolhardy) act of violence threatened to expose not only the moral, but also the practical consequences of slavery's continuation. In the end, however, the awful losses and suffering of war were no match in the popular imagination for the self-mythologizing, bloodless Romance that Brown cultivated at trial. The second cultural anxiety we will encounter is epistemological anxiety, as manifest in the 1875 adultery trial of Henry Ward Beecher, the most renowned religious and moral leader of his generation. Beecher's lawyers shrewdly exploited the anxiety many people felt at the time when faced with the possibility that they could no longer trust outward appearances. Better to give a man like Beecher the benefit of the doubt, his lawyers would argue, than to risk universal skepticism and the subsequent collapse of society's ruling Victorian ethos.[3]

With the turn of the century a third kind of cultural anxiety would grip the nation, a destabilizing and oppressive anxiety caused by gross social and economic inequality. I call it socioeconomic anxiety. We see its effects in the 1907 trial of Harry Thaw, the man who shot and killed renowned architect and wealthy New York socialite Stanford White. Charged with murder, Thaw would never be convicted. A fantasy of heroic proportions would rescue him from that harsher reality—a strange outcome, helped along, I will suggest, by a potent dose of retributive fury aimed at the wealthy class.

There is, I believe, a general lesson to be derived from the nation's effort in the course of historic notorious trials to find safe haven in collective fantasies that fend off, by distorting or denying, the urgencies of deep cultural and social conflict. These shared fictions help contain the outbreak of the uncanny in everyday life. They function in a way akin to what Frank Kermode, in *The Sense of an Ending,* calls "the consoling plot." Their purpose is not so much to get the right ending as to make a particular plight bearable by making it comprehensible. But there is an additional lesson here. The denied or distorted urgency returns. A Romantic hero may be narratively created at trial for the sake of the moral force he embodies. But as the trial of John Brown revealed, trading upon that force in the absence of actual commitment consigns moral reality to the status of shared fantasy. A transaction of this sort carries hidden social costs. For when fantasy's debt to reality lies in unenacted commitment, the price to be paid may consist either in the surrender of cherished values falsely obtained or in the completion, by legal or other means, of the socially transformative, perhaps even violent task of ensuring their historic fulfillment. Simply stated, the lesson learned is that for every denial of factual reality, for every fantasy falsely purchased at trial, there remains a cultural debt that must be paid. That debt serves as a driving force behind notorious trials to come. Like a symptom, the hidden costs of collective fantasy can come back to haunt us.

Notorious trials in this respect are double trials. On the manifest level a particular event, some transgressive act of violence, let us say, is in dispute. Whodunit? Why? How? But on a symbolic level it is not about this particular victim or this particular defendant. It is about what it means, in some larger sense, for the event in question to have occurred at all. In approaching such trials we must be on the lookout for conflict in the way individuals and events are depicted. What kind of story is being told? What metaphors and stock characters are being evoked or silenced? In the clash of discourse, in court and out, lie clues to the battle of beliefs, values, and expectations that is being waged. For one of the hallmarks of the notorious case is its staging of competing world views (what Robert Cover has referred to as the *nomos*—that discrete world of meaning—that law brings into or ushers out of being[4]). By trial's end some meanings will reign triumphant, some will hold on but for a little time longer, some may be nostalgically called into being within the mythic moment of trial and its publicly resonant aftermath, while still others will give way to the urgency of the new. As Slavoj Žižek notes, "The easiest way to detect changes in the so-called *Zeitgeist* is to pay careful attention to the moment when a certain (literary, etc.) form becomes impossible."[5]

In this view, then, notorious trials provide moments of great opportunity for collective insight and normative clarification. They are catalysts for increased dialogue and movement toward social and cultural change. Yet they often fail to realize that potential. Having been inadequately worked through, like a neurotic symptom, the underlying symbolic conflict is fated to return to haunt the public imagination anew. The ghost of unattended conflict will not rest until the urgency of its need subsides.

Referring to the silence of the Catholic Church during the Nazi Holocaust, Olivier de Berranger, the Archbishop of France, poignantly stated: "No society, no individual, can be at peace with himself if his past is repressed or dishonest."[6] This is surely so when it comes to law. It is this unrest that helps us understand why law is continually haunted by ghosts of the past, and the present. They persist in their unrest, awaiting the sentence that will finally set things right, the legal utterance that will finally allow them to be still. These spectral presences remind us of something urgent, something that clamors to be heard, something that may well seem too difficult or too terrible to address. Yet, when such failure occurs, when silence or disguise diverts our gaze, the apparition returns. Similarly, the trial that disposes of deeper urgencies with evasive truths and inadequate justice may claim but a temporary respite from the forces of disorder it seeks to repel. In the face of every *Dred Scott* the ghost of *Brown v. Board of Education* restlessly waits to be heard. Less comfortingly, in the face of every Rodney King the specter of Reginald Denny may also lie in wait.

In what follows we will see how legal meaning responds to the urgency of powerful cultural and social forces. It is in this sense that notorious cases serve as barometers of their time. To study these legal conflicts and their social reception offers a unique and valuable way of doing cultural history.

We turn first to what has been referred to as the first mass-mediated notorious trial in American history: namely, the 1859 trial of John Brown. At issue in this historic case were profound cultural tensions spawned by the peculiar American institution of slavery. Since the birth of the American nation many members of the populace managed to repress the contradiction inherent in the ideological claims and the historic reality surrounding its origin. By no less authority than God's law, the Declaration of Independence boldly proclaimed to the world that all men are created equal. Yet the United States Supreme Court saw fit to affirm the law of the land in the matter of slavery. The high court would not presume to gainsay its legality under the Constitution. And therein lies the historical genesis of moral anxiety and the urgency that suffuses this profound cultural conflict.

By 1859, the tension between moral aspiration and legal reality could no longer be contained. In that year John Brown led his disastrous raid on a federal arsenal at Harper's Ferry in the Blue Ridge Mountains of Virginia. Brown had convinced himself that this violent action would immediately trigger a spontaneous slave revolt across the South. Brown and his poorly armed band of seventeen followers, which included two of his sons, were intent on firing the first shots of that rebellion. They attacked, unperturbed by the fact that few slaves were to be found in the district.[7] They were quickly subdued. Many in the party were wounded or killed outright. Afterwards Brown, who himself had been seriously wounded in the raid, was put on trial for insurrection.

Brown's trial received intense and daily coverage that spread quickly across the nation's newly laid telegraph lines. Brown shrewdly manipulated that coverage to bring to the nation a narrative useful to his purpose. It was meant to be a tale of spiritual courage and moral fortitude that would awaken the country from its complacency about slavery. The role Brown played in the courtroom and the lines he recited in his own defense could have come straight out of the most

popular cultural genre of the time: the heroic Romance.[8] There is
Brown, dramatically lifting up his wounded body from the cot court
officials had provided, speaking words like these:

> Now if it is deemed necessary that I forfeit my life for the furtherance
> of the ends of justice, and mingle my blood further with the blood of
> my children and with the blood of millions in this slave country whose
> rights are disregarded by wicked, cruel, and unjust enactments, I say let
> it be done.[9]

And it was. With his conviction at trial and his death by public hang-
ing Brown's heroic fate was sealed in the popular imagination. Ralph
Waldo Emerson would say of Brown, "Thus was formed a romantic
character absolutely without vulgar trait, living to ideal ends, without
any mixture of self-indulgence or compromise"; and Henry David
Thoreau, echoing the Romance genre ideal, would praise Brown for
forgetting "human laws" and doing homage "to an idea."[10] Armed
with the smoothing power of the Romantic ideal, commentators were
able to transform or elide inconsistent details from the story of
Brown's heroic sacrifice. As Robert Ferguson has written: "Insensitiv-
ity appeared as fixed principle, financial failure became superiority to
material concern, atrocities blurred and then reinforced the image of
the veteran warrior defending freedom in Kansas."[11] Never mind that
Brown's rampage in Kansas on the night of May 23–24, 1856, later
to be known as "the Pottawatomi massacre," included the unprovoked
murder of five pro-slavery men. Never mind that Brown falsified his
motives in his final burst of courtroom eloquence, denying any intention to incite insurrection when that was precisely his objective. On
the strength of Brown's self-serving, highly romanticized account at
trial such "petty details" merged into "higher truth": the narrative
truth of a man willing to die for his cause. As in John Ford's classic
film, *The Man Who Shot Liberty Valance,* history went with the leg-
end. "The man himself," Brown's biographer Stephen Oates would
conclude, "was all but forgotten."[12]

Need begat the man. But what was that need? And whose need was
it that Brown's trial-court Romance expressed? The irony is that the
urgency felt by many for moral suasion in this time of deep cultural
conflict would be met with a collective fantasy, but at a hidden cost.
Lofty sentiment and symbolic truth seemed, for the moment at least,
to have drowned out a more difficult reality: the unjust reality of slavery itself. It was as if Brown's sacrifice would provide the effect of

moral redemption without the commitment necessary to earn it. This moral debt would soon come due. But in the meantime, denial would prevail in a fantasy of disembodied ("transcendental") heroics. The Romance that transformed the present would triumph over both past and future. The historic details of Brown's dismal life of repeated failures, including the raid he led on Harper's Ferry, like the future prospect of slavery itself, would give way to the orchestrated theatricality of the trial and the larger-than-life persona that its mass media coverage helped to create. Brown's persona struck a highly resonant chord in the popular imagination of the country. The public, having been narratively primed by the familiar strategies of the Romance genre, was ready to receive what Brown and his admirers offered.

But it is not simply the narrative preconceptions it fulfilled that account for the phenomenal cultural impact of Brown's Romantic trial story. What fueled the public's need and quickened its receptivity was a strong undercurrent of moral anxiety. Brown's trial held open a domain between reality and fiction in which a protective symbolic fantasy could, at least momentarily, prevail. Fear and denial (of the true cost of moral commitment) and desire (to attain lofty moral ideals) would provide fertile ground for a collective, bloodless fantasy that would reconstruct both factual and legal reality.

More than the factual inconsistencies of Brown's life were smoothed away for the sake of his Romance. So too was the legal meaning of the trial itself. The law's truth—about murder, treason, and conspiracy—would now yield to symbolic truth. Having knowingly and intentionally caused the deaths of seventeen men at Harper's Ferry, John Brown was found guilty. Yet the trial and its outcome would be condemned by Brown and his supporters as the very proof of law's injustice: "[T]his mockery of a trial," would be Brown's oft-repeated refrain. The need for sympathy, to facilitate the public act of identifying with this heroic protagonist—the noble, suffering martyr that was John Brown—would thus occasion a broad-based condemnation of the legal process itself. For was it not that process that had brought about Brown's conviction and death?

The legal reality of factual guilt and due process, like the factual reality of Brown's unheroic past and his manifestly impractical (if not insane) raid upon Harper's Ferry, would ultimately bow to a more compelling symbolic reality. In its popular version, then, the trial and conviction of John Brown would recount an entirely familiar tale. It is the prototypical Romance of a martyr's death, featuring justice sacrificed upon the cold altar of legal formality.

For Ferguson this conflation of fact and fiction at the trial of John Brown illustrates how meaning "migrates" in accordance with the historic demands of narrative necessity. The dominant narrative of the day exercises the power to retranscribe the meaning of a case in accordance with the prevailing mode of self and social understanding. As Ferguson says, "We can only tell the stories we know how to tell." Or as Laura Hanft Korobkin puts it, "[A]ll litigation is essentially conducted by constructing, presenting, and interpreting narrative versions of past events. . . . The particular story told, and the way it is told, represents the teller's best guess about what will persuade the specific audience for who it is constructed." [13] Meanings that fall outside the dominant mode of discourse may either change to meet the narrative demand, or fall into silence. Factual or legal truth notwithstanding, a claim that cannot be heard must fail.

But there is even greater irony at work here. According to Thoreau, Brown "forgot human laws, and did homage to an idea." Yet Thoreau and Emerson and their transcendentalist followers were also paying homage to an idea, even as they were engaged in an act of forgetting. They paid homage to an idea of themselves, leaving Brown's more disquieting ideas all but forgotten. In the end, the romanticized ("transcendental") retranscription of the John Brown trial eclipsed the intolerable reality for which Brown gave his life, the reality of human suffering that was slavery itself. The sentimental reception of Brown's trial may have met a deeply felt public need for moral solace, but it was purchased on the margin of conscience. This is moral capital generated by a shared fantasy: the transcendental Self-ideal borrowing against an account of justice that, as John Brown insisted, would only come due in concrete acts of moral commitment. In short, the transcendentalists' debt to Brown's moral cause remained concealed and for the most part unfulfilled. It would take a willingness to commit to principle, in blood if need be, to test the "lawfulness" of a *nomos,* a world of living meaning. [14]

Of course the transcendentalists' sentimental dodge did not succeed in diverting all eyes from the practical reality of Brown's violent deed, including its predictable failure. For example, the eloquent abolitionist spokesman, and former slave, Frederick Douglass could only refuse Brown's invitation to participate in so reckless and foolhardy a venture. Nor do we hear Douglass's voice among the chorus of Brown's admirers in the aftermath of the Harper's Ferry debacle. What was there for Douglass to admire? Notwithstanding Brown's "glorious" sacrifice, the slaves remained exactly as they were before. It is as if the white community had enacted this Romance all for themselves. And, in fact, Emerson would candidly concede as much: "The absence of moral feeling in the whiteman is the very calamity I deplore. The captivity of a thousand negroes is nothing to me."[15] Or as Thoreau would say, in celebration of what had been won as a result of John Brown's martyrdom, "the North, I mean the living North, was suddenly all transcendental."[16] Such lofty sentiment comes in sharp contrast to abolitionist Wendell Phillips's down-to-earth cry: "The lesson of the hour is insurrection!" For Phillips the matter could only be settled by resort to arms.

Here, then, is the received ("retranscribed") message of Brown's Romantic example. It consists in the lofty, abstract principle of "eternal justice and glory." On so abstract a plain, it is little wonder that the futility of Brown's action would blur into insignificance. For the transcendentalists the raid and its immediate purpose had become irrelevant. Its details, like the details of Brown's life, were an inconvenience that could be smoothed away. It is the same fate that awaited Brown's biblically inspired message from the courtroom. For that message, too, ultimately was supplanted by something else, something altogether "transcendental." No, it is not the vision of Christ's Sermon on the Mount, of which Brown eloquently spoke at trial, that resonates within Emerson's and Thoreau's romance of the transcendental Self. It is not Brown's biblical injunction to stand with God's "despised poor" of which his admirers speak. It is decidedly not Brown's explicit identification with those in bondage, or his willingness to mingle his blood with "the blood of millions in this slave country whose rights are disregarded," on which Emerson or Thoreau stake their ideas. They are on a different plane altogether, serving a different mission. The aspirations they follow bind them to their own transcendental Self.

In short, it is not the black man's suffering about which Emerson and Thoreau sing. They sing of themselves. Nothing nearly so poetic or uplifting abides in isolated acts of violence or in the waging of war—a reality suffused with loss and destruction, suffering and death. Yet it is the ugly reality of violent conflict that would ultimately have to be faced before the evil of slavery could be purged from the land. The transcendentalists' comparatively cool fantasy of an idealized ("transcendental") Self takes flight against this historical backdrop of imminent violence. It is a fantasy licensed perhaps by the false assurance that Brown's act had in fact *failed* to ignite the fuse of insurrection or civil war. Indeed, it may be this failure that allows the price of moral principle to seem so affordable to so many.

On this view, it is hardly surprising that Brown's eloquent evocation at trial of his sense of shame as a white man for colluding with the institution of slavery and his guilt in the face of compromised moral principles is nowhere to be found in the romanticized version of his trial. No such humbling sentiment mars his admirers' self-congratulatory spirit. Yet it is precisely this omission that leaves intact the terrible moral urgency that obliged Brown to act in the first place. If the emancipatory credo that gave birth to America is true, if all men are created equal and are endowed by their Creator with the inalienable rights of life, liberty, and the pursuit of happiness, then a dark contradiction surely remains at the heart of the republic so long as slavery and its cognate injustices continue.

What is perhaps most striking, then, about the public's highly romanticized reception of Brown's character and conduct is its denial of guilt or shame. Nowhere in Emerson's or Thoreau's elevated account do we find even a trace of Brown's empathic identification with "the despised and poor," the suffering lot of the black slave. Having failed to identify as Brown had, these transcendental admirers do not miss the guilt that Brown could not avoid. Nor are they concerned with what Brown regarded as the urgent need to act. From this posture, then, all that remains of Brown is an abstraction, a disembodied Romantic figure, a man who was "already dead" even while he lived, as Thoreau revealingly put it. In short, Brown's reality, like the reality of the violent and destabilizing threat he presents, is subject to the same denial as the plight of the slaves themselves. Absent Brown's empathic identification with the slave's oppressed condition, and his concomitant sense of moral guilt in the event that such gross injustice is left unaddressed, the transcendental response remains all pride and glory. One may object that surely it is a false pride that seeks solace in such disembodied principle. Surely it is but a fantasy of glory that denies the moral guilt that compels action and that urges no course of action whatsoever. But such objections, however well founded, miss the point. If the harsh and unsettling reality of Brown's violent deed and self-humbling message has been traded in for its opposite, if a morally uplifting transcendental ideal with no disagreeable consequences has been left to triumph in the end, we should not be surprised. This is precisely what fantasies are for. Their job is to displace anxiety. Through fantasy an imminent sense of displeasure and self-loathing gives way to a reassuring sense of self-gratification and esteem. In this respect, the popular reception of the trial of John Brown was a success. The respite from moral anxiety, however, was fleeting. The frightening prospect of uncontrollable violence would soon become all too real.

The sentimental evasion that characterized the popular reception of John Brown's trial and conviction left in its wake an unpaid moral debt. It is a debt to the biblical vision for which John Brown died. Even the Civil War would not fully repay it—not so long as the inequities of which Brown so eloquently spoke remained insufficiently addressed by the nation; not so long as Brown's identification with the slave (and the acceptance of guilt such identification produced) as well as with those who shared in the benefits of slavery (and the sense of shame this produced) remained beyond the reach of many. Continued denial in the face of Jim Crow segregation and continued racial strife would outlive the Civil War, harking back to the narrow objectives that initially launched it. For as history records, it was not the injustice of slavery that roused Union statesmen like Daniel Webster to their feet in the halls of Congress along with the vast majority of Union soldiers who marched to the fields of war. Rather, it was the calamity of disunion, the fear of anarchy and the self-interest that it threatened. Even Lincoln, who recognized as early as the 1850s the moral anxiety that hung over the land, who eloquently proclaimed that "a house divided against itself cannot stand," compromised principle when necessary. He was too savvy a leader to consign an inadequately committed nation to war in the name of equality.[17] Only later, after the terrible bloodletting had begun, would Lincoln issue the Preliminary Emancipation Proclamation. By 1865, when the Thirteenth Amendment made emancipation a reality for all of America's slaves, the Romantic evasion of the nation's moral debt technically ended—although the full account would take many more years to be paid.

A ghost has stalked more than one notorious trial in the days since the trial of John Brown—from the postbellum days of *Plessy v. Ferguson*'s "separate but equal" doctrine,[18] to the Supreme Court's formalistic condemnation of Martin Luther King's "civil disobedience" in the face of continued discriminatory practices,[19] to more recent currents of racial strife.[20] And as we look back, who can say if the specter that hangs over these legal dramas is not the restless spirit of John Brown seeking repose in a moral reckoning that is balanced at last?

The strength of the Romantic genre's grip on the popular imagination would not be the same following the unremitting violence, suffering, and loss of the Civil War years. And amid the post-traumatic shock of the postwar era and the violent disruptions occasioned by profound social and economic changes, a new cultural conflict would come to haunt the nation's collective imagination. We see it play out at trial in a narrative clash between a nostalgic longing for Romantic faith and the triumph of conventional mores on the one hand, and a disabused skepticism toward deceptive appearances foreshadowing the emergence of modern realism on the other.

The main players in this legal drama were Henry Ward Beecher, his friend Theodore Tilton, and Tilton's wife, Elizabeth. The catalyst was adultery. Tilton accused Beecher of carrying on an affair with Tilton's wife. The issue was this: would Henry Ward Beecher, the most re-spected and idealized religious figure of the day, prove to be yet one more confidence man in a nation of incipient hucksters and deal mak-ers? Had he too betrayed others' trust, captivating admirers by deceit, harboring, against all outward appearances, a secret core of moral decay within? Yes, Tilton's lawyers would loudly proclaim. Do not be taken in, they would urge in summation before Beecher's jury. And the defense? Their response might well have come straight from Groucho Marx: "So who are you going to believe, me or your own eyes?" Bee-cher's counsel, you see, was betting on the fragility of facts before the urgency of belief. Would the jury let this icon of faith fall, and with him faith, trust, and civility itself? Or would they do what had to be done, sustain our most cherished values by affirming Beecher's inno-cence? Today we might say it could have been a line straight out of the O. J. Simpson defense: Will you rush to judgment? Do you have the courage and fortitude to send a message? Will you let it be known that the evils of official corruption will not be tolerated? Will you, by your verdict of acquittal, help to end it?

The spectacular adultery trial of *Tilton vs. Beecher* pitted claims of factual truth against urgencies of belief too strong to be denied. The genre of the sentimental hero would now do battle in open court (and with the media's help, before the public at large) against a new protag-onist: the anonymous, disbelieving antihero of modernity. It was no secret that the sentimental faith in outward appearances had begun to fail. The mystery and the anxiety lay in what would come after. Intimations of a post-Romantic sensibility were at hand. Melville had announced the theme as early as 1857 in his poorly received final novel, *The Confidence Man*. The seemingly endless ambiguity and moral skepticism this protomodernist work announced struck fear in the Victorian soul. The dark modern vision, with its subversive insight

that the more we inquire the stranger things become, the human heart
(or soul) being the strangest, most unfathomable thing of all, was resisted on a variety of fronts. Yet by century's end the reality of self-
estrangement would become a commonplace of popular belief and
experience. The shift would be helped along by the prominence of this
theme in the work of writers ranging from Robert Louis Stevenson to
Dostoevsky, Kafka, and Freud. According to this new sensibility, no
one escapes the vicissitudes of the violent and disruptive unconscious
forces that rage within. How then can we not feel like strangers in our
own skins? As Stevenson would intuit hardly more than a decade after
the Beecher affair, within every mild-mannered Dr. Jekyll there lurks
a Mr. Hyde.[21] In this sense, Freud's work would define the modern
sensibility par excellence.

But that would come later. In 1875, when Henry Ward Beecher,
America's leading moral and spiritual teacher, came under a cloud,
the nation would show itself unready to give up its simpler sentimental
faith. Still, the deep current of anxiety that gave the Beecher trial its
almost unbearable intensity betrayed something more. A recognition
was dawning that the sentimental belief in unitary character (as without, so within) could no longer be maintained. At first blush it might
seem that to say as much is belied by the jury's failure to condemn
Beecher. But it was a desperate measure already couched in ambivalence. It could buy peace of mind, but for a short while only. Too
much was already known by too many. It would take but a short time
before that knowledge would be admitted. Then the spirit of modernity, having escaped the grip of Victorian denial, would move swiftly
upon the face of the nation. Many would experience its unique blend
of personal alienation and freedom—fruits of the anonymity and increased privacy that city life allowed. Passing among strangers sorely
tested the Victorian virtue of trust in outward appearances. For who
knew for sure the true nature of the people one encountered in everyday life? A new, post-sentimental sensibility was needed to better
equip people for this new urban reality. Before that could happen,
however, a profound cultural anxiety hung over society. It was this
anxiety (who can one trust? how does one read the signs of personal
integrity and virtue?) that the Beecher case enacted. And here too collective fantasy, steeped in denial and distortion, would take shape in
the hope of staving off currents of change that threatened to unsettle
too soon conventional moral and social expectations.

On this reading the Beecher-Tilton affair shows us the face of denial, but a denial that winks. Could a man like the much esteemed

Henry Ward Beecher commit adultery with his best friend's wife? Could someone so virtuous without hide such perfidy within? That was the question the jury, together with avid trial watchers, would obsessively ponder. In doing so they would follow a classic sentimental story line, the very one held out by lawyers in Beecher's defense. The question would nudge up against, but ultimately repel a concomitant anxiety, one that already haunted the trial, and the nation: if outward appearances cannot be trusted, who then can we trust? What then is to stop society from sliding down into the chaos and corruption of manipulative deceit and empty nihilism? In response, Tilton's lawyers would ask for greater sophistication from their audience. "You must dig beneath the surface of appearances with tools of reason; you must induce the truth from the clues presented, and follow them wherever they may lead," they would insist. Thus did Tilton's attorneys hope to wrap their client's cause around the narrative armature of a prototypically modernist tale. It was a story that cast jurors and the public at large as skeptical, uncertainty-plagued detectives. And in their search for truth they were to go wherever the trial led— even if it took them into the most private inner sanctum of human personality.[22] For it was there, after all, that the lie to Beecher's outward virtue was to be found. But it was a place few wished to go— certainly no decent folk would admit such a wish, at least not in public.

The Beecher-Tilton trial, it must be recalled, played to a nation not only recently torn by a devastating and deeply unsettling civil war, but also one currently beset by confusion and uncertainty occasioned by significant social and cultural transition. In this respect, then, the Beecher trial may be viewed as helping to play out a larger social, economic, and cultural shift that was under way at the time. The changes came as part of the nation's postbellum shift from an agrarian to an urban-industrial society. The transition was especially marked by rapidly increasing numbers of city dwellers. Traditional mores under these new circumstances were being strained beyond their limits. City life held out new freedoms. An unprecedented vista of individual privacy grappled with a concomitant sense of alienation in a largely depersonalized urban environment. With the evisceration of traditional networks for reputation (such as local venues for gossip), trust among strangers was never more sorely needed, or more sorely tried.

Little wonder that Henry Ward Beecher's advice to this new, transitional generation, in his numerous pamphlets and sermons, was so warmly welcomed. Beecher was speaking to changing needs. As old conventions grew increasingly strained, Beecher touted a whole new set of values—values of the heart. Privacy was a glorious thing, Beecher preached, for it offered new intimacy, new richness of feeling. This was Beecher's self-professed "gospel of love." It is almost as if Timothy Leary had been born a century early. For today it is not difficult to recognize in Beecher's celebration of emotional spontaneity and spiritual and physical intimacy, in his brusque repudiation of the formal rules and coercive conventions imposed by official authority, a Victorian-era precursor to the 1960s hippie counterculture.[23]

So was it vice or was it part and parcel of the new virtue of intimacy, the gospel of love, if Beecher put into practice in his own private life the sermons he passionately preached in public? Or would his gospel finally stumble upon an unpaid debt to the conventional mores it so boldly challenged? Beecher would stumble, but he would not fall. Not if he could transform himself quickly enough in the public's perception. And that is precisely what he did, or at least what his lawyers did for him. He transformed.

One fantasy was about to trade places with another. Ironically, Beecher's popular fantasy of intimacy in the privacy of the heart's sincere urgings would now collapse into a trial-spawned fantasy designed for denial. Beecher had made a mistake. He had gone real with the fantasy, and his public was unwilling to follow. Nor would they be willing to be held accountable for having imagined such a thing. This was adultery after all. The new Beecher on the block would have to be anything but society's reformer. He would need to become a man of plain old country virtue. But what the heck, if he was now repudiating everything he had stood for in the past, if he was pretending to be someone else, at least it was for a good cause. He'd dissemble at trial so that sincerity might be preserved.

Beecher's enormous popularity suggests a populace ready for the freedoms he offered. But perhaps it was rather the fantasy of freedom, a vicarious emancipation acted out through the lives of larger-than-life figures like the celebrity figure of Beecher himself, that they fancied. In this respect Beecher's celebrity trial casts a strikingly modern shadow, prefiguring in some respects what the nation would encounter 120 years later in the O. J. Simpson double murder trial. For in Beecher as in the Simpson case the narratives proffered at trial operated on the basis of publicly traded personae. Beecher would trade in one public persona (the man of free love gospel) for another (the man of conventional virtue). Simpson would strive to retain his old public persona throughout the trial (Simpson the celebrity athlete, the media personality, the black entrepreneur and magnanimous supporter of worthy public causes). In the new age of media-spawned personae this much had suddenly become clear: public personae may not only be won and lost, they may also be traded, like commodities, in the market of public opinion. The Beecher defense would hawk "the new Beecher" at trial nearly a century before "the new Nixon" staged his political comeback in the presidential campaign of 1968. It was a historic moment for the still inchoate field of public relations. Still, in 1875, as the population of urban strangers grew alongside a new breed of get-rich-quick schemers, who could doubt that the old ethos of trust in appearances was anything but anachronistic? And who could deny that the Victorian epistemological anxiety was anything but well-founded? As it turned out, nearly an entire nation could.

Beecher had been caught short. By acting out his gospel with another man's wife—an intimacy that Mrs. Tilton herself would finally concede three years after the trial[24]—Beecher had run roughshod over the most basic conventional mores of his day. At trial it would seem that the fantasy he espoused was about to be called into account. The irony is that Beecher's social survival depended on denial and distortion—of his own conduct with Elizabeth Tilton, and of the very message with which he had preached his way into the nation's heart. The double irony is that only such deceit would allow him to champion the conventional Victorian virtue of sincerity.

Beecher's defense rested squarely upon just such a triumph. It was his embodiment of virtue and religious faith per se, never mind the particulars, that would win the day for him. Little wonder that Victoria Woodhull, a well-known women's rights and free-love advocate of the time, would denounce Beecher as "a poltroon, a coward and a sneak . . . for failing to stand shoulder to shoulder with me and others who are endeavoring to hasten social regeneration which he believes in."[25] Had he not become a con man after all? Beecher's position at trial is more than a little paradoxical. Tapping into a deep need for faith to counter the anxiety of epistemological uncertainty and moral decay, Beecher's lawyers would now invite the public (consisting of jurors and general consumers of the mass media's hysteria-pitched trial coverage) to identify with a sentimental world view that was utterly familiar. Repudiating his former role as spiritual idealist and social reformer, Beecher would now play to the public's need for reassurance. It would not be Beecher who would throw them into the abyss of uncertainty, unable to disentangle outward signs of integrity and sincerity from privacy-ensconced truths utterly at odds with appearances. Rather, Beecher would consign himself to hypocrisy—if only to assure the jury and the public at large that he was no hypocrite, so that sincerity itself might triumph against the corrosive impact of omnipresent con artistry.[26]

The figure of Beecher painted by his lawyers at trial neatly fit the stock character of popular Romance. Here was a man of virtue besieged, a hero who had devoted his life to public service, and to God, only to become the victim of the most personal of attacks targeting the heretofore protected domain of private life. To attack Beecher's outward appearance of sincerity in this way, argued the defense, must be viewed as an attack on all who hold themselves out to be as they claim. It is to subject friends, mentors, and spouses to a pernicious and unquenchable suspicion. In this manner Beecher's lawyers left no doubt that this case was not simply about Henry Ward Beecher, one man who had been singled out to suffer the indignities of such inflammatory and intrusive charges concerning his private life. It was not simply a matter of protecting this man's dignity and honor from such reckless invasion. Rather, it was an indictment of an entire way of life. Here is Beecher's defense lawyer in summation:

> The attack is not that there are wolves in sheep's clothing, that vicious men dissemble and that they hide themselves under the cloak of sanctity to prowl on the society that they thus impose upon . . . it is that the favored, approved, tried, best results of this social scheme of ours, which includes marriage, and of this religious faith of ours, which adopts Christianity, is false to the core; that the saintly man and the apostolic woman are delivered over to the lower intelligences; and that being proved, the scheme itself is discredited and ready to be dissolved. . . .
>
> Why do you look at the growing beauty of [your wives' and daughters'] face and form, and feel safe? . . . Why, all the while it may be going on in all our families, and nobody knows anything about it. What, shall we then discard all this, shall we believe that these sins come only by power against which no morality can guard, that there is no necessary connection between character and conduct; that these sins do not come from within, but that with all this purity they may arise? . . .[27]

As Korobkin notes, the logic of sentimental romance would now be elevated at trial to the status of evidentiary principle. "By the time [defense counsel] Evarts is done, it is the jurors' values, loved ones, and principles of judgment that are being tested by this trial—the jurors' security of mind that hangs precariously on the verdict, not Beecher." A vote for acquittal thus became a vote for virtue writ large. The anxiety of epistemological uncertainty (what can we believe? where lies the truth? and where does it end when one is willing to inquire into the innermost reaches of private life?) is thereby evaded. And the modernist anguish of uncertainty, isolation, and distrust is thereby put off, at least for a while.[28]

In the defense narrative, the symbolic value of "honesty" is made to triumph over a particular factual truth. The question thus becomes not whether this man Beecher is a hypocrite, but rather are we to continue to believe in the virtue of honesty itself? To identify Beecher as corrupt would be to subject everyone to a similar state of corruption. Who would be exempt from such probings into their private life? And who would be exempt then from the threat of hidden corruption? The gist of the defense is clear: We must believe in the honesty of others whether or not they are actually honest because belief makes civilization possible.[29] This is the triumph of symbolic truth, a shared fantasy in a necessary fiction.

Beecher's adversaries, by contrast, are caught between two disparate worlds. This conflict is evident in the clash of narrative lines that infects Tilton's lawyers' summation. On the one hand they too would exploit the popular sentimental romance. They too would have their client, Theodore Tilton, perceived as the long-suffering hero, the victim of Beecher's false friendship, of his betrayal and moral debauchery. As Tilton's attorney put it in his opening statement to the jury: "We come here from a blighted and desolate home. The children of my client are scattered in different parts. He will return tonight to as cold, as cheerless, and as desolate a home as there is in the land."[30] At the same time, however, in addition to evoking the jury's pity and compassion by the use of these familiar sentimental images, Tilton's attorney also sought to invoke critical inferences about Beecher's private immorality. By pursuing the latter tack the plaintiffs could not but risk heightening the modernist (epistemological) anxiety after all. For if Tilton is right, then the widely shared conventional belief in appearances must be deemed naive. Similarly vulnerable is the popular belief in the easy availability of meaning. The plaintiff's trial strategy thus risked thrusting the jury further into a strange antisentimental, modern world where the traditional notion of integral character could no longer be assumed—not when the unknowable depths of the human heart must be deemed a part of the landscape of conventional knowledge and expectation.

In short, Tilton's lawyers may have activated the simplified narrative line of sentimental reality to their own detriment. For to the extent that Tilton is identified with a characteristically modern anxiety, the virtue and familiarity of sentimental truths lies with Beecher. Tilton cannot have it both ways. And faced with factual and moral ambiguity—can we ever really know what goes on in private between two people? Can we afford to question outward appearances based on such elusive [and intrusive] grounds?—the more consoling narrative reality lies with the defense. The jury's inability to reach a judgment in the Beecher case (they hung—nine votes to acquit, three to condemn) reflects their unwillingness, whether by conscious refusal or unwitting inability, to enter into the problematic realm of inward realities. For these were realities unpredictably and perhaps incomprehensibly at odds with outward signs to the contrary. Simply stated, the modernist narrative was too threatening at the time to win the jury's (or the general public's) adherence. In the end, the conventional popular sentimental fantasy, with Henry Ward Beecher as its unlikely defender, had won the day. The urgency to believe in Beecher, the heroic man of virtue besieged, was more acceptable than the anxiety let loose by belief in a contradictory truth. It was a truth that called too much into question, including the collective fantasy that had borne Reverend Beecher to the heights of celebrity. Francis Williams, in his contemporary account of Beecher's life and tribulations, may have said it best:

> It is simply incredible that the man who thus wrote and lived, with the eyes of the world upon him, should be a liar, a sneak, a perjurer, a debauchee, and a confirmed, persistent hypocrite. The millions who during this long period have been cheered and strengthened by his words cannot believe it.[31]

How could millions have been wrong? What would that say about the public? Surely their motives have always been of the purest sort. Even as they obsessively followed for months on end every detail of this nonexistent debauch, details that played and replayed across the psychic terrain of the nation, with unacknowledged illicit pleasure, the pleasure that is all too familiar to (who else could it be?) the voyeur.

With Beecher's technical exoneration, a legal model for denial and distortion had been set. Vicarious identification with illicit desire had been washed clean. The urgency of epistemological anxiety had been met and evaded. Uncertainty was denied. But the debt this whitewash created to a shared, albeit disguised, psychic reality would come due in time. The modern novel was waiting in the wings. The core of self-doubt and uncertainty could not be wished away without cost. Yet, whatever price remained to be paid, the Beecher trial would nevertheless remain a paradigmatic reenactment of untrustworthy appearances. It ended up staging what the nation feared most: the deceptiveness of outward appearances. The need to overcome doubt seemed to have triumphed in the end; Beecher was not convicted. But then again, neither was he wholly exonerated. The trial's residual ambivalence is nicely captured by the symbol of the hung jury. The almost-met need to overcome doubt belies in its ambivalence an even deeper anxiety that doubt remains intact in the end.

In this sense, then, the Beecher trial was a charade in which the jury and the public were all too willing to collude. Beecher would become a hypocrite so that the triumph of sincerity could be achieved. On the plane of symbolic reality the defense fought the unacceptable truth that even a man of such high social standing and accomplishment as the Reverend Henry Ward Beecher cannot really be trusted. Their victory, founded as it was upon the paradoxical enactment of hypocrisy, remains ambivalent. And one cannot but wonder whether Richard Wightman Fox was right in concluding that the Beecher trial "helped detach American culture from its familiar mooring and set it on a new course that no contemporary navigator could chart."[32] With the Tilton-Beecher affair the nation winked at the anxiety of disbelief, but one eye remained open. Perhaps intimations of the modern era of public relations con artistry soon to come[33] were enough to shore up the narrative fiction of sentimental faith in appearances, if only to stave off the inevitable a bit longer. With the adultery trial of Henry Ward Beecher the American public felt the future and tightened their grip on a fantasy that was about to pass.

Not that even by century's end the Victorian sentimental Romance had given up the ghost for good. Compelling urgencies of the time would yet call it back. But its return would come on the heels of a new anxiety. This is what we see in the 1907 murder trial of Harry Thaw, where the anxieties of moral uncertainty and socioeconomic imbalance combined forces to produce strange legal results. As the Beecher-Tilton affair had shown, the tensions the Romantic cultural ideal faced were particularly pronounced when it came to male-female relations. That conflict would only increase in the ensuing years with the advent of the women's suffrage movement, increasing attacks on the oppressive impact on women in particular of the double standard embedded in the Victorian moral code, and the widening search for emancipation through economic security in the work force. In narrative terms, the sentimental Victorian ideal of female innocence, uncorrupted by the harsh realities of a man's world, was slowly giving way to a new ethos. Modernity would offer a counterimage of womanhood featuring independence, sexual freedom, and an enterprising, pragmatic attitude toward a career. This cultural transition, however, would be anything but smooth. As author Kate Chopin disconcertingly discovered when her short novel *The Awakening* appeared in 1899.

As the century turned, the genre of sentimental Romance and, more generally, the familiar features of the novel itself—including plot, character, and narrative—were about to yield to the new demands of modernity. In this respect, Chopin's novel can be read as a symbolic tale depicting the profound cultural transitions that were under way at the time. At issue were traditional societal constraints that had unduly limited a woman's political, intellectual, and physically expressive capacities. However, critics and the reading public in general greeted Chopin's novel with virtually universal disdain and derision.

On its surface *The Awakening* tells the tale of a woman who grows increasingly estranged from the conventional norms of family life and middle-class values. The story simultaneously recounts her flight from ordinary expectations regarding female domesticity. On a symbolic level the novel offers a stark repudiation of the sentimentality of the Romantic novel. The harsh vision of modern realism has set in. Chopin's main character may attain her freedom by breaking away from conventional middle-class role expectations as wife and mother. ("Mr. Pontellier had been a rather courteous husband so long as he met a certain tacit submissiveness in his wife. . . . [H]er absolute disregard for her duties as a wife angered him."[34]) Yet, with her newly won freedom also come loneliness and a disturbing sense of emptiness. Her awakening to a life of the senses thus takes on an ironic aspect, for it turns out that in the end Romantic idealization will not do. Liberation from society's unnatural constraints for the sake of mythic solitude and fantasies of unconstrained freedom may feed the Romantic imagination ("As she swam she seemed to be reaching out for the unlimited in which to lose herself"[35]), but it is a dead end. "Self-fulfillment" in these isolated and rarefied terms is not a livable ideal. The Romantic transcendental vision of the ideal self fails—for man and woman alike. Mrs. Pontellier's final, suicidal swim into the sea tells us as much. If cultural transformation is to come, we will have to seek it in other parts. The sentimental Romantic ideal is done for.

Much to Chopin's surprise, and dismay, however, the public reception of her novel confined its content to a curiously literal reading. The larger significance of the work was lost. Chopin was in trouble: critics excoriated her for courting social anarchy; she was charged with inviting young and impressionable women down a path of domestic irresponsibility and hopeless emotional self-indulgence; and many libraries banned her book altogether. Chopin's writing career was all but over.

Notwithstanding the public's response, however, the need persisted for an alternative to the increasingly unsatisfying moral and social conventions of Victorian culture, and to the fantasy of escape embodied in the nearly moribund sentimental genre of Romance. Twentieth-century art, split between the modernist impulses of Dadaism and surrealism on the one hand, and the incipient action-, machinery-, and war-obsessed antimodernist esthetic of Italian futurism (which would fuel fascist ideology) on the other, reflects the deep-seated turmoil of the times.

The conflict went beyond shifting cultural ideals. Material needs and class disparities had now become a significant issue. With the turn of the century the nation's optimistic faith in the open market had begun to wane. It was a time marked by the rise of socialism, unionism, and the anarchist movement. Writers of the day not only protested the great "octopus" of Standard Oil and other behemoth corporations, with their vast networks of market-enveloping tentacles; they also expressed a fear of the marketplace itself. For was it not the market that was "making machines of men, robbing them of their humanity and turning them into cool calculators of personal advantage?"[36] And was it not the great disparity between the advantaged few and the disadvantaged many that led decent men to desperate acts? As Earl Rogers put it in his defense of that great man of the people, Clarence Darrow:

> If I had walked the streets all day long, offering to sell my hands or head to feed my hungry, crying baby, and couldn't get work, and knew there were others living on bee's knee's and hummingbirds' tongues, and giving monkey dinners, I'd commit violence. I'd tear off the First National Bank with my fingernails. In this country of ours there are

many things that must be settled and settled quick. We can't go on like this. We can't do it.[37]

It was against this backdrop of growing socioeconomic anxiety, as the middle class perceived its prospects to be dwindling, that the 1907 trial of Harry Thaw unfolded. In important respects, the trial would reenact many of the same social and cultural themes and expressions of public resistance that greeted the publication of Chopin's novel. This time, however, the outcome would be different. A jury, with the avid support of the popular press and the public at large, would manage to get the story right. The threat of feminist emancipation would merge with a widespread fear of economic paralysis in the face of an impregnable elite. But a strange nostalgia for the twin Victorian virtues of male honor and female fidelity would prevail in the end. These traditional values would disguise and subdue the threat. And in the process, as in the trials of John Brown and Henry Ward Beecher, disagreeable facts would be forced to yield to a deeper cultural need. A Romantic saga of honor and vengeance would transform the players in the Thaw case, together with the meaning of their acts. But while Romance played out on the surface of the trial, underneath that surface deeper anxieties roiled. A fear of systemic injustice manifest in the growing disparities in wealth and power between the well-placed few and the immobilized many fueled the nostalgia for Romance. But it also signaled the presence of an underlying melodrama. In this typically modern narrative we confront a mystery that must be solved. Society's norms have grown corrupt, and the source of that corruption must be found; only then can it be effectively rooted out. It is this underlying melodrama that gives the Thaw trial its distinctly modern cast.

If the Beecher trial, gripped by epistemological anxiety, helped to repress a pervasive fear that outward appearances could no longer be trusted, the Thaw trial marked a radical reversal. Thirty-two years after the Beecher-Tilton affair had pushed its generation's corrupt "Hydes" back into the shadows of private life, we now find an audience ravenous for public exposure. By 1907, the question is no longer "Does Hyde exist?" but rather whose Hyde will be gored—whose private demons will be publicly targeted in the service of public needs? The trial would constitute a hallmark event in the popular history of modernity.

The three main players at the Thaw trial were Stanford White, Harry Thaw, and Evelyn Nesbit. White, to all outward appearances at least, was at the pinnacle of his career as the leading architect of his generation. He had been honored as a great artist in his own country and abroad. He moved easily among the highest ranks of New York society. But White also had a darker side. His appreciation for physical beauty apparently also found expression in an appetite for adolescent girls. Among his numerous conquests was sixteen-year-old Evelyn Nesbit.

White had used his persuasive powers (including substantial wealth and a magnetic personality) to sweep the penniless and fatherless Nesbit off her feet. He introduced her to a world of high society she could never otherwise have known. He helped Nesbit with her education, her appearance, and her career on the stage. He even removed Nesbit and her mother to finer housing, and paid all the bills. These efforts succeeded—only too well. Nesbit's feelings toward White were strong. She loved him. But that would not be the nature of her testimony at trial. For by then, she had long since been replaced by others, White's fresh young conquests. And of course by then she had also become Mrs. Harry Thaw.

Harry Thaw desperately craved the life Stanford White led. Yet it was a goal that would forever elude him. To be sure, it was not for lack of resources. Thaw, at age thirty-five, was a direct heir to his late father's $40 million railroad fortune. But he had also acquired something else, a personality that, due to drug use or congenital abnormality, or perhaps a combination of the two, had led to bizarre and violent behavior. Thaw had on more than one occasion used whips to gratify his perverse sexual needs. It would cost him thousands to keep this dark side of his character hidden. For all his wealth, however, Thaw could gain no foothold within the fashionable circles of New York society. He remained an outcast, scorned by the likes of Stanford White.

Nesbit was aware of Thaw's peculiarities, and of his obsession with White. Thaw had pursued Nesbit from early on, even from the time of White's own infatuation with her youth and her beauty. To gain the affections of Nesbit, the woman everyone knew as Stanford White's protegée (though that she was also his mistress had remained secret), would represent a great personal coup for Thaw. But he simply could not compete with the acclaimed Stanford White. Nesbit rejected Thaw's advances from the outset, repelled by his oddness and by a prescient suspicion of the danger he presented. But then White's fervor cooled, and Thaw's solicitations persisted. Though she should have, and most likely did know better, eventually Nesbit yielded to Thaw's relentless pursuit. She traveled with him abroad twice, although she still kept in touch with (and even upon occasion received money from) White. On returning from their second European excursion, Nesbit and Thaw married.

During his early pursuit of Nesbit—who had been making her way at the time first as a young artist's model and then as a chorus girl—Thaw had used private detectives to spy on her activities. Thus Thaw probably was aware that Nesbit had spent many an evening in the company of Stanford White—at parties and alone in one of White's elaborate romantic hideaways around the city. Yet, after his marriage to Nesbit, Thaw insistently questioned her about her relationship with White—until, at last, she told him what he apparently wanted to hear. After Nesbit recounted the story of the first time she, an inexperienced sixteen-year-old girl, had spent the night in the embrace of the famous fifty-two-year-old White, Thaw wept. Then he got his gun.

Thaw shot Stanford White during a theater performance at the Madison Square Roof Gardens, a building White had designed. Three shots in the head at point blank range. White died instantly. At Thaw's subsequent trial for murder, the defense was an odd, seemingly contradictory blend of temporary insanity and justification. Thaw's lawyers were apparently playing upon the thin line between the insanity standard (did he know his act was wrong? did he believe his will had been overborne by a higher power which overruled the dictates of law?) and moral righteousness (there is a higher natural law, an unwritten moral law, that did in fact overpower Thaw, turning him into a passive agent of its force).[38] In essence, Thaw's defense was that even an insane man was entitled to act in defense of his honor. In this way, Thaw's lawyers were asking the jury to see Thaw's homicide as both honorable (and thus deliberate) and mad (and thus without volition). The strategy worked with enough jurors to result in a hung jury. At the second trial the defense won on the strength of the insanity defense alone.

The Harry Thaw murder trial mesmerized the nation—not least for the spectacle of illicit sex and violence it provided. What the trial also provided, however, was a rare glimpse at the private life of one of society's most renowned and admired figures. The Thaw trial swept aside the curtain of privacy that had previously kept hidden from view what it meant to lead a life of wealth and privilege in the upper crust of New York society. An increasingly resentful public had finally hit pay dirt. The corruption and moral decay at the top was there for all to see. This sentiment would serve the defense well.

The story of White's murder was of course far more complicated than Thaw's lawyers would have liked people to believe. This was not a simple tale of a husband acting in the heat of passion upon finding his wife in a sexual dalliance with another man. After all, White's affair with Nesbit had been over for years. Nor was Nesbit's relationship with White likely to have been unknown to Thaw when Thaw asked her to marry him. To complicate matters further, Thaw himself had lived "immorally" with the then nineteen-year-old Nesbit—an indictable offense at the time. If Thaw's homicidal act was to be seen as a passion-steeped, honor-saving act of vengeance, clearly the defense had its work cut out for it.

The question the lawyers faced was plain: What kind of narrative were they dealing with? How were the main players in the drama to be depicted? The formula the defense seized upon was instantly recognizable. It was a story of moral retribution, with Harry Thaw as the knight-errant, Evelyn Nesbit as the young and innocent damsel in distress, and Stanford White as the rich and immoral blackguard. Thaw's lawyers would boldly characterize Thaw's violent act as "Dementia Americana," "that species of insanity that inspires every American to believe that his home is sacred."[39]

In short, what we find here is a compelling fantasy of male honor and female fidelity triumphing over corruption, greed, and the abuse of power. In this sentimental tale, Thaw's violent act would give new life to an unwritten law. As the defense put it:

> He knew not but struck as the tigress strikes the invader who comes to rob her of her young. He struck for the purity of the home, for the purity of American womanhood, for the purity of American wives and daughters, and if he believed on that occasion that he was the instrument of Divine Providence, who shall say he was in error? . . .
>
> On that night he had raised his eyes to God, and God at last answered the cry of the poor fatherless child, as He had promised thousands of years ago to the children of Israel that He would hear and that He would answer that cry. And God redeemed the promise that He had then made, that those who afflicted the fatherless child He would smite and kill them with the sword.

Harry Thaw as avenging angel—a strange transformation to be sure. Yet the strategy worked. To many among the jurors and the public at large Thaw was a hero. To reach this judgment, however, a good number of conflicting facts would have to be discarded or changed. The question is, why were so many prepared to go along with the defense's transformation? Why target White's Hyde when there were so many Hydes to choose from? Consider the possibilities:

- Thaw kills to wipe away a stain on his honor; yet he is also a man who, on more than one occasion, acted upon violent and perverse sexual impulses.
- White is drawn to physical beauty in all its forms; but he also places himself above society's moral and legal norms by subjecting minors like Nesbit to his sexual needs.
- But, of course, Nesbit too is no innocent. She shrewdly uses her relationships with wealthy and well-connected men to better her social and economic condition. The District Attorney made the point well in his summation before the jury:

> The angel child that [the defense] would paint her to be, reared chastely and purely . . . drugged and despoiled! Why, what nonsense . . . what does she do? She meets him again and again and again—this human ogre that had drugged her. She meets him at the Tower. Eight or ten times she goes to this Twenty-fourth Street place. . . .
>
> There is a difference between the man who errs and the man who brutally despoils. My own information is that there is an explanation to this as consistent with the facts as [the defense's] marvelous Jekyl[l] and Hyde theory. Her own words have ruined that theory. . . .

Having attacked Nesbit's credibility, the prosecution next turned upon Thaw, identifying him as the true "monster" in the drama. For example, the prosecutor recounted how immediately upon her return from abroad with Thaw, Nesbit fled—and the man to whom she fled, bearing tales of Thaw's brutal and perverse sexual practices, was none other than Stanford White. The real "Hyde," according to the D.A., cannot be in doubt. "Sir Galahad!" the prosecutor sarcastically sneers. "This is your protector of the home . . . [this] dope fiend. . . ."

The groundwork done, the prosecution stood poised to lay bare the real dynamic underlying this fateful triangle:

> The married man [White] getting away with the girl [Nesbit] from the unmarried one [Thaw], and the unmarried one taking her back and living with her, and finally marrying her; and fearful that the married man would get her back again—the man whom he [Thaw] hated, the

man who kept him out of clubs . . . who said that he [White] could get
the girl back . . . and the girl [Nesbit] lying between them like a tiger
egging them on. With Thaw she is wronged by White; with White she
is lashed by Thaw. . . .

In short, the driving force behind the murder is none other than
Evelyn Nesbit.[40] Little wonder the D.A. had initially intended to indict
Nesbit for her part in the murder. Had she not fanned Thaw's hatred
of White, knowing full well how Thaw was likely to react to her distorted depiction of White's "ravishment" of her? She loved White, and
she also hated him—a classic instance of what the ancient Greeks
called *philos-aphilos,* or love-in-hate, the very force of contradiction
itself. No, it probably wasn't just the money Harry's mother had promised her (but apparently later reneged on) that led Nesbit to remain
loyal to her husband at trial. She owed him. After all, it was Thaw
who had released her from the torturous grip of her unrequited love
for White.[41] Perhaps this is why Nesbit testified dishonestly to save
Thaw's hide. Looking even younger than her twenty-two years, she
dramatically embellished White's first act of seduction. She spoke of
having been drugged and of her uncontrollable screaming afterwards,
once she realized what had occurred—"while she slept." Thus, according to Nesbit's depiction, the true victimizer is clearly not Harry
Thaw, but the murdered scoundrel, Stanford White.[42]

The defense strategy worked. The district attorney's more complex
tale of deceit and collusion failed to take hold. Yet, in retrospect, one
is struck by the acuity of the prosecution's analysis. Surely Evelyn
Nesbit was not the innocent victim the defense had depicted, nor was
the deviant Harry Thaw anything like an avenging Sir Galahad. Still,
these were the images that stuck. Again, one is led to ask why? Why
were White's demons more damnable in so many people's eyes than
Thaw's—or, for that matter, Evelyn Nesbit's?

I believe that part of the answer emerges when we consider the
trial's historical backdrop. Socioeconomic inequality and the threat of
widespread disempowerment of the many by the few cried out for a
response. The Harry Thaw trial provided an ideal opportunity for a
suitable response. In the fantasy the Thaw defense effectively aroused,
Stanford White came to stand for all the ignoble, corrosive, and uncontrolled appetites of the wealthy class writ large. As for her part,
the young and innocent-looking Evelyn Nesbit was exceptionally well
suited to the role of exploited, working-class victim.

Profound social and economic inequalities had made the middle and lower middle classes increasingly restless.[43] To many, upward mobility seemed a thing of the past. The new industrialists, in an age of neo-Darwinian laissez-faire economics, not only dominated the marketplace; they did so with a "rationalized" sense of entitlement. Didn't their economic success prove their superiority over others and their right to reap the spoils of the marketplace as they saw fit? The Supreme Court seemed to agree. In the justices' view the supreme law of the land, the United States Constitution, proscribed legislators from interfering with natural market forces. Clearly, the law would offer no help to those who felt increasingly exploited and helpless in the face of untrammeled big business. A source of power would have to be sought elsewhere.[44]

If conventional legal norms and procedures failed to address the growing perception of gross social and economic disparities—worse still, if wealth and class appeared to place the advantaged few beyond the reach of ordinary ethical and moral norms, would not recourse to alternative, extralegal sources of authority become necessary to set things right? This is the line of argument one hears echoing within Thaw's "natural law" defense. The unwritten law of the frontier unfurls its banner so that the Romance of popular justice may play out. "And if [Thaw] believed on that occasion that he was the instrument of Divine Providence, who shall say he was in error?" Here is Thaw as everyman, acting in righteous anger; Thaw in the grip of "that species of insanity that inspires every American to believe that his home is sacred." Here too lies the source of that motive force that would encourage so many people to repress inconvenient details and to fill in the defense's Romance with more suitable facts of the matter. Only in this way would the story of Harry Thaw's triumph over Stanford White's evil be complete. Only then could the fear of impotence turn into righteous rebellion, and the symbolic suffering of the oppressed change into moral triumph.

In short, the defense's symbolic narrative provided the perfect script for popular vindication: the people's triumph over corruption by the evil forces of social injustice. The power of victimizers like White over victims like Nesbit had to be countered. A means to resist had to be found. To achieve this goal would require heroic strength. In order to fulfill his part in the drama, therefore, Thaw would have to be transformed. In order to gain the victory they desired the audience would have to turn Thaw into Sir Galahad, the knight of male honor, protector of female purity, defender of the unwritten law of vengeance. And so they did.

Here then is a double drama, a tale within a tale. On its surface an anachronistic Romance plays out. But this show of fidelity to traditional values (male honor, female fidelity) masks an underlying melodrama, a modern play in which profound social ills are diagnosed and in which a symbolic cure is offered. It is Stanford White, symbol of all that is corrupt and askew in modern life, who must be violently excised from the body politic. The Romance is but a cover story for the melodrama that lies at the trial's heart. This is the matter of central concern Reverend George Chalmers Richmond expressed when, in a sermon preached shortly after Thaw's acquittal, he tells his listeners, "Thaw had the courage to free this world of a moral hypocrite.... Thaw played the role of a savior to society."[45] Here sounds the popular theme of Thaw's defense: Thaw's violent heroic act constituted a symbolic blow against a corrupt social and economic elite. In short, it was perceived as a defensive (albeit fantasized) response to the pervasive socioeconomic anxiety of the time.

We have seen that in the course of Henry Ward Beecher's trial the denial of modern skepticism toward outward appearances ultimately served to reinforce the still regnant sentimental ethos of the time. With the trial of Harry Thaw that ethos was finally giving way, but only to a degree. At this early stage of its emergence, the more skeptical spirit of modernity could be openly acknowledged. But it would only be allowed to go so far. Private demons came into plain view. The gap between public appearances and hidden defects had become less threatening than in Beecher's day. But the public's toleration had its limits. Taken too far the new modernism threatened to leave no one unscathed. Powerful and uncontrollable forces might be lurking within us all. And if that were the case, how then could we condemn any act without condemning in the same judgment a comparable force within ourselves? Thus whispers the fear of uncertainty that grips the modern soul—yet another reason for traditional sentimental values to do the moral work of condemnation in the Thaw trial. For by their very assertion the specter of full-blown modern skepticism may be kept at bay.

The nature of the prosecution's difficulty in the Thaw case may now be discerned with greater clarity. The state's more complex picture of Thaw's violence and Nesbit's collusion failed to do justice either to the widely felt need for sentimental purity (and moral triumph) on the one hand, or the urge for some retributive payoff (proof of the power to act) on the other. For what moral good is served by a Sir Galahad in defense of a damsel who is willfully, indeed, manipulatively impure?

Moreover, what retributive payoff may come from a "hero" who turns out to be a plain old crackpot? The prosecution's harshly skeptical, more typically modern narrative punctures the defense's sentimental tale. However, in doing so it offers little solace. According to the state's account it is demons all around. Such a narrative denies its audience the comfort of closure. Taken on its own terms, it appears nothing may be gained from the act of condemning Thaw. In order to obtain a moral payoff one needs a contrasting "good"—a good that allows one to glory in evil's defeat. Yet the prosecution's skeptical account seems to leave little room for goodness to triumph. Worse, it poses a danger of loss. If we are all haunted by demons, how can any of us escape condemnation?

It is this narrative weakness in the state's presentation of its case against Thaw that the defense shrewdly exploited at trial. Of course, to do so the defense had to make certain factual adjustments. I refer not simply to the incongruity of Thaw in the role of knight-errant; there is also the discordant fact that Harry Thaw stood to inherit the Thaw family's colossal railroad fortune. This hardly provides a suitable counterpoint to Stanford White's symbolic embodiment of the corruption of the privileged few in the upper strata of society. A more fitting image would have to be proffered at trial: the image of Thaw as "everyman," the man who struck, as the defense said, "for the purity of the home, for the purity of American womanhood, for the purity of American wives and daughters." Here, then, lies an effective counterpart to White: Harry Thaw as a larger-than-life figure battling against the most dangerous and corrosive forces in American society.

In sum, what the Thaw defense gave the jury and the public at large was "modernity lite." It is modern skepticism cut with a little sentimental romance and moral indignation (at the high and mighty oppressor) to ward off the fear of collusion and to ease the pain of self-judgment. But even more, it is a version that gives pleasure—the melodramatic pleasure of heaping self-righteous condemnation upon the demonic other. For so long as Harry Thaw remains one of us, and so long as Stanford White's hidden Hyde-like self holds him apart, White may be condemned with impunity.

If the doubt-laden genre of modernity met with only partial acceptance at the opening of the twentieth century, by century's end a more thoroughgoing skepticism would take hold. Now Hydes and Jekylls freely exchange places, as the post-Freudian, post-unitary self fragments into multiple identities. And as private goes public as readily as the actual goes virtual, what reality cannot be played and replayed at will—or at need? Melodrama's confident detection and straightfor-ward resolution of social ills will now have to share the stage with a far less optimistic outlook, an outlook that will also be couched in a novel form of esthetic expression. For simplicity's sake, we may call it postmodernism—though, as the following chapter will suggest, post-modern storytelling is anything but simple or clear-cut. Still, amid its notoriously protean forms and the confusions to which they lead, a critical cleavage may be discerned—a thin, wavering line along which postmodern skeptics and affirmers clash and divide.

"You reasoned it out beautifully," [Dr. Watson] exclaimed in unfeigned admiration. "It is so long a chain, and yet every link rings true."

The Adventures of Sherlock Holmes

The matter of interest seems to be the configuration formed by chance events in the moment of observation, and not at all the hypothetical reasons that seemingly account for the coincidence.

CARL GUSTAV JUNG, Foreword to *The I Ching*

FIVE

The Postmodern Challenge
A Case Study

People prefer stories neat. Recognizable characters, familiar motives, and recurring scenarios of conflict and resolution are typical elements of our workaday narrative world. Legal narratives are no different.[1] And trial lawyers, especially prosecutors and criminal defense attorneys, are only too glad to indulge a preferred image or story line if it will help win a case.

The trouble with having one's stories neat, however, is that they tend to leave things out—the things that make a story messy, hard to keep in mind. Of course, such infelicitous details can be dealt with. That's what recurring story lines, familiar genres and plots, and typical characters, conflicts, and resolutions are for. They keep the mess out. It simply won't do to be telling a story and have it trail off, or break up, or have another story poke its nose in. When you tell a story, you make a choice. That's the story you're telling. It could have been otherwise, but it isn't. The story told, in order to be told, represses other possibilities.

Since stories are supposed to make sense, and since the sense they make is supposed to be believable, it helps if the recounted events, actions, characters, and backgrounds involved seem necessary. If it were otherwise, if it seemed that other stories could just as easily be told, perhaps with equal truth (or incredibility), who'd want to accept the offered version as true? When making meaning happen, it helps to suppress chance and multiplicity. That, at least, is the lesson of narrative necessity.

This chapter is about a murder, the murder of a Dallas police officer named Robert Wood. It is also about the different stories that were subsequently told about that crime. First there were the stories told at trial, which ended in the conviction of Randall Dale Adams and his sentence of death by electrocution. Then there were the stories told by filmmaker Errol Morris in his so-called documentary about the Adams case, *The Thin Blue Line*.[2] Morris's lead story in that film made so many people disbelieve the state's trial story that the courts eventually reexamined the case. That reexamination led to Randall Adams's release from prison. Adams had served twelve years, a good part of it on death row. In many people's eyes Morris's film served as the key catalyst in righting a terrible wrong. By helping to set Randall Dale Adams free the film also helped set the Dallas criminal justice system straight.[3]

How did these different stories achieve such disparate outcomes? By what craft? And what are we to think when a legal reality, freedom for a supposed cop killer, follows hard upon the heels of a cinematic "docudrama"? It is this strange mingling of forms, art on the one hand, legal reality on the other, this shifting back and forth between ways of making meaning in narrative and the ways people see and make judgments about reality, that drives this chapter's inquiry.

In what follows, we will explore how it happens that law's demand for truth and justice can clash with the modernist mindset's demand for closure and certainty. When truth defies certainty and becomes complex, justice requires difficult decisions on the basis of that doubt. The struggle between shifting cognitive needs and legal duty is commonplace, and without a way to question how a given narrative shapes and informs our desire for certain and tidy justice, that desire, and competing ones, cannot be adequately understood. As a result, the kind of justice operating in a particular case at a given cultural juncture may remain confused or hidden from view. The emergence in our time of new, arguably postmodern narratives of justice, ones that are spontaneous, contingent, and irrepressibly messy, provides a case in point.

In some of what follows, I shall be arguing uphill, in favor of complexity, insinuating ambivalence about the kind of order legal stories typically create. I shall approach the disorder that lurks beyond the bounds of these well-told tales. Perhaps more unforgivably, I shall question whether the specific tale of Randall Dale Adams might be less tidy than we'd prefer. What if the modernist penchant for dichotomies that produces starkly polar choices like guilt/innocence, frame-up/frame-up undone, injustice/injustice corrected—the very mindset that gives us such satisfaction in seeing justice's scales finally balanced—were part of the problem? I want to suggest that the simplicity of these polarities, and the calm they induce, are at least partly responsible for making us leave things out. The messy things, the things that leave a sense of disorder and lack of control, the unsettling things we refuse to see or discuss. These are the things that make it hard to make legal decisions, decisions that can have irrevocable effects upon the body and soul of a person: prison, prison life, perhaps even death. No less grave, they are decisions that could lead to erroneous acquittal and the recurrence of violence done by the liberated defendant. It is precisely because the stakes are so high that I want to examine how we might guard against facile resolutions without getting mired in indecision and meaninglessness. In particular, I want to explore a form of postmodern legal storytelling that can sustain a coherent sense of justice as well as order. But to follow this path we must learn to question our own complicity in making truth appear overly neat. Thus, rather than share in the triumph of having seen the system set straight, we must ask ourselves whether we might be accomplices in a form of reality-making that let the Adams frame-up occur in the first place and that could let similar frame-ups occur in the future.

Ironically, my effort in this chapter to pursue the topics of order and disorder in legal storytelling risks the same fate as the film I set out to describe. *The Thin Blue Line* has become a cultural symbol. It is, after all, Morris's story that helped free a man from the corrupt grip of an ugly frame-up. But Morris's film is not simply an exposé of injustice. It also confronts the complexity of seeking the truth and the multiplicity of its forms. Like the film, whatever is simple in this account, or can be made by popular preference to seem so, risks eclipsing what is not. Each of us is well equipped to deny complexity, particularly when it threatens to destabilize what we want or need to believe about ourselves, others, and the world around us.

But to beat that temptation I had better get on with my story and tell you more about the event that spawned so many stories, including this one, which is also a story about legal storytelling in criminal cases.

The Event: Murder in Dallas

> We still haven't reached any consensus on the specifics of the crime: the number of gunmen, the number of shots . . . the list goes on and on. Beyond this confusion of data, people have developed a sense that history has been secretly manipulated . . . I think we've developed a much more deeply unsettled feeling about our grip on reality.
>
> DON DELILLO

I begin this way, but it could be otherwise[4]:

On Thanksgiving night, November 25, 1976, Randall Dale Adams and his brother arrived in Dallas, Texas. The two were heading to California from their home in Ohio. Meantime, they took up residence in a Dallas motel. The day after their arrival, Adams landed a job at an abandoned airport near Fort Worth.

On that same day, Friday, November 26, 1976, a month after his sixteenth birthday, David Harris decided to run away from home. That afternoon, he broke into a neighbor's home and stole some money. Later that evening, Harris also stole his neighbor's 1972 blue Mercury Comet. He packed some clothes, a 12-gauge shotgun, and his father's .22-caliber nine-shot pistol. Harris put the fully loaded pistol and a plastic box of .22-caliber ammunition underneath the driver's seat of the Comet and then left his hometown of Vidor, Texas.

Harris drove late into the night, finally stopping in the northern outskirts of Houston where, parked in a department store lot, he slept. When he awoke, it was daylight. Harris proceeded to Dallas, arriving sometime Saturday afternoon. It was his first time in the city.

After purchasing brake fluid and gasoline, Harris picked up a hitchhiker. The twenty-eight-year-old man who entered Harris's car, wearing blue jeans and a dark jacket and sporting bushy brown hair and a drooping mustache, was Randall Dale Adams. Adams, whose car had run out of gas, thanked Harris for the lift.

The boy and the man proceeded to find a gas station and returned to fill Adams's car. Adams then drove his car, with Harris following, to the Dallas motel where Adams and his brother were staying.

Adams and Harris went in. Adams's brother was watching TV. Adams changed his shirt and left with Harris in Harris's car. Adams brought some stereo equipment and three 8-track tapes. Harris had some electrician's tools in the car. They drove to several pawn shops in an effort to get money for the things they had with them. Along the way, Harris showed Adams the loaded handgun under the driver's seat. They did not pawn the gun; either Harris told Adams that it was not for sale[5] or he asked Adams to pawn it, and Adams refused.[6]

With the pawn money in hand, Adams and Harris hung out together for the rest of the day and evening. They drove to the airport where Adams worked, smoked some marijuana, drank some beer. They went back to town, to the Bronco Bowl, to have some lunch, some beer, and perhaps to play some pool. After, they went to a store to buy more beer, wandered around a shopping mall, drank the beer. Adams asked Harris if he would like to see a film. They went to a drive-in. *The Swinging Cheerleaders* was playing—soft porn. Maybe Harris chose the film, or maybe Adams did. They drank beer, smoked more pot. The next film, *The Student Body,* came on, and they watched that one too.

Adams wanted to go. It was close to midnight now, or maybe it was only 10 P.M. They left the drive-in.

Then, according to Harris:

Adams drives the Comet down Inwood Road. Soon, a police car, lights flashing, appears behind them. Adams pulls over, tells Harris to get down. A policeman approaches the driver. Adams rolls down the window, reaches beneath the seat for the pistol and, as the officer comes up to the car, fires five or six shots. Adams and Harris drive off, returning to the motel. Adams asks Harris if he needs a place to sleep. Harris says he does. Adams goes in to get the okay from his brother. Once Adams is inside, Harris slides behind the wheel and drives off.

According to Adams, it happened like this:

They leave the drive-in and head back to the motel. Adams picks up some cigarettes and a newspaper at the convenience store next to the motel. Maybe Harris asks Adams if he can stay at the motel with him. Maybe Adams says no.[7] Adams says he will see if he can get Harris a job at the place where he works. They arrange to meet on Monday morning. Adams goes in. His brother is asleep with the TV on. It's the end of *The Carol Burnett Show.*

Later, while in police custody, Adams will say in an illegally obtained statement that he drove that evening onto Inwood Road, the site of the murder. Adams will say in the statement that he remembers nothing more until he turned left onto Fort Worth Avenue.

Years later, while on death row for a different murder, David Harris will tell an interviewer that he was alone in the car when Officer Wood was shot and that he held the gun when the five bullets were fired.

The Trial: Conviction and Appeal

> Many techniques of the effective advocate . . . involve
> the undermining of rational argument rather than its
> promotion: they include techniques for keeping relevant
> information out, for trapping or confusing witnesses,
> for "laundering" the facts, for diverting attention or
> interrupting the flow of argument, and for exploiting
> means of non-rational persuasion.
> WILLIAM TWINING

Initially, the trial sets up a swearing contest: David Harris's word against Randall Dale Adams's. Each accuses the other of the shooting. The Adams defense is fairly confident. Adams has no prior criminal record, and there appear to be no eyewitnesses to the shooting. The slain police officer's partner cannot describe the lone occupant of the car they stopped that night for driving without headlights. The sole witness against Adams is David Harris, who at sixteen already has a criminal record that includes three burglaries. After returning to Vidor, Harris was also involved in yet another series of crimes, including burglary and armed robbery. And it was Harris himself who led the police to the murder weapon, and to his own arrest.

After the shooting of Officer Wood, Harris had given the pistol to his friend Alvin "Hooty" Nelson. Nelson and his brother Frank say Harris claimed at the time to have shot the Dallas officer, but they figured he was just joking around. Alvin and Frank Nelson's father subsequently found the gun in the house and dumped it in a swamp after his sons told him it had been used to shoot a policeman.

In the meantime, Harris's father reported his gun stolen. Someone else reported to police that David Harris had been bragging about killing a cop in Dallas. The Vidor police visited Harris, and he told them that he gave the gun to the Nelsons. The police then convinced Charles Nelson to take them to the swamp where he dumped the gun.

With this information in hand, the defense feels it has a decent chance of creating a reasonable doubt about Adams's guilt in the minds of the jurors. It is a matter of discrediting Harris and the three polygraph tests reportedly showing that Adams lied when he denied shooting the officer and denied that Harris told the truth when he claimed Adams was responsible. But then the trial takes a different turn.

Contrary to defense requests, the trial judge refuses to admit evidence of Harris's prior criminal convictions or of the post-shooting offenses then pending in the courts. The Vidor sheriff's office claims it cannot locate any of the Nelsons, so the defense subpoena for their testimony remains unexecuted. Then the prosecution introduces three surprise rebuttal witnesses. Suddenly, there they are in the courtroom, ready to be sworn in.

Each of the new witnesses claims to have been driving by the scene of the murder just as the shooting took place. Each identifies Adams in court as the man who shot Officer Wood. The defense seeks to discredit the alleged eyewitnesses on cross-examination. But Adams's attorneys have nothing with which to impeach their testimony—the district attorney has unlawfully withheld the witnesses' prior written statements. It is not until the recess before closing arguments that one statement is finally turned over and another is read to the defense over the telephone. According to the written statement, one eyewitness had described the gunman to police as a Mexican or light-skinned black man. The only possible gunmen, however, were Harris and Adams, both white. The statement received by telephone casts doubt on another eyewitness. Yet when Adams's attorney seeks to confront these two witnesses with their prior inconsistent statements, the trial judge accepts the prosecution's argument that the statements are consistent and refuses to admit them for impeachment.

The legally admissible evidence is now in; the attorneys' closing arguments end. The jurors leave to deliberate. When they return, they read their verdict: Randall Dale Adams is guilty of capital murder.

The state requests the death sentence. The jury now hears from two psychiatrists, Dr. John Holbrook and Dr. James Grigson, both of whom interviewed Adams in prison. Dr. Grigson, known as "Dr. Death" for his repeat performances in capital sentencing cases, gives his standard testimony: Randall Dale Adams is a killer who, if released into the community, will almost certainly kill again. In a similar vein, Dr. Holbrook tells the jury that Adams is a sociopath, a predator without conscience. The jury has all it needs. Randall Dale Adams is sentenced to death for the murder of Dallas police officer Robert Wood.

Several months after sentencing, the defense team files a motion for retrial. They have uncovered evidence indicating that the three alleged eyewitnesses committed perjury in court. But the information comes too late; as a matter of state law, this kind of impeachment evidence must be presented within thirty days after sentencing to warrant a new trial.[8] Adams waits on death row as his appeals continue, moving first through the state judicial system, where he loses, then through the federal system.

On June 25, 1980, three and a half years after Adams's arrest in Dallas, the United States Supreme Court declares unconstitutional the Texas death penalty statute under which Adams was sentenced.[9] The state now has the option of trying Adams for capital murder a second time under a corrected sentencing procedure.[10] Instead, the Dallas district attorney, the trial judge who presided over Adams's trial, and the Dallas sheriff petition the governor for a commutation of Adams's sentence to life imprisonment. On July 11, 1980, the governor complies. And that proclamation of commutation removes the only legal taint remaining in Adams's case. All the irregularities and potential due process violations at trial have been dismissed; Adams's legal remedies have run out.

And there the story would end, but for a strange and serendipitous event. In the course of making a film about the infamous "Dr. Death," Errol Morris hears the story of an inmate named Randall Dale Adams. Intrigued, he decides to change the focus of his film. The film Morris makes and releases narrates the frame-up of Randall Adams. It is this story that ignites the public's attention, but the film also takes up a larger theme. According to Morris, the film is also about the contingency of truth and the manifold ways in which truth may be constructed. It is to this process of meaning making that we now turn.

Framing the Frame-up: Detection and Complicity

> [The detective] reassures us of an ultimate rationality, "a benevolent and knowable universe," "a world that can be interpreted by human reason, embodied in the superior intellect of the detective." . . . The detective's skill is precisely the ability to code "seemingly unrelated data into a coherent system of signs, a text identifying the malefactor." . . . [T]o the degree the crime novel puts the signification process into doubt or even exploits the gap between socially accepted signification and ultimate reality, it subverts the reassurances of the detective novel.
>
> TONY HILFER

The prosecutors at the trial of Randall Dale Adams told a convincing story about a hitchhiker, a drifter up to no good, who smoked marijuana and drank no mean amount of beer with a sixteen-year-old kid, took the kid to a soft-porn drive-in and then to his motel. They described a guy whose luck ran out late that night when he happened to be seen by five local Texans, including the young David Harris and the slain officer's partner, each of whom either saw Adams shoot Officer Wood or could place him at the scene of the murder. Adams denied his guilt, but there were no witnesses to support his claims at trial.

Now, according to the popular media, and in the minds of many who saw it, *The Thin Blue Line* correctly resolved a murder case. Perhaps it did, and perhaps it didn't. From the point of view of the legal system, of course, it did just that. The film triggered an official inquiry

into the case that culminated in Adams's release from prison[11] as an
innocent man scapegoated by a corrupt D.A. and a biased judge. But
I believe there is more to it than that. The film tells us a good deal
about how people—lawyers, jurors, judges, witnesses, police officers,
criminal defendants—typically make sense of guilt and innocence in
a criminal case.[12] But it also presents a way of making meaning that
we tend to reject. In fact, I believe the film elucidates my contention
that our habits of making meaning are so entrenched when it comes
to matters like determining guilt or innocence that to oppose them
becomes a highly subversive act—assuming that we allow such oppo-
sition to register at all.

As it turns out, Morris's film lays out two contemporaneous but
opposing plot lines: the story as told in a classically linear fashion
(beginning, development, conclusion), and a provocative, unresolved
nonlinear narrative. The classic linear story line is perhaps best ex-
emplified by the familiar genre of the detective story wherein the
detective-hero, by identifying and combining significant clues, resolves
a disturbing mystery. In Morris's film, the audience as detective/juror
traces the clues that point to a sinister plot by state officials to frame
Randall Dale Adams. The clues fit neatly into a story that ends when
the mystery of the frame-up is revealed and solved. Once revealed, the
plot is obvious and familiar. Lies, corruption, and abuse of power
made Adams a scapegoat for a crime he did not commit.

The film's opposing plot line operates within the context of a less
familiar, nonlinear (arguably postmodern) narrative form. Rather than
offering closure, this form leaves a disquieting sense of inadequate
resolution and residual mystery. Was Harris the gunman? If he was,
is that all there is to the story? What about the loose ends? Where was
Adams at the time of the murder? What were the two of them up to
that day? Does it take a serendipitous interview with an artful filmmaker to save a prisoner from life in jail or death by electrocution?
What if the plotting of chance or fate actually played a larger part in
the criminal justice system?[13] Surely such uncontrollability of events
and human actions dissipates, in rather short order, the complacent
"all's right with the world because truth and justice will out in the
end" attitude that the linear story would have us believe.

In short, there are two tales here, and one subverts the other. When
framed as a causal-linear documentary and detective story, Morris's
film employs conventional wisdom (including schemata, scripts, and
stereotypes) about lying, madness, official corruption, local prejudice,
and psychological trauma. It takes us along a straight path of mean-

ing: from mystery (why is this man in jail?) to resolution (because he was framed!). Within this frame, we know that human nature and the world operate according to causal-linear principles. Things make sense, and judgments are not difficult. When the film is framed as a nonlinear composite of symbols, however, we find ourselves in a universe of fate and fortune, circularity and irresolution. The nonlinear story about the murder of Officer Wood suggests that our conventional knowledge about causation and meaning may not be sufficient. It suggests that while the conventional mystery genre often shapes and informs the way lawyers tell their clients' tales, it may not do justice to what is going in the world.[14] As distasteful as it may be, it suggests that it may not be possible for us to account fully for truth and justice within a conventional, causally sequenced story line. Perhaps the mythic narratives of ancient Western (and even some current non-Western) cultures, most notably the classical culture of Sophocles and Aeschylus, with their vast interjaculating array of nonrational forces, are also (perhaps have always been) shaping our world.[15] If so, coming to grips with disruptive forces like deceit, corruption, and pathology is not enough—not if chance and necessity must also be reckoned with when assessing individual accountability.

But if more than one story about Officer Wood's murder is believable, which one do we choose as a matter of law? Surely the legal system, which enforces official decisions about truth and justice with the power of the state, can be expected to resist judgments that take root in shifting standards of style and taste. Little wonder, then, that after vacillating between linear resolution and nonlinear complexity, so many will succumb to the pull of the familiar, the path of least dissonance, with a preferred sense of resolute justice, or redress, or right outcome. For here we witness the actualization of deep modernist beliefs about what justice is and how it gets done in the world. Yet, at the same time, these beliefs operate so deeply that the way they shape our understanding and our practical judgments remains largely hidden from view. Perhaps this is so because we deal here with things that could not be otherwise. The beliefs at stake may be so necessary to a particularly culture's or community's collective sense of order and coherence that, like gravity or causality, once they are questioned the universe seems irrevocably disturbed. Perhaps that is why we do not let them be questioned. In law, as elsewhere, radical change rarely comes without resistance.

The Thin Blue Line is curious in that it simultaneously enacts and refutes the classic modern narrative of straight-arrow truth and constant justice. Morris activates this polarity by directly implicating the viewer (as juror) in the frame-up of reality. Unlike some of its more distant forebears in classical tragedy, however, *The Thin Blue Line* offers no transcendent resolution. The gods do not intervene when meaning fails. In this respect, the film's existential credentials might appear impeccable. Yet such a comparison misses the mark. It is the existential hero who anchors our faith in the human will to meaning. But here, no such hero can be found. No, Morris does not chant with Sartre, God is dead—long live humanity! Rather, he moves us closer to the postmodern world of Beckett. We go on, yes, but not because we understand why.[16]

In this view, there is no longer a straight path to truth and justice, no longer the autonomous will to meaning. More than one frame for meaning now lies before us. And while surely it is up to us to decide which frame to believe in, the task of choosing which to accept grows increasingly difficult. Standards are clouded, meaning's possibilities proliferate, while human agency itself seems close to dissolution.

In the arena of criminal law, however, such indeterminacy of meaning can be fatal to judgment. Even the criminal defense attorney, who deliberately sets out to activate uncertainty in order to establish that the state has failed to carry its burden of proving guilt beyond a reasonable doubt, may go too far. For uncertainty, by itself, is highly volatile. It is a state that cannot be maintained. Jurors in its grip will seek relief elsewhere, in any respite of meaning, grasping for a way to tolerate the difficult responsibility of deciding whether to acquit or condemn.

Uncertainty alone, under the onerous strictures of the law, will not do. The defense must buttress any uncertainty it induces with something stable, or risk sending the jurors scurrying for any scrap of certainty the prosecution offers. And to be sure, the prosecution will be offering certainty. After all, it is the prosecution's task to provide a smooth and easy ride on the currents of historical truth and legal necessity.

The Causal-Linear Frame: A Documentary Exposé

> [I] did not get my picture of the world by satisfying myself of its correctness; nor do I have it because I am satisfied of its correctness. No: it is the inherited background against which I distinguish between true and false.
>
> LUDWIG WITTGENSTEIN

Just because the framework for our beliefs is invisible does not mean it is not actively shaping the way we see and understand ourselves, others, and the world around us. So it is with common sense. And so it is with common sense that Errol Morris molds our perception of the official frame-up that landed Randall Dale Adams in prison. Morris makes deceit and corruption look simple; each of the characters' motives fits the archetypal plot of a frame-up.

Consider first official corruption. Everyone knows that unchecked power breeds corruption and oppression. And everyone knows what oppression looks like. We recognize it in the film's opening image: Randall Adams sitting incommunicado in police custody, a false confession placed before him, the barrel of an officer's revolver held inches from Adams's face. Yes, that's what oppression looks like. And when Adams talks about a nightmare from which he cannot awaken, we tend to agree: Yes. That's what oppression must feel like. It's Kafkaesque.

So, too, do we recognize the confident, smiling face of the interviewing officer when he smugly describes the same interrogation scene as a "casual friendly conversation." Yes. This is what one would expect an oppressor to look like. And when the officer can't see through his own bias and we can, when an accused's protestation of innocence is taken to signify only a lack of conscience, we are persuaded. Adams had it right when he said, "They did not want to believe me."

Everyone knows consistency bespeaks truth, and contradiction lying. What Adams says about his situation is consistent with what we are shown—a gun, a false confession, threats. Thus we are inclined to believe him. In contrast, the police officer's words reflect contradiction: there was nothing friendly about that initial encounter between them. But what can you expect? Oppressors lie. It makes sense. Adams is in the hand of oppressive liars. The frame-up has begun.

Knowing what we know so early on in the film, we are not surprised to learn later that the district attorney got David Harris to lie about the exchange of immunity for his testimony against Adams. Or that the D.A. "reminded" Harris of the chronology of events leading up to the murder. Yes. That's what official corruption is like. And when Adams describes what it's like to be caught in such a mechanism, that it's like living in a "Hell on Earth"—that's the right image for oppression. That's true. Adams is telling the truth. Power corrupts, everyone knows that. Now consider greed. Greed, too, corrupts. And like oppression, greed has familiar guises. Consider Mr. Miller, one of the eyewitnesses that got Adams convicted. Mr. Miller was heard to have said that for enough money, he would testify to anything. Yes, that's what a greedy and corrupt person would say. We also discover that Mr. Miller and his wife only decided to testify against Adams after they had already been in police custody following three days of domestic violence. They'd been booked for disorderly conduct and drunkenness. Besides, their cooperation got their daughter out of some robbery charges that could've landed her a life sentence. These folks are indeed the sort who would lie for money. Greed, deceit, corruption. They fit the image and they fit the script.

As does that other eyewitness, Michael Randall. As a black man in Dallas, he knows the score: "The D.A. will put something in your mouth if he wants to. That's why they call it the 'Hall of Justice'—the scales are not balanced. The scales are in the hall and they go up and down." Randall's behavior is consistent with his experience of the world, and his experience has been awash in corruption and deceit. And again, there is the persuasive image of a quid pro quo. Randall, too, lied to get what was his for the taking—his share of the reward money.

Greed and power corrupt. But then there is madness, which needs no reward. And anyone with eyes in her head could see that Mrs. Miller, the third eyewitness, is mad. She sees crimes happening all around her. "[I]t's always happening to me, everywhere I go, you know. Lots of times there's killings or anything, even around my house." And it's Miller who wants to solve the crime, quicker than the cops. Anyone can recognize such blatant pathology. Even her husband, whom she once had arrested for carrying fantasized drugs in the trunk of his car, said: "[O]h man, she's. . . ." Though he chuckles without finishing the sentence, it's not hard for us to fill in the blank: yeah, she's crazy.

Almost all the main players in the frame-up are before us now. The corrupt officials, from Dallas cops to the district attorney, as well as the greedy, self-interested, or delusional eyewitnesses. The only characters that remain are the trial judge and David Harris himself. And common sense, Morris shows, has no trouble placing them in the thick of the plot.

Everyone knows that arbitrary justice is no justice at all. When a person can be sentenced to death simply because he's an unwanted outsider, and his sacrifice will save the neck of a local boy, common sense stirs our outrage. And outrage at local prejudice could hardly find a better catalyst than in the person of Judge Metcalfe.

Metcalfe knows who the good guys are. He's known since child-hood, for he's been taught the greatest respect for law enforcement. You see, his dad was a G-man in the days of gangsters like Baby Face Nelson and John Dillinger. Judge Metcalfe has a personal understanding of what it's like to risk life and limb in service to law and order. He learned it from his dad. We are not surprised that he choked up during the D.A.'s summation. We know what side Metcalfe is on.

And who is Randall Dale Adams, anyway? As Metcalfe puts it, he's just a drifter. Not worth blotting the perfect win record of a legendary D.A. Besides, it's a matter of local justice. Consider Metcalfe's response to the United States Supreme Court's reversal of the death sentence he'd imposed: "[I]n Austin, in our State Appeals Court, I was nine [votes] to nothing correct and in Washington I was one to eight incorrect. If you tally all those votes, I come out ten to eight, and yet the case was reversed." For Metcalfe, it's as if the Civil War went the other way. The federal Constitution remains on par with state law. It is what you'd expect of an old-boy network: insiders count more. And when Randall Dale Adams, with his bushy hair and drooping mustache, stops off in Dallas on his way to California, a better outsider would be hard to imagine.

Last but not least, there's David Harris, the local boy from Vidor. Common sense tells us he committed the murder. Morris even gets Harris to say that Adams is innocent. Harris says he's the one who should know. And we believe him. After all, hasn't he been straight with us? Hasn't he come clean about the deceitful way that he played into the hands of the authorities in the Adams case? We understand Harris. His behavior makes sense. Everyone knows that a terrible trauma at a tender age can lay down a pattern of aggressive behavior for the rest of one's life. And just look what happened to him when he was a little kid. His older brother drowned in a neighbor's pool when Harris was only three years old. His father, who was supposed to be watching them, never dealt with the guilt. And when a new child took the deceased sibling's place, Harris never could gain his father's acceptance. As Harris says, "There you go." The pattern was laid down. Harris became the kind of person who would beat up his commanding officer or shoot a cop. Uncontrolled aggression against authority figures. It was like he was acting out his hatred toward his father and then punishing himself by making sure he got caught. It doesn't take Freud. Common sense tells you Harris is the kind of person who would shoot a cop.

It's common sense. In a world of official corruption, greed, cynical self-interest, madness, local prejudice, and profound psychological trauma, these things happen. Innocent outsiders get framed, and local sociopaths go free. It makes sense. Randall Dale Adams should never have been in prison at all. The film sets the record straight. Justice miscarried, but truth will out in the end. The causal-linear metaphysics of common sense triumphs. Morris's exposé allows us to rest easy: error can be corrected, order can be reimposed, and above all, our belief in the ultimate triumph of justice can be confirmed.

Within the documentary frame of the film, Morris's techniques are persuasive. We want to believe Adams is innocent; he fits our image of a likely victim of official abuse. Similarly, it is easy for us to distrust the people who participate in the frame-up; they fit the script for the corrupt and deceitful. Nevertheless, Morris's linear exposé frame is not without fissures and unanswered questions. Even this narrative, which offers certainty, does not banish doubt. In a film about the different forms of deception, Morris leaves room to realize that certainty often demands self-deception.

Consider, for example, the following factual ambiguities: Officer Turko (the slain officer's partner), David Harris, Harris's friend Dennis Johnson, and two local officials all claimed that there were two people in the car when the shooting occurred. And Adams, who conceded that the statement he made while in custody was "basically what I liked," seems to admit at one point that he was driving when he and Harris turned onto Inwood Road, the scene of the murder. Why did Adams have nothing to say about the period of time between turning onto Inwood Road and his arrival back at his motel room ten minutes later? Did he really forget? Was Adams with Harris at the time of the shooting? Why did so many different people say there were two people in the car? In one account, Harris says he and Adams returned to the motel and Adams went in to ask his brother if Harris could stay with them that night. According to Harris, the brother "[didn't] like to do that." So Harris left. In another version offered by Harris, he drove off without waiting for the brother's word.

But why didn't Adams's brother confirm Adams's story, or at least verify one of Harris's versions of events at the trial? If Harris made it all up, why such detail? The climax of the movie comes when Harris mysteriously proclaims that Adams might only be in jail because "he didn't have no place for somebody to stay that helped him that night. . . . That might be the only, total reason why he's where he's at today." Consider the ambiguity of this statement. It might mean that had Adams's brother agreed to let Harris stay over, the shooting would not have occurred. It might mean that had Harris stayed over, Adams would not have found himself on Inwood Road that night with David Harris. It might mean that there would have been no grudge, no reason to pin the murder on Adams.

But why would Adams drive off at night with David Harris? Perhaps the answer comes in response to a broader question: what was twenty-eight-year-old Adams doing spending the day with sixteen-year-old Harris, drinking and smoking dope, going to a soft-porn drive-in movie? The sexual connotations fit the schema we have for such things, that sort of thing of which Adams's brother disapproved. Why were the car's lights off that night on Inwood Road? Some connection between a tryst that night along a dark road and the shooting of the police officer cannot be ruled out. It may be the sort of thing neither Harris nor Adams would care to own up to. We do not know. But the film invites this sort of speculation and does not resolve it.

So, was Randall Dale Adams in the car at the time of the shooting? Even if he did not pull the trigger, was he an accomplice in the murder of Officer Wood? Even within the linear framework of Morris's documentary, these uncertainties remain, defying the reassuring conclusiveness of the genre. Such doubt invites us to confront our desire to be taken in by the metaphysics of linear resolution, our desire to suppress all of the messy and disturbing details. For is it not more important to have a simple frame-up, with the concomitant certainty about truth and justice, than to wind up with a set of mysteries?

If a certain amount of denial framing out unpleasant, dissonant details for the sake of a neat and reaffirming ending attends even the linear exposé frame of the film, it should come as little surprise that the film's nonlinear, antidocumentary frame may be met with denial on an even grander scale. Is it seen at all? Seen or not, there it is: an acausal theme, presented both discursively and stylistically, pervades this work.

To appreciate Morris's acausal counterplot we must leave the ordered world of the detective for the mystery of the crime novel. We must abandon the causal thinking that has long dominated common sense. But if this antidocumentary frame isn't commonsensical, then what is it? What must one believe in order for Morris's counterplot to make sense? To address this question we must explore the metaphysics of acausality. This analysis will sweep us into Morris's antidocumentary frame.

The Acausal/Nonlinear Frame: Fateful Reversions

> The heavens themselves, the planets, and this centre
> Observe degree, priority, and place,
> Take but degree away, untune that string,
> And, hark! what discord follows . . .
> Force should be right; or rather, right and wrong—
> Between whose endless jar justice resides—
> Should lose their names, and so should justice too.
> WILLIAM SHAKESPEARE

As a paradigm of how we make sense of social reality, the Adams case draws our attention not only to how we recognize truth and justice, but also to those underlying shared beliefs that allow us to agree upon a particular interpretation or meaning of an event. The discrete mental representations that constitute our social knowledge, our common sense, tell us why Harris is guilty and Adams innocent.[17] A deep belief in the straight path of truth and justice convinces us that the mystery of the Adams frame-up has finally been solved.

But the Sherlock Holmes world of linear logic is not the only one Morris puts before us. He also has us ponder: what if rationality, rather than being a triumphant force in the world, turned out to be the loser? What if chance (coincidence) or fate (necessity) were instead the dominant forces? Then human agency would be greatly diminished, and human responsibility along with it. Things would "just happen" to us.[18] This vision is one of the emplotting threads that runs through *The Thin Blue Line*. It is a vision that leads us into a peculiarly nonlinear, antidocumentary frame.

If Morris had wanted to tell a purely linear tale, he certainly would have proceeded differently. Consider, for example, the film's failure to provide captions identifying who is speaking. Why this blatant defiance of the conventional documentary style? Instead of telling us how to take the words of the speaker in terms of his or her social or legal status, we are left with the words themselves. And perhaps also with the felt need to know the speaker's status in order to know how to take what he or she is saying. This technique of nondisclosure provokes a feeling of disorientation.[19] And this disorientation is only the beginning. Morris goes much further to knock us out of the standard causal-linear cognitive loop.

Consider how fate and chance are introduced early on in the film and maintained discursively throughout. At the very outset we have the classic image of endless possibility in America: like so many others before them, Randall Adams and his brother are making their way across the country. Possibility—or destiny? Destiny—or chance? The main characters in the film, Harris and Adams, play up both the necessity and the fortuity of the circumstances. For example, Adams muses at the beginning: "I'm not in town a half a day and I've got a job. It[s] just . . . everything clicked. It's as if I was meant to be [in Dallas]." Adams's gloss on fate is immediately followed in the film's opening sequence by Harris: "[T]his all started when David was running away from home. And he takes . . . I took a pistol from my dad's, a shotgun. . . . Ended up coming to Dallas." Thus, a strange pattern is set. At times the dominant operative force for both Adams and Harris seems to be fate as necessity; at other times it seems to be fate as chance. But the upshot remains the same: both Adams and Harris appear to suffer events rather than cause them to happen. Things are simply playing themselves out. As Adams says: "[W]hy did I meet this kid? I don't know. Why did I run out of gas at that time? I don't know. But it happened. It happened."

For Harris, fate is the dominant force in the universe. At one point he states, "Everybody's life's going to take some kind of path regardless of what happens." He seems to be saying that whether his violent behavior was an effort to "get back at [his father] for the way he treated me" or was "nothing but hurting myself," he had no choice in the matter. It's as if he'd been born into a life predestined to unfold as it did. And it's not just Harris's life that's dominated by fate rather than reason. Harris says, "There's probably been thousands of innocent people convicted and there will probably be thousands more. Why? Who knows."

Who knows? Things just happen. The only problem is that in a universe run by fate, truth and justice may be impossible. Truth requires a reasonable basis for certainty, and justice requires a reasonable basis for assigning responsibility. In their own discursive accounts, Harris and Adams question the possibility of both individual responsibility and certainty. Moreover, the film's stylistic techniques in what I call its nonlinear antidocumentary frame do much to reinforce this theme.

Morris conveys the film's nonlinearity through recurring metaphors of reversion. We keep seeing the endlessly circling red police light; we keep returning to the scene of the shooting—obviously fictional but replayed again and again, as if seeing it one more time would tell us something new. The film offers other breaks from representational reality. For example, Morris splices in black-and-white clips of Hollywood detective movies from the 1940s—a Tinseltown landscape of crime solving offered to illustrate the mental reality that Mrs. Miller inhabited. Or consider the G-man and gangster images offered to convey the trial judge's mental construction of the world. And permeating the film is that reversionary score by composer Philip Glass in which chords melt into one another like floating arabesques in an opium dream.

These pervasive figures of reversion do not tell us anything specific about the events themselves. Rather, they are metaphysical tropes that tell us something about how reality is framed in both life and art. Part of this story, they tell us, is about storytelling itself. The film offers not just one frame-up, the causal-linear frame-up of Randall Dale Adams, but perpetual, repeat frame-ups, leading us to wonder: What world are we in? What sense does it make?

In sum, *The Thin Blue Line,* in its antidocumentary, antidetective frame, implicates not just a few deranged or corrupt folks around Dallas, the kind we like to condemn in the service of our own dedication to truth and justice in a causal-linear world. The film implicates all of us in our complacency about how easily we employ ready-made notions of truth and justice to save ourselves from the anxiety and doubt that might otherwise plague our judgments. By exposing some of the epistemological devices we all use to make meaning out of chaotic life, the film makes it more difficult to laugh contentedly at Mrs. Miller's pathetic inner world of Hollywood gangsters and her delusions about her own ace detective skills. Such laughter is a defense, a way to distance ourselves from other people's seemingly bizarre internal scripts and views of the world. Surely no ill-conceived constructs filter *our* view of reality, no odd cultural artifacts interfere with *our* discernment of who's who and what's what.

Informed by the film's acausal, nonlinear frame, we come to see that the same common-sense wisdom that allowed us to solve a mystery now breaks reality into fragments we cannot neatly reassemble. The discrete elements of the Adams case, each rotating on its own axis of impersonal truth and necessity, may invite too many stories, each of whose meanings are too overdetermined, potent, and varied to allow any confidence in the overarching order of things. The nonlinear frame leaves us uncertain, mystified. What really happened, and why? What might it mean? Who can we blame?

Faced with radically different ways of seeing and making sense of the world—the causal-logical system of the documentary genre on the one hand, and the acausal-reversionary system of the antidocumentary on the other—we are left to wonder which frame to choose. That we are able to ask this question confirms the artistic triumph and social importance of Morris's film. *The Thin Blue Line* is undoubtedly important as an exposé of injustice and official corruption in the Dallas criminal justice system. But on an allegorical level, the film depicts a battle that rages back and forth, moment by moment, across a thin blue line of representational order. It is a battle against chaos, fate, and deception, forces that could easily destroy human agency and make individual responsibility impossible. Metaphorically, the film asks a fundamental and daring question: who (or what) polices meaning?

It is a daring question that Morris does not quite follow through. For in the end, the counterplot does not take hold. Having raised the specter of unaccountability, of the unknowability (or perhaps the untellability) of truth, the film ultimately reverts back into linear certainty and resolution. After all, we know Randall Adams was framed. Or do we? The postmodern challenge Errol Morris masterfully raises, yet ultimately abandons, has yet to be adequately reckoned with. And so it is to postmodernism and its relevance to legal storytelling that we must now turn.

Skeptical Versus Affirmative Postmodernism

> With all due respect, Justice Brennan's proposed ending to this lawsuit is as unsatisfying as the conclusion of a bad mystery novel: we learn on the last page that the victim has been done in by a suspect heretofore unknown, for reasons unrevealed.
> JUSTICE BYRON S. WHITE

> There is no inside story; there are only images.
> JAMES B. TWITCHELL

Conventional wisdom dictates that although criminal defense lawyers may pursue a variety of different trial tactics, three reliable strategies stand out: "[I]f you've got the facts on your side, argue the facts to the jury. If you've got the law on your side, argue the law to the judge. If you've got neither, confuse the issue with other parties."[20] The first strategy is that of the good historian. Defense counsel reconstructs the past and shows the jurors that the defendant "didn't do it" and must be found innocent. Or she establishes the fact of another's guilt. The defense thus battles the prosecution on the prosecution's own turf: the playing field of historical truth and legal necessity. This is the site of the imperative, linear story frame, for here a particular historical truth mandates a particular legal outcome.

The third strategy of "confusing the issue" is consistent with an acausal, nonlinear frame and often employs postmodern tactics. The defense attempts to attack the prosecutor's history, impeach the credibility of the state's witnesses, and deconstruct the linear narrative the prosecutor offers, breaking it up until it is transformed into a nonsensical, incredible tale too full of inconsistencies and loose ends to withstand the onslaught of reasonable doubt. Unlike historical narration, the most important time frame for historical deconstruction is the present, not the past. A good historical narrative account is temporally closed off and can simply be accepted. ("Makes sense to me. That must've been the way it happened.") A good deconstruction, by introducing hesitation, emphasizes and dilates the present moment of doubt. ("Hey, wait a minute. First he said it was 10 P.M., then he said midnight. He must be lying.") The believable history is what already happened; the deconstructed history is what happens in the courtroom.

In *The Thin Blue Line*, Morris adopts the first and third of these defense tactics. With the film's viewer cast as juror, Morris not only deconstructs the state's causal-linear history ("Those witnesses are lying! They didn't see Adams shoot anyone that night"); he also substitutes a linear, prosecutorial history of his own, pointing to someone else ("It's Harris, not Adams, who shot Police Officer Wood"). The film's linear plot shows us why the witnesses lied (greed, delusion) and why the frame-up was set in motion in the first place (the only suspect old enough to electrocute was Adams). At the film's close, the historical truth of David Harris's guilt is sealed with Harris's own words:

> MORRIS: [W]hat do you think about whether or not he's innocent?
> HARRIS: I'm sure he is. . . . 'Cause I'm the one that knows.

It is partly due to the strength of Morris's linear plot that his counterplot fails. When I say it fails, I mean that it does not stimulate us sufficiently to question the certainty the linear plot induces; without such stimulation, the audience is borne along with much the same ease that created the frame-up in the first place. Ironically, by simply stranding the viewer in a domain of echoing reversions and uncertainty, the practical effect of the film's nonlinear techniques is to reinforce its linear plot—strengthening our willingness to blame Harris and exonerate the long-suffering Adams. These techniques fail to take us in when they are in plain view as servants of radical subversion. Put differently, the counterplot does not hold our imaginations because its techniques are those of a skeptical rather than an affirmative postmodernism.

Skeptical Postmodernism

As an example of the kind of postmodernism I have in mind here, consider contemporary sociologist Jean Baudrillard's assertion that in the current media age, conventional dialogue has become too slow: "Looking is much faster; it is the medium of the media. . . . Everything must come into play instantaneously. We never communicate. In the to-and-fro of communication, the instantaneity of looking, light and seduction is already lost."[21] In Baudrillard's view, our culture is rapidly slipping from communication with content into "simulation," what he calls the "ecstasy of the real."[22] According to Baudrillard, this state of ecstasy is a state of empty form; it is reality esthetically heightened to the point that it is stripped of all meaning and becomes pure seduction. Like pornography; like fashion. When the ecstatic form absorbs all the energy of its opposite, that which gives it meaning, the result is sheer simulation.

But simulation is not the endpoint of the cultural development now under way. According to Baudrillard, we are seeing a shift from pure "simulation" (the failed representation of the real) to pure "simulacrum" (the impenetrable commingling of fiction and reality). This transition takes us to a point where representations no longer need to be rooted in reality. It is sufficient for images simply to reflect other images. Once the image itself comes to stand for the real, the need for reality is lost. This marks the birth of the simulacrum. When the simulacrum reigns, external reality no longer matters. As a result, however, fiction and reality alike are called into question. The commercial mass media of film and television best embody this absorption of reality into the "hyperreality" of the simulacrum.[23]

The cultural vision shared by writers like Baudrillard may be called "skeptical postmodernism." Skeptical postmodernism manifests a marked inclination toward pessimism and disenchantment. In this view, truth, meaning, and reality itself are no longer discernible.[24] The jolt of novel juxtapositions and the sensations they produce may thus readily displace cognitive content. The unified self and human agency come to be seen as illusory. Autonomous authority and representation are invariably deceptive; no normative stance seems worthy of commitment. Yet without intentionality and causation, or the means with which to reliably narrate and assess human activity, individuals can no longer be held accountable for having "authored" their acts or caused an event to happen. Little wonder, then, that in the end the skeptical postmodern is left with nothing more than endless play and detached irony.

To the extent that Errol Morris's acausal, nonlinear counterplot in *The Thin Blue Line* evokes such a vision, it is bound to fail. Indeed, the film's counterplot fails in the same way that skeptical postmodernism fails in law and lawyering generally. In a legal context, the reality it portrays is esthetically and psychologically untenable. In matters of life and death, whether it be the execution of the accused or the possibility of his killing again, we instinctively reject the message of skeptical postmodernism. Human traits like prejudice, deceit, greed, abuse of power, and the reality of a deliberate frame-up are things we can understand. But mystification, time's circularity, fate, and coincidence defeat the practical demands of human judgment. We become strangers in a strange and incomprehensible land.

In *The Thin Blue Line* the threat of incomprehensibility that is presented by the acausal counterplot serves only to enhance the persuasive power of the film's conventional mystery plot. In fact, Morris employs a variety of bizarre imaging techniques for the explicit purpose of solving the mystery, to persuade viewers that Adams was framed. For example, we see the cartoonish cops-and-robbers clip that accompanies Mrs. Miller's account of the Dallas shooting, bringing us into her delusional world of commingled fact and fiction. We see the Chicago gangster shootout scene that overlays Judge Metcalfe's wistful reflections on law and order and his dad's golden days, making plain the judge's bias in favor of the state. In short, these images engage the viewer in an act of deconstruction. We see why the defense case for Adams makes sense: the judge and Mrs. Miller cannot be trusted; police and prosecutorial corruption fueled the state's frame-up of Adams.

But now consider the equally obvious and deliberately cartoonish reenactment of the shooting: the chocolate malt flying in slo-mo and oozing like blood on the ground; the single-framed revolver flame lighting up the night; the slam of the gun echoing off the butt-littered interrogation room table; the lonely echo of cowboy boots in the early morning hours of Randall Adams's ordeal. These parodic, postmodern, self-conscious images are effectively eclipsed by the linear detective plot. The viewer resists the invitation to find problems in the film's linear development. We refuse to entertain the possibility that the purported "documentary" nature of the film is itself merely another dramatic reenactment. We reject the parody and prefer to play it straight.

The counterplot fails on both esthetic and psychological grounds to make us question our craving for certainty and the ease with which we embrace it. Esthetically, the causal-linear frame of the detective story is familiar and easy to follow; it is built from and produces conventional, contextualized, graspable meanings. In contrast, the counterplot operates within the strange and mystifying domain of the crime novel. It is a world that appears to be dominated by chance and fate. It is a place where events are difficult, if not impossible, to explain, a place where causal reasoning breaks down; where things just happen. Stories about events in this world can offer no final outcome, no closure; the only constant is uncertainty.

Such unresolved mystery points to a second ground for the failure of Morris's counterplot—a psychological one. Psychologically, we crave meaning. Meaning lends order and control. Chaos is disorienting and unpleasant, especially in matters of life and death. There is no place in decisions of such consequence for epistemological conundrums or esthetic musings. Thus, once nestled in the sobering frame of a criminal trial, storytelling fictions such as Morris's self-consciously cartoonish images have a boomerang effect. These caricatures of reality only send us running back to a "truer" reality, one the linear plot alone is able to provide.[25] Faced with untenable disorder on the one hand, and a meaningful drama on the other, we have no choice. There is no meaning in a story in which Adams just happens to meet Harris on the side of a Dallas highway; in which Harris happens to act out the rage of a father's rejection; in which a filmmaker happens to hear a story that culminates in a movie that happens to get a convicted murderer out of prison. Such acausal "happenings" take and leave us nowhere. They conjure a world robbed of personality, motivation, intentionality, and a story robbed of a structure that allows the listener to make sense of human actions and interactions. Such psychological fatality is intolerable to those—judges, jurors, lawyers, victims, suspects, spectators, and media producers—who face the law's demand for public judgment. Without coherent stories, judgment becomes impossible.

The Thin Blue Line's esthetic and psychological failures offer a cautionary lesson about the art of persuasive legal storytelling: the law has little use for the kind of skeptical, radically subversive postmodernism that has been featured of late in some legal and much nonlegal scholarship. However, there is another kind of postmodernism that may not be so easily dismissed.

Affirmative Postmodernism

Postmodernism need not be skeptical. A postmodern story might close around a coherent meaning, or at least point to one in the mind of the audience. Thus the story may be postmodern in its nonlinear use of popular cultural images and symbols, but need not employ these images and symbols in an insular or exclusively self-referential manner. A story might concede the demise of the autonomous modern subject, but still find meaning through the distributed self: an identity made up of multiple cultural and social constructs shared by others in particular communities. It might, in this postmodern but nonskeptical spirit, recognize the irreducibility of truth and justice to any abstract metanarrative (e.g., a system based on axiomatic principles such as fairness, liberty, or some utilitarian calculus), but still see truth and justice as coherent. Abstraction may give way to particularity, contextuality, multiplicity; judgment may turn toward characteristic voices and localized accounts. But localization and contextualization are not fatal to meaning. It remains possible to seek rather than abandon meaning for concepts like truth and justice—even in the face of contingency, unpredictability, and spontaneity.

Consequently, when the demand for judgment arises we may respond to it not with skepticism, but pragmatically, drawing from known storytelling genres, social stereotypes, and deeply rooted cultural myths. The meanings thus narrated may be postmodern in that they lack classic linear form, but may nevertheless compel belief and commitment. Persuasiveness may come from a variety of discrete logics, including the associative logic in which one encounters the sudden power of an isolated phrase or image or cluster of novel juxtapositions of familiar mental representations. Such meanings are irreducible to, though they may not be wholly cut off from, traditional forms of deductive and inductive reasoning.

In this way, human depth remains. Internal forces (like motivation and intention) rather than wholly external forces (like chance or fate) still account for events and provide a basis for narrative coherence and accountability. Of course to say as much is not to deny the presence of strange irrational forces within and without—forces that can never be fully mastered. Nevertheless, the ability to embrace meaning, to say "yes" to enchantment, remains intact. Indeed, rather than deny the contingency and ultimate fragility of meaning, these now become the very conditions that inform our shared responsibility for meaning's construction, maintenance, and change.[26]

To gain a better sense of what might be called the "affirmative post-modern" account, consider the story told at an actual homicide trial by a criminal defense attorney who framed reasonable doubt within a meaningful myth-based narrative. After having thoroughly deconstructed the linear history of the crime, the defense attorney went on to provide the jury with a meaningful exit from the chaos and unremitting uncertainty that such an attack might leave behind. The proffered exit would lead the jury into a drama of compelling significance—a drama enacted in the real time of trial. Playing upon the deep, persistent cultural myth of the hero called to the difficult task of solving the riddle of the evidence, the defense sought to seduce the jury away from the state's straightforward historical narrative about what happened before trial into the present performance of a heroic courtroom drama. As the defense put it at the end of closing argument:

> So what I'm really asking you to do is to do what I think will probably be one of the hardest things that you have ever been required to do in public, which is to stand up and at some point look over at [the defendant] and while looking at him vote not guilty of charges brought against him. Thank you.

We have seen this before in the mythic dramas enacted by defense attorneys Johnnie Cochran and Gerry Spence. Here, too, the challenge for the jurors is the same one faced by the mythic quest hero.[27] They must resist the temptation to resign themselves to the ordinary. Here this means they must not summarily convict despite the passions the crime may arouse or the common sense of justice a conviction may inspire. Instead, they must stay true to their heroic and sworn duty to convict only in the absence of reasonable doubt. Notably, this mythic counter-frame is mobilized and sustained by unreflective associations to popular cultural images of the heroic quest, images that derive from classical as well as contemporary sources, including film and television.

This too is an example of postmodern storytelling, but it is affirmative rather than skeptical. The defense employs mythic images that resonate deeply within the juror's mind. The purpose is to create a dramatic tension sufficient to draw the decision maker into a personal drama, a drama that operates according to its own narrative logic and necessity. This differs from the lawyer's conventional recourse to the rule-based linear logic of deductive and inductive argument. There are no explicit syllogisms or analogies at work here. Instead, seeking to induce the jury to believe that the defendant lacked the requisite intent to murder, the defense challenges the jurors to act out, then and there inside the courtroom, the role of quest hero.

In *The Thin Blue Line,* Morris uses familiar gangster filmstrips and cops-and-robbers film clips in an attempt to create a similar dramatic tension. He draws upon popular caricatures of reality to communicate the absurdity of the prosecution's case against Randall Adams. Such associative, nonlinear storytelling techniques are persuasive if they are used in the service of a discrete and coherent story line. Thus, Morris's postmodern storytelling succeeds when it serves the film's mystery plot but fails when it is used in the service of the film's radically skeptical, acausal counterplot. In this respect, one can imagine similar postmodern storytelling techniques being used in support of a more coherent skeptical thesis. For when all is said and done can we say with certainty that we know what really happened on that fateful night when police officer Robert Wood approached a car parked on the side of a local Dallas highway? Can we (should we) be so confident in our reasonable doubts about the guilt of Randall Dale Adams?

Errol Morris's Revisions Revisited

Although the more subversive techniques of Morris's film fail to affect the credibility of the linear frame-up story, one could imagine a different counterplot, one made of the same material but fashioned to fit the affirmative postmodernist frame I have described above. Imagine the same techniques of the nonlinear narrative harnessed to reach the opposite outcome: in defense of Harris. Around what tropes or myths would the film's images circle?

The character trope of the trickster fits Harris well: the playful prankster, the shadowmaster and shapeshifter, always in control, always mocking, especially those invested with authority (like police officers and documentary filmmakers). The film could easily portray Harris as acting out a drama of manipulation. Consider, for example, the following re-edited sequence from Morris's film:

ADAMS: The kid scares me. Kid scares me.

[Cut to Harris, in dirty saffron prison garb, smiling inscrutably.]

HARRIS: Everybody's life's going to take some kind of path regardless of what happens.

MORRIS: Is he innocent?

HARRIS: Did you ask him?

MORRIS: Well he's always said he's been innocent.

HARRIS: Didn't believe him, huh? Criminals always lie.

Cut to a film clip as Harris speaks: a sequence in which we see a familiar trickster figure, perhaps the mischievous Coyote, foil yet again the hapless aggressor.[28] Watching from this reconstructed skeptical perspective, do we really believe that Harris, the perennial trickster-sociopath, has suddenly decided to tell the truth on film if not at trial? Has Harris really seen the light? Has he experienced, as one of his self-serving film monologues suggests, real psychological insight? Is this real remorse, or just another form of mockery? And what is this introspective voice we hear, telling us about how Harris's father blamed Harris for his younger brother's accidental death and how Harris forever thereafter could never win his father's love—is this Harris's "true" voice? Or is it just another prank, a parody of psychological insight in which "psychobabble" mocks the fateful necessity of tragic action arising from early family trauma?

We could also imagine a narrative discrediting Harris that tracks the prosecution's causal-linear style. This argument might emulate defense lawyer Barry Slotnick's strategy in his successful defense of Bernhard Goetz, the man who shot four black youths he claimed were about to rob him on a New York subway. The argument, which seeks to discredit the defendant's own incriminating statements, might run something like this:

> Ladies and gentlemen of the jury, you cannot trust this man, speaking to you on tape from prison. In fact, David Harris is his own worst witness. What we know of him establishes that what he says is of questionable reliability. Consider the previous lies; the desperate need to get people's attention; the pitiful show of bravado. It makes sense that he'd try to claim yet another macho, anti-authoritarian act. There was a reason his friends didn't believe him when he bragged about killing a cop. He had a lot of hot air but no guts. Harris would say anything.
>
> So what are we to expect when opportunity knocks, and suddenly Harris gets to speak to the largest audience in his life? And you know,

even if we were to take seriously Harris's account of these events, what has he really told us? For all his show of bravado, Harris's statements still carefully stop short of actual confession. Like he says, "Criminals always lie."

So on what basis can you confidently conclude that Harris rather than Adams committed this crime? Adams's denial of guilt is obviously self-serving. And if the two of them were in that parked car together, the natural culmination of an entire day shared by this 27-year-old man and 16-year-old boy, doing what Adams's brother refused to let them do at Adams' motel? (Remember the brother saying he didn't like that sort of thing? And by the way, how come Adams's brother didn't stick around to buttress his brother's story? 'Cause maybe he was afraid of a perjury charge?)

So what do you think? Is it so surprising Harris wouldn't admit to why he and Adams were in that car together? Is it so surprising why Adams would deny being there? (After all, this isn't San Francisco or Greenwich Village. It's Dallas, Texas.) And there's your motive, ladies and gentlemen. There it is. You find it in the absolute necessity of Adams denying why he was pursuing Harris from the get-go, the reason why he was with Harris in that parked car. Adams shot in order to silence the one witness who could testify to what Adams desperately wanted nobody to know. That witness, ladies and gentlemen, was Officer Wood. . . .

In short, whether we take the conventional linear path, or the unconventional, affirmative postmodern one, or take the two together, is it so clear that Adams was simply the innocent victim of a prosecutorial frame-up? Is it possible that Harris didn't do it after all? Could it be that our desire for certainty and closure is powerful enough to induce us to believe in another frame-up, the frame-up conjured by Morris's film (rather than the Dallas D.A.)? Except that Morris's frame-up gives us a different scapegoat. Now it is David Harris who steps in to take the rap for the "long-suffering" Adams. If we had sworn an oath not to convict in the presence of reasonable doubt, would we now choose to reject both Morris's and the state's frame-ups alike, electing to convict neither Harris nor Adams? Or would we convict both for their joint participation in the fatal shooting of Officer Robert Wood?

Fortunately for us, we need not decide this case one way or the other. My point here is simply this: set within an affirmative postmodern frame, *The Thin Blue Line*'s skeptical counterplot might have induced more uncertainty than its unsuccessful skeptical postmodern

frame allowed. For the affirmative postmodern story to work, however, there must be a coherent story line to cling to. There must be
something to make us feel, if not heroic, at least gratified and confident that justice has been done—whether it is a sense of justice as
retribution or as the triumph of procedural norms and the heroic repudiation of deceptive practices in whatever form they may take. When
faced with the unavoidable demands of judgment, a claim to truth
(Adams's? Harris's? Morris's? mine?) coupled with a believable tale
(scapegoat? trickster? hero?) is apt to be preferred to a claim backed
by no coherent story at all.

The array of deeply ingrained, culturally inherited, and socially in-
stilled story lines that we carry in our heads, often subconsciously,
recapitulate an equally deep sense of how truth and justice operate in
the world. We believe truth travels a straight line and deceit curves.
We believe justice will out in the end because the law's machinery,
once set in motion, ensures that it must, and because the narrative
demands of the story promise that it will. Yet we can also tolerate a
nonlinear tale, as long as it embodies or invokes a truth that sustains
belief. Just as we can tolerate the justice in factual ambiguity, in reasonable doubt, as long as we locate it in a tale that lets us feel certain
about something—even if it is only the certainty that we are heroic in
resisting the temptation to yield to a false certainty.

Although I have focused in this chapter on the meaning of one
criminal case, the capital murder case against Randall Dale Adams,
far more is at stake here. The rationalist view, dominant in our culture
since the Enlightenment, has taught us to discard rhetoric as mere
window dressing, that which obscures reality. This bias against rhetoric distracts us from the rational, scientific rhetoric that champions of
the Enlightenment have used so effectively. According to the rationalist, credible persuasion proceeds on the basis of a causal-linear frame
of meaning. Anything else is fiction, myth, or just plain nonsense. As
a result, the sciences have long dominated our legal reasoning and our
beliefs about truth. With the advent of postmodernism we are able to
see that the causal preference of scientific modernism is but one
among many rhetorical strategies. In today's complex culture, the
challenge has become to articulate the appropriate limits and contexts
within which to use the multiple forms of narrative meaning making
at our disposal. The challenge may be greater than before, but this is,
after all, the price to be paid, if we are willing, for the responsible
exercise of enhanced freedom in the creation of meaning.

In both mainstream and legal culture, fear and uncertainty have accompanied an awareness of the multiplicity of narrative frames. The temptation is to lock ourselves within a familiar world of parochial meanings. But a world of forced certainty is a dangerous one. As I have attempted to show in the case of Randall Adams, popular local notions of truth and justice may unwittingly coincide with prejudice, deceit, and corruption. Exposing such injustices to popular scrutiny does not guarantee their elimination. There is no guarantee, but cautionary steps may be taken. We must learn to discern and guard against the more repugnant forms of narrative manipulation. For ordinarily, only our own prejudices, our ingrained perceptions, understandings, and beliefs, stand between narratives of truth and justice and the exercise of power over the criminal defendant. Sometimes, perhaps, all that stands between such narratives and a person's death is fate.

Forces beyond our reckoning and control, forces like chance and fate, seem to have no place in the legal system. For how could we judge in a universe that does not recognize human agency? What could judgment mean in a world without motivation and intentionality, in a world where things just happen? Without order and certainty about the past (historical truth) and the present (narrative necessity), there is no place for us. Fear of human obsolescence and chaos may thus make even the lie a haven. At least there, there is a place to be in, and a place from which judgments can be made.

The ancient Greeks wondered whether it was fate or chance that ruled our lives and dictated justice.[29] Others in the Judeo-Christian tradition have wondered whether the secular order allows for revelatory insights into justice. Or, if prophecy fails, does justice then depend on individual virtue and heroic imagination? Or is justice simply another futile fiction in a world governed by chance?

Errol Morris's film about the capital murder case of Randall Dale Adams provokes these sorts of musings. By offering us two opposing narrative frameworks for the organization of meaning, the causal-linear detective story and the acausal tale of unresolvable mystery, Morris invites us to see how reality can be fashioned in very different ways. He also depicts the lapses and manipulations that plague each of these framings. In the comforting form of linear narrative, all the clues add up. Its narrative necessity assures us that truth and justice will triumph in the end. We want so much for it to be so that we forget or ignore the details that get in the way. Especially in a case of capital murder, we prefer causality, closure, and factual resolution to the discomfort of unending mystery.

I have argued that this desire for order effectively buries the nonlinear and mystifying aspects of Morris's film. I advocate a far less comforting complexity. The Adams case should make us uneasy. To leave unchallenged our belief that "truth and justice will out in the end" ignores the tapestry of interwoven yet opposing frameworks Morris skillfully invites us to contemplate. As Morris suggests, that tapestry, its acausal threads no less than the causal, is a product of the mind.

The Adams "frame-up" highlights the need to scrutinize more closely the different ways in which we perceive and assess events and others' actions. It is simply not enough to see and judge. If we are to guard against our unwitting participation in convenient and comforting frame-ups of reality, we must be better acquainted with the linguistic and cognitive constructs we use to see and evaluate people and events in the world. How do we hear another's story? How do we translate it into terms consonant with our own experience, desires, and preferences? What do we tend to omit or distort in an effort to tell a smoother tale, a tale whose prototype waits in the mind to be triggered?

This heightened sociocultural and psychological knowledge may also enable us to expand our meaning-making capacities, adding new resources, cognitive tools, and mental representations to the narrative repertoire. For example, we may be better able to appreciate how someone who lives outside the range of our ordinary experience makes sense of a particular situation. Such an enhanced capacity for localized seeing and understanding can also expand our ability to translate from one cultural context to another, perhaps cultivating more widely shared notions of individual dignity and equal justice under law. Without such knowledge, I do not believe we can take adequate responsibility for the judgments we make, or for the concrete consequences our narratives of truth and justice produce.

Better training in the possibilities of narrative meaning making is likely to leave lawyers, judges, and jurors as well as the public at large more sensitive to multiple forms of legal proof and persuasion. This is also likely to provoke increased critical reflection upon those forms of proof and persuasion that look like unacceptable manipulation, triggers for judgmental error. Lawyers, judges, scholars, and the public at large may thus more readily recognize unacceptable stereotypes (e.g., Harris as the good old local boy, Adams as just a drifter), false closure based on a denial of uncertainty, and unsupported assumptions about what truth and justice look like. Because any frame-up of legal reality implicates us all, we must accept greater responsibility for the legal realities we help to establish when we tell or accept one legal story rather than another.

Aristotle reminds us of the enormous creativity and responsibility in the human act of making meaning: midway between the unintelligible and the commonplace, it is metaphor that most produces knowledge.[30] Classical or postmodern, it is the metaphor, the mental image, the deeply rooted mythic tale, the resonant story form, by which we take account of others' and our own actions. These judgments, these accounts, may become most truly ours when we knowingly claim them as ours. Yet to do this we must understand the mechanisms by which we judge: what cognitive tools, what stock narratives, what assumptions about truth and justice make up the legal stories that capture belief?

In the next chapter, we will turn our attention to the critical issue with which Morris ultimately fails to deal. For we have yet to come to grips with the extent to which law *has already gone pop*. Which is to say, the extent to which it has become a pure simulacrum, where surface meanings alone prevail. This will take us to a realm where desire and consumption are mediated by fantasy: namely, the popular domain of the visual mass media, television in particular. As we will see, this is the realm of law as commodity, where images are consumed for whatever immediate payoffs they allow, a realm where law and entertainment become one.

It is only the notorious trial which will be broadcast because of the necessity for paid sponsorship.

Estes v. Texas

Surface appearances are more likely to conceal than reveal how the judicial system operates. Television will create popular spectacles of great appeal but deceptive authenticity as it selects and interprets trials to fit the existing pattern of law in the world of television.

GEORGE GERBNER

The crimes that dominate the public consciousness and policy debates are not common crimes but the rarest ones. Whether in entertainment or news, the crimes that define criminality are the acts of predator criminals. . . . Predator crime is a metaphor for a world gone berserk.

RAY SURETTE

The Jurisprudence of Appearances
Law as Commodity

Let us begin with a rule of thumb. It will sound the theme that resounds throughout this chapter. Whatever the visual mass media
touch bears the mark of reality/fiction confusion. There is also a corollary to the rule: once you enter the realm of appearances it may be
difficult to control how the image spins. In what follows, I offer illustrations of the rule and its corollary in the field of contemporary legal
practice. Here we will encounter what has come to be known as litigation public relations. I will also trace the rule to its historic origin.
This effort will lead us to the United States Supreme Court itself, the
institutional source of the jurisprudence of appearances. In the course
of this analysis we will see what happens to law when it comes to be
dominated by image and perception. It is what happens when law
enters the domain of the hyperreal, a realm in which appearances battle appearances for the sake of appearances—and where images risk
spinning out of control.

In the preceding chapter, we saw that the words and images used
in Errol Morris's film about the fate of Randall Dale Adams generally
succeeded in capturing the viewer's belief. A docudrama came to stand
for reality. A general insight about human cognition helps to account
for this phenomenon. What we recognize amid the flux of events
around us recapitulates what we are already capable of knowing. We
are always screening out the inessential, the unfamiliar, that for which
no word or category has prepared us. In this way, culture lends us eyes
and ears; it teaches us to perceive, to speak, to think, and to feel. In
this way we are prepared to project back into the arena of action and
events (either real or simulated) the familiar forms of everyday world
knowledge with which we have been provided. Order and conflict resolution, the heart and soul of law, need these cultural forms as well as
a shared cognitive tool kit so that our knowledge and discourse may
be adapted to the demands of specific cases.

It is important to recall that this understanding of the way reality is constructed and maintained had a practical origin, and payoff, long before it received the empirical and theoretical treatment that fills the pages of much recent psychological and cultural analysis. Prior to its becoming the focus of the "New Look" movement in cognitive psychology,[1] and a virtual trademark of postmodern writing, the "social construction of reality" served as the guiding insight of the American public relations movement. As Ivy L. Lee, a founding member of that movement, said in 1916: "It is not the facts alone that strike the public mind, but the way in which they take place and in which they are published that kindle imagination. . . . The effort to state an absolute fact is simply an attempt to . . . give you my interpretation."[2] We find a similar thought even more strikingly expressed by Walter Lippmann, a prominent American theorist in the 1920s and a strong advocate of public opinion management:

> For the most part we do not first see, and then define. We define first and then see. In the great blooming, buzzing confusion of the outer world we pick out what our culture has already defined for us, and we tend to perceive that which we have picked out in the form stereotyped for us by our culture.[3]

This insight carries tremendous power for those who are able to recognize (and act on) its ramifications, those who see that culture is a two-way street. The ad man's logic of power goes like this: if popular culture helps to inform and shape popular belief, then those who are able to control or influence popular culture will be able to do the same with respect to public opinion.

What came to be known as the "engineering of consent" was a direct byproduct of this logic. The thought that launched a thousand and more ads, the prize insight of American public relations, tells us that it is possible to establish an essential tie between commercial consumption and the perception of personal and social reality. The same school of thought, bent on the manipulation of public perceptions through mass media spin control and the belief that there is no "there" there outside the world of images, would later come to dominate American politics. Television would prove to be a central player in this development. As Robert MacNeil notes:

> It should not surprise us that television, which has modified all our institutions, should be altering the conduct of public and international affairs. . . . In medieval Europe, the church was a matrix of thought,

the boundary of popular imagination: It explained everything. Today, television sets the boundaries of popular imagination. . . .[4]

And what dominates television? It is no secret. What gets on the air, and stays on, is that which attracts viewers and keeps them watching, the kind of entertainment that combines quick gratification through intellectual relaxation, emotional excitement, and escapism. Law stories, especially those featuring violent and/or sexual crimes, seem to fit the bill well. The single largest portion of news air time is taken up by such stories.[5] They have also consistently occupied a significant percentage of prime time programming.[6]

The sharp demands of market-share competition and television advertising may be driving the visual format, but the format itself is nearly universal. For example, whether it is prime time drama, docudrama, reality television, or news, the number of shifts in image ("shots") per minute is increasing. According to recent research, if the average shot lasts longer than four seconds the viewer's attention is likely to drift. Even educational television for children mimics the format and at times even the imagery of standard commercial programming. In this way, children are taught from an early age to operate in discrete, rapidly paced time segments. Locked into this kind of fast-paced media format, learning must produce a quick payoff. More time-consuming learning tasks, as well as the viewer's capacity to grasp broader political, social, and legal issues, are thus placed at risk.[7] Defense attorney Leslie Abramson, who became a media celebrity as a result of her work in the Menendez brothers' patricide and matricide case, may have put it best when she said in terse understatement, the media "have trouble with complexity."

There is a clear commercial payoff associated with this esthetic development. Rapid image consumption and the immediate gratification it brings usefully model what commercial sponsors are after. The format trains viewers to equate consumption with pleasure. Whether the object of consumption is a particular product—or a particular identity or way of life that has been visually associated with it—the result is the same. Consumption, as a primary cultural norm, is reinforced. The format also serves a manifestly practical need. It caters to the highly competitive demands of the market. With the quickening pace of image shifts, the viewer's eye becomes riveted to the screen. This visual technique exploits the organism's atavistic reflexive response to sudden changes in the environment. When the pace and incessant interruption of images make it impossible to keep up with the flow, much less consider what they might mean, the viewer ends up simply submitting. This passive state has been lauded by advertising experts, who see it as "the right mental condition for the placement of images."[8]

Image placement also works off another simple, but profound insight: we tend to like, and believe, what is familiar, that which makes us feel comfortable. As Edward L. Bernays, America's premier public relations theorist-practitioner, understood so well, a publicist must comprehend "the mental process" of the public and adjust his propaganda "to the mentality of the masses." So-called "impulse buying" can be accounted for in precisely these terms. It is based, as ex-ad man and arch media campaign strategist Tony Schwartz has observed, on the fact that the things we see in the store "evoke the recall of our experience."[9] The ad conjures a familiar positive feeling or experience (comfort, affluence, sexuality) and then compellingly associates it with a product. The act of consumption consummates the feeling, bestowing possession by way of the product. In the process, the viewer is also taught to think associatively (from image to memory/sensation to product) and to seek the promised payoff, immediate gratification, in concrete terms (the act of consumption).

The sense of detachment, irony, and cynicism many consumers cultivate to defend against this pervasive commercial onslaught, a posture many postmodern intellectuals have championed since the 1980s, turns out to be no defense at all. For irony itself is readily exploitable. As one advertising executive put it: "It seems to me that when an advertiser makes fun of advertising it endears him to the consumer, who says, yeah, you're right. It's a way of getting the consumer on your side." Like the popular Subaru car campaign in which, with tongue in cheek, "Joe Isuzu" mocked the stereotypical slick car salesman's pitch. Mark Crispin Miller puts the matter well when he observes: "Today, within the television environment, you prove your superiority to TV's garbage not by criticizing it or refusing it, but by feeding on it, taken in by its oblique assurances that you're too smart to swallow any of it."[10] A posture of apparent detachment is similarly unavailing. As Herbert E. Krugman, a leading researcher in the field of advertising, notes, "The public lets down its guard to the repetitive commercial use of the television medium . . . [and it] easily changes its ways of perceiving products and brands and its purchasing behavior without thinking very much about it." Krugman calls this process "learning without involvement."[11] In short, whether one adopts a posture of ironic superiority or passive detachment, the result is the same. Either stance is easily coopted by the commercial media.

We have increasingly witnessed the same development in contemporary politics. Perhaps the watershed year was 1960, the year John F. Kennedy was elected president, defeating Richard Nixon by less than 1 percent of the popular vote. That percentage might well have been accounted for by the share of voters swayed by Kennedy's superior appearance during the candidates' televised debate. Radio listeners gave the edge to Nixon. But Nixon's shifty-looking five-o'clock shadow and baggy suit were no match for Kennedy's telegenic vitality and youthful good looks. As Marshall McLuhan would later comment: "Without TV, Nixon had it made." It was a lesson that would not be lost on the candidate next time around.

Two presidential terms later, in 1968, Nixon became the nation's chief executive. Many people were startled to learn shortly thereafter that he had done so by marketing himself as one would market any commodity. Nixon's backstage manipulations of the visual mass media, first revealed in Joe McGuinniss's best-selling book *The Selling of the President*,[12] prompted indignation at the time, although Nixon's advertising stratagems are surely tame by contemporary standards. McGuinniss showed that during the 1968 campaign Nixon had surrounded himself with people who understood the craft and impact of image making. For example, there was William Gavin, who advised Nixon to avoid being televised in the artificial air of the TV studio. The public would see the new Nixon in situations carefully staged to appear unstaged. And there were H. R. "Bob" Haldeman, former account executive in the advertising firm of J. Walter Thompson, and Roger Ailes, former producer of TV's popular *Mike Douglas Show*. It was Ailes who orchestrated Nixon's media events in time for the evening news and who staged Nixon's television commercials, placing the candidate in the open air among concerned citizens, skillfully fielding their questions and addressing their deepest concerns.

Public attitudes have changed. The outrage that greeted "the selling of the president" in 1968 has not only cooled, it has transformed into a strange mixture of complacency and even admiration, the admiration we reserve for a clever commercial. But perhaps this is to be expected. Today politics mostly takes place on the screen. It is in terms of the images at play there that politics is discussed and analyzed. Consider: between 1968 and 1988 the time the networks devoted to the candidates' visuals, unaccompanied by their words, increased by more than 300 percent.[13] Moreover, as Kiku Adatto notes, "political reporting today is filled with accounts of staging and backdrops, camera angles and scripts, sound bites and spin control, photo opportunities and media gurus."[14] The dominant tone of these "news" accounts is one of detachment and playful irony.[15]

What is significant here is the declining importance of the source of the image or the extent of its truth (if any) as compared to its power to stick in the mind. This phenomenon comports with the findings of psychologist Richard Gerrig, who has shown that it is the strength of the association between even a fictional representation and the world-knowledge it calls forth that is important.[16] As we saw in chapter 3, fictional constructs like the film *Jaws* have real effects—as was made clear by the many film viewers who subsequently avoided the ocean. Similarly, if a novel or a vivid commercial or political image succeeds in evoking real feelings, or the memory of real experiences, these personal responses help to validate the image that triggered them. The more of ourselves we invest in a story, the more real it seems. Verisimilitude works best when it works off what's in our heads, in our own terms of belief. It is harder to argue with one's own feelings and memories than with someone else's. And it is precisely that sense of personal reality that helps make the evocative image seem real. Italian linguist and novelist Umberto Eco has expressed this idea in more piquant terms: "Everything looks real, and therefore it is real; in any case the fact that it seems real is real, and the thing is real even if, like *Alice in Wonderland*, it never existed." In cognitive terms we might simply say, fictional models permeate factual discourse.[17] And law is no exception.

For a number of years now the same public relations appreciation of popular culture's "use value" that has been operating on the political front has also been at work in the domain of law. And law too is now being afflicted with some of the same problems. Chief among them are the problems that come with the conflation of truth and fiction, image and reality, fact and fantasy. We see this inside the courtroom as savvy litigators with increasing frequency emulate the popular cultural constructs and visual storytelling techniques that dominate the culture at large. But we see it outside the courtroom as well, as a growing number of lawyers deploy the strategies of public relations—using soundbites, photo ops, and a variety of spin control tactics—to win their cases in the court of public opinion. By gaining public support in a "phantom" (or virtual) trial prior to and concurrent with the real trial, prosecutors and defense attorneys seek to reap benefits inside the courtroom itself.[18]

In order to get on the air, however, trial attorneys must package their message so that it is suitable for screening. As one trial lawyer has said, "It's a lot more interesting to a TV audience to see pictures of a genuinely weeping mother and father than a scientist or engineer saying, 'Here are the statistics with regard to [defective] pickup trucks'. . . . The parents make an indelible impression." To illustrate the point, consider the lawsuit that was triggered by the death of Cheryl Fleischner. Fleischner's husband attributed the cause of death to an anti-inflammatory drug, Voltaren, which Fleischner had been taking for a liver problem. When the story reaches CNN its opening sequence takes us to a cemetery. There's Mr. Fleischner, kneeling at his wife's gravesite. He's distraught, calling his wife's name, crying as he strokes her gravestone. Then he recounts what it was like toward the end: "She was begging—she was screaming at the top of her lungs, 'Joe, make them take it out of me!' She didn't know what it was, but what it was was her liver self-destructing." "There should have been things to prevent this from happening," he adds. It is a sentiment with which Fleischner's attorney is quick to agree: "It makes me angry that there was absolutely no knowledge of, you know, she, here she is taking it with a glass of water every day not knowing that she actually is poisoning her system."

Compelling images, real emotion, good TV—and unquestionably a good thing for the Fleischner lawsuit. Little wonder that lawyers and their clients are increasingly willing to take advantage of the media's need for this kind of dramatic programming. Like the parents of the coed who was raped and murdered in her college dormitory. Their $25 million lawsuit against both the murderer and the university gained force as the parents, with the help of their publicist, made the rounds on the TV talk-show circuit. As they grieved, and railed, unopposed, against the alleged insensitivity of the college president, millions watched—among them students, alumni, the Board of Trustees, and presumably the college president himself, not to mention prospective jurors and other potential trial participants.

The cottage industry of litigation services offering to package trials, from pretrial publicity to the production of persuasive visuals for the jury, testifies to the appeal the mass media and spin control tactics hold for present-day litigators. Reflecting this spirit, Robert Clifford, a Chicago-based personal injury lawyer, has said, "Publicity is an is-

sue in civil and criminal cases all the time." One attorney has described such pretrial publicity as "a free kick" that can force companies to settle quickly "before their stock price drops."[19] But corporate
defendants are no less savvy. They are increasingly realizing that negative public perceptions can seriously affect business operations.[20]
Those perceptions, however, may be altered. As John Budd, a public
relations advisor for companies facing litigation, notes, "People can
more easily relate to the small victim than the large, faceless company.
The companies need to develop common-man support; rebut with
passion, not just facts."[21] And that is precisely what they are doing.

Consider, for example, the lawsuit against American Airlines.
Faced with federal antitrust claims accusing the airline of restructur-
ing its fares in order to force two weaker carriers out of business,
American launched a massive public relations campaign several weeks
prior to trial. Their goal, they said, was to convince the public that the
airline had done nothing wrong. As Tim Doke, American's managing
director of corporate communications, put it: "If we allow the imagery that the attorneys and the spokesmen for our competitors have
laid out for the news media to absorb and to linger, we would be
paying many kinds of costs in correcting that damage in the perception of the general public." But American might also have had another,
albeit unstated, goal in mind. Their spin doctoring in the weeks and
days immediately prior to trial might also have been used to influence
prospective jurors. As Philadelphia attorney Ralph Wellington has
noted, it may be useful to employ the media "for predisposition and
saturation in an area so those living there have already seen one side
of the story."

In short, legal spin control has come to be viewed as but another
tool in the lawyer's toolbox. And like the use of visuals inside the
courtroom, when one side's got it, the other side is often well advised
to do the same. As one practitioner warned, "Sound bites can kill.
They can destroy reputations, or they can communicate a positive
message to a vast audience. . . . How does a lawyer meet this new
challenge? Those savvy to the risks facing their client, often engage
the help of a communications consultant with expertise in litigation
support."[22]

There are a number of different messages, serving different strategic
purposes, that lawyers may wish to convey via the mass media. For
example, federal and state prosecutors may use negative publicity
prior to trial to antagonize or "demoralize" the accused, making it
easier for the government to convict, or likelier that the accused will

forsake trial for the benefits of plea bargaining, aided perhaps by his having cooperated with the government. One may consider in this regard the arrest, on criminal charges of inside trading, of Richard Wigton in 1987, at the direction of then United States Attorney for the Southern District Rudolph Giuliani. Giuliani deliberately exploited the image of Wigton being dragged away in handcuffs from the trading floor before waiting television cameras. Wigton's dramatic televised arrest, together with the subsequent, and also media-coordinated, arrest of Robert Freeman in his office at the established investment banking firm Goldman, Sachs, were meant to send a clear signal to others currently under investigation—a group that included Dennis Levine, Ivan Boesky, and Michael Milken—federal prosecutor Giuliani meant business.

Under the public pressure generated by Giuliani, Milken, dismissed by his brokerage firm, Drexel Burnham Lambert, which would later be forced into bankruptcy, admitted a share of wrongdoing. Milken offered to cooperate with the government and eventually succeeded in working out a deal with Giuliani, as did Ivan Boesky, who found himself in a similar situation. The information Giuliani had fed the media, both through press conferences and via "unnamed sources," helped him to publicize and control the direction of his campaign against white-collar crime. And though some charges, like the ones against Richard Wigton and Robert Freeman, were quietly dropped later on, it hardly mattered. By that time Giuliani had already left the U.S. Attorney's office—in preparation for his run for the higher public office of mayor of New York. The dramatic images of his days as a federal prosecutor ensured that Giuliani's reputation for crime-busting would be securely imprinted in the public's mind.

Aside from seeking to influence the accused, lawyers may also use the media to mobilize public opinion in the hope that pressures from that source will influence other trial participants, such as jurors, prosecutors, judges, and publicity-sensitive lawyers and witnesses in the case.[23] For example, in the course of defending alleged Nazi war criminal John Demjanjuk, Michael Tigar followed a strategy of cultivating media attention that would reflect poorly on the prosecution's case. His goal was to disseminate the message that the power of extradition had been abused or mistakenly used against Demjanjuk. According to Tigar, the message was specifically directed at senior officials in the United States Department of Justice in the hope that they might conclude that they would be better off simply to "cut their losses" and preserve the discretionary power that they maintained rather than risk an adverse ruling in the *Demjanjuk* case that might impose additional restrictions on their field of operation. In another case, when prominent attorneys Clark Clifford and Robert Altman were prosecuted for lying to bank regulators, defense lawyers sought out the public relations services of Hill & Knowlton to fight the charges in the media. This ensured that the defendants' story would gain broad public exposure.[24] Such efforts typically seek either to stave off indictment altogether or at least to create conditions conducive to a favorable plea agreement.

Judges may also be susceptible to this kind of influence, for they too (particularly those who are elected) are sensitive to adverse as well as laudatory publicity. Notably, the kind of influence that may be sought in this regard need not focus on a judge's ultimate ruling in the case. It may be sufficient to use an extrajudicially generated atmosphere to affect how the judge presides over the trial. A judge may affect the outcome of a case in a number of different ways: by projecting an air of skepticism (or support) toward a particular witness or attorney or evidentiary submission; by supporting (or denying) an attorney's objections concerning the admission of evidence or the examination of witnesses or the instructions the jury will receive on the law. By affecting any of these judicial functions, extrajudicial publicity can have an effect on the outcome of a trial. Litigators may also use the mass media to help ensure that judges hear their arguments in as many places as possible.

The manipulation of images in the court of public opinion need not be confined to news leaks, press conferences, and the TV talk-show circuit. Even fictional representations, like the TV docudrama, may be susceptible to influence. Consider, for example, the pressure defense attorney Leslie Abramson brought to bear against CBS and Fox Television. Both networks had produced trial dramas that depicted Lyle and Erik Menendez in the act of killing their parents. Apparently, neither movie subscribed to the defense theory that the brothers had been sexually molested by their father, Jose, and that they feared for their own lives when they killed their parents. Abramson insisted on a "fairer" picture of events. After all, both dramas were set for broadcast prior to the Menendez brothers' retrial. But the producers refused to make any changes. In response, Abramson threatened to sabotage the broadcasts by booking Erik Menendez for a live jailhouse interview on a rival network. Apparently, the risk that jurors would confuse fiction with reality was too great for Abramson to ignore. As she put it: "The power of these entertainment creeps to completely position the public view when these boys' lives are depending on public opinion is just appalling. . . . They're insisting on a vicious fictionalization of everything that bolsters the prosecution case—nothing else exists. There's no favorable fictionalization of the defense and the defendants."[25]

Abramson's tactic deserved to be rebuffed. But her apprehension is understandable. In fact, the time lag between court reality and TV docudrama seems to be shrinking. Millions of viewers (including prospective jurors) find themselves watching "real" trial stories before the real trial has actually taken place.[26] Under these circumstances, can we be sure which reality they will bring with them into court when their turn to serve comes around? Can we be sure what effect upon legal reality unconsciously held fictional images might exert at trial?[27]

Trial attorneys who package their cases to fit into designated news holes or to meet the insatiable demand for human drama and emotion that drives the TV talk-show circuit leave no doubt that the interests of lawyers and those of media producers may overlap. As Oklahoma attorney Gary Richardson has advised, lawyers "need to understand where the media is coming from. Reporters are after as much information as possible to cause a story to be sensationalized."[28] Sol Wachtler, former chief judge of New York's highest appellate court, apparently got the message. Upon being brought up on criminal charges for terrorizing his former mistress, Wachtler immediately fought back in the media. His first move was to disseminate the classic "scheming seductress" story. The fruits of Wachtler's efforts were apparent when news accounts incorporated his spin, describing Wachtler's victim, in the words of one journalist, as "a cross between Alexis from [the TV program] *Dynasty*, [celebrity pop star] Madonna, and Carolyn Wormus, Westchester's *Fatal Attraction* wacko killer."

In theory, of course, there are rules against trial by spin control. According to the American Bar Association's Model Rules of Professional Conduct for lawyers, a lawyer is prohibited from making an out-of-court statement that "will have a substantial likelihood of materially influencing an adjudicative proceeding." That standard has been upheld by the Supreme Court, and a majority of the states subscribe to it. Indeed, according to the Supreme Court, "Few, if any, interests under the Constitution are more fundamental than the right to a fair trial by 'impartial jurors.'" And it is precisely this right that lawyers' "extrajudicial statements" put at risk. As the Court explained:

The outcome of a criminal trial is to be decided by impartial jurors, who know as little as possible of the case, based on material admitted into evidence before them in a court proceeding. Extra-judicial comments on, or discussion of, evidence which might never be admitted at trial and *ex parte* statements by counsel giving their version of the facts obviously threaten to undermine this basic tenet.[29]

Yet, as a practical matter, the operative standard ("materially influencing an adjudicative proceeding") is notoriously elusive and difficult to prove. In any event, nothing in the current legal ethical canon directly forbids lawyers from disseminating fictions outside the courtroom. Nor do they ignore the need for extrajudicial communications. For example, the model rules explicitly recognize that communications of this kind are permissible where "a reasonable lawyer would believe a public response is required in order to avoid prejudice to the lawyer's client."[30] In a culture of adversarial justice, where competitive pressures insistently remind lawyers of the need to maintain and grow their client base, strategies that serve the client's interest are hardly likely to be disregarded. Litigation public relations has clearly become such a strategy. The rules that currently govern lawyer behavior are unlikely to stop it.

So far we have been dealing with this chapter's rule of thumb—whatever the visual mass media touch bears the mark of reality/fiction confusion—as it plays out in contemporary legal practice. With the advent of litigation public relations we see how legal advocates exploit the visual mass media's tendency to blur the line between reality and fiction. As it turns out, however, this leap into image-bound hyperreality is not simply the work of savvy trial lawyers in league with ratings-sensitive media journalists and producers. Nor is it simply a reflection of the thoroughness with which the public relations mindset has come to pervade our society. What is perhaps even more remarkable is that a significant stimulus catapulting law into the world of appearances has come from no less an authority than the United States Supreme Court.

The high court has long maintained a concern for the appearance of justice, insisting not only that justice must be done, but that the public must also perceive it to have been done.[31] This concern with appearances assumed a more exaggerated and dubious form, however, in two cases decided sixteen years apart: *Estes v. Texas* (1965), and *Chandler v. Florida* (1981). I believe that the story these two cases tell captures an inaugural moment in the ongoing development of the jurisprudence of appearances. Rather appropriately, both cases deal with televising criminal trials. They are all about appearances. In fact, they offer a cautionary tale about what happens to law when appearances are used to counter appearances for appearances' sake. That is the jurisprudence of appearances in a nutshell.

Billie Sol Estes was a financier and confidant of President Lyndon Johnson who was prosecuted on swindling charges. It was a big deal at the time and drew a lot of media attention. In plain terms it was a classic notorious case. The problem was that Estes did not want his trial to be televised. It was anyway. The legal question presented to the Supreme Court was this: did the presence of TV cameras deprive Estes of a fair trial? A majority of the Supreme Court concluded that it did. Televising notorious criminal trials, they said, is inherently prejudicial to the defendant and thus violates due process.

Sixteen years later, the question came up again. This time the trial was in Florida and involved some corrupt cops who got caught pulling off a burglary in a well-known Miami Beach restaurant. Unbeknownst to the burglars, an amateur radio operator had fortuitously managed to record their walkie-talkie conversations as the crime was under way. This material made for some compelling media coverage. But when the defendants protested against the presence of cameras in the courtroom during their trial, the matter went all the way to the Supreme Court. And this time, in 1981, the Court said no problem; cameras in the courtroom are fine with us. But what about the Court's earlier decision in *Estes v. Texas*? Didn't a majority of the justices say in that earlier case that TV cameras were constitutionally prohibited in this sort of notorious criminal case? The matter calls for closer scrutiny.

Writing for the Court in *Chandler*, Chief Justice Warren Burger had an opportunity to revisit *Estes*. And by the time the visit was over, that case was no longer the same. In fact, Burger stood *Estes* on its head and then lied about it. His distortions live on in a surprisingly large number of law review articles as well as state and federal decisions which mimic Burger's account.[32] At the core of that account is a falsified description of what Billie Estes's trial was like. In *Chandler*, Burger looks back upon that trial and sees utter chaos, a courtroom out of control. For example, Burger describes the snaking cables that ran through the courtroom, the distracting klieg lights, the technicians scurrying under foot—a regular circus. That's the word he uses, and the one that keeps getting repeated. Estes's trial, Burger tells us, was a "Roman circus." Of course, Burger goes on to note, that was back in 1965, the early days of television. Things have changed since then. In 1981, telecasting trials doesn't produce that kind of disruption. Television has evolved; it's much less obtrusive now than in the old days.

There is only one problem with the analysis of *Estes* Chief Justice Burger provides in *Chandler*. It gets the facts and the law of *Estes* completely wrong. Burger is right about the snaking cables and technicians under foot. But that was at Estes's pretrial hearing on the motion to bar cameras from the courtroom. The trial looked nothing like that. That's because the trial judge had ruled that a camera could be present at Estes's trial only if it was hidden behind a specially constructed booth in the rear of the courtroom. And that is precisely what was done. In short, no lights, no wires, no technicians, no circus. So what gives?

It is at this point in the *Estes* story that the rule of thumb makes its first entrance. As it turns out, Chief Justice Earl Warren did something novel in his concurring opinion in *Estes*. He appended a series of shocking oversized photographs. What they showed was a courtroom packed with camera tripods, cameras, cameramen, cables, lighting devices—in short, it was a circus, a scene one would associate more with a press conference than with a court of law. Warren relied on these images to bolster his view that televising trials was a bad idea. But there was only one problem. The photos he used were not of Estes's trial. They were taken from Estes's pretrial hearing. Apparently, what Warren had in mind was to show what criminal trials might look like if the Court allowed them to be televised. In other words, Warren used especially vivid visual images to convey what he feared, not what had in fact occurred in Estes's case. In doing so he led the way into the realm of appearances, the domain of the hyperreal. Warren wanted people to see the way television mocks the solemn atmosphere of the trial. He wanted people to grasp the inherently prejudicial nature of such a spectacle. So he used appearances to stand for the reality that he feared.

It is the rule of thumb at work. Warren was counting on the vividness of the images he showed to stick in the viewer's mind. Their power would overshadow their unreality. Once firmly embedded in memory, they would come to stand in for the real. Warren's stratagem succeeded. Warren apparently had grasped something important about the cultural and cognitive shift from print to visual evidence. Photographic and video-based evidence tends to enjoy a presumption of accuracy that is qualitatively different from print-based evidence.

As Walter Lippmann put it: "Photographs have a kind of authority over the imagination today which the printed word had yesterday, and the spoken word before that. They seem utterly real. They come, we imagine, directly to us without human meddling, and they are the most effortless food for the mind conceivable."[33] In our current visual culture the most powerful images acquire an iconic quality. Iconic images distill complex details into what Barthes has called "a blissful clarity."[34] S. Paige Baty calls these kinds of images "mediaphemes" or quick encapsulations: "Once a story, person, or event is translated into mediapheme form, it ricochets through the channels of mass mediation with ease."[35] The face of Willie Horton, the figure of Rodney King, and the chaos of Billie Sol Estes's "Roman circus" trial are all examples of mediaphemes in this sense. Notably, the truthfulness of these images is not essential to the meanings with which they are commonly invested within the culture at large.

Warren put this insight to good use in *Estes*. However, in *Chandler*, sixteen years later, Chief Justice Burger took a step further. Burger, too, understood the rule of thumb, but unlike Warren he was also aware of its corollary: once you enter the realm of appearances it may be difficult to control how the image spins. Burger would now seize Warren's images and turn them against him. The same images, spun in the opposite direction, would now open rather than close the courthouse doors to television. In taking this step, Burger thought he could master the corollary to the rule of thumb. But his confidence was misplaced. There was a price to be paid after all.

This is how it worked. For Warren and the *Estes* majority, cameras in the courtroom do two things that are bad. They not only adversely influence participants in the trial (including the lawyers, witnesses, and the judge), but they also taint the entire trial process by causing the public to confuse law with entertainment. As the *Estes* majority put it, only by featuring certain kinds of defendants (such as fallen idols or celebrity figures) and certain kinds of cases (such as those offering particularly grisly details to satisfy the public's voyeuristic impulses) would "TV law" attract the commercial support necessary to sponsor courtroom television.[36] Televising trials would thus encourage the public to associate the trials they see on television with "the commercial objectives of the television industry." When law marries entertainment a legitimation crisis is in the offing. Not a bad prophesy—though the Burger Court would surely beg to differ.

In fact when the issue of cameras in the courtroom came up again sixteen years later, the political and legal landscape had changed dramatically from the Warren years. The new majority, under Chief Justice Warren Burger, were not so much worried about TV cameras prejudicing criminal defendants. Their concern was a growing public perception that the judicial system was lurching out of control. Consider the historical backdrop:

- Richard Nixon's strong crime control and antijudicial activist rhetoric during the 1968 presidential campaign had convinced a significant number of Americans that the Warren Court's "pro-criminal" rulings had in fact made life a lot more dangerous than before; ironically, this created a popular anti-Court backlash that the Burger Court inherited.
- Following the assassination of Martin Luther King Jr., domestic unrest over race relations surged; many feared that a new militancy would supplant Dr. King's politics of passive resistance. At the same time, the protest movement against the war in Vietnam fueled a counterculture that had little trust of government and at times responded with skepticism toward the rule of law itself. This sentiment was vividly expressed by the absurdist ("guerrilla theater") tactics defendants used to mock judicial proceedings in the Chicago Seven conspiracy trial in 1969.
- Revelations about political corruption stemming from the Watergate crisis that broke in 1972 enhanced public skepticism not only toward political institutions, but also toward lawyers. After all, hadn't the nation's highest-ranking attorneys—from Attorney General John Mitchell to presidential counsel John Dean—shown themselves perfectly willing to advance the President's unlawful designs?
- Finally, only two years before *Chandler* was decided, investigative reporters Bob Woodward and Scott Armstrong published the first ever behind-the-scenes look at the Supreme Court itself. *The Brethren,* which had a long run on the bestseller list, produced many disconcerting revelations about the Court under Chief Justice Burger's leadership. Indeed, the picture of Burger that emerged was of a judge obsessed with appearances, often to the exclusion of all other values. Take for example the scene in which Burger openly voices his concern to an amazed Justice Harlan about how a particular Court decision might play out in the media. Or accounts of Burger

circulating outrageous opinions simply to draw the attention of the media.[37]

With images such as these dominating the popular imagination, a new anxiety hung over the high court. It looked as if the judiciary was losing control over appearances. Something had to be done.

Burger realized that the best way to counter bad images was to oppose them with good ones. But where could such images be found? Burger had an answer. Permit TV cameras inside the courtroom. Let the public see orderly criminal proceedings with convictions being swiftly and surely dealt out. This would not only provide the sought-after images of judicial order and stability; it would also reinforce the crime control values that Burger championed.

Burger had good reason to believe these "confidence-building" images would prevail once cameras were allowed inside the courtroom. After all, it was logical to assume that only the strongest cases, the ones the government was most certain of winning, would be broadcast to the public. Weaker cases would most likely never reach the trial stage; they would be resolved by negotiated guilty plea settlements. As for those cases where publicity might influence the state's decision to proceed to trial, surely they would receive the most government resources and be handled by the most experienced prosecutors. Criminal defendants arc rarely in a position to match this level of investigative and adversarial power. And if a case threatened to send the public the wrong message, if it placed the appearance of order and solemnity in the courtroom at risk, trial judges were likely to be responsive to the prosecutor's call for the cameras to be shut off.[38]

But even if Burger had good reason to expect favorable, confidence-building images to play on the air, a problem remained. The Court's earlier decision in *Estes* had concluded that it was precisely the highly publicized criminal case that could not be televised without violating the defendant's constitutional right to a fair trial. Clearly, something would have to be done about *Estes*—preferably in a way that would leave the appearance of justice intact.

Burger proved himself up to the task. Working off of Warren's deceptive images of Billie Sol Estes's trial in chaos, in *Chandler* Burger disingenuously explains why Estes's conviction had to be reversed. It was like being tried in "Yankee Stadium," he says. By contrast, Chandler's trial was nothing like that. And that's why his conviction must stand. What is more, now we can go on televising criminal trials—so long as they don't look like they are out of control. In short, it's the bad images, the ones that (regardless of their source or accuracy) show a lack of proper decorum and respect for the judicial process, that violate due process. They are the ones that must be shut off.

In this way, Burger subverts both the facts and the law of *Estes*. For he not only treats Warren's deceptive images as if they were accurate, but he also makes it seem as if the *Estes* majority were mainly troubled by the cameras' physical obtrusiveness. They were not. The subdued atmosphere at Estes's trial hardly raised that issue. What they were concerned about were television's psychological effects. Televising notorious criminal trials, they said, changes the way people behave in the courtroom. It is these effects, in conjunction with distortions in the way the public perceives the judicial process, that are inherently prejudicial to the defendant. In the wake of *Chandler,* however, that conclusion was erased from the books. Burger's analysis in effect gutted *Estes* as a matter of law and fact—without saying so. Having entered the hyperreal courtroom Warren's images conjured, Burger effectively exploited their fiction/reality confusion to suit his own purposes. As Burger would put it, tracking Warren's deceptive images of cumbersome cameras, cables, and technicians underfoot, the "negative factors found in *Estes*" are "less substantial today than they were at that time." In other words, with the evolution of technology complaints like Chandler's had become all but anachronistic.

Fearing what criminal trials might become with the advent of cameras in the courtroom, Chief Justice Warren sought to superimpose upon the reality of Billie Sol Estes's trial vivid photographic images of a courtroom in chaos. These images were meant to legitimate Warren's fears. In *Chandler,* however, Burger reversed their spin. The same images were now used to avoid what Burger feared most: namely, conveying to the public the appearance of a court out of control. As Charles Nesson aptly observes, "To one deeply concerned with the image of the courts, it would make little difference whether the default in judicial decorum occurred at a pretrial hearing or an actual trial. Either situation would call for a correction."[39] Burger's lack of concern about getting the facts of Estes right seems to have carried over to his legal analysis as well. Here, too, it is the appearance of justice that counts most.

If the popular perception was that Billie Sol Estes's trial was a "Roman circus," Burger was content to let it be so. In a similar vein, if the popular perception was that only liberal ("activist") judges break with recent past rulings, Burger would let that be so too. It would not do to risk the impression that the Court was reversing *Estes* simply to gratify its own ideological preferences. That was the bane of the Warren Court years. No, if the legal effect of *Estes* was to be avoided it would have to be done covertly. And this is precisely how Burger proceeded. Consider, for example, his chief legal claim in *Chandler*— namely: that the whole matter was really out of the Court's hands. You see, Burger explains, the case is governed by the principle of "federalism." And what federalism says is that even if a bunch of federal judges are convinced that it's a bad idea for cases like Chandler's to be televised, it's not really for them to say. Federal judges cannot elevate their own prejudices into rules of law. Here, then, is Burger as champion of states' rights, the living antithesis of liberal activism. Let the states decide whether or not to televise criminal trials, he humbly concludes. If problems arise it is only through "continuing experimentation" by the various states, not by federal intervention, that we will come to know what they are.

Burger's analysis is fine as far as it goes—with one reservation: the view he is espousing comes from the *Estes* dissent. It was Justice Stewart in dissent who attacked the *Estes* majority for "escalating" their "personal views" into a "constitutional rule," just as it was Stewart's dissenting claim that "the Constitution does not make us arbiters of the image that a televised state criminal trial projects to the public." He hasn't said so, but in his talk about federalism Burger has actually assumed the voice of *Estes*'s staunchest opponents. Nor is that all.

Aside from relying upon the "governing principle" of federalism, Burger's opinion in *Chandler* also expressly notes the absence of any showing of "specific prejudice" suffered by the defendant as a result of his trial being televised. But here too Burger is speaking in the voice of the *Estes* dissent, not the majority. It was Justice White writing in dissent who criticized the *Estes* majority for finding in Estes's favor despite Estes's failure to show specific prejudice. Of course what makes White's criticism possible is precisely its rejection of the majority's view that cameras in the courtroom are inherently prejudicial. Inherent prejudice means that showing specific prejudice is unnecessary. By the same token, White also rejected the *Estes* majority's contention that a showing of actual prejudice in these kinds of cases is impossible.[40] On this view, then, what White in his *Estes* dissent and Burger writing for the majority in *Chandler* are really doing is placing an impossible burden of proof on defendants who claim that TV cameras have prejudiced their trial. It is equivalent to saying that such defen-

dants are bound to lose. Of course, that is precisely the result Burger
wanted. His goal was to open the courtroom to cameras, even if the
law of *Estes* had to appear other than it was.

Indeed, even when Burger is procedurally correct, as when he notes
that since Justice Harlan's concurring opinion in *Estes* provided "the
fifth vote necessary in support of the judgment" it "must be read as
defining the scope of that holding," Burger still gets the substance of
that opinion wrong. For example, in *Chandler* Burger claims that
Harlan had never endorsed prohibiting cameras from the courtroom
because of their inherently prejudicial effects. But that isn't so. In Harlan's view it is publicity that makes televising trials inherently prejudicial or, to use Harlan's phrase, "unacceptably dangerous." For it is
publicity, Harlan says, that causes people to become "emotionally involved" in a case—thus introducing the risk of undue influence and
the related danger of a "popular verdict." As Harlan puts it:

> [Publicity] introduces into the conduct of a criminal trial the element of
> "professional showmanship" and extraneous influences whose subtle
> capacities for serious mischief in a case of this sort will not be underesti-
> mated by any lawyer experienced in the elusive imponderables of the
> trial arena. . . . The critical element is the knowledge of the trial partici-
> pants that they are subject to such visual observation.

In short, for Harlan when it comes to notorious criminal trials—
by which Harlan means highly publicized trials in which the participants have good reason to believe they are being observed by a large
audience—the risk of prejudice and unfairness is too great to ignore.[41]
Harlan's crucial "fifth vote" in *Estes* thus holds that when it comes to
notorious criminal cases cameras in the courtroom are constitutionally impermissible. That is as far as Harlan felt he needed to go in
Estes, for on the specific facts of that case there could be no doubt
that the justices were dealing with a "notorious" criminal case. Thus,
if Harlan's "fifth vote" is dispositive of *Estes'* outcome, as Burger
rightly concedes, *Estes* must stand for the legal proposition that televising notorious criminal trials is inherently prejudicial and thus in
violation of due process. Under such circumstances, Harlan goes on
to note, the absence of specific prejudice "does not matter."

If *Estes* had been left intact, as Burger claims, the proper inquiry
for the *Chandler* Court would have been the following: are we dealing
here with a notorious criminal case? If the answer is yes, the rule in
Estes says that the presence of TV cameras violates due process, and

accordingly, the defendant's trial conviction would have to be reversed. But the *Chandler* Court never confronted that question. Indeed, if they had there is good reason to believe that an affirmative answer would follow. For it is difficult to imagine that the participants in this botched police burglary trial would have been unaware of the fact that they were being observed by a large television audience. In Harlan's view nothing more is needed to establish an unacceptable risk of prejudice. And that is precisely why, notwithstanding Burger's claim to the contrary, *Estes* and *Chandler* are essentially alike. Chandler was surely justified in his reliance upon *Estes* when he asked the courts to reverse his conviction. Even Justice White (who dissented in *Estes*) conceded as much in his concurring opinion in *Chandler*. White simply could not understand why Burger did not reverse *Estes* outright. Why the need for such subterfuge and distortion?

Unlike Burger, White wanted to play the game straight. But Burger was playing according to a different set of rules. He was playing by the rule of thumb and its corollary. Having entered the hyperreal courtroom that Warren's images conjured, Burger effectively exploited their fiction/reality confusion to suit his own purposes. He reversed Warren's spin, using hyperreal facts to generate *Chandler*'s hyperreal law. As a result, *Estes* remained legally intact but practically irrelevant. The quiet and decorum of *Estes*'s actual trial had now been replaced by the more compelling fiction of a courtroom out of control. Chandler's trial would thus stand in stark contrast to the "circus" that Billie Sol Estes supposedly had to endure. Having framed the matter in this way, Burger's conclusion seems inevitable. Since the televised trial that Chandler received was nothing like the "circus" in the infamous *Estes* case, there is no reason to rule now as the Court had in *Estes*. In short, no circus, no prejudice, no constitutional taint, no need to reverse the conviction. Chandler stays in prison, and *Estes* stays on the books as a matter of law. Meanwhile, the television cameras are free to roll. After all, they're new and improved. Television has been made safe for due process.

In *Richmond Newspapers v. Virginia,* an opinion handed down by the Court a year before *Chandler,* Burger shed light on the core beliefs that inform what I am calling his jurisprudence of appearances. In that case Burger wrote:

> Civilized societies withdraw both from the victim and the vigilante the enforcement of criminal laws, but they cannot erase from people's consciousness the fundamental, natural yearning to see justice done—or

even the urge for retribution. . . . [N]o community catharsis can occur
if justice is done in a corner or in a covert manner. . . . To work effectively, it is important that society's criminal process "satisfy the appearance of justice," and satisfying the appearance of justice can best be
provided by allowing people to observe it.[42]

The logical corollary is not hard to figure: the more people who see
it, the better.[43] Rather than serving as the paradigm case for inherent prejudice, as Justice Harlan believed, the notorious criminal trial
has now come to embody the ideal vehicle for "community catharsis." On the basis of that broadly shared experience, Burger believed,
public faith in the legal system would be restored. People would see
that the courts are doing their job, obtaining swift and sure justice
and in the process placating the urge for retribution. In short, the
notorious criminal case had now become the cornerstone of law's
legitimacy.

But an unforeseen problem remained. Burger may have been savvy
about the rule of thumb, but he was naïve when it came to the rule's
corollary. What he didn't realize was how easy it is for images to spin
out of his control. And that is precisely what we have seen in the aftermath of *Chandler*. The corollary to the rule of thumb has turned
against Burger, even as it turned against Warren before him.

Consider first in this regard the impression television gives of being
there, live, inside the courtroom. TV makes viewers feel like a thirteenth juror. But of course they are not. Few television viewers actually
see all that the jury sees—from the parties' opening statements, to the
complete presentation of evidence, to the attorneys' complete closing
arguments, to the judge's full instructions on the law. And of course
no TV viewer swears an oath to follow the law and uphold his or her
duties as a juror. In any event, things may be changed when they play
on the screen. For example, Professor Peter Arenella of UCLA Law
School has noted that Detective Mark Fuhrman in the O. J. Simpson
criminal trial looked far more credible on television than he did inside
the courtroom.[44] Arenella also suggests that television has a tendency
to exaggerate insignificant matters while trivializing important ones.
Take Simpson's not-so-famous houseguest Kato Kaelin. There was
something about this struggling actor that worked on the screen. His
mannerisms, his speaking style, his man-boy image struck a chord
with the viewing public. There was something about his appearance
that charmed some and revolted others. It was a visceral response,
more emotional, in keeping with the electronic medium, than any-

thing else. Yet, despite his having become a major "character" in the Simpson drama, his actual contribution to the case was minor.

TV viewers' confidence in their opinions about how a case should come out persists not only in the face of gaps and distortions in what they see and hear, but also despite the fact that they often see and hear things that are kept away from the jury. This includes legally inadmissible evidence as well as expert commentaries on various aspects of the trial, such as a particular witness's credibility or a particular attorney's trial strategy. Notwithstanding these discrepancies, however, when a jury's verdict is not what the viewer expects, it is the jury that is to blame as well as the legal system that allowed their mistakes to occur. The public's largely skeptical response to the Simpson verdict illustrates the point. Disparities between TV-trial viewers' expectations and actual trial outcomes tend to erode public confidence in the judicial system. Nor is this the only risk associated with Burger's notion of televisual catharsis.

Let us pause a moment to consider more closely Burger's claim. If television is our surrogate, if images on the screen really do end up informing the public's perceptions of legal reality, it seems appropriate to consider the images of law that are being shown. As it turns out, rather than serve Burger's strategic ("confidence-building") objectives, TV-law tends to subvert them.

It is not simply that the real trials that show up on TV distort legal reality. For example, Steve Brill knew perfectly well when he established the Court TV network that his main competitors were CNN and afternoon soap operas. He would have to combine the best of both if he was to make his commercial venture a success. Little wonder, then, that a vastly disproportionate number of the trials viewers see on Court TV are criminal trials of the most titillating sort: murders, sex crimes, and if an occasional civil case sneaks through odds are it will involve a celebrity. For example, actress Pamela Anderson of *Baywatch* fame appeared in a rarely featured contract dispute case. This allowed the network to promote its coverage of the case by showing scenes of the bikini-clad defendant from the internationally popular TV series in which she starred.

Violence, voyeuristic titillation, the cult of celebrity: this is regular TV fare. Now if this familiar programmatic expectation drives Court TV (which disingenuously bills itself as "justice without scripts"), consider what we see when we turn to "reality TV's" eye on law and crime. I am referring to the spate of TV programs that allegedly show us the police in action. As more than one media scholar has shown, there are unmistakable patterns at work here as well. Take, for example, the prototypical "predatory criminal." We know him when we see him, and so do the police. He's violent and his violence is usually of the most irrational sort. The world he inhabits is utterly unlike the world we know. The message that these images convey is clear. Criminals aren't like the rest of us. They are the deviant Other among us.

As criminologist Ray Surette writes: "The crimes that dominate the public consciousness and policy debates are not common crimes but the rarest ones. Whether in entertainment or news, the crimes that define criminality are the acts of predator criminals. . . . Predator criminals are modern icons of the mass media."[45] What the screen shows us is plain: the criminal predator's acts of violence are impulsive, unpredictable, without reason. In this way, the criminal as social predator not only enhances the TV viewer's sense of fear in the face of what is perceived by many as pervasive social disorder, but it also makes the strictest punitive response the most desirable measure for coping with the threat. Surely one cannot expect to "rehabilitate" such irrational beings. And since the criminal predator is usually presented without personal history or any semblance of having come from a normal social milieu, since they are depicted, in short, as abstract threats divorced from the rest of society, their punishment is hardly likely to prompt sympathy or regret.

Thank God for the police, these TV shows teach us to realize. For it's their street smarts that keep the rest of us safe. We have but to rely upon their instinctive and seemingly infallible ability to quickly identify crimes that are either in progress or just about to happen and to seize the criminals who are pulling them off. The carefully chosen and carefully edited footage on these shows leaves no doubt in the viewer's mind: the police invariably get it right. The people they stop really are criminals.

But there is a problem associated with this sort of programming. Because viewers never get to see the police battering down doors to the wrong apartment or arresting (or even shooting) the wrong man, there appears to be no reason to place legal checks on how they do their job. Why should there be, since they're doing so well? In short, on this view legal rules invariably appear to hamper the police needlessly. Law's formal demands appear only to get in the way of effective law enforcement. It is "legal technicalities" like these that keep incriminating evidence from juries and that discourage guilty suspects from confessing their crimes to the police. In other words, once the criminal accused becomes the deviant Other, someone who is utterly unlike the rest of us, constitutional safeguards make no sense. Who needs them if they only help criminals? In this respect, then, popular TV images of the reality of crime and law enforcement argue against the rule of law. Based on what we see on TV, the rule of [police] men seems to be doing just fine—until legal formalities enter into the picture and mess things up.

These popular representations of crime and of the need to punish serve multiple purposes. For one thing, they reflect the electronic medium's need for striking images, such as extreme criminal violence and/or sexual abuse, to rivet the viewer's attention. As we have seen, even the most realistic of televisual portrayals of the judicial system, the predominantly criminal trials featured on Court TV, are disproportionately violent and eroticized. Murders, rapes, and familial abuse are represented here in numbers far exceeding statistical reality. As a consequence of this misrepresentation, the impression that television gives is of a far more violent world, populated by far more violent criminal predators than is actually the case.[46]

The irrationally violent criminal predator also serves as a potent symbol of what Surette calls "a world gone berserk, for life out of control." In this sense, the images we are dealing with here are not about law or even about reality, strictly speaking. They are about hidden fears, deep uncertainties—in short, the predominant cultural anxieties of our time. These images tell us about our intense need to stave off what are perceived as potent chaotic forces (both within and without). They tell about the struggle to feel more in control of our lives. These needs are especially acute nowadays, for there is a growing sense that our ability to govern our lives in the face of powerful irrational forces is diminishing. At the same time, our ability to find security within an identifiable moral community seems increasingly elusive. This is what many political conservatives as well as new communitarian republicans, like Harvard political scientist Michael Sandel, are so concerned about.[47]

Based on what has been said so far, their concerns are well placed. For in the absence of more self-reflectively affirmed values we are at risk of falling victim to symptoms, of promulgating laws and policies, for example, that act upon the "reality effects" of repressed or distorted fears, impulses, and desires. This is law imitating appearances prompted by denial. The predatory criminal icon may be a media construct, but it is also a construct that the law has increasingly adopted as its own. The problem is that no matter how hard we try, no matter

how many new laws we create, no matter how great the punitive measures they hold out, the predatory Other cannot be subdued. Nor
should we be surprised at this outcome—he is, after all, a phantom,
the virtual offspring of law's dalliance with the commercial media.
The predator criminal is a spur to desire—the very fuel that helps
make the media's images flow. In this respect, every short-term victory
over the Other represents a battle in a larger war that cannot and
indeed must not be won. For in the current scheme of things such a
victory would ultimately spell law's defeat. The engine of desire would
then come to a halt. The image flow would stop, leaving no place for
law to appear in, no place for it to be consumed like the commodity
it has become. That is the price for deriving law's legitimacy from the
screen. It is the price society must pay for making law's legitimacy
depend upon broad public consumption of popular images, like the
highly charged images we consume when notorious criminal cases are
on the air.

Chief Justice Burger spoke of the need for "community catharsis"
in the service of law's legitimation. But by associating the judicial process and the retributive impulse with other images (and other impulses) to be found on the screen, what he gave us was something else
entirely. Call it "hyper-catharsis," the illusion of catharsis, catharsis in
appearances only. In real catharsis repressed fears, wishes, and desires
are confronted and consciously worked through. Hyper-catharsis does
the reverse. Like the TV trials that produce it, hyper-catharsis is a
spectacle that masks rather than reveals unconscious impulses and the
fantasies they produce. In this way it perpetuates the repression and
displacement of illicit gratifications that drive the flow of appearances.
Burger's jurisprudence of appearances exploits images—of victims
and aggressors alike—for the sake of their emotional payoff, converting them into fuel for the viewer's sensation. This demeans the
dignity and authenticity of viewer and viewed alike. For surely one
who colludes in the exploitation of others can hardly hope to escape
its effects. But it does more than this. Hyper-catharsis also perverts
the enchantment of meaning itself. This is what we see when meaning
collapses into mere sensation—meaning's "use value." In this sense
the clash between hyper-catharsis and real catharsis points up a corre-
sponding distinction between skeptical and affirmative postmodernism. Two opposing forms of enchantment are at work here: one in the
service of deceit, illicit desire, and self-gratification, the other in the
service of feelings, beliefs, and values that we consciously aspire to
affirm.

In a world where the mass media love nothing so much as the mass media, it is the media's own images that are the most certain means to catch the camera's eye. It is hardly surprising, then, that lawyers often find their dramatic, real-life stories of loss, suffering, and death welcome on the air. Passion sells; images of grief, horror, and violence are in high demand. They fill television news holes, docudramas, and fictional police, crime, and law dramas, as well as the "reality TV" shows that millions of Americans watch daily. Yet, amid the intertwining of law, crime, and media, significant problems arise—the problems that come with the conflation of truth and fiction, image and reality, fact and fantasy. The mutually assured seduction between trial lawyers and the commercial mass media has created a feedback loop that elides the real and legitimates the fanciful.

The process goes like this. The trial stories that offer the most familiar images, characters, and plot forms are the ones most likely to get on the air. Once ensconced there, they are more likely to stick in the viewer's mind (including actual or prospective jurors). In fact, the more they stick the more credible they become. This encourages lawyers and their public relations agents to pitch their clients' stories in terms of TV reality. In this way, the media's law stories lend credence not only to the legal reality they portray, but also to the media that portray them. By lending its badge of authority to the popular images and stories it embraces, law enhances not only its own persuasiveness and legitimacy, but also the persuasiveness and legitimacy of the media themselves.

As popular stock images, character types, and plot lines from commercial television acquire enhanced verisimilitude, TV's commerce-driven, attention-riveting programming increasingly comes to provide models for legal reality. It is as if the familiar images, categories, and story lines disseminated by the visual mass media are supplying cognitive heuristics for society as a whole. And whether true or not, it is on the basis of these compelling images that public policies, criminal statutes, and sentencing guidelines are being drafted and passed into law.

Chief Justice Burger thought TV would be good for law. But he didn't realize how good for TV law could be. Or how legal appearances could be made to spin in commercial currents that exploit the public's unconscious fears and desires. Contrary to Burger's naive confidence, the courts cannot control appearances on TV. And to the extent that TV has become our surrogate, confidence in the judicial process and respect for the rule of law have, contrary to Burger's design, only declined. If current trends continue, they are likely to decline even further.

Here then is a cautionary tale about what happens to law when it becomes beholden to commercial pop culture for its legitimacy. It is an account of what becomes of law, and society as a whole, when symbolic dramas involving law enforcement agents, lawyers, and the system of justice in general cycle through media-fueled expectations, fantasies, and desires. We have seen this before in the mutually assured seduction between media and law that plays out in litigation public relations. And there too there is no guarantee that law's strategic objectives, as opposed to the media's, will come out on top.

In the end, paradox remains. Today prisons abound, yet the cry for more imprisonment has not softened. The prison population soars, even as the proportion of nonviolent offenders increases—making prison the remedy of choice for nonviolent crime. Executions increase, yet the desire for more capital offenses continues to grow. The chain gang is back; the demand for public shaming is on the rise. Indeed, we are reaching a point where shunning the deviant Other may no longer require a criminal act. As the United States Supreme Court has recently said, sexual offenders who "cannot control their behavior and who thereby pose a danger to the public health and safety" may be civilly confined against their will.[48] Notably, such forcible confinement is not a response to a specific act. It is a precautionary measure, in response to what a particular offender might do in the future. For the so-called "mentally abnormal," the Other among us, there is no escaping character as fate. The Other's expulsion from society is required by the kind of person he is—or the kind our irrational fear and uncertainty, our frustration and rage, have made him out to be.

In recent years, we have seen a concerted effort by ad masters, political spin doctors, public-relations-minded litigators, and Supreme Court justices to exploit the power of the mass media, particularly television. Their willingness to use the media to manipulate desire, to conflate fantasy and reality, and to merge self-identity with self-gratifying acts of consumption—regardless of whether the commodity consumed is a product, a political candidate, or a matter of law—is contributing to a significant cultural crisis. Powerful irrational forces seem to be irrupting all around us. Chance events and uncontrollable impulses threaten to subvert rational explanation, throwing causation itself into doubt. New forms of associative thinking and disparate logics are eroding conventional notions of modern reason and the autonomous self. An emerging sense of contingency—of the

historical, cultural, and psychological constructedness of self and social reality—is making it harder to agree upon shared moral and ethical standards for community life.

In short, the very rudiments of law in the Western liberal tradition
seem to be up for grabs: causation, the autonomy and moral responsibility of the individual, and the coherence of reason itself. In the next
chapter, we will study more closely the impact on law of this sweeping
cultural development. It is here that we will encounter what I take to
be the foremost legal challenge of our time. We must begin to reconceptualize law in a way that is consonant with current lived realities,
which is to say, with the cultural constructs and anxieties actually circulating in society. Also at issue here is the need to provide a new basis
for law's legitimation. That effort will lead us from hyper-catharsis
to real catharsis—in the face of tragic suffering and the affirmative
potential of legal enchantment.

What is happening is not merely the breakdown of law, but, more importantly, the breakdown of the underlying order upon which law is based.

ALVIN TOFFLER

We are living in a time of frailty, fear, and morbidity.

LUIS BUÑUEL

When Law Goes Pop
Strange Forces, Trauma, and Catharsis

There are times in the life of a nation when law is needed to check popular sentiments. In Alexis de Tocqueville's words, law must serve as a "brake" when the people "let themselves get intoxicated by their passions or carried away by their ideas." The mass media, by contrast, function best with the gas pedal pressed down. The more movement—the speedier the image flow and the greater the emotional intensity it produces—the better. When law goes *pop* it yields to the media's logic. As a result, its capacity to serve as a necessary brake upon popular passions and impulses is lost. This failure is accompanied by increased disillusionment, a heightened sense of skepticism or disenchantment concerning law's ability to seek the truth or render justice in the particular case.

In this chapter I examine the recent trend in popular culture toward disenchantment, primarily as manifest in contemporary film. My working assumption is that film, like notorious cases, provides a reasonably reliable indicator of shared, conflicted, and newly emerging beliefs, values, and expectations. For example, we see signs of significant cultural change in the course of the nearly three decades that separate the original *Cape Fear* (1962) and Martin Scorsese's 1991 remake. Across that arc of years major shifts have occurred in both the *Cape Fear* story and the storytelling process itself. Skepticism sounds the key note here in a cultural move toward failing faith in the ability of law and lawyers to do the work that justice requires. That note will deepen beyond rational reckoning as we move on to examine David Lynch's *Twin Peaks* (1990) and *Lost Highway* (1996).

I want to suggest through these film studies that the cultural trend toward disenchantment is operating on several levels at once. In one sense, it is a part of a growing tide of disillusionment with American institutions in general, including the institutions of marriage, politics, mass media journalism, and law. Film director Martin Scorsese vividly depicts this skeptical spirit in his scathing version of *Cape Fear,* as we will see shortly. But in another sense the skeptical spirit that is at work goes even further. In this respect, I believe we are also witnessing the effects on law of a widespread cultural movement that I identify as radical disenchantment (or skeptical postmodernism).

It is in illustration of this deeper, more thoroughgoing skeptical impulse that I draw upon the films of writer/director David Lynch. In Lynch's highly disturbing work we see how the outbreak of powerful but blind irrational forces—such as chance, fate, rage, and desire—undercut human agency, making meaningful action and judgment all but impossible. The implications of this movement for law are nothing short of devastating. Put simply, skeptical postmodernism leads to law's vanishing point. The all-encompassing chaos it depicts leaves no way out. The meager coping strategies it offers are understandably desperate and unsure.

The path of skeptical postmodernism invites alternative options. The temptations of denial on the one hand and nostalgia for the naive realism of an idealized past on the other are strong. But I shall suggest another option: the affirmative postmodern option that I endorse in this book. For I believe that radical disenchantment represents but one take on what postmodernity has to offer. Within contemporary culture we also find a competing take. In the interest of illustrating such an alternative, I will close this chapter with yet another film, Philip Haas's *The Music of Chance*. Here we glimpse, at an inchoate stage perhaps, crucial elements of an affirmative postmodern take on the advent of meaning. It is "affirmative" because pulsing within it is a rejuvenating urge toward enchantment and belief. This affirmative possibility ultimately invites us to consider anew the constructive power and importance of myth. And not just for popular culture alone.

But before pursuing further the possible connections between law and mythic enchantment, we must first take up a competing impulse: namely, the strong cultural trend toward disillusionment and disbelief.

Cultural Skepticism and the Law

> The truth tragedy tells is that we cannot protect
> ourselves, neither through the wisdom of self-control nor
> through the magic of wish. There is no defense against
> the self in its fate.
>
> RICHARD KUHNS[1]

It is one of the crueler ironies of our time that uncertainty, fear, and a sense of human frailty can be so great in an era when science and technology have advanced so far. Never before have so many enjoyed so much in the way of material security and comfort and in refuge from sickness and calamity. Yet it is as if our intolerance of loss, pain and suffering, and even death itself only increases in proportion to our collective power, and desire, to triumph even more completely over the vicissitudes of everyday life. In law it is no different. In many ways, law today offers more protection against loss and suffering than in any previous era. Yet public outrage, even in the face of diminishing criminal activity and attenuated civil wrongdoing (such as exposing others to secondhand tobacco smoke) seems never to have been greater.[2] Laws proliferate. But the forces of irrationality and disorder are not so easily tamed. And as the perception of law's defeat grows, the modern faith in progress, rationality, and the human ability to ensure order and security unravels a bit more—prompting more uncertainty, more resentment, and more law.

It wasn't always this way. Indeed, to judge by director J. Lee Thompson's 1962 version of *Cape Fear,* the law's—and by extension society's and our own characterological—center holds even in the face of violent, irrational attack. Thompson's plot is straightforward, his message neat. It can be simply summarized: law has its limitations, and so does rational self-restraint; but in the end, law and rationality prevail.

For Thompson, the story goes like this: immediately upon his release from prison, Max Cady (Robert Mitchum) tracks down the man who testified against him in court eight years earlier. That man, an upstanding lawyer by the name of Sam Bowden (Gregory Peck), happened to witness Cady's violent assault upon a young woman in a parking lot. Ever since his conviction, Cady has been plotting his revenge against Sam. For seven years he has fantasized Bowden's death. By his eighth year of prison, however, Cady has managed to go a step further: the lawyer's death will no longer suffice. That would be too simple, too easy. No, Sam Bowden, that exemplary citizen and family man, will have to undergo something more painful than that. He is going to have to suffer, the way Cady has suffered. And that means Sam is going to have to witness the violent loss of his family.

Cady's plan for revenge is as simple as it is sinister: he'll track Sam down, violate Sam's wife and fifteen-year-old daughter before Sam's tortured eyes, and then, presumably, finish Sam off with a fitting death.

As the film proceeds, we see Cady's plan put into action. First he introduces himself to Sam, insinuating the menace that he has in mind for Sam and his family. Cady then kills the family dog, unseen but known. Next, he stalks Sam and his family. He seeks out Sam's daughter in front of her school and he explicitly threatens Sam and Leigh Bowden with specific acts of violence. As the Bowdens' terror mounts, Sam (and the audience, which cannot but sympathize with his plight) realizes that the law is simply unable to handle this kind of threat to normal, civilized life. As the town's sheriff tells Sam, "It's a dictatorship to arrest someone for what they might do."

Sam gradually comes to grips with the fact that it is up to him to stave off Cady's menace. But Cady is smart. He has used his prison years to educate himself, to study up on the ins and outs of the law. He hires an attorney who is determined to end the strip searches, vagrancy allegations, and station-house lineups through which the local police are arguably violating Cady's civil rights. The police are stymied by the law, and as Cady's threats mount, Sam finally succumbs to the need for unofficial, unlawful action. He hires three thugs to send Cady a message, armed with chains and sticks for emphasis. But Cady fights off the paid assailants' attack, and when one of the assailants "talks" to the authorities about who hired him, it is Cady now who has the legal upper hand, and he knows it. Cady's lawyer moves quickly to institute disbarment proceedings against Sam Bowden.

Hamstrung by the law he has served his whole professional life, Sam now moves to set a trap for Cady. Sam lures Cady to his houseboat on the river Cape Fear. Using his wife and daughter as bait, Sam, armed with a gun, waits for Cady to show. Cady takes the bait. He confronts Sam's wife on the boat, threatens to rape her, and then leaves in order to pursue the Bowdens' young daughter. Sam goes after him, and when he finds Cady the two men fight. Sam gains the upper hand, gets the gun, trains it on Cady, but doesn't fire. No, death would be too simple, too easy, says Sam, consciously echoing Cady's own threatening words to Sam. It's prison for life, Sam tells Cady. Life in a cage, that'll be Cady's just desserts.

And so the film ends, with Cady evidently on his way to a criminal trial that'll put him away for good.

The film's message is not hard to decipher: even the most upstanding citizen, a dutiful attorney committed to the lawful demands of due process, a virtuous man beloved by wife and daughter, a well-respected citizen in his community, can be driven to violence. In the face of an antagonist's unabated fury, sometimes only an equally forceful fury will serve to counter the threat presented. All of us, the film seems to be telling us, are capable of such fury under the right circumstances.

Yet, in the end the film leaves us with a significant assurance: even when such fury is provoked, it can be checked by reason, and the law can then take its proper course. We do not have to act on our rage; we do not have to kill. Like Sam Bowden, we can depend on law to do the work of retribution without the need for self-help. In this way, law appears to be properly calibrated to meet our felt need for punishment in proportion to the menace and outright violence perpetrated by the likes of Max Cady.

In short, *Cape Fear* in the original 1962 version presents a picture of violent rage and the law's inability to stave off its threat. Law clearly has its limitations; it cannot insulate us completely from the risk of antisocial violence. But it can do justice when such violence ultimately erupts.

None of these assurances survive the nearly thirty years from Thompson's original *Cape Fear* to Martin Scorsese's brilliant, and far more unsettling, 1991 remake. The world has changed radically from what it was. Now, neither law, nor family, nor the virtues of individual character, nor even justice itself can be trusted to prevail in the face of irrational violence. The force of corruption has grown pervasive. And the shadow world from which Max Cady emerges has now become a place to which none of us can claim to be a stranger. According to Scorsese's vision, we are all living at least partly submerged in the shadow of violence, guilt, and denial.

Max Cady (Robert De Niro) too has changed. He has become a far more complex symbol than in his former incarnation. The early sexual, violent menace now mixes with biblical prophecy, Nietzschean philosophy, and an empathic (self-described "feminine") sensitivity to the life of the emotions. Cady does more than threaten. He is a guide to worldly and unworldly suffering, a mock Virgil out to show Sam Bowden (Nick Nolte) the way to righteousness. As he tells Sam's fifteen-year-old daughter Danielle (Juliette Lewis): "Every man carries a circle of hell around his head like a halo. . . . Every man has to go through hell to reach his paradise." Every man, and every woman. This is what the Bowdens will have to learn by the film's anguished denouement. In Scorsese's hands, the story of *Cape Fear* has become a parable for our time, a symbolic tale of the violent clash between desire and reality, magic and strife, childhood and childhood's end, and between fantasy and its consequences.

The story begins not as a straight, chronological narrative, but as a

story within a story. It is Danielle's ("Danny's") story. "My Reminiscence," she recites as the film begins.[3] And indeed it is. The story that
unfolds before us is, we shall later learn, a homework assignment
Danny offhandedly mentions to her father. "What are you working
on?" he will casually ask. "We have to write something in the style
of Thomas Wolfe's *Look Homeward, Angel*. A reminiscence," she'll
reply. Hers will be of the houseboat, on the river Cape Fear. At the
time she announces what her topic will be, she apparently has in mind
the halcyon days of summer vacation. Those days will be taken over,
however, by memories of a different sort, memories of Max Cady terrorizing the Bowden family on the very same houseboat, threatening
sexual violence and death, as the boat swirls out of control in a storm-
swollen river whose raging violence breaks it asunder, sending it down
to the unseen river bottom—together with whatever halcyon memories Danny might once have recalled.

For Danny, the magic of her youth is about to end, is already ending, has ended, the magic of those early, carefree summer days on Cape
Fear. She is a young woman now; her sexuality is in full blossom.
And with the onset of adulthood she is about to learn adult things:
knowledge of social transgression, illicit sexuality, and moral and
emotional suffering. This is knowledge her parents, and Max Cady,
and seemingly everyone else in this bleak film, already possess. It is a
form of knowledge that makes remembrance of the past, of the time
before adulthood, a kind of death—the death of youth's illusion of
immortality, the death of innocence and uncompromised rapture. In
her remembrance, Danny already knows this, just as she knows it is
best to forget, lest "you die a little every day."

To gain a better sense of Scorsese's skeptical vision, let us consider
some vignettes from the new *Cape Fear*.

We begin with Sam Bowden, Esq. There he is, walking down the
courthouse steps, briefcase in hand. Calmly, almost distractedly, he
reports his success to his client walking beside him, another attorney,
Sam's law partner as it turns out. It's a matrimonial matter. The client's
son-in-law apparently is trying to stash away assets in order to avoid
a fair divorce settlement with the law partner's daughter. Sam has
managed to get a 21-day extension in the proceeding. Good! This will
give the client the time he needs to launch a private investigation to
find out what savings and loan accounts his son-in-law is using.

Ah, just another day in the life of a modern-day attorney. No longer
do we see the lawyer's virtuous concern for his client's desperate financial need—as in the tort case Sam Bowden (Gregory Peck) han-

dled thirty years before. Gone, too, is the attorney's virtuous concern for the well-being of an elderly witness. Now we have legal maneuverings, private investigations to counter deceptions, corrupted Savings & Loans—the familiar landscape of social corruption and private scandal. Indeed, soon we'll see Sam's law partner try to persuade Sam to undertake some unspecified, but clearly unethical, perhaps illegal, action in the divorce case Sam is handling. "No, that's bullshit, and I'm not doing it," we'll hear Sam say.

Perhaps Sam's law partner was encouraged to think otherwise based on his knowledge of Sam's own unethical actions in the past. Like the one he committed fourteen years ago, when he was a public defender handling a rape case. The defendant at the time was one Max Cady. Cady had a record of violent sexual assaults against young women. In this particular case, however, Sam learned that the victim's sexual history report contained references to sexual promiscuity. The victim had two or three lovers during the same month as her involvement with Cady. The report could have helped Cady's case. But Sam buried it. Cady got fourteen years on a plea-bargained conviction, a conviction bargained down from rape to aggravated assault. So gone too, we see, is the lawyer's innocent, fortuitous tie to Cady's criminal case. Thirty years ago Sam just happened to witness Cady's crime and testified against him; now, the lawyer cannot escape complicity in the matter.

Here then is the face of modern law that Scorsese shows us. The trial never takes place, just the conviction—a normal event. Today, in well over 90 percent of all criminal cases convictions are obtained on the basis of plea bargaining between the prosecution and defense counsel. What we also see in the film is professional betrayal of the client in lieu of professional commitment. Who will ever know? After all, the plea agreement is a private affair, the records are buried. It will take Max Cady seven years of jailhouse legal study before he learns how to obtain those records, before he learns how his own attorney sabotaged his case, turning from zealous defender to judge and jury, determining from his own private viewpoint (after all, who likes sex offenders?) what the case was really worth. And who knows? If you negotiate the market value of enough criminal cases for a living perhaps that's the appraiser's mentality that eventually takes over.

So much for the decline of the legal profession. But what about family life? Thirty years ago movie viewers saw Sam Bowden leave the courtroom to go bowling with his loving, devoted wife and adoring daughter. But that too has changed.

As it turns out, like Max Cady himself, the Bowdens are up to their necks in barely repressed violence. Consider the following scene: the Bowdens have gone to a local ice cream parlor after watching a movie together. Danielle is telling her dad how he should've "punched out" that rude guy with the cigar who was making such a disturbance in the theater. (Prescient girl, unbeknownst to them that man was Max Cady, and in time her dad will do exactly as Danielle wished.) But for now, Dad (stung by Danny's implicit blow to his male ego?) simply retorts, "Yeah, but I can take you!" And without so much as a blink of an eye he takes Danny into a headlock, his arm firmly screwed around her neck. Leigh calmly looks upon the scene, smiling wanly, then offers her husband a jab of her own: "You know how to fight dirty. You do that for a living." Blow two. Sam punctuates Leigh's sarcastic comment with a final twist of the arm. (Is it Danny, or Leigh, that he's choking?) Mouth agape, reaching vainly to unlock dad's grip about her neck, Danny coughs, gags. There's a startled expression on his face. Sam lets go, commenting: "Real cute, Leigh."

This little family transaction takes but a couple of seconds to complete. But packed within it is the baggage of shared aggression and resentment that the Bowdens have been lugging around with them for some time now. Don't let the happy surface fool you. It's all well documented.

We see as much in the next scene. Sam is locked in an aggressive game of racquetball with an attractive young woman. Sam knows Laurie from the courthouse where they both work. Their physical contacts during the game match their flirtatious banter. It is not clear at this point whether Sam is on his way to an adulterous relationship with Laurie, or whether it has already occurred. To be sure, the sexual tension between them is clear. (Laurie will later admit to Max Cady in a bar where, feeling jilted by Sam, she'll tell him, before letting him pick her up, that Sam was "her first," by which she apparently means her first affair with a married man.) But it's not Sam's first time. Sam's last adulterous affair almost wrecked his marriage. Leigh suffered a near, or actual, emotional breakdown: crying all day, staying in her room, doing no work, preparing no meals for the family. Sam stayed on—fearing Leigh's precarious state of mind, anxious about the possibility that she might even commit suicide. Sam stayed on, through the marriage counseling sessions and the family's hopeful new beginning after they moved to another town.

Why did he stay? Was it love, or guilt perhaps? It's what Leigh wants to know when she later learns of what she'll call Sam's "pathetic infidelity" with Laurie, when she mournfully asks: "Why didn't you have the balls to just walk out?" Love? No, Sam's response to Leigh is plain enough. It was guilt, and the fear that she'd do herself in. Oh, the arrogance, Leigh responds. Yes, thirty years is a long time in the history of the modern family. We've come a long way, so that a spurned wife can identify with an avenger's rage against an infidel husband. And when Sam vainly attempts to bring Leigh into a common struggle against Cady by confessing to her that he is afraid, Leigh can only respond with that wan smile of hers and the almost gloating words: "So, someone has finally got to you." No, not Leigh. On her own Leigh couldn't get to Sam. But Max Cady can.

In short, all of the women in Sam Bowden's life seem to be drawn for their own hidden reasons to Sam's nemesis, Max Cady. There is something about Max Cady, something that he embodies, that he offers, something forbidden, and therefore denied. But the repressed wish returns in the person of Max Cady. Furious vengeance for Leigh; the titillation of raw sexuality for Danielle; sexual revenge for Laurie (little did she know that it would be Cady's revenge against Sam, not hers, that would be acted out when she and Cady lay down together). In short, they all seem to be haunted by a dark double, that classic Gothic trope, so pervasive in contemporary pop culture. As Rikki Schubart explains:

> In horror the repressed desires, manifested in the monster, are disguised as the ultimate in fears. . . . Desires are projected outward on to a clearly external monster which functions not as a Body Double but a Soul Double, a classic doppel-ganger symbolizing the repressed. The fight between man and the monster is in this phase a psychomachia, a fight between reason and desires of a sexual nature.[4]

No, Max Cady hasn't come for Sam Bowden alone. He's there for everyone. The summons of impermissible rage and desire dogs the entire Bowden family. Perhaps we should get a gun, Sam muses. "We'd probably end up using it on each other," Leigh replies. To which Sam shoots back: "Or Danny would." Illicit desire is equally close at hand. Throughout the film Scorsese is careful to emphasize Danielle's budding, provocative sexuality. We hear her discuss Henry Miller with Max Cady (who recalls Miller's description of an erection as a lead pipe). And when Cady describes her parents' hypocrisy, their not letting her grow up, their "deflection of their own guilt" onto her, he succeeds in making the emotional connection with Danny that he has been seeking. She even allows him to touch her, and to kiss her.

Later that day, her dad will learn of the encounter. She'll smile provocatively when he asks if Cady put his hands on her. She'll even come to Cady's defense, insisting that he was only trying to make a connection with her. Is it her smile or her desire (or Cady's, or Sam's for that matter) that Sam cannot tolerate? To what is Sam reacting when he shakes his adolescent daughter violently, shouting, "There will never be a connection between you and Max Cady." Is it Cady alone that Sam fears? Have his own forbidden wishes somehow gotten involved? ("Put some clothes on," we hear Sam say upon entering Danny's room, "you're not a kid any more.") But Sam's aggression once again has gone too far. (Deflecting his guilt onto her?) He catches himself, realizing how inappropriate, how disproportionate, is his response. Too late. If there had existed any possibility for Sam to make a connection with his teenage daughter, it's gone now. "Get out!" Danny shouts, in tears. And in silence, he leaves.

The once united and loving Bowden family, a model of virtue, stability, and devotion, has now become a model of pervasive dysfunctionality. Judging by Scorsese's vision, life has grown considerably more complex in the years since *Cape Fear* first made its appearance on the silver screen. The Bowden family, the lawyers, the official law enforcement agents and their unofficial counterparts—all have been inverted, reversed in polarity, turned inside out from what they once were. And they are a thoroughly blemished lot, assuredly not the characters they were in J. Lee Thompson's more secure world. The change is no less striking in the character of Max Cady himself. Of course, Max Cady has always been there. But now he seems closer. His rage for revenge blends more readily with the retributive and increasingly punitive impulses of our time.[5] But there is also another dimension to Cady, a less obvious one. It is as if he were the embodiment, or perhaps the agent, of secret wishes, forbidden fantasies. It is as if he were acting out the Bowden family's frustration and rage in the face of thwarted desire and aggression—like Sam's barely repressed attraction to his daughter's budding sexuality and his hostility toward women generally, impulses Cady explicitly carries out. The same way Cady also takes further Sam's own willingness to subvert the law, a willingness that is apparently shared by Sam's law partners, as well as the law enforcement agents with whom Sam works. It is as if the hidden violence and corruption of the entire social and legal system were finally breaking out into the open.

By film's end we come to realize that Sam's imperious act of vigilantism, his decision to assume the role of judge and jury, condemning his client when he should have been the client's most zealous advocate, has unleashed an even more violent retributive force. Sam has triggered the vengeful fury of Max Cady. And in this too we see an inversion of Thompson's original *Cape Fear*. It is an inversion that sets Aeschylus' great tale of law and vengeance in the *Eumenides* on its head. In that classic Greek drama, the hideous fury of retribution was tamed, and brought into the law.[6] Through this civilizing process was born the trial and its formalized procedures (the swearing in of witnesses, the submission of evidence, adversarial argument before a jury of twelve citizens)—a process that has been handed down to our own day.

Yet when the civilizing effect of law is reversed, when those who are sworn to uphold the law willfully defy its rules and principled procedures, the ancient fury is let loose again, free from law's civilizing constraints. From this viewpoint, then, we might say that Scorsese's is, at heart, a conservative message. Beware the dark forces within. Beware the return of the repressed. Beware the loss of the reality principle when confronted with the chthonic agency of desire, fantasy, and magical thinking.

In this respect, Scorsese's *Cape Fear* might be read as an updated version of Freud's *Civilization and its Discontents*. If we do not stand up to the ego-smothering claim of instinct ("where it [the id] was there I [the ego] shall be!"), we will leave civilization in shambles. It is a fear Freud suffered all too compellingly in the last years of his life as he witnessed in exile the rise of Nazism.

But there is more to Scorsese's vision than simply expressing the need to repress basic instincts while also acknowledging their inescapable presence in our lives. He also forces upon us the vital question: what will secure us from the deep imbalances, the familial and social dysfunctions, with which we have grown so familiar? If law and lawyers are as corrupt as they seem, if private ethics and the corrosion of character are as pervasive as they appear to be, how do we chart a course out of the present social and familial morass?

Scorsese holds out no reason to hope that law or justice can save us. It is, after all, only blind fate that prevents Sam Bowden from becoming a killer in the end, the same force of circumstance that drags Max Cady to his death beneath the waters of Cape Fear. In the penultimate scene in the film, Sam is prepared to kill Cady; indeed, he wishes it with all his being. There he stands, with a rock heaved above his head, ready to smash it down on Cady's face, crushing bone and brain. And so things would have turned out but for the fact that the broken fragment of houseboat to which Cady had been handcuffed suddenly breaks free of the shore—perhaps it is the wind, or the natural force of the river's current—and Cady is out of Sam's reach. The stone will crash down, but it will miss its target. But for the wind, the current, Sam might have killed. So easily could things have been different.

But if this is the way of "justice," how can we be sure that it will work the next time we need it? How do we know the currents will shift then? Can justice as capricious as this be just?

Sam does not kill Cady in the end, but it is not hard to imagine things working out otherwise. Sam might well have preempted and transgressed the law, for if he did kill Cady when Cady no longer presented a threat, how could this be a justified form of homicide? Surely there is no triumph of law here. How stark is the contrast between this ending and the one presented in the original *Cape Fear* when Sam Bowden (Gregory Peck) heroically concludes: "No I won't kill you, you'll go to prison for the rest of your life." Which is to say, not I, but the law will be the agency of your punishment, the law will serve my need and the felt need of society for just deserts.

Thirty years ago perhaps we could be assured. Law would do its job in the end. But today we are not. Today we must depend upon purely circumstantial forces, a wind, a current—something more in keeping with a theory of chaos than of rational order. In the end we are left with fateful justice, justice as chance, justice as contingent upon irrational forces beyond our control. But what kind of justice is that? What possibilities for humanity does it hold out? And how does one live in such a world?

Scorsese's updated vision of the limits of law, character, and community is dark, to be sure, but it is not so dark as to be bereft of the possibility of redemption. Consider the Bowdens after their ordeal. They have seen and experienced much. It has been traumatic, yes. Yet there is also the chance that for the first time in their lives they now stand poised to take stock of themselves and of the way they interact with each other and others in the community around them. They've been humbled, broken down. But it is also possible that they are ready now to grasp the extent of their collusion with the likes of Max Cady and the dark forces he embodies. The terrible rage, the forbidden wishes and desires, hidden yet haunting them for so long, have been revealed for all to see. Will this traumatic event become an opportunity for insight, perhaps even wisdom? Will trauma provide a basis for cathartic working through of previously repressed impulses? Will it foster a sense of compassion built upon terrible knowledge? (For who does not harbor similar impulses and desires within?) Will understanding now enable the Bowdens to forgive themselves and each other? Will it bring pity and compassion into the hearts and minds of those of us who look on?

In the epilogue to Scorsese's *Cape Fear*—a story that has been, we now learn, her reminiscence—Danny recites the lessons she has learned. She tells us that we must battle not to let Cady into our dreams. But neither can we cling to naive dreams of the past, dreams of idyllic childhood days, of innocence, and unadulterated joy. But how is he to be kept out when he is so close? And how are we not to despair when we forget to forget, and memories of bygone days surge back to consciousness?

According to Danny, the proper fear is not that the magic will end.[7] As adults, we all know that it will. No, the more appropriate fear is that the magic might be unnaturally prolonged, held onto, in the service of desire. "If you hang onto the past," Danny recites, "you die a little every day." Here speaks the wisdom of the reality principle, checking fantasy and unabated instinct. As philosopher Richard Kuhns writes: "Catharsis [is] the descriptive term for clarifying, separating out, and getting centered upon the right emotion."[8] This is the voice of tragic knowledge, the proper fruit of catharsis. But as Danny and her parents know—and as do we, the audience, who have let Cady and the Bowden family into our own lives (at least for a while)—catharsis will not come without terrible suffering, without trauma.

The riddle of Max Cady's being is that he is, and must not be. His rage and desire are real, but too terrible to accept. His violence is brutal, intolerable, but not totally bereft of justice. If only we could be free of the infuriating contradictions he embodies.[9] Yet, Scorsese insists that Cady does exist and will not be denied, nor will his contradictions so easily be chased from the scene. He may sink back into the dark depths from whence he came, but—like the primitive threat of Freddy Krueger—this offers no guarantee that he will not surface again without warning sometime later on.

If, for the law to function, we need the Other to channel illicit desire or to find a permissible place for unconstrained fury, we will find him; if we cannot find him, we will create him. And to a significant extent that is precisely what we are doing.[10] By law we define the nature and scope of criminality. But when the fiction of law's sanitized violence comes into view, or merely threatens to do so, the more criminals we create the better. As René Girard has observed, "For the basis of violence to be effective, it must remain hidden."[11] We hide law's violence by displacing it onto the deviant Other. And as law's violence increases, so too does the number of deviant Others, and the laws that create them. As does the distance that separates the Other from the rest of us. In short, by legitimating in this way its growing violence, law also represses the "forbidden knowledge" of illicit violence within us all.

On this analysis, the current movement toward increased criminalization and enhanced (often mandatory) sentencing calls for serious reevaluation. If there is a source of hope in this regard I suggest that it may be found in the form of tragic understanding and the effect tragedy has on the quickened sensibilities of those caught up in its traumatic, destabilizing grip. Through tragedy, and the deep, wrenching catharsis it produces, the work of repression and denial, the ceaseless cycling of hidden rage and desire, may be interrupted. As Kuhns puts it, tragic knowledge "draws moral distinctions that help us in growing up."[12] Like the ancient Greeks before us, we too must come to grips with the urge to deny the fury within us, and the fictions with which we pretend to maintain control over our fears and desires.[13] The tragic sufferer is us. And the cause of the tragedy unleashed upon the sufferer is, at least in part, also us. We can no more wholly alienate ourselves from the forces of the victim's victimization than we can shut out the sympathy we feel for the innocent victim.

Nothing said here is meant to deny the reality of antisocial aggression and the pressing need for law to punish and deter criminal acts. At the same time, however, it is surely an illusion to think that "putting away" the Others among us will make the irrational forces that we fear just as simply disappear. That fiction, reflecting the urge to neutralize and sanitize the violence without as well as within, only invites the return of the repressed, the return of the one who, like Max Cady, comes into our midst as the wholly Other, but who turns out to be the dark double that we carry deep within ourselves.

If social healing is to occur, as tragic-fated Oedipus and the Bowden family in the aftermath of their ordeal stood ready to comprehend, perhaps it will come by way of trauma and catharsis. Healing in this sense refers to the way suffering helps to repair pathological splitting. We are the Bowdens, and we are Max Cady. The challenge of adulthood, it seems, is to learn to accept unacceptable contradictions, to consciously forge a livable balance between our self-aspirations and ideals (about who we would be) and our darkest terrors and anguish (about who we are in our innermost depths). The fictions with which we deny our fears ultimately serve only to ramify and enlarge them. As Kuhns puts it: "[T]he means to the mastery of splitting yields the pleasure we find in the harshest scenes of suffering. It is the mastery of this process and the knowledge it makes manifest that allow us to become cultural beings."[14]

If we can see ourselves in the other, if we allow the other's story to reveal his humanity, perhaps the compelling need to intensify law's violence, to criminalize more acts, to isolate more others as "wholly Other" will be eased. Perhaps it will be recognized for what, to a significant extent, it covertly embodies: a form of denial, the repression of what we fear most within ourselves. That task, making that connection, hard as it is, is perhaps harder still for us postmoderns. As Kuhns again incisively puts the matter: "Living as we do today, more and more in images and stories, we have obscured the line that separates fantasy from reality, internal psychological entertainments from external natural events."[15]

In this view, the greatest risk is that we will not be alarmed enough. The danger is that we will not experience within ourselves the terror that gives rise to cathartic justice, that instead of healing the pathological splitting to which we are prone we will continue to externalize our demons, blindly creating newly deviant Others in our midst. Yet that Other, a Gothic monster made up of fantasy and thwarted desire, cannot—precisely because it is imaginary—be destroyed. We who continue in the vain attempt to do so, though, are not so invincible. We can become the unwitting victims of our own dark and uncanny double.

These are the tantalizing possibilities with which Scorsese's terrifying vision in *Cape Fear* leaves us as the final scene fades. In a general sense, the question that remains is not whether law will escape the consequences of postmodernism, but rather what those consequences will be. My claim is that in taking up this question we must give careful consideration to the kind of postmodernism to which law will adapt and, in so doing, to the kind of self and social reality it will help to create.

Before we can explore these questions further, however, we must first come to grips with the full extent of the skeptical postmodern challenge. As the following film examples will suggest, that challenge takes us to law's vanishing point.

The Skeptical Postmodern Vision: Law at the Vanishing Point

> If doings such as these receive honor, why should I join
> the holy dance?
> *Oedipus Rex*[16]

Sudden violent upheavals in cultural life, or slower, but similarly deep
cultural transitions, lead one to reencounter the forgotten history of
order's mythic origin. During such times habits of thought and perception are shaken, accepted social arrangements grow suspect, uncertainty becomes the culture's hallmark. During such times the myth
(*mythos*) of reason (*logos*) and the reason of myth commingle freely,
if uneasily, in the mind's musings.[17] Signs are that ours is such a time.

Call it the counter-Enlightenment, an era apparently lacking the
secular faith—in the free and autonomous self; in reason and reason's
handmaids, science and technology—that inspired the modern break
with medieval sectarianism. If the moderns loved God less and humanity more than their premodern forebears, the postmoderns fall
short on both accounts. They have no more love of God than the moderns; and no more love of reason, for all its material productions and
reshapings of the natural world, than the premoderns before them.
The postmoderns are in love—or perhaps it is an obsession—with
flux and desire. Today material objects proliferate and the plastic self
adjusts quickly to absorb their use. But when the product's use is up,
as it inevitably will be, shapeless consuming desire remains. The experience of the postmodern subject is like that: contingent upon immediate uses, constantly in danger of being used up.

It is the same with meanings as it is with things. Information pro-
liferates. The desire to maximize the speed and quantity of data consumption increases daily at a dizzying pace. Global informational
networks spread from screen to screen in homes and offices. We're all
linked up. And everywhere talking heads are busily revealing our
world: in accumulated tonnage of toxic wastes, in total inches of rain-
fall from coast to coast, in disconnected images of violence and death,
in the latest sex scandals among politicians and Hollywood stars. . . .
Day after day. What does it mean? Never mind. It is hard enough just
to keep up.

But beneath the onslaught of information there flows a deepening
current of cultural anxiety. Basic beliefs are unstable, and the rush to
distraction does not wholly succeed in covering up the accompanying
confusion. Uncertainty is growing regarding our ability to control

events, to choose a particular path through life, to claim a discrete identity and bear responsibility for it. Works of our culture, in art, music, literature, and film today are telling us this. As the mind gropes for meaning, new stories are being told: narrative offerings seeking to frame the elusive self, the unknowable other, the fractured reality that is our social world.

Consider in this regard the work of David Lynch. In *The Thin Blue Line* Errol Morris nudged up against skeptical postmodern reality only to revert back in the end to the comforts of a conventional modern mystery story. While viewers were led to discern the constructed nature of meaning and truth, they were encouraged to do so only so long as the insights this produced proved useful in deconstructing the corrupted versions of truth and justice proffered by the Dallas district attorney. The risk of perpetual deconstruction was thus held in check. For Morris, deconstruction proves a useful tool—in the service of conventional notions of factual truth and causal-linear justice, notions that escape a similar critique. Conveniently, the constructed nature of Morris's preferences for truth and justice remain safely hidden from view. Viewers of David Lynch's "mystery" stories enjoy no such leeway. For here there is no escaping the terrifying effects of chance, fate, rage, and desire on our ability to know the truth and judge what is to be done. Lynch breaks free of the modern craving for certainty and closure. And in so doing he shows us the underlying mutability and contingency of truth and identity itself.

Take, for example, Lynch's popular film and nighttime television series *Twin Peaks* (1990) and his even more unsettling film *Lost Highway* (1996). Murder sets Lynch's stories in motion. In *Twin Peaks* the plot engine comes in the form of an apparently straightforward query: who killed Laura Palmer, an innocent-looking, well-liked teenager? But this is no ordinary whodunit. As Lynch's drama unfolds the viewer discovers that crime and pathology are uncomfortably common in the seemingly peaceful, rural town of Twin Peaks. We soon learn about other murders, acts of arson, drug trafficking. The town is also awash in bizarre characters—like the log lady, so called because she carries a small log with her everywhere she goes. It is her friend. She believes it hears and sees and speaks like anyone else.[18] Or consider Big Ed's wife, a woman with a patch who possesses superhuman strength and whose lifelong obsessions include developing a soundless curtain rod.

And of course there are FBI agents Cooper and Rosenfield, who have come to Twin Peaks to solve the mystery of Laura Palmer's death. Rosenfield is everything you'd expect a rational criminal investigator to be. He's full of sharp observations and masterful logical deductions. Except that, unlike Sherlock Holmes in the orderly world of Arthur Conan Doyle, he's always wrong. When evidence logically points to a particular suspect, it inevitably turns out to be a false lead. In Lynch's skeptical postmodern domain, it is Agent Cooper's irrational techniques that must guide us: mystical intuitions, dreams, riddles. Like the giants and dwarves who provide Cooper with clues while he sleeps; or the "deductive technique," which came to him in a dream about Tibet, that calls for tossing stones at a bottle in the woods while someone recites possible suspects' names. A clue is produced when a hit and a name coincide.

But if *Twin Peaks* teaches us to solve crimes the irrational way, in *Lost Highway* Lynch leaves us wondering whether crime can be solved at all. What we now face is not simply the inadequacy of the rational mind to solve a crime. It is the inability of rationality to penetrate the mystery of identity and representation itself. The distinction between cause and effect, representation and reality, self and other, or among the disparate fragments of the multiple self, is blurred beyond recognition. It is, in short, the quintessential skeptical postmodern condition.

Once again it is murder that sets things in motion. We learn as much from the film's opening scene, which begins with the mysterious announcement on saxophonist Fred Madison's home intercom that "Dick Laurent is dead." Only in the film's final scene will we learn that it is Fred himself who utters these words. By then we will also know whodunit. That too is Fred. The circular flow of events frames Lynch's postmodern vision. Past and future intermingle as characters double, transform, and change back again. The pillars of reason—causality, objective representation, moral agency, and the unified self—have crumbled. In their absence, anything can happen. And as the story's players are drawn now this way, now that, by strange and terrible forces that they can neither understand nor control, it seems as if all are guilty, and innocent, at the same time—if guilt and innocence (or judgment, for that matter) can mean anything in such a lawless world. For when identity has become so utterly mutable, how can we know whom we are judging?[19]

The flashback with which *Lost Highway* begins immediately sends us into a strange time loop, signaling the breakdown of causal-linear sequencing. A murder has already occurred, and another is about to happen. Fred doesn't know it, but he will commit, perhaps has already committed, both. Then the clues appear. Mysteriously, three videotapes are deposited on Fred's doorstep. One per day. The first shows

Fred's house as it appears from outside. The second shows Fred and his wife Renee asleep in bed. The third shows Fred, steeped in blood, in the act of butchering Renee's naked, mutilated body. It is the third video that will convict Fred of murder. The apparent objectivity of the images is all the law needs. And though Fred has no independent recollection of the crime, over time his memory will close around the images that he has seen, making them his own. This is how the image becomes real.

But is it? In prison, following his conviction, Fred continues to play the horrifying images in his head. But then something strange occurs. A pounding headache afflicts him. Its intensity makes Fred want to leap out of his skin. He writhes in agony, and finally loses consciousness. When he awakens he is someone else, a younger man named Pete. A fat knot on his forehead is all that remains of the ordeal of metamorphosis, as if the images within had violently torn their way out of his skull. But Pete knows nothing of Fred. And the authorities know nothing of Pete. Baffled, they are forced to let him go.

Later, Pete, an auto mechanic by trade, will encounter a woman named Alice. It's Fred's wife Renee, or perhaps her double. They're identical, except that Renee was dark-haired and Alice is blonde. Alice and Pete find themselves instantly locked in a gaze of intense mutual attraction. Alice will return to Pete's garage later and will lure him into a world of searing sexuality and violence. Pete's craving for Alice is insatiable. And though she gives herself to him, she ultimately remains elusive. In his quest to possess her, Pete will kill and rob her pimp-pornographer friend, Andy. It's for the money, and perhaps the only way Alice can get away, so they can start a new life together. But it doesn't pan out. Pete's desire for Alice is too great. He wants to *have* her, to possess her completely. Desire this pure craves eternity. Here is where *eros* and *thanatos* meet. For only when the boundaries of self (the obstacle of "I" and "other") dissolve completely will Pete find release from the prison of finitude and his desperate dependence upon another for desire's fulfillment. He tells Alice as much, almost involuntarily, in a moan of hopeless yearning after lovemaking. But Alice is quick to reply in a fierce whisper: "You'll never have me." And she disappears from view.

That is when Pete changes back into Fred. And a mystery man, in whiteface and dressed in black, appears in Alice's place. A classic trickster figure, and shapeshifter. Someone who can be in two places at once, who seems to know past and future. Just as he seems to know the hidden impulses that rage within people's minds. He's the man with the video camera, who shows people scenes from their lives, scenes latent in consciousness and perhaps in time. Presumably, it was the mystery man who delivered to Fred's home the tape showing Fred's murder of Renee. Just as it was the mystery man who led Fred to Renee's secret lover, the man he also helps Fred to kill. It's Dick Laurent, whose death in the film's final scene Fred Madison announces over his home intercom. To himself, it turns out, as we recall from the film's opening scene when Fred stands listening to a mysterious announcement, "*Dick Laurent is dead.*"

What is real? What is cause and what is effect? Who is guilty and who is innocent? With whose act are we concerned, and who exactly is the actor?[20] Are the recorded images of Renee's murder on the mystery man's tape real, or are they images of Fred's hidden, internally percolating rage? For though at the time of the murder Fred may have had reason to suspect Renee of infidelity, his suspicions are confirmed only afterward, when the mystery man leads him to Dick Laurent in bed with Renee. Is the fact that Fred's jealous rage and the associated impulse to kill were already present in his mind enough to justify his conviction? (As Freud would say, from the vantage point of the super-ego it hardly matters whether the illicit impulse is acted upon or merely conceived in the mind; both are equally deserving of punishment.) Or could it be that the mystery man, rather than revealing Renee's murder, has in fact *goaded Fred into killing her* by leading him to discover her together with her lover? Are the images of murder depicted on the tape real, in a documentary sense, or is it enough simply to play them in our heads, to turn them into memory, so that they may then become real? Or perhaps the images that convicted Fred were not real *yet*. Perhaps they are, like Max Cady, the externalized living embodiment of hidden wishes, thwarted desire and the rage to which it gives rise. In this sense, perhaps they set in motion a series of events that subsequently caused them to become real.

Acausality, disjointed time flow, and the mutability of identity play havoc with our capacity for judgment. For example, did Fred's transformation into Pete while in prison cause a guilty man (Fred) to go free, or did it allow an innocent man (Pete) to kill someone else— namely, Alice's and Renee's pimp-pornographer friend, Andy? Does it matter *who commits the act,* or when it occurs, if it is simply waiting to occur, is as good as done, by virtue of the power of fantasy or irrepressible desire or fate? Was Oedipus innocent? What does innocence (or guilt) mean amid such irrefutable and infallible forces? Forces like desire, that most primitive and irrational of forces that

Alice lasciviously embodies and that Pete seems utterly incapable of resisting. But did Pete kill *because of* desire (because he lacked the strength of will to resist Alice's wishes), or *for* desire (so that his craving for Alice might be fulfilled)? Or does such a distinction even matter?

The implications of Lynch's skeptical postmodern vision unfurl with dizzying effect. What are we to make of law in such a world, where primitive forces, like blind rage and insatiable desire, rule? For plainly these are forces that can be neither governed nor halted. Fred may strike at desire's source (the adulterous Renee), but it comes back stronger than ever (the irresistibly seductive Alice). And even when our impulses—such as erotic desire and the rage that its frustration produces—remain hidden from ourselves and others, they are there, waiting to break out of our minds into the world. This is what the mystery man knows. It is his natural element, it is what he takes delight in. There is no escape from the endless cycling of irrational forces. If it isn't Fred, it will be Pete; if it isn't Renee, it will be Alice. The names change, perhaps even the faces. But it really doesn't matter. Deeper, more powerful forces flow through these changes, linking them, making the details incidental, beside the point.

It is as if we were dealing with elementary powers, basic principles of the cosmos. Like the universal flux of Heraclitus, or the chaotic and creative rapture of Nietzsche's Dionysus.[21] Or like Kali, the Hindu goddess of disorder and destruction who, much like Lynch's mystery man/trickster figure, finds supreme delight in mischief and catastrophe. Yet it is also Kali's erotic dance with princely Shiva (like the one between Alice and Pete?) that brings the world into being and sustains it. The same erotic dance that might also incite in Shiva such riotous impulses as to cause all things to fracture into primordial chaos. Like Kali, the mystery man who takes Alice's place is indifferent to Time. And as in his world, in hers too everything exists in tension with its opposite, with everything constantly at risk of losing its balance and cascading back into Unbeing.

In Lynch's skeptical postmodern world law surely acquires a curious aspect. If it can be understood at all, perhaps it is only possible in terms of powerful impersonal forces, strange forms of reason, and unfamiliar ritual practices—practices attuned to an entirely different causal order than the one known to us in the modern Western cultural tradition. In this realm, internal realities have very real effects in the world of action and consequences; at the same time, external realities are symbolic of internal impulses, desires, and fantasies. This is the law of the supernatural, where enchantment, divination, witchcraft, and prophetic revelation prevail. Nor is this without precedent.

The eminent sociologist Max Weber has written about the movement in Western culture from premodern (or "primitive") law, which is based on faith, magic, and divination, to modern rational law, which is based on universally applied rules and procedures. On this view, it may be that we are entering a new cultural phase. Call it "postmodern-primitive." It is reminiscent of Claude Lévi-Strauss's "bricoleur," whose premodern mind is steeped in associative and magical thinking rather than the universalistic, abstract, rule-based thinking we associate with modernity.

To the extent this may be so, it is hardly surprising that dreams and riddles, as Lynch suggests in *Twin Peaks,* become law's tools. Indeed, in the face of unfathomable and ungovernable forces one might well expect renewed expressions of religious faith or a renaissance of magic and superstition to emerge as a response to our profound bewilderment. As we find ourselves being forced to submit to larger impersonal powers it is only natural to want to assign them new names. For in the act of naming we might (like the premoderns before us) discover new tools of reason, tap new resources of knowledge and power, which would allow us to curry favor, to repel misfortune, to divine the will of the gods. It is also to be expected that new beliefs will produce new rituals in which those beliefs may be enacted. As in medieval times, when people believed God's will would be made manifest: the innocent accused would not be burned by holding hot irons or touching scalding water. Nor would he be cast out of the river (for surely the water would reject only the guilty) or defeated in physical combat against an unjust accuser.[22] In this respect, prayer, votary appeasement, and ritualistic divination make sense as practicable "legal" devices designed to influence the outcome of trial.

Clearly a cultural turn toward such premodern forms of reason and the occult practices they invite would carry drastic consequences for law. For one thing, as pressure mounted against conventional forms of Western rationality we would be confronted with diminishing means of regularizing and thus stabilizing the rule of law. Inevitably there would arise a keenly felt need for alternative sources of authority as well as alternative means of interpreting and implementing its demands. Thus instead of relying upon the deductive logic of Sherlock Holmes we might well turn to *Twin Peaks*'s Agent Cooper. In a time of primitive superstition and magical thinking, those who wield what anthropologist Mary Douglas, in *Risk and Blame,* calls "fetish power" are the most likely to step forward. They are the ones with the power to influence or perhaps even control the strange forces around (and within) us. If the social scientists and psychoanalysts no longer seem able to do the job, perhaps the shaman, the magician, the channeler, the media celebrity, the person with natural charisma or special allies can.

Television's elevation of magically intuitive officers of the law who may readily dispense with the technicalities of legal procedure may be considered part of this development. For surely intuitive justice (regarding the factually guilty) and swift deterrent action (to expel whatever is polluting the community) provide a far more immediate sense of reassurance and gratification than drawn-out and increasingly suspect procedural requirements allow. Nor is this the only expression of magical thinking to be found in the popular legal imagination today. The jurisprudence of appearances thrives on magical ideas. It is what we see, for example, when a handful of virtual (highly mediatized) cases generate a virtual, thoroughly self-referential caselaw wholly divorced from the authority of traditional common law. The criminal case involving black defendant Damian Williams illustrates the point.

Williams was tried and convicted for his savage attack on white truck driver Reginald Denny. The attack occurred during the civil unrest that broke out following the acquittal of the white police officers who beat black motorist Rodney King. The meaning many observers subsequently assigned to Williams's ten-year prison sentence for mayhem and assault can be directly traced to their view of King's fate. Those who viewed the acquittal of King's attackers as a travesty of justice regarded Williams's "lenient" sentence as an expression of popular ("reparative") justice. On the other hand, those who saw justice in the officers' acquittal viewed Williams's sentence as inappropriately "soft." In short, through the power of associative logic, virtual ("image-based") justice in one case seems to magically counter virtual injustice in the other. The actual facts and applicable caselaw are simply swept away. And why not? In the jurisprudence of appearances, as elsewhere in the domain of the hyperreal, "reality" is the result of preferred images selectively juxtaposed. It's the magic of television.

It has been my contention in this chapter that the kind of skeptical postmodernism from which Errol Morris shied away, and upon which David Lynch firmly fixed his gaze, is fatal to law as we know it. In such a world, if law functions at all it does so in the primitive (premodern) sense described by Weber and Lévi-Strauss. It functions, that is, in the service of the irrational, as an agency of the supernatural. Unlike the premoderns, however, what skeptical postmodernists leave

out of the picture is the more affirmative dimension of human experience: the ability, regardless of how reason or causality may be config-
ured, to say "yes" to commitment, choice, relationship, meaning,
value, love. Because of this crucial omission, I believe the skeptical
postmodern vision is a reality that ought to be resisted.

To say as much, however, is not to dismiss skeptical postmodernism
out of hand or to encourage its suppression. As we have seen before,
repressed realities have a way of returning. Symptoms of the repressed
tend to strike back. This is why defending against a repugnant or even
terrifying reality by means of denial and displacement will not succeed. To the contrary, as Sam Bowden discovered in his battle against
Max Cady, such defenses are more likely to intensify the battle and
ultimately strengthen the forces they resist. The better course, then, is
to treat skeptical postmodernism as a symptom of our current cultural
condition, to recognize and assess its truth. To do this we must ask:
What is it a sign of? What cultural work does it perform? What lack
or imbalance is it responding to?

Yet, even were we to understand what is behind the skeptical impulse in contemporary culture, the most effective response is most
likely to come not from critical reason alone. What is needed is an
affirmative counterforce of even greater magnitude than the skeptical
impulse it opposes. Such an alternative cultural framework must be
capacious, since it will have to encompass great polarities (such as
the Nietzschean oscillation between Apollonian form and Dionysian
rapture). The affirmative postmodern response I propose seeks to address real cultural needs, and in so doing to seize and nourish the
popular imagination to an even greater degree than its skeptical counterpart.

Of course cultural developments of this kind cannot simply be "leg-
islated" into place. In matters of cultural production we are dealing
with creative vision, the province of the artist, the poet, the writer, the
filmmaker—and also of the advertiser, the public relations expert, the
blockbuster film producer, and the television programmer striving to
maximize audience share. For surely the needs and aspirations of high
art have no lock on the creative impulse. Creativity pulses through
popular culture, where it amply serves the commercial needs of the
marketplace. Indeed, in the current era of the celebrity icon and his
dark double, the deviant Other, these commercial interests have
proven to be the definitive and most pervasive influence of our time.
They are manifestly a dominant force in the production of American
(and global) culture today.

It has always been the task of creative expression to translate the living moment as it is, to give voice and image to what is felt but unthought, feared but unworded, desired but repressed. This task is left unfulfilled, however, when the discrete logic of the commercial mass media force out more complex forms of expression, forms that fail to offer immediate or clear-cut emotional or psychological pay-offs. Of course, by acknowledging the difficulty of broadly communicating critical insights into current social, cultural, and psychological conditions I do not mean to write off the effort altogether. Important cultural expressions may elude popular notice, but this does not stop them from being made. It is the obligation of the cultural observer, and more generally of anyone seeking a more developed understanding of the shifting and multiple realities of self and society, to take note of such works and what they have to tell us about our lives and practices and institutions—including law.

It is with this sense of purpose in mind that I propose we turn our attention next to signs within the current culture that run counter to the skeptical postmodern vision. The vision that informs these cultural trends helps us to see more clearly what law may be like when viewed from the sort of affirmative postmodern perspective I have endorsed throughout this book. This next stage of our inquiry will take us to fundamentals. It urges upon us such questions as, what is criminal after all? Is guilt-by-misfortune still guilt, or simply misfortune? Must the actor be able to change the consequences of his act before the law will condemn him? How much chance will (should) the law bear before it may take away a person's freedom, or his life? It is with these questions in mind that we turn to an examination of Philip Haas's film adaptation of Paul Auster's novel, *The Music of Chance*. Here I believe we see the door to mythic enchantment mysteriously open.

The Affirmative Postmodern Vision: Chancing Upon Order and the Power of Myth

> You tampered with the universe, my friend, and once a
> man does that, he's got to pay the price.
> POZZI

In *The Music of Chance* the power of fate and accident is assumed from the outset. The question now becomes, given such a premise, how are we to find order? Close on the heels of that query is another: is law still possible?

Philip Haas's film begins with a blind leap into the unknown. Jim Nashe, an ex-fireman, has been aimlessly driving around the country for months. He's been kept afloat on money he inherited when his father died. He drives not to arrive anywhere but for the sense of un-burdened momentum that driving allows. Nashe has become truly postmodern: a placeless, will-less subject in a world in which nothing lasts for longer than a moment. He simply follows the road before him.

As his cash runs out, however, Nashe realizes that things can't con-tinue as they have. So when he spots a stranger stumbling along the roadside he doesn't hesitate. Nashe picks him up. His passenger is Pozzi, a professional card player. Pozzi tells Nashe that he was robbed and beaten during a high stakes poker game. The shame of it, Pozzi relates, is that because he's now penniless he'll have to miss the game of his life. Turns out that he was supposed to play poker with a couple of millionaires named Flower and Stone who, according to Pozzi, know nothing about the game. He stood to win a good forty, maybe fifty grand off those two, he says.

Nashe, a man without plans or prospects, is quick to leap onto the path Pozzi lays down. Nashe will use his remaining cash, ten grand, to get Pozzi into the game with Flower and Stone. In exchange Pozzi will split his winnings with Nashe fifty-fifty. And off they go.

As it turns out Flower and Stone are no ordinary millionaires. Re-spectively an accountant and an optometrist by trade, they won their first millions in the lottery. They chose primes: primary numbers, "numbers that refuse to cooperate, that don't change or divide, num-bers that remain themselves for all eternity." Flower adds: "It was the magic combination, the key to the gates of heaven." So it would seem, for ever since hitting the jackpot they can't seem to stop making money. Flower describes it this way: "No matter what we do, every-thing seems to turn out right. . . . It's as though God has singled us out from other men. He's showered us with good fortune and lifted us to the heights of happiness. I know this might sound presumptuous to you, but at times I feel that we've become immortal."

Besides their extraordinary luck, Flower and Stone also have un-usual interests. Stone is a collector. But his collection is crazy: a tele-phone that once belonged to Woodrow Wilson, a pearl earring worn by Sir Walter Raleigh, a half-smoked cigar filched from an ashtray in Winston Churchill's office, William Seward's Bible. Random, beside-the-point stuff. But to Stone it is something else: "Motes of dust that have slipped through the cracks." He preserves things for what they are; their purpose is irrelevant. And now Stone has branched out. He recently purchased a fifteenth-century Irish castle and had the stones, all ten thousand of them, shipped back to America. They're sitting on his property in a heap. He plans to build a wall out of them. Just a straight wall.

Flower's interest is different. Rather than collect, he builds. Flower is an artist. He is constructing a perfect replica, in miniature, of a city. He calls it the City of the World. There are scenes here from Flower's childhood and more recent history. Tiny figures, of Flower and Stone and others. There's the Hall of Justice, the Library, the Bank, the Prison. Everything in the city is in harmony. Even the prisoners are happy, glad they've been punished for their crimes. For now, as Stone admiringly puts it, "they're learning how to recover the goodness within them through hard work."

Surely by now we realize this is no ordinary story about people about to play a game of cards. Surely this is a mythic tale, a parable. Consider the setting: from the outset we are thrust into a world in which choice and direction have disappeared. Nashe doesn't plan, he reacts. Pozzi has made a life out of luck and instinct. And Stone and Flower have gone a step further. Propelled by luck to a mastery of the material world, they have now assumed an almost godlike status. (Perhaps they are immortal, as Stone muses. Perhaps God *has* singled them out.) In Stone's philosophy things need no purpose. It is enough that they exist as they are. That is why he can snatch odds and ends from beneath the black veil of history and render them, well, eternal. For Flower it has become possible to orchestrate reality itself, to shape events according to harmonious principles: law (the Hall of Justice), economy (the Bank), knowledge (the Library), and penitence (the Prison). And, stranger still, it is not only the past that is represented in his City of the World. So, too, as we shall see, is the future: Pozzi's and Nashe's.

If Nashe has relinquished all efforts to control his life, yielding instead to fate, if fate has placed beside him Pozzi, a more experienced player in the field of chance, Flower and Stone turn out to be the oracles of fate's domain. It is as if they already knew Pozzi and Nashe would come, lose all their money at cards, and be forced to pay back the debt with money earned by working for Flower and Stone. What work? Why, to build the stone wall, of course. And that is precisely what transpires. With one additional detail well worth noting.

When the card games begin Pozzi's good fortune is running high. He is in gear, and can hear luck's music playing. He is sure he can't go wrong. But then something happens that stops the music cold. Some hours into playing, Nashe decides to stretch his legs. Where does he go? Back to the room with Flower's City of the World. And what does Nashe do? Why, he snatches up a miniature Flower and a miniature Stone and stows them in his pocket. Mementos of a strange and glorious day, he thinks. Wrong. As Pozzi will later observe: "It's like committing a sin to do a thing like that, it's like violating a fundamental law. . . . You tampered with the universe, my friend, and once a man does that, he's got to pay the price."

And, indeed, from that moment on Pozzi's luck could not be worse. Upon Nashe's return he finds Pozzi losing without end, until finally he is in serious debt to his hosts. In a last desperate measure Nashe puts his car into the pot. But Pozzi loses that too. That's when Nashe arranges the work contract: he and Pozzi will build the wall with Stone's ten thousand stones for an hourly wage, for as long as it takes to pay off the card debt. What choice do they have? After all, Stone has threatened to use his influence to ensure trouble with the authorities if they refused. So their work begins.

There is but one brief stretch to cover now before the story ends. Nashe and Pozzi have consigned themselves to manual labor on Stone's and Flower's property. The wall goes up. The debt goes down. But then there's a snag. Pozzi and Nashe thought that small expenses like food and entertainment would be covered by their employers. But that turns out not to be the case. It seems they'll have to work a few weeks longer than they thought.

Pozzi buckles under the idea of more forced labor. And Nashe agrees that Pozzi, fragile to begin with, probably isn't up to the task. Nashe suggests that Pozzi make a break for it while Nashe stays on to finish out the contract. They say their goodbyes and Pozzi escapes. Early the next morning, however, Nashe wakes to find Pozzi lying outside in the cold grass, bruised and unconscious. He's been beaten silly. Now comes the caretaker with his son-in-law to take Pozzi to the hospital, they say. Nashe is convinced that it was the caretaker, probably with the help of the son-in-law, who were responsible for Pozzi's beating. Retribution for the escape, Nashe figures.

The next days and weeks are hard for Nashe. Without his companion, of whom he had grown fond during their time of shared labor, Nashe battles with guilt, sadness, loneliness, and thoughts of revenge. As times passes, the caretaker begins to take pity on Nashe's solitary duty. So when the wall is nearly completed the caretaker invites Nashe to a tavern for a friendly, celebratory drink with him and his son-in-law. Nashe agrees to go. They drive there together in Nashe's car, the one he lost in cards, which Flower and Stone have apparently given to the caretaker.

A few drinks at the tavern, some friendly talk, and a couple of low stakes games of pool with the son-in-law, with this catch. When the son-in-law loses to Nashe and Nashe waves away his winnings, the son-in-law is not to be outdone. He insists on returning the favor. What'll it be, Nashe? Why, how about a chance to drive his old car back to the house? So be it. Nashe takes the wheel. The old feelings of aimless freedom flood back. Just motion and distance, with a musical score courtesy of the car stereo. Gradually Nashe increases the speed. When he's past seventy the caretaker panics. He snaps off the music. The caretaker's sudden move breaks Nashe's concentration. He's going too fast. There's a headlight ahead, closing in like lightning. Nashe loses control and crashes into some bushes on the side of the road. The caretaker is dead. Injured and stumbling along the roadside, Nashe spots a passing car. It stops, Nashe gets in. The story ends.

A mythic gem. In the land of chance, as it was in the beginning, so it is in the end. One injured chance passenger replaces another. And who knows what adventure is about to unfold, what Stone- and Flower-like design is waiting to be realized? For if things just happen, by fate or chance, the film tells us, there are also the chance gods who have laid up the patterns of fate. Destiny is already made out, in advance—in replica, so to speak.

But in this parable of fate we also learn that there is harmony in destiny's order. The affirmative postmodern story of Pozzi and Nashe confirms it. It is as Stone said about Flower's city: the prisoners are happy in their labor, learning to recover the goodness within them. Just as Nashe did. There was nothing to be found in his aimless and solitary driving. Nashe was no *Easy Rider*. He realized that his shielded existence on the road was an empty fantasy that could not be sustained. It was only when he began his labor with Pozzi that Nashe found what he had previously lacked: human companionship, a sense of sharing with and caring for another human being, the basis for community. Moreover, forced labor though it was, Nashe's work with Pozzi provided him with a sense of worth and purpose. As the wall grew, he and Pozzi took pride in their efforts, and those efforts were plain to see—they were tangible, made in stone.

Fate is strange: in aimless freedom Nashe was a lonely prisoner of placeless speed and empty distance; in forced labor he found solidarity, freedom, and peace of mind. But then the order of things was

disturbed again. Doing penance to pay off their card debt was in harmony with basic principles. But when Nashe, convinced that Pozzi
could no longer take it, coaxed Pozzi to escape, that harmony was
shattered. As in the card game before, and the car ride with the caretaker later, once the music shuts off a payment has to be made. When
Nashe by his rash act stopped the music of harmonious penance, he
could not avoid paying the price, as Pozzi would for his own dishar-
monious repudiation of penance altogether.

And so it goes. From car to car on the road of chance and necessity.
Yet even if human will, the ability to govern or design one's fate, is
forfeited, responsibility for one's actions does not disappear. There is
it seems an order deeper than human designs can go. As the ancient
Greek philosopher Anaximander said more than two thousand years
ago: and into that from which things arise they pass away once more,
according to necessity; for they pay penalty and retribution to each
other for their injustice according to the assessment of Time.[23] If we
breach the natural order, our fate is sealed. Best is it then to seek
harmony; failing that, it is best to seek happiness in penance. So
speaks the wisdom of the fate gods in this contemporary myth of the
invisible, but not indiscernible music of chance.

I believe one may discern here a movement toward affirmation that
has a bearing on law's response to the skeptical postmodern challenge.
Perhaps most striking amid the familiar array of constructed meanings, contingent truths, and strange impersonal forces with which
these films deal is an emerging sense of the deeply felt need to recover
law's mythic dimension. But what can it mean to speak of myth in
this context, and how does mythic thinking figure in the development
of an affirmative postmodern framework for law? On the heels of that
inquiry comes another: how can we be sure that the premodern (or
postmodern-primitive) impulse will not land us in the skeptical postmodern world of *Twin Peaks* and *Lost Highway,* a world of magic
and divination in which detective-shamans and lawyer-priests rule by
intuition and charisma, as ordained by the law of the supernatural?

With increasing skepticism toward the modern ideal of ceaseless
technological progress and the ability to impose reason upon disorder,
with the growing realization that much of what goes on in society
and in our own psyches will never yield to human control, it may not
be surprising to witness renewed attempts within popular culture to
come to grips with nonrational forces—forces like unbounded rage,
desire, chance, and fate. This is what we are seeing in films by
Scorsese, Lynch, Haas, and others.

The modern era has gone into decline, and faith in modern calculative rationality and its instrumental ideals has diminished. The marvels of modern technology? Yes, of course. But what of machines of mass destruction? What of technological waste and resource depletion? As for the rational engineering of society by the state, the fall of Communism has attested to the fallacy of that ideal. And while free economies have no doubt fared better, uninterrupted progress is hardly assured. Neither governments nor transnational corporations are able confidently to predict, much less control, the direction of the market forces that govern their fate.[24] Moving from the "macro" to the "micro" level, what we now see is that the model of the rational agent as the best generator of social wealth is being overtaken by other, far less rational images of the multiple self.

Suffice it to say, if the mysterious invisible forces of the free market are still perceived to be active in the world today, it seems likely that they are not operating alone. What names and attributes such other nonrational forces will acquire remains to be seen.[25] But it seems clear enough that the prospect ahead is for more mythic tales about them. Granted, this may not be the naive (unreflective/credulous) mythicizing of Homer and Ovid. The (hyper-)self-reflectivity and habitual self-questioning that characterize the current postmodern era are hardly likely to carve out an exception for mythic storytelling. More akin to the post-Homeric spirit of Greek tragedy, the myths we tell, infused as they may also be with strange irrational and impersonal powers, will nevertheless remain ours: *we know that we make them.* Just as we know that this does not rob them of their reality and truth—notwithstanding their partiality, their ambiguity, and their infuriating contradictions.

Here, then, is the heart of the constructivist ethos: gripped by the boundless, ever cognizant of the limits of our knowledge, language, and understanding, we are left with no choice but to redefine the bounds of meaning and experience again and again, without end, without completion. And today it is precisely this kind of self-conscious mythicizing, in order to establish an order we can live in, that is in store for law and justice as well.

One such mythic construct has already attained special prominence in mainstream culture today: the Gothic revival.[26] The public's fascination with dark, supernatural forces—vampires,[27] werewolves, witches, demons, and of course Satan himself, as well as a variety of Frankensteinian monsters, aliens, and hybrids—is a clear indication of this cultural trend. The ungovernable rage and passion these creatures embody evidently haunt the postmodern psyche.[28] It bears noting, however, that what we are seeing is significantly different from other historic periods when the horror genre gained such cultural prominence. As Mark Edmundson points out, visionaries like Blake and Shelley perceived Gothic forces as obstacles to fuller self-integration. In their quest for a loftier vision of Selfhood, these late-eighteenth-century poets were compelled to confront their own destructive, sadomasochistic impulses. They consciously staged battles on a mythic terrain where opposing forces of light and darkness fought for dominion over the soul.[29] By deliberately confronting their greatest fears they hoped to achieve "a great release of power for good."[30] Yet this kind of deliberate confrontation is precisely what contemporary American Gothic lacks.

Rather than healthfully confronting the illicit impulse for what it is, terrifying the popular imagination today seems more like a form of temporary relief from pressing, albeit undiagnosed anxieties. Worse, it appears to be a form of unconscious titillation. In this respect, the rise in preoccupation with sadomasochism and the rise of draconian legal measures against alien Others appear to be related. As Edmundson observes: "In a culture that is in many ways dominated by Gothic, the sadomasochistic mode, in love and all other human relations as well, will come progressively to the fore. For S & M is Gothic uncontested by an effective alternative drive; S & M is where Gothic . . . wants to go."[31] This development is part and parcel of the jurisprudence of appearances. We need the deviant Other to pay the price for our sins. Thus we continue to generate increasingly punitive legal measures and more intuitive law enforcement, to the detriment of the rule of law. The mounting fury that fuels this self-defeating cycle is precisely what Shelley and Blake warned against. It leads not to self-integration but to additional psychic splitting.

Thus we return to the pivotal question: How is the cycle of repression and displacement to be broken? How might we tap into a cultural counterforce, embodied in a self-reflectively posited mythic framework, for belief and understanding that is strong enough to invite terrible knowledge (of strange forces within and without) without simultaneously inducing despair, denial, or radical skepticism? This is the perennial task of mythic affirmation: to confront what we fear most, to transform anxiety and denial into wisdom and affirmation. It is a task that the skeptical postmodern vision cannot fulfill.

To live with such tragic wisdom no doubt requires a robust constitution. As Edmundson has said: "It takes considerable power, intellectual and moral, to both express one's own obsessions in the most eloquently passioned language, and to take up a critical listening position."[32] But where is such power to be encountered today? And are our cultural and psychological resources for enchantment and belief sufficient for such a task?

[And one day the Muses of Olympus, daughters of Zeus, taught Hesiod glorious song; and this word first the goddesses said: W]e know how to speak many false things as though they were true; but we know, when we will, to utter true things.

HESIOD (c. eighth century B.C.)

Whereas the historian, in his commitment to the facts, can mislead the seeker of truth, the poet, like the lawyer, aims at an altogether different kind of truth, which is most aptly expressed by a fiction.

PHILIP SIDNEY (c. 1580)

EIGHT

Law's Need for Enchantment
Perils and Possibilities

We crave enchantment, but fear deceit. In an ultimate sense we all share the predicament of Scheherazade of *The Thousand and One Nights:* sentenced to death, seeking a stay. Like Scheherazade, we tell stories in the hope of deferring the final sentence long enough to learn and perhaps leave traces of who we are. Long enough, if we are lucky, to acquire moral wisdom and spiritual fulfillment. Meanwhile, along the way, a world of meaning is born. As the stories we hear and tell grow and weave their way into a larger mosaic, a discrete culture takes shape. There we find the archive of images, characters, plot lines, and scenarios with which we make sense of ourselves and others and the world around us. And there too lie the various tools of narrative, the techniques of meaning making, of persuasion and critical interpretation, which prompt (or perhaps alter) our opinions, produce knowledge, and cultivate judgment.

The culture into which we are born teaches us specific narrative practices and expectations. What kinds of stories may be told to whom, when, in what way and with what effect? Through such practices we acquire degrees of communicative competency in the various spheres of professional, commercial, and personal interaction that make up our daily lives. At the same time we learn the limits of our competency and the need to seek out experts to help us achieve our goals.

Lawyers are experts of this sort. They are, among other things, professional interpreters of the law's stories and professional storytellers in their own right. Lawyers are privy to words and images and narrative techniques whose power may bring the full force of law to bear upon others or prevent that force from affecting those who have availed themselves of the lawyer's protection. In short, lawyers are professional persuaders trained to know which words and images work best when. They also know where words of power may be found (in what statutes, regulations, and court opinions) and how to artfully knit the formal words of law together with words of their own. The results of such handiwork are narratives that integrate legal claims with the most persuasive story that can be devised under the circumstances. This is the *techne* (or art) of persuasion Aristotle studied in his *Poetics, Rhetoric,* and *Prior Analytics.* Notably, in cataloguing the various methods of proof Aristotle was fully aware of the convergence between legal persuasion and dramatic construction. He understood, as did the early Renaissance lawyer Sir Philip Sidney, that the so-called fictional method of the tragic poets is essential to the lawyer's profession. The great American novelist John Barth conveyed the gist of what binds and impels lawyers and poets alike when he wrote: "It's in words that the magic is . . . but the words in one story aren't magical in the next. The real magic is to understand which words work, and when, and for what; the trick is to learn the trick." [1]

Here is the magic and the trick of legal persuasion. Lawyers are storytellers. It has always been so. And though the stories lawyers tell and the ways of telling surely change over time—whether oral, printed, audiovisual, or digitally synthesized, or in the form of mystery, melodrama, or heroic myth—the endeavor itself remains the same. Worlds of meaning are being cast upon the public stage for others to share. And for each world we may be induced to enter there is a truth and a sense of justice for judgment's sake. But that is not all. For we must also come to see that as law's stories change so too do reason and judgment itself. The way we understand truth, fiction, reason, and desire and how each stands in relation to the other is also contingent upon the kind of story we tell (or enter). But what stories does our culture allow? Stories that allow us to discern the truth that may be found in desire or the desire that resides in and gives shape to truth? Stories that help us to recognize the fictions contained in reason or the truths (within fiction and desire) that reason often represses?

We crave enchantment and fear deceit, but with different intensities at different points in time. The history of culture may be viewed as a history of reason's oscillation between *mythos* and *logos,* magic and logic, inspiration and *techne,* irrational desire and rational calculation, enchantment and suspicion. And one lesson history teaches is that prolonged imbalances at one end of the rationalist-irrationalist spectrum tend to invite destabilizing oscillations toward the opposite extreme. The reign of unconstrained irrationality produces cultural bursts of repressive rationality just as repressive rationality leads to outbreaks of immoderate irrationality. Thus, for example, we witness Plato's harsh response to the irrational enchantments of Gorgias and the other Sophists of his generation during the fifth century B.C. in

Athens. As the century waned, the beguiling word magic of the Sophists gave way to a highly rationalized philosophy based on the logic of syllogistic reasoning.

In their renunciation of rhetoric and poetry Plato and his philosophical descendants sought to discredit (if they could not banish outright) those who publicly practiced the "truth-subverting" art of persuasion through seduction and the manipulation of desire. And in this aim they were largely successful. Yet, the ensuing divorcement of reason and desire would in time break down. Such was the case, for example, during the first and second century A.D. when a new generation of rhetoricians revived the Gorgian and Pythagorean traditions of magic and inspiration in a movement that came to be known as the "second sophistic."[2] But we needn't travel so far to find similar patterns and reversals in reason's oscillation between magic and logic.

Consider, for example, the advent of modernity in the era of the European Enlightenment. With the triumph of Cartesian rationality (which celebrated universal truths through the scientific method of clear and distinct ideas), the ancient and medieval rhetorical tradition slid into near oblivion. As Descartes would say: "Those who have the strongest power of reasoning, and who most skillfully arrange their thoughts in order to render them clear and intelligible, have the best power of persuasion even if they can but speak the language of lower Brittany and have never learned Rhetoric."[3] For rationalists like Newton and Descartes, truth needs no embellishment; in its natural state it is naked and pure. The language in which one finds it is but a superficial, inessential dressing that may be cast away with no loss to truth itself. And if truth but awaits discovery it is the deductive logic of causal reasoning that will find it. Newton metaphorically set the universe running like a giant clockwork, and ever since scientists and philosophers have been calculating the causal mechanics of observable human behavior and natural events. Absent rigorous quantitative methods, they said, nothing could be reliably known. What escaped the calculus was all but meaningless.

In this way, scientific truth came to be pitted against the nonquantifiable knowledge of the arts and humanities, just as the deductive logic of scientific reason came to be pitted against the irrationality of emotion and desire. To embrace the poet's fictional method would now become tantamount to embracing deceit. Hence the (still) popular sentiment of the modern era: if the lawyer is like the poet it is because they both lie. Both move the passions with their honeyed words, using eloquence to divert us from the unadulterated truth that lies beneath their veil of rhetoric. Both seek to twist the truth the better to serve their own fictions and deceits. In short, from within the rationalist narrative of the modern era it becomes evident that the emotions can never produce knowledge, nor can fiction ever be a source of truth.

In more recent times, however, we have new narratives about these matters. As a result, the rationalist premises of modernity have been significantly eroded. Today even Descartes's skillful deployment of rhetoric no longer remains hidden from view.[4] Indeed, everywhere we look there are signs of the return of the repressed. Irrational forces (both within and without) have broken free of modernity's rational censor. As Jonathan Lear writes, "Enlightenment consciousness abandons itself to thinking. One might view the postmodern consciousness as originating in the collapse of this defense."[5] The power and presence of chance, fate, fury, and desire have come crashing into contemporary consciousness. To be sure, modernity's repression of these forces had never been entirely successful. Newton and Descartes had their detractors from the beginning: those who felt left out of the scientists' systematized, mechanical world. They were the poets and free spirits of their age, writers like Blake, Wordsworth, Goethe, and the later German Romantics—Schiller, Heine, and Holderlin, to mention only a few. What of the spirit? they cried. What of the human genius for living the life of feelings, passions, heroics, novelty, invention, sacrifice? Where within the quantified world of the scientists is there room for this kind of experience, this sense of reality?

The Romantic rebellion against the repressive and reductionist impulses of modern rationality was but one sign of modernity's rationalist imbalance. By the end of the nineteenth century Dostoevsky's underground man would proclaim outright: better insanity than to become a cipher in someone else's system. It is a sentiment Kafka would refine further in his disorienting tales of bureaucratic rationality gone awry. It is a sentiment that was born of and that bred rebellion. It is in this spirit that writers as different from one another as Hermann Hesse, Nikos Kazantzakis, Henry Miller, James Joyce, and Albert Camus could be joined. For each was driven by a profound sense of cultural lack; each in his own way was seeking a force powerful enough to oppose the desiccating and repressive effects of immoderate rationalism. Not surprisingly, the play of the irrational, particularly chance and desire, figured prominently in their work. And not theirs alone.

Whether it is the incantatory magic in the poetry of Mallarmé, the "magic dictation" in the writings of André Breton, the magic of chance operations in the musical compositions of John Cage or the arbitrary cut-ups of William Burroughs or the paint drippings of Jackson Pollock or the plot configurations of Paul Auster, whether it is the deep mystery of Being's self-disclosure and withholding in the philosophy of Heidegger or the theater of cruelty of Antonin Artaud, or the strange curative powers (the *pharmicon*) of the *logos* in the works of Freud or Derrida or Lacan, the resurgence of the irrational in contemporary culture is unmistakable. Nor have legal theorists escaped from this antirationalist tide. One need only consider such recent developments as the critical legal studies movement to see that this is so. It turns out that a driving force behind much of the scholarly work the movement produced lay in the felt need to expose irrationality: in the caselaw, in traditional legal scholarship, and even in legal reasoning and causal analysis itself.

In this respect the advent of postmodernity may be viewed as ushering in a period of both danger and opportunity. The danger is that it invites a new excess, a surge of the irrational. In terms of opportunity, it offers an important corrective to the distortions and unduly repressive impulses at work within the modern Enlightenment ideals of objective truth and universal reason. For example, language now comes to be seen as much more than mere dressing. Many thoughtful scholars today across a broad range of disciplines reject the traditional modern view that objective truth rides into human understanding like freight on the backs of verbal boxcars. The emerging view is that truth is not something that can be disengaged from language and scooped up pure. What we know about ourselves, others, and the world around us is inextricably embedded in cultural forms of understanding.

The various language practices in which we engage every day are constitutive not only of social reality, but also of our own self-identity. As cognitive psychologist Jerome Bruner has put it, our understanding of self is both "situated" and "distributed."[6] In other words, the meanings we carry inside our heads are to a significant extent continuous with the cultural world around us. They are constantly being affirmed and negotiated anew in our various interactions with others. Shifts in self-identity follow shifts in our language practices, in the stories we tell ourselves and others in specific contexts. This is what it means to talk about the multiple (or "narratively distributed") self. Put simply, mind and self are part of the cultural world in which we live. The universal autonomous self is not a given in nature, something we are born with, as the Enlightenment perspective held out. It is contingent, multiple, and actively constructed in discretely contextualized narrative practices.

In addition to substituting a more complex understanding for modernity's naive idealizations regarding the purportedly "prepackaged" natural state of truth, reason, and the autonomous self, the recent cultural developments I have been describing manifest an emancipatory quality. For example, one finds here a concerted effort to break free of the unproductive, anxiety-producing dichotomies that pervade the modernist mindset. The postmodern perspective shuns simplistic "either-or" distinctions between truth and fiction, reason and desire, logic and myth, self and other. Here too a new complexity has settled in. It is not uncommon to encounter within postmodern scholarship, literature, and art a multiplicity of discrete truths, disparate logics, and multiple selves. This enhanced awareness of plurality carries with it a heightened sensitivity to how discrete realities—different senses of truth, logic, or self—may interpenetrate one another.

Once we come to view our sense of self and social reality as something that is situated and distributed through the stories we tell ourselves and share with others, it becomes far easier to acknowledge and self-consciously grapple with its constructed, multiple, and overlapping characteristics. Enhanced sensitivity to the different ways in which discrete communicative practices shape and inform reality invites the query: what stories and images do people use under what circumstances (as lawyers, judges, and jurors) to establish a particular normative reality or effect? This kind of critical inquiry is useful in a variety of contexts, from media fluency (what are advertisers, newscasters, docudrama makers telling us about ourselves, others, and society?) to political decision making and legal judgment. It calls upon us to become more active interpreters of the symbolic forms of meaning and communication (rational and irrational, conscious and unconscious) that help to make up our sense of self and social reality.

In this respect, I believe that postmodern thought may be viewed as carrying forward in new and sophisticated ways important attributes of the premodern rhetorical tradition. Indeed, one of the definitive attributes of a rhetorically sophisticated culture is its emphasis upon learning the diverse strategies of meaning- and world-making. Postmodern deconstruction, in this sense, teaches the art of discerning how discrete social, political, legal, and self realities are constituted and sustained based on concrete practices. What are the assumptions, beliefs, feelings, and expectations, the express or hidden desires and ideologies that make up a community's social, political, legal, and popular cultural forms of communication? And how do these forms influence, conflict with, or strive to suppress one another?

Cultural and cognitive psychologists, linguists, anthropologists, and philosophers, among others, are addressing these questions in a variety of discrete social and cultural contexts. What we are learning is the extent to which what we know (as true) is constructed by the communal language practices and cognitive tool kits we inherit and adapt from the culture we live in. These cultural and linguistic competencies ready us to interpret in particular ways our experience of ourselves, others, and the world around us. This is not to deny the universality of certain physical laws or emotional states. Rather, it is to account for the different ways in which people make sense of things at different points in time and in different cultural settings. In this way, understanding culture in rhetorical terms also comports with key constructivist insights.

In order to appreciate adequately how discrete cognitive and cultural constructs ready us for particular kinds of meanings, truths, and realities, we must increase our awareness of the various beliefs, desires, motives, and expectations, among other intentional states, that are involved in the meaning-making process. Such a study focuses not only on what people think and say in specific contexts while engaging in particular communicative practices, but also on the specific cognitive and cultural tools they think and speak with. If we ignore this cultural and cognitive dimension we lose a vital component of what Dilthey calls "lived experience," the meanings that make us who we are. In this respect, then, philosophers intent on exploring the ramifications of posited rationalist ideals cannot escape a significant degree of artificiality. For along the way they will need to assume away the messy details of lived experience, including the obstinate irrationality of the human mind. The stories they tell will not speak about the unconscious, about explosive desire and violent rage, or about the forces of chance and fate that also condition human actions and judgments.

In short, undue rationality unduly represses what it cannot make sense of. This lesson was learned the hard way by the great Liberal philosopher John Stuart Mill. Mill's father, a staunch believer in Jeremy Bentham's utilitarian calculus, set out to mold his son into the perfect rational chooser. In retrospect, Mill's ensuing mental breakdown is hardly surprising. As he subsequently wrote in his *Autobiography:*

> [I]t occurred to me to put the question directly to myself, "Suppose that all your objects in life were realized; that all the changes in institutions and opinions which you are looking forward to, could be completely effected at this very instant: would this be a great joy and happiness to you?" And an irrepressible self-consciousness distinctly answered,

"No!" At this my heart sank within me: the whole foundation on which my life was constructed fell down.[7]

It was the Romantic poetry of William Wordsworth to which Mill ultimately turned in an effort to restore a more compelling sense of life's drama, a sense that rational calculation had all but drained away.

Mill's experience alerts us to a crucial reason why we crave enchantment: on an individual level, because it is what gives meaning to our existence, and on a communal level, because no culture can flourish for long if its core beliefs are not periodically reenacted in shared symbolic forms. The unconscious empowers the life of the mind, the meanings and beliefs that we live by, just as myth empowers shared meanings and beliefs in cultural life. This power, however, must be at least periodically revivified in shared rituals and social dramas. One might say it takes art to animate belief. We need forms of creative expression that integrate the conscious and unconscious mind.

This is something that savvy lawyers, like all savvy storytellers, know. It is the poet's fictional method that animates reality, that gives meaning and life to naked facts and in so doing compels action and judgment. As Kathy Eden notes, it is only in recent years that we have come to recognize "how much the tragic stage and the law courts of fifth- and fourth-century Athens owe to one another."[8]

That debt, as Sidney argued in the late sixteenth century, includes the imaginative ground-plots of the fictional method. This is the lesson that the prosecutor in the first trial involving the police officers who beat Rodney King failed to learn. Like a quintessential modern rationalist, Assistant District Attorney White thought that the truth was simply "out there." The jury had but to look at the "reality" that George Holliday's amateur video displayed. White paid a price for such naive realism. For it was naiveté in this respect that led him to overlook the compelling narrative package in which the defendants' attorneys had skillfully woven Holliday's images. The jury "looked" at the video, as White told them to do, but when they did it was the defense story that the images played out. What had White missed? The existence of the defense team's imaginative ground-plot. In short, he failed to engage the fictional method. That failure was twofold, for he neither constructed a compelling narrative of his own nor even attempted to deconstruct the compelling plot design of opposing counsel's narrative strategy. The latter failure is the inevitable consequence of being oblivious to the use of the fictional method to give life to reality inside (and outside) the courtroom.

In saying as much I mean for it to be clearly understood that endorsing the fictional method is not equivalent to sanctioning lies and deception. Once the modern proclivity for dichotomous thinking has been overcome, the simplistic notion that one is dealing with either objective truth or subjective fallacy may be similarly avoided. What we are talking about are the practical necessities of legal persuasion: how to make physical and testimonial evidence into a compelling narrative for the sake of legal judgment. Legal conflicts typically concern events that must be reconstructed. The jury therefore needs to "see" as clearly and compellingly as possible what happened and, most importantly, why. This is what the fictional method is for. It is not for the sake of deceit, but in recognition of the necessity for dramatic recreation. Facts do not speak for themselves; neither do values.

The key question thus becomes, how does an advocate create a just representation of the human actions that lie at the heart of the legal controversy at issue? The lawyer's job is, as Aristotle wrote, to consider intelligently what are the best available means of persuasion. What Aristotle did not go on to specify, as did the Sophists and rhetoricians who carefully studied the power and techniques of the fictional method, was precisely how a particular persuasive strategy might be most effectively implemented under a given set of circumstances.

The trial is a test of truth and justice within a specific concrete context. In our adversarial tradition, following the principles Aeschylus laid down twenty-five hundred years ago in his tragic drama the *Eumenides,* opposing truth claims are publicly tried in the search for justice. As Philip Sidney argued five hundred years ago, there is nothing deceitful in testing out claims to truth and justice that may or may not ultimately be deemed worthy of belief. Indeed, under the conditions of uncertainty that typically prevail in such situations, all we have is good judgment. Absent any better guarantee, our best hope for truth and justice rests in the most persuasive warrants for believing particular claims under particular circumstances.

Such claims in a court of law may be warranted by factual truths or by legal fictions, or perhaps they will be warranted by symbolic truths or by the claims of higher legal principle. This is not the case insofar as historical or scientific studies are concerned. Historians, for example, traditionally rely upon factual truth claims warranted by painstaking archival research (though to an increasing extent postmodern historians are resorting to the fictional method in an effort to animate the past). For lawyers, however, the situation is different. In legal contests of truth facts must be animated in order to bring to life not simply the actions in question, but also the motives underlying those actions. As Kathy Eden has written, the fictional method includes "both the equitable and the tragic reconstruction of past events in the light of the agents' inherently irrecoverable intentions."[9] Only through such "fictional" reconstructions may judgment actively meld the potentially disparate claims of factual truth, legal rules, and a sense of what justice requires.

In short, legal judgment requires an understanding not simply of what occurred, but of why. It takes the inventiveness of art, the linchpin of the fictional method, to produce vivid words and images that will allow a decision maker to enter into the experience of another, to feel what someone else (whether victim or accused wrongdoer) must have been feeling under the circumstances in question. Indeed, it is precisely in this respect that Sidney regards the fictional method as superior to history and philosophy. For only the former has the power to evoke the reasons for action. In so doing the fictional method empowers the advocate to move others to rage or fear or pity and to the kind of judgment that does justice to such feelings. Consider, for example, the following scenario.

A man mistakenly shoots a police officer who was actually coming to his aid. Immediately prior to the shooting, however, the gunman had chased a rowdy gang of would-be robbers from his home, though not before they had broken into his sister's bedroom. It was nighttime and the street was poorly lit. A melee was in progress. The shooter sees a man with a gun walking toward him from the group of malefactors that had just accosted him. He shoots. Should the law condemn him outright for wounding a police officer, or should it permit a jury of his peers to assess whether this was an understandable and perhaps excusable act of self-defense under the circumstances? Only by permitting the jury an opportunity to enter into the actor's state of mind, to feel what he was feeling at the time, may the law "correct" factual and legal wrongdoing (he shot an innocent man) with a more just result (but it wasn't his fault).[10]

Factual truth claims (about such matters as intent, motive, or individual accountability) cannot resolve recurring questions about the demands of justice in the particular case. But even beyond the realm of factual truth alone, the fictional method has an essential role to play in the pursuit of justice. And in this respect as well the lawyer (unlike the traditional historian) cannot be limited to the claim of facts alone. For to do so would be to abrogate the lawyer's responsibility to other forms of truth or truth-trumping principles that may be no less essential to justice in the particular case. Here, too, it takes the inventiveness of art, the vividness of image and character, to lift a decision maker out of the banal temporality of everyday life so that heroic truths or principles may be realized (perhaps in mythic time) inside the courtroom. Only in this way may a decision maker be moved to assume the role—to feel the feelings—of the hero. Someone with the strength of will to set aside factual truths for the sake of a higher mandate. Someone who is able to say that the state's factual truth claims will not count if they have not been proven beyond a reasonable doubt or if they were obtained in violation of the accused's privacy or dignity rights and thus in violation of the constitutional limits that have been set upon the potentially tyrannical powers of the state.

We witness this kind of principled resistance to the common-sense insistence upon factual truth, for example, in cases involving the Fifth Amendment right against compelled self-incrimination. It is well settled that criminal confessions obtained by state coercion must be excluded from evidence at trial. This is so even if the confession proves to be factually reliable. As one legal commentator has observed, what is at stake here is "an almost metaphysical notion that encouraging a person to participate in his own 'downfall,' i.e., his criminal conviction, is inconsistent with the person's inherent dignity as a human being, whether or not he is guilty." [11] In a similar vein, Justice Byron White wrote in the path-breaking United States Supreme Court decision *Jackson v. Denno:* "[I]mportant human values are sacrificed where an agency of the government, in the course of securing a conviction, wrings a confession out of an accused against his will." [12] Justice White went on to note the "deep-rooted feeling that the police must obey the law while enforcing the law; that in the end life and liberty can be as much endangered from illegal methods used to convict those thought to be criminals as from the actual criminals themselves." [13]

It is the peculiar virtue of the judiciary to articulate precisely this sort of counter-majoritarian (and counterintuitive) principle. When in the heat of the moment popular sentiment cries out for convictions based on factual guilt no matter how such guilt may have been ascertained, the judiciary's role as constitutional caretaker becomes most evident. Higher legal principles must at times check popular sentiments, like the felt need for retribution, if individual rights, due process, and other constitutional safeguards against excessive state power are to retain practical meaning.

To be sure, popular sentiment and the everyday wisdom of common sense have virtues of their own. This is why ordinary members of the community are called upon (and in some cases, such as the criminal trial, are constitutionally *required*) to assess the reliability of the physical evidence, the credibility of the witnesses who testify, and the persuasiveness of the parties' competing claims. In undertaking this crucial role, jurors are expected to be guided by their own common experience: what "everyone knows" about the way things are and how people usually behave in the world around us.

In this way, our system of law plainly refuses to privilege a single source of knowledge (whether it is based on unexamined opinions or technical legal or other forms of expertise) over other sources. It achieves this diversity by authorizing different cognitive and discursive practices (whether ordinary common sense or judicial prudence) inside the courtroom. In short, multiple forms of discourse, knowledge, and power are deemed to be necessary to reckon with the complex demands of truth and justice in the particular case. The trial in this sense is a contest among disparate warrants for belief. Its genius lies in allowing the discrete virtues of different forms of knowledge and discourse to compete in the struggle of persuasion. Factual truth competes with symbolic truth, and both compete with the demands of higher legal principle. Yet it is also a system that is susceptible to various kinds of failure. This is what we see, for example, when the virtues of a particular source of knowledge couched in a particular form of discourse are either silenced or ignored. This is what occurs when legal principles such as the presumption of innocence or the requirement of proof beyond a reasonable doubt are drowned out by popular passions and the irrational craving for retribution. And it is what happens when the unpopular judicial task of repudiating factual guilt on the basis of some counterintuitive principle of law is forsaken as politically risky or undesirable.

When a court fails to uphold its responsibilities as constitutional caretaker, when in fear of public censure or of losing an election a judge sets popularity as a benchmark for judgment, the rights of all citizens are in danger of being diminished. For how else is the meaning of constitutionally specified individual rights to be tested and affirmed if not in cases involving state overreaching? And what practical meaning can such rights retain if factual truth continues to trump or silence their claims in particular cases? When we prefer criminal convictions even if they require condoning unlawful police invasions of individual privacy (or violations of the right against unreasonable search and seizure or the right against self-incrimination or the right to a jury trial or the right to confront one's accusers), then those rights lose whatever meaning they may once have had.

A general observation may be offered here. When the special virtues of a particular source of knowledge as expressed in a particular form of discourse are ignored or silenced, the special virtues of the triumphant discourse may turn into defects. This is what we see, for example, when common sense rather than judicial prudence governs constitutional interpretation.[14] It happens when a jury's ordinary common sense is shaped and informed by mass media images, when it becomes the product of manipulative public relations campaigns, including hyperreal, emotionally charged media events, spawned and driven by the *mutually assured seduction* between journalists and lawyers. Simply put, when a lawyer's adversarial interests and the needs of the marketplace merge, the virtues of common sense are at risk. For it is in the nature of such media spectacles to exploit stereotypes, intensify passions, and manipulate hidden or disguised rage and desire. This is achieved on the basis of principles well known to media advertisers and public relations experts whose stock in trade consists of highly charged, immediately compelling images and discourse. The danger is that such techniques tend to supplant the realities of lived experience with media-realities, which is to say, with realities constructed to meet the demands of the marketplace.

Truth may never be guaranteed, but there are discrete strategies that may be undertaken in its behalf. The first step is to determine the kind of truth being sought, and the means by which we seek it. As we have seen, adversaries may lay claim to different kinds of truth in any given set of circumstances. Factual truth, symbolic truth, or some overriding legal principle may be warranted. That is a matter for the decision maker in question, whether judge or juror, to determine. Similarly, the means undertaken in its behalf may be tested: is the chosen strategy of persuasion illicit? Does it do justice to the kind of truth that it serves, or does it rely upon skewed data, hidden impulses, or illegitimate claims to irrelevant self-gratification?

Natural truths—the necessary laws of physics or geometry, say—are rarely dispositive in legal dramas. For example, while it may be true that physical laws determine how a person actually falls down a flight of stairs, it requires human testimony, and the ensuing variables of conflicting narratives, to establish whether someone fell or was deliberately pushed. In legal matters, therefore, the objective certainty of a logical syllogism typically gives way to probabilities, to judging under conditions of uncertainty. This brings us to the domain of what Aristotle called the enthymeme. According to Aristotle, "[m]ost of the things about which we make decisions, and into which therefore we inquire, present us with alternative possibilities. For it is about our actions that we deliberate and inquire, and all our actions have a contingent character; hardly any of them are determined by necessity." In other words, judgments typically made under conditions of uncertainty are typically arrived at on the basis of what people generally tend to take as true in the ordinary case. This is where the enthymeme comes in.

Enthymemes may be understood as the common constructs we carry around in our heads that help us make sense of what happens in our own experience and in the world around us. Call it common sense, for the stock of enthymemes is but the storehouse of our everyday knowledge. It is here that we find the various unconsciously deployed cultural and cognitive constructs—the recurrent scripts and simplified worlds, the familiar stories and scenarios, the popular character types and plot lines—that serve as the building blocks of reality making. This is the stuff out of which we make sense of our lives and the world around us in our everyday practices. These are the raw materials out of which lawyers, like all storytellers, create compelling narratives. When Gerry Spence establishes his character before a jury as authentic and reliable he is tapping a basic cognitive construct: namely, that it is easier to believe people we trust. When Barry Slotnick establishes the character of his client, Bernhard Goetz, as just like you and me, he is tapping a basic cognitive construct: namely, that it is easier to sympathize with someone's fears and motives when you can put yourself in their shoes (or "walk around in someone's hide," as Spence likes to put it). Conversely, when the person in question is cast as wholly Other, in the image of the predatory criminal that we see in film and on TV, it is far easier to condemn his actions (perhaps to death) without sympathy or mercy.

This, then, is the way of the enthymeme in the practice of common sense. It functions by evoking what everybody knows: "This is the way this kind of person may be expected to behave." "This is the way heroic characters rise to the challenge of historic judgment." "This is the way we achieve 'total justice' in this kind of case." "This is the way stories of this kind—be it melodrama, mystery, or heroic myth—are expected to come out." In short, by prompting discrete elements of ordinary common sense in the minds of decision makers the legal advocate endeavors to create in court a replica of the world we know from our lived experience. That is what persuasive narratives are for: by conjuring the familiar principles and images, the causal or associative, the logical or emotional links between character and action, motive and judgment, historic event and courtroom drama, legal narratives provide the means and impetus for judgment. The stories lawyers tell lead decision makers to identify with or distance themselves from the players in question, to enter into a recreated drama of the past or a live drama contemporaneously taking place inside the court. In this way, advocates guide the decision maker to a particular understanding, a discrete state of mind that includes the cognitive content emotions provide, that, all things considered, provides the most compelling grounds for judgment.

To be sure, the ordinary expectations and various meaning-making tools or constructs that may be tapped in a particular case may serve a number of different truth claims set within a variety of narrative frames. As we have seen, lawyers may invoke the mystery genre as the imaginary ground-plot for fact-based truth (as prosecutors Marcia Clark and Christopher Darden attempted to do in the O. J. Simpson double murder case). Or perhaps they will seek to tap the heroic genre for the sake of "symbolic" truth (as Johnnie Cochran did in Simpson's defense and as Gerry Spence did in defense of Randy Weaver). Alternatively, lawyers may also tap the heroic genre in an effort to narrate law's "higher" truths. Notions like the presumption of innocence, guilt beyond a reasonable doubt, the need to limit state power and to protect individual privacy, autonomy, and dignity may in the end trump factual truth (as defense lawyers sought in behalf of Ernesto Miranda before the United States Supreme Court).

Regardless of the kind of truth one is pursuing, however, whether factual, legal, or symbolic, the need for an imaginative ground-plot (which is to say, for the art of the fictional method) remains constant. It is unrealistic to think otherwise. Truth in the service of justice will not speak for itself. It is up to the advocate, like the playwright, the poet, the novelist, to give it voice, motive, plot, and drama. It is this that gives life to a particular truth claim and the sense of a just outcome in a given case. It is this narrative choice that allows the force of mercy or of some counterintuitive legal principle (such as the right to be shielded from improper state violence) to trump if need be the naked demands of factual truth.

To establish the verisimilitude of a given truth claim one must go beyond naked (which is to say, unnarrated) facts or arid logic alone. What we are also dealing with here is the stuff of desire. As Aristotle wrote, "the cause of action and the cause of choice is desire and reasoning directed to some end."[15] Motion is impossible without desire— including the motion of legal drama. And it is the power of desire, rage, pity, fear, mercy that provides the magic, enchantment, or seduction rhetoricians like Gorgias studied and taught others to master and thus manipulate at will. To manipulate, but to what end? Here we come to the crux of the matter. For if the advent of postmodernity may be viewed as ushering in a period of great opportunity, that is not to say it is without profound dangers of its own.

For one thing, postmodern insights about the "constructedness" of meaning introduce a new sense of radical contingency. If meanings are constructed, surely they may be deconstructed and reconstructed at will. What guarantee, then, is there to stave off the threat of the malevolent manipulation of "fictions"? In short, the constructivist perspective of postmodernism raises the fear of a collapse in standards for reliable reality testing. If it is all being constructed, we can hear postmodern anxiety whisper, isn't one construction as true (or as false) as any other? This fear is fueled by advances in communication technology that increasingly blur the line between fiction and reality (from digitally manipulated photography and videos to computerized simulations of reality), and by the shrewd exploitation of that confusion by savvy advertisers, politicians, and lawyers alike.

In sum, as the modernist benchmark for ideal truth and objectivist rationality gives way to constructivist insights, the task of judgment becomes a far more complicated matter. For now the search for objective truth must give way to the task of choosing among competing warrants for a variety of disparate truth claims. But radical contingency and the anxiety that attends it are not the only dangers postmodernity presents. As the repressive impulses of modernity ease, a variety of irrational forces flood into consciousness. The contingencies of fate, chance, fury, and desire threaten to overwhelm the mind, oppressing it with feelings of helpless passivity. Thus in place of hyper-repression a new excess is born, an excess that skeptical postmodernism vividly embodies. Faced with an onslaught of uncontrollable forces both within and without, the subject faces a crisis of identity and a foreboding sense that individual agency itself may no longer make sense. For how can one expect to direct events or even control one's own actions when irrational forces like chance and desire mock the best efforts of deliberation and intentionality?

In response to such fears, skeptical postmodernism offers a strategy of bemused irony, a more or less stable posture of guarded detachment, to defend against the dual dangers of incessant deception on the one hand and destabilizing incoherence on the other. Failing that, of course, it also holds out the alternative option of simply diving into the flow, in a triumph of Sadean or Nietzschean rapture. The skeptical postmodern thus confronts a grim dilemma: to play (or at least bemusedly watch) the manipulative games of language or to leap beyond language into the primary, incommunicable flux of irrational forces that surround and infuse our words and images.[16]

I believe that this kind of Hobson's choice is as unnecessary and illusory as many of the dichotomies posited by modernist rationality.[17] Which is why I believe that in posing this kind of false dilemma skeptical postmoderns unwittingly betray a secret alliance with modern rationality itself. For when they say no middle ground exists between dispassionate rationality on the one hand and the esthetics of enchantment on the other, are they not mimicking the rationalist rhetoric of Plato and Descartes? But there is a middle way, a way in which opposing forces and disparate modes of knowing, thinking, and talking interpenetrate in varied and complex fashion. This is what the affirmative postmodern perspective allows us to discern.

The affirmative postmodern stance adopted in this book embodies what Ernst Cassirer has usefully referred to as a "mature constructivism."[18] In the postmodern era we are burdened with the awareness that we live within forms of knowledge and belief that we both inherit and create. Thus, unlike those who dwelled among the Homeric myths, we know that the mythic forms in which we live, that establish our world, are subject to critical scrutiny. They may be deliberately affirmed or disavowed. The responsibility for meaning operates on both a collective (cultural) and an individual (cognitive) level.[19] We needn't accept the proffered warrants for enchantment. But we may. The question, therefore, is not whether we should be suspicious of enchantment. Rather, we must ask under what conditions should suspicion as opposed to belief prevail?

From the very dawn of Western culture knowledge of the magic power of words and images has been dogged by fears of trickery and deceit. In ancient times it was said that the voice of persuasion was a gift of the Muses that mortals could neither cast away nor confidently construe. This strange gift combined the powers of healing and entertainment. The voice of persuasion might speak things as they are or be a manifestation of *eris,* the power of strife, falsehood, and dispute.[20] For the Muses, so the ancients believed, often tell lies that look like truths. This suspicion is evident in the ancient Greek word for persuading, *paraiphamenoi,* which carries the sense of "speaking to deflect," "to deviate someone," to bend the mind or will of another. As Homer said of the great counselor Nestor, his words are like "honey." Their "sweetness" makes them easy to swallow, an easiness that might also disguise their distortions. When persuasion distorts it acts as a *dolos,* or trick. At the same time, the power "to sweeten" may also be said to soften truth thus opening the way to peace from strife, a form of enchantment and healing that leads to oblivion.[21]

Trickery, beguilement, oblivion, a force that overtakes the mind: how like the power of desire is the enchantment of persuasion.[22] In this sense it should hardly surprise us to find Milton in *Paradise Lost* describing Satan as "the Father of lies," the rhetor who prompts man's fall. Enchantment is a force that reason fears—the way the men in Bram Stoker's *Dracula* fear Lucy. Dead yet living, she cries out to her fiancé: "Come to me, Arthur. . . . My arms are hungry for you." But Arthur's blood runs cold. "There was something diabolically sweet in her tones," the narrator observes, "something of the tingling of glass when struck, which rang through the brains even of us who heard the words addressed to another."[23] It is the diabolical sweetness of desire, a force larger than death, yet closely related. This is what David Lynch is depicting in *Lost Highway*'s disturbing evocation of the irresistible and unattainable nature of desire. Desire in the form of *Kali,* or *Persephone,* the destroyers. Those who would capture *eros* (the feminine) turn desire into *thanatos:* the death of self that marks the final loss of desire.

Psuchagogein is the ancient Greek word for "raising spirits." It is a word that evokes the magic of *logos,* the mysterious power of language itself. It is this power that claims us in words and images—in poetic utterance, the gift of the Muses.[24] Such words and images instill sorrow and longing, pity and fear, or perhaps joy, pleasure, ecstatic delight in the heart and soul of the one who listens. And here we approach the essence of the rhetorician's art: to move the soul where he will. It is here as well where rhetoric and tragedy converge. As John Kerrigan notes, referring to the ancient Dionysian ritual of ecstatic sacrifice: killing purges evil from the world, just as it cathartically purges feelings of horror, pity, and fear that ill-fated malefactors arouse. The victim's spirit from beneath the earth cries out for revenge. It is the whelming cry of blood-lust, the fury of Aeschylus' Erinyes, goddesses of retribution. The spirit must be appeased, in blood. That is why, Kerrigan reminds us, the word "tragedy" takes its meaning from "goat song." "At the source of tragedy . . . is an act of solidarity reaching the dead through repayment of the god's wine in blood."[25] In the ancient Dionysian ritual the wine-god Dionysus drinks the blood of the sacrificial goat. Wine and blood are poured to satiate the fury of the restless spirits. Again, those sweet and viscous liquids: elixirs that lead the way across the threshold that separates the living from the dead. Gothic meets the tragic on a stained dark field of retribution.[26]

But raising the spirits of the dead can be a risky business. One might, it is true, commune with great heroic souls, bringing to life for a time at least, prompted by the moment's dire need, undying virtues of strength, courage, and wisdom. Perhaps it will be the spirits of Washington or Jefferson or Adams (as Gerry Spence invoked in the Randy Weaver case). But it could just as well be darker spirits, the spirit of retributive blood-lust through which the community may seek purgative bliss in the sacrifice of some unlucky scapegoat, the hapless outsider, drifters on the margins of society—like Randall Dale Adams. How can we tell in the course of our legal rituals of retribution the kind of blood that flows? (Dracula or Christ?)

This of course raises the *logos/mythos*, philosophy/rhetoric, reason/desire dilemma in yet another form. In the highly ritualized social dramas of Greek tragedy fundamental cultural norms were brought to life and actively shared among members of a unified community. A common language of chance and fate, violence and desire, pity and fear, mercy and purgation linked fragile souls together. In the grip of tragic enchantment individual identity was in flux. While in such a state the fate of Oedipus or Orestes or Medea might well be one's own. But we do not find terror being depicted here for its own sake alone, for the thrill that such an experience might provide. Rather, shared identification with the source of terror leads beyond: to the assimilation and transcendence of terror. Therein lies the true power and wisdom of tragic catharsis. That which we fear most, and most wish to deny, disguise, or repress in some other way—perhaps by displacing its source onto predatory Others, misfits or aliens in our midst—is now inescapably lodged in consciousness. It does not, it cannot, go away. Instead, it is directly confronted, accepted, and made part of understanding our (tragic) human condition.

Thus the question arises: we may risk the power of enchantment for the sake of revitalizing basic beliefs and shared cultural norms, for the sake of a more unified community, but in so doing what spirits do we risk raising? One needn't pause long to realize the danger. Memory of the mythic power of the spirits and unifying ritual practices embodied in Germany's National Socialist movement hovers like a dark cloud over the twentieth century. We cannot forget how that power gripped the minds of so many, great minds among them, like the philosopher Martin Heidegger, whose life work was a meditation on the mysterious power of Being's poetic call through living language.

Could it be that Heidegger's knowledge of these matters enhanced his susceptibility to the Nazi "calling"? Once having opened himself to the enchantment of Being in language, how could he (and why didn't he and so many others besides) avoid the *dolos* (or trick) that diverted his thinking onto the path of evil?

We have seen this kind of thing before: in Italian futurism and the associated social movement that culminated in Mussolini's fascist cult of personality. As Simonetta Falasca-Zamponi has noted: "[R]ituals, myths, cults, and speeches were fundamental to the construction of fascist power, its specific physiognomy, its political vision."[27] That vision included the statesman as artist and perhaps most significantly the estheticization of violence. It is a sentiment readily expressed in the futurist writings of Filipo Tommaso Marinetti:

> War is beautiful because it establishes dominion over the subjugated machinery by means of gas masks, terrifying megaphones, flame throwers and small tanks. War is beautiful because it initiates the dreamt-of metalization of the human body. War is beautiful because it enriches a flowering meadow with the fiery orchids of machine guns. . . .[28]

Notably, this effort to estheticize war itself represented an effort to break out of what was perceived by many at the time as the modern stupor of disenchantment and technology-induced alienation.[29] It is also significant to recall that Mussolini's esthetic conception of politics drew upon turn-of-the-century theories of mass psychology and the crowd that had been developed by such writers as Gabriel Tarde and Gustave Le Bon. According to Le Bon, words have "a truly magical power." Thus, as Falasca-Zamponi observes, "By emphasizing magic in the leader's relation to crowds, Le Bon instituted a doctrine of mystification. Since he believed he had scientifically proven crowds' irrational nature, Le Bon in effect advised the orators to appeal to their 'sentiments, and never to their reason'."[30] Notably, these are precisely the same insights that gave birth to the twentieth-century art of propaganda, mass advertising, and the American public relations movement. As Edward Bernays, the self-styled father of that movement, said: "The appeal to the instincts and the universal desires is the basic method through which [the public relations expert] produces his results."[31]

This hyper-estheticized and radically amoral perspective has been championed in more recent times as well. In a general sense, I believe it is the dominant esthetic of those who assume the posture of skeptical postmodernism—people like *Pulp Fiction* filmmaker Quentin Tarantino, for example. These are people who inhabit Gorgias' world, a world where knowledge is deemed to be impossible. Everything thus comes to be seen as an image within a vast flux of multiple, disparate images, a surface upon which our gaze falls seeking a response to the central reality-defining query: how does it make me feel? This is the image as commodity. If I consume it, what is its payoff? In short, the sensation it offers is its own reward. And in that reward lies the only truth we may lay claim to. It is in the context of such a morally depleted, wholly estheticized perspective that Tarantino may be understood when he says:

> I don't take violence very seriously. I find violence funny, especially in the stories I've been telling recently. Violence is part of this world and I am drawn to the outrageousness of real-life violence. It isn't about lowering people from helicopters on to speeding trains, or about terrorists hijacking something or other. Real life violence is, you're in a restaurant and a man and his wife are having an argument and all of a sudden that guy gets so mad at her, he picks up a fork and stabs her in the face. That's really crazy and comic bookish—but it also happens. . . . To me, violence is a totally aesthetic subject.[32]

This statement neatly sums up Tarantino's esthetic in a film like *Pulp Fiction* where random murder and sadomasochistic violence are used for purely esthetic purposes, most notably for comic effect. Tarantino reacts to life as a series of random images, surfaces to be gazed at for the gratifications they allow. It is a profoundly televisual esthetic: the kind of representation that leaches out of the picture both moral depth and meaningful critical reflection. Perceiving the real world through such a skeptical postmodern screen turns reality into TV reality: surfaces to gaze on, to consume, for the sake of immediate (albeit free-floating) gratification. This is what filmmaker Oliver Stone seems to have had in mind when he referred to the mass media's effort to arouse everywhere "a fascination without scruples" resulting in "a paralysis of meaning, to the profit of a single scenario."[33] It is the same skeptical postmodern esthetic that prompts audiences to laugh in the face of horror and perversion. As when the young man in *Braindead* (1992) enters a house full of zombies and triumphantly says, "The party's over." While he makes mincemeat of the monsters his girlfriend is in the kitchen cutting zombie parts in a food processor. The gruesome becomes a joke, as if once we see the genre, the construction, there's nothing left to fear.[34]

Here is the skeptical postmodern defense in action. Faced with a
surge of powerful irrational forces, ironic deconstruction strives to sap
symbolic violence of meaning. It's as if the unconscious itself were
being denied, as if savvy deconstruction could rob it of its destabilizing
and frightening power. In laughter and irony skeptical postmoderns
seek safety and control. They would have us believe that there is no
choice but to oscillate between irrational excess on the one hand and
skeptical disenchantment on the other. But the cost of their strategy
is high. For when the price of safety and control is generalized (*anes-
thetized?*) disenchantment, meaning itself is endangered. From the
Simpson double murder trial to the constitutional crisis of the Clinton impeachment proceeding the danger is the same. Estheticized responses (*what does the image make us feel?*) and estheticized judgments (*how does it create that effect?*) threaten to take the place of
reflective judgment (*what self, social, legal, and political reality are
these images constructing? to what end? how do they make power
flow? who benefits? who loses?*). The flow of power in society is real,
with real effects; it's no joke. We cannot afford to feel superior, in an
ironically detached way, to the symbolic cultural forms that help to
make up who we are and the reality we live in.

The jurisprudence of appearances I described in chapter 6 has much
in common with this estheticization process. Indeed, by incorpor-
ating the insights and techniques that inform contemporary commercial mass media, particularly television, the jurisprudence of appearances takes to heart the insights of Bernays, and by extension, of Tarde
and Le Bon as well. On this view, the jurisprudence of appearances is
a direct byproduct of the convergence of law and popular culture:
it is what we see when law's need for legitimation and the media's
converge on the same set of images. This is why even the most realistic of televisual portrayals of law, like the predominantly criminal
trials broadcast on Court TV, are disproportionately eroticized and
violent. This is what it means for the mass media to become, in Justice
Burger's phrase, "the law's surrogate." And this, too, is how law comes
to inherit the baggage of postmodern anxiety: the lurking suspicion
that illusion and manipulated rage and desire increasingly make up
the law.

Surely, then, it is not without good reason that the controversy surrounding rhetoric, with its honeyed words and compelling images, its
mysterious power to enchant and beguile the mind, has throughout
history hit the legal community especially hard. For what do we fear
most if not the danger of surrendering law and politics to the deceitful

seductions of the self-interested few (particularly those few who have
the financial means to dominate popular cultural communications)?
For with the sanction of law behind them it is their interests then that
will be backed by the full power of the state. Surely this is what Plato
feared: that the illusions sown by rhetoric-wielding Sophists would
some day ensnare and dominate all Athenian politics and law. The
fear that pleasure, personal ambition, and the will to power would
rule in place of justice; that mercy and piety would collapse into base
self-interest. Similarly, what is it that we fear most when law goes *pop*
if not that we too might suffer such a fate: the fate of pervasive deceit
and, concomitantly, pervasive disenchantment?

When skeptical postmodern theory, communications technology,
and the demands of the marketplace converge, as they are now doing,
the fear of deceit and the spirit of disenchantment hang over law and
culture alike. We suffer today from too many images, too many meanings, too many warrants beseeching belief in the service of disguised
rage, hidden desire, and transient gratification. No sentiment or aspiration, no matter how lofty or admirable—not love, not pity, not generosity, not courage or concern for the dispossessed and disempow-
ered, not fear for an endangered global ecology—is immune to the
deflationary, skepticism-building exploitation of mass advertising,
public relations, or hyperreal media events in the service of specific
commercial or political interests.

If we cannot know reality, as many skeptical postmoderns believe,
then all that remains is opinion. Moreover, once words and images
devolve into a homogenized flux of coequal stimuli—what we recognize today as the global "matrix" of electronic data flow—nothing is
exempt from exploitation in the interests of persuasion. The ancient
Greek rhetorician Gorgias was perhaps the first to perceive the human
world in terms of free-floating beliefs subject to manipulation.[35] His
life's work was dedicated to perfecting the enchantments of public
persuasion, the art of swaying people's everyday beliefs. In this respect
one may rightly regard Gorgias as the father of the mass advertising
and public relations movements[36] that exert such a powerful influence
on our world today: in the production of popular culture, and in the
communicative practices of politics and law.

No wonder the craving for enchantment is so great when the promise of fulfillment is so meager, when it has been reduced to what Andy
Warhol sardonically and presciently referred to as the fifteen minutes
of fame to which we are all entitled or, worse still, when enchantment
shrinks to fit the demands of a fifteen-second spot on TV. No wonder

the popular urge is so great to as quickly tear down what the culture of celebrity so speedily builds up—the better to avoid or (more likely) to preempt at the earliest moment the disenchantment that is sure to follow. To stave off the deflation that comes with the discovery that it is all hype, illusion, *dolos*—and what is more, that it was deliberately constructed that way from the beginning.

The extent of our need dictates our willingness to yield to the spell of belief, just as the extent of our fear of deceit dictates the speed with which disenchantment, detached irony, and passive resignation will soon follow. The magic power (the *eros* or seduction) of words and images remains, but we are increasingly ill-disposed to risk yielding to its call. This is how it is in a culture of superficial stimulation and simulation. The quick enchantments and meager payoffs that they allow require the rapidity and constancy of information and image flow to stand in for (perhaps to divert us from) the depth and stability of meaning that the culture lacks. Needless to say, this state of affairs poses significant dangers. For without the means of experiencing more profound enchantments, without communal rituals and social dramas through which the culture's deepest beliefs and values may be brought to life and collectively reenacted, those beliefs ultimately lose their meaning and die. And at that point we will have become what mass commercial communication practices encourage us to be: scattered impulses alert to each moment's promise of immediate gratification.

On this analysis, then, it is not in the magic of belief or the enchantment of esthetic seduction per se that the greatest danger lies, but in the ends or interests or values that they embody and promote. Simply rooting out the irrationality of seduction is no answer. This was the road Plato chose: as if truth (*aleithea*) and esthetics (*terpsis*) were utterly antithetical and irreducible. Here is the paradigm for the dichotomizing and repressive rationalist impulse of modernity. Modern thinkers also sought to banish the irrational forces of chance (*tyche*), fate (*ananke*), enchantment (*peitho*), and desire (*bia*) by intellectual fiat. Yet, as history teaches, the dictates of critical reason in this regard are but an invitation to repression and the various disguises and externalizations to which denial typically gives rise. Put simply, the stronger the impulse to repress, the greater its impact will be when the repressed returns. As it inevitably will.

It may be that current developments in culture, technology, and the history of ideas have led us to a fork in the road similar to the one Plato faced. Down one path reason and desire, truth and rhetoric, ethics and esthetics are sharply divided; down another they are not.

Plato chose the first way, the path of irreconcilable divisions and highly rationalized ideals. We know the history that it spawned. The untaken path lies open before us. Its future is uncertain, but its present is reminiscent of fifth-century Athens—a time when, in Charles Segal's words, there was still "a coherence between the aesthetic and moral spheres of human life, when the arts can still be felt as reinforcing the communal and moral aims of the *polis*." [37]

I believe that the affirmative postmodern perspective that I have described in these pages has much in common with this pre-Platonic perspective. Postmodern constructivist insights have shown us in a broad range of social and cultural and even scientific contexts that the particular form of expression—the discourse, the metaphor, the visual image that is used—is essential to the kind of truth that may be expressed. This is not to say that truth is reducible to esthetics, that content equals style, as the fifth-century Gorgian Sophists and their contemporary skeptical postmodern counterparts seem to believe. Rather, it is to acknowledge the complexity, contingency, and multiplicity of truth and reason. It is to accept the interpenetration of truth, morality, and esthetics as well as of reason and the irrational in all its varied forms and disguises. And it is to affirm responsibility for choosing among the disparate claims to truth and reason that confront us when conflicts demand resolution. [38]

On this view, it becomes apparent that we share a deep insight with rhetoricians like Isocrates and Philip Sidney. Without the fictional method, without the efficacy of verisimilitude and the motivating power of emotion, truth may simply fail to come to life in the mind. Denying that efficacy robs truth of its motivating power just as it robs us of the capacity to discern and understand that power when it is being exerted. Indeed, ignorance or naiveté of this kind is precisely what insulates the rhetoric of truth's "nonesthetic purity" from critical scrutiny. In a similar sense, it is precisely our ignorance of the process and effects of repression of the irrational that blinds us to the symbolic forms and specific cultural and legal effects that it assumes when the repressed returns.

It is the function of art, poetry, and rhetoric alike to make a particular form of truth (and reason and justice) compelling. Sufficiently compelling, ultimately, to lead the subject to a specific judgment or course of action in a particular context. It is the particular function of tragic poetry and narrative to make the contingency, multiplicity, and complexity of truth and reason compelling. Indeed, it must do so even in the face of the irrational forces that surround us (both within and without). Forces like chance, fate, and the whelming enchant-ments of rage and desire, love and mercy. Tragic wisdom urges us to critically discern the reality- or meaning-making power and technique of rhetoric, but it also compels us to acknowledge the limits of reason and the contingency of truth and meaning. By describing in dramatic detail the effects of forces like chance and desire on human life, tragic narrative delineates the bounds of rationality. In this way, it invokes a sense of finitude, humility, fear, and pity. And in doing so the tragic view brings into focus the shifting patterns of meaning and mystery that rationality and irrationality create in dynamic disequilibrium. These patterns constitute the lived realities of truth and reason, law and justice in our time. However, unlike skeptical postmodernism, tragic wisdom seeks to go beyond the critical capacity to recognize the rhetorical (or esthetic) forms of cultural and cognitive meaning making. It also seeks to cultivate our capacity for enchantment, the ability to feel and affirm the normative force of meaning's appeal. This is what it means to accept the responsibility of a mature as opposed to a naive constructivism.

This is also what it means to adopt an affirmative postmodern understanding of the interpenetration of law and culture. We must struggle to integrate critical constructivist insights regarding how the meanings we live by are made and disseminated (by whom? and with what effect?) with the human capacity to affirm deep cultural values and beliefs. Only then may we avoid the dangers posed by pervasive dis-enchantment: whether in the form of detached irony (as we find in the skeptical postmodern response to irrational excess) or in denial of the "magic" of words and images (as we find in the Enlightenment's hyper-rationalist response).

Culture, like art and (as I have tried to show throughout this book) like law, cannot flourish without the enchantment of esthetics, what the ancient Greeks called *terpsis*. We need the enchanting power of images and words for the sake of belief and to motivate judgment. As cultural anthropologist Victor Turner has written, conflict prompts social dramas and redressive rituals that raise to the surface of the community's collective consciousness beliefs and values that are ade-quate to the task of conflict resolution.[39] In this respect, there is always a symbolic as well as a practical dimension to legal adjudication. For without a public articulation of the symbolic forms that regulate the process of conflict resolution and legitimate specific outcomes, both process and outcome ultimately grow suspect.

Legal rituals that have become rigid, stale, deprived of the dynamism of symbolic drama, are easily perceived as sites for the exercise of naked power and illicit prejudice alone. By contrast, notorious cases are the most highly symbolic of legal dramas precisely because at the time of their unfolding the public's need for clarification and affirmation of specific normative claims is so great. Conflict resolution under these conditions will provide the public with words and images of truth, reason, law, and justice not simply in the particular case but more generally for the culture as a whole. These heightened legal dramas serve as a "medium": they raise invisible spirits, the usually hidden ("antistructural") norms that constitute *communitas*.[40]

In this view, notorious cases provide society with an opportunity to articulate and breathe new life into shared beliefs and values. When they succeed the community gains renewed faith in law's ability to give meaning to the claims of truth and justice. Of course, as we have seen in chapter 3, this does not always happen. Sometimes a particular cultural anxiety will distort, repress, or displace some underlying cultural urgency in the way of belief. In this sense, notorious cases also serve as effective barometers of the current-day conflicts, confusions, and anxieties that disguise or distort *communitas*, that prevent it from coming into view. When that occurs the trial's symbolic conflict-resolution process breaks down. Left unconfronted, unarticulated, and ultimately unresolved, the repressed is bound to return again. More effective symbolic conflict resolution must await some future legal controversy. In the meantime, however, the community is fated to endure continued anxiety regarding law's ability to give meaning to the unanswered demands of truth and justice. In this way the failed notorious case is a potent breeding ground for legitimation crisis.

By virtue of its symbolic function law gives voice to irrational impulses, needs, and desires, the mysterious urgency of repressed cultural conflicts. In this sense, the real trick of legal persuasion is not to separate out the rational from the irrational, but rather to discern the discrete patterns created by the interpenetration of the one by the other. Forms of enchantment in the service of deceit, illicit desire, and self-gratification alone must be separated out from forms of enchantment in the service of feelings, beliefs, and values that we aspire to affirm in light of the self, social, and legal realities they help to construct and maintain. This is the esthetics of deliberate normative construction. And it is this that most keenly distinguishes skeptical from affirmative postmodernism. It is one thing to identify and effectively implement the best means of persuasion available in the particular case when the objective is a potentially valid or warrantable truth claim in the pursuit of justice. However, as we have seen in chapter 6 with the advent of the jurisprudence of appearances, it is something else again when a particular physical or emotional or other psychic gratification is exploited for the sake of benefits or objectives that are extraneous to the case in question.

Today, as in Socrates' day, experts profess to have reduced the persuasive power of communication to a science. Like the ancient Greek Sophists Gorgias and Protagoras, jury consultants, public relations professionals, and the legal advocates they serve understand the power of words and images and sounds to enchant the mind and move the passions according to the enchanter's will. Moreover, as in Socrates' day, these techniques of persuasion have spread from mainstream culture into all major areas of social practice. As a result, law, like politics, is now in danger of merging into the culture of spectacle and sensation, the realm of contrived media events and calculated appearances. And as adulterated desire cycles into law, for a growing number of people enchantment has become a form of perverse seduction. In sum, the ideal of narrative *eros* as rooted in a noninstrumental love-relation between storyteller and audience, and as a vital source of the myths, philosophies, and art works through which we define and experience self, social, and legal reality, is at risk—the victim of suspicion, skepticism, unrestrained cynicism, and ironic detachment.

Yet, the affirmative power of enchantment persists. It is a power that poets and rhetoricians have championed throughout history. From Isocrates to Sidney to Vico to Chaim Perelman and James Boyd White, the claim that rhetoricians must surely deceive when they deploy the fictional method has been vigorously challenged. It is in the service of warrantable truth claims and justice, not violence and pleasure, that the techniques of rhetorical persuasion have been most persuasively defended. After all, is it not rhetoric that protects the weak against the stronger? Is it not rhetoric that allows them to be heard, thus making rhetoric the ethical source of all laws?[41]

By repressing the practical necessities of the fictional method, the modern Enlightenment's rational model for truth has caused needless anxiety. As if to say, when the rationalist's unreasonable expectations of unadorned objectivity are not met skepticism or cynicism must follow. Or that one must greet the lawyer's "fictions" with condemnation and renewed determination to achieve a purer (less "subjective") truth. The irony here is that it is precisely this kind of naive realism that invites the very perils the rationalist mindset fears most. The trick, in response to such impractical expectations and the fears they produce, is to rediscover what the classical and medieval tradition of rhetoric has taught all along: testing out diverse notions of truth does not cause us to descend into nihilism and despair. Indeed, it is the chief virtue of the adversarial culture to take uncertainty as its point of departure and effective persuasion as its chief means of realizing the best chance we have for truth and justice. In this sense learning the ways of meaning making and reality construction is ultimately less an invitation to anxiety than an invitation to a more sophisticated sense of responsibility for the realities and meanings that we affirm or deny. It is, in short, an invitation to a heightened sense of responsibility for the world we live in.

Still, if enchantment, seduction, beguilement, magic—in sum, the trick of making meaning—has long been the lawyer's stock in trade, alongside (rather than to the exclusion of) dispassionate reason and the straightforward logic of deduction and proof, the controversy remains. As Jacqueline de Romilly aptly notes: "When one begins with the irrational, it is hard to know where to stop."[42] Where do we draw the line between lofty inspiration on the one hand and a fascination with occultism on the other? Socrates trusted the mystical spirit of the *daimon* within. But how can we be sure that one man's *daimon* is not another's *dolos* (trick), or evil spirit in disguise (Descartes's "*malin genie*")? How are we to know that we haven't been tricked by illicit means in the service of illicit goals? What of desire, power, and the purely esthetic gratification that comes with gazing upon an image or getting inside a well-told tale and liking the way it feels to be there?

I believe that these questions ultimately prompt a pivotal query: is it possible reflectively to reframe the myth of modernity in a way that allows us to avoid the excesses of skeptical postmodern irrationalism and disenchantment on the one hand, and of modernist rationality and repression on the other? Put differently: how are we to affirm a world of meaning in which law and democracy may flourish? For even if disenchantment were to be held at bay we still need to articulate clearly and affirm the founding "myth" or establishing narrative that determines (and in so doing legitimates) law's stories. What forms of legal discourse, knowledge, and power does that mythic source establish (or suppress), under what circumstances? According to what measure do we regulate law's profusion or judge the difference between licit and illicit forms of legal persuasion in the face of particular conflicts? These are the issues to which we must turn in the final chapter.

[R]hetoric implies both serious thinking and the defense of justice, as opposed to violent action: it protects the weak against the stronger, since it allows them to be heard, and is the source of all laws.

JACQUELINE DE ROMILLY,
Magic and Rhetoric in Ancient Greece

[D]emocracy is able to take cognizance of the fact that its limit lies in itself, in its internal "antagonism." This is why it can avoid the fate of "totalitarianism," which is condemned to invent external "enemies" to account for its failures.

SLAVOJ ŽIŽEK, *Looking Awry*

Conclusion
Redrawing the Line between Belief and Suspicion

In this concluding chapter I aim to provide a general overview for the concrete studies that make up the bulk of this book. My working hypothesis throughout has been that law cannot be adequately understood without a careful examination of specific linguistic, cognitive, and cultural practices. By making that hypothesis explicit here I hope to make plain that in undertaking a highly contextualized approach to law I have been doing theory all along: postmodern theory, of the affirmative kind.

In the main, I have been arguing that a cultural constructivist perspective carries with it an enhanced awareness of contingency, chance, uncertainty, and multiplicity (of truth and reason and of self and social reality). As the repressive impulses of modernity ease, our awareness of irrational forces—rage and desire within, chance and fate without—comes more readily into view. Tragic consciousness is an offshoot of this heightened awareness. Yet, obstacles to its development abound.

The obstacles range from nostalgia for the rationalist faith of the modern Enlightenment (in the form of some utilitarian, autonomy, or discourse ideal) to radical skepticism and the wholesale repudiation of reason and the efficacy of human will. Ironically, both extremes share the modernist proclivity for dichotomous thinking. For while the skeptic's and the rationalist's choices will undoubtedly differ, both seem to insist that the choice itself is inevitable. Either reason or desire, *logos* or *mythos,* logic or enchantment, truth or esthetics—one must triumph over the other. What this kind of rigid dichotomizing tends to overlook, however, is the extent to which the one interpenetrates the other.

As Jean-François Lyotard has observed, language itself joins and divides at one and the same time. In John Kerrigan's words: "Dialogue is imbalance. There is, at best, an oscillation of subject and object positions, at worst the violence of two language games at odds."[1] This insight points up the limitations in such recent rationalist claims as Jürgen Habermas's regarding idealized speech conditions.[2] For example, Habermas writes:

> Indeed one can say that the general and unavoidable—in this sense transcendental—conditions of possible understanding have a normative content when one has in mind not only the binding character of norms of action or even the binding character of rules in general, but the validity basis of speech across its entire spectrum.

But the barrier of localized differences, not to mention the limits of rationality itself, are far more obstinate than Habermas seems willing to acknowledge. When rational idealists like Habermas, Kant, and Rawls lay claim to universal principles of morality and reason, it is precisely the transcultural nature of their appeal that falls short. The reason is not hard to state. Quite simply, their claims fail to give due consideration to the particular linguistic, cultural, and cognitive competencies by which those who advocate the norms in question, and those whose actions are judged accordingly, construct their own disparate senses of self and social reality. As cultural anthropologist Richard Shweder writes,

> How we are involved with the world and react to it depends on our representation of the ambient facts of reality. . . . People live differently in the world of Kali from the way they live in the world of the Virgin Mary. It is a supposition of cultural psychology that when people live in the world differently, it may be that they live in different worlds.[3]

In other words, Habermas's notion of an ideal speech condition, like Kant's notion of an ideal moral law, fails to account for the diverse ways in which discrete cultural, cognitive, and linguistic constructs give rise to various kinds of meaning making. It simply will not do to impose abstract notions of "the right," "the just," and "the true" from the top down, so to speak, without inquiring into how those notions (and conflicting ones) are actually understood at the level of local belief, discourse, and practice.

Thus, for example, whether the use of peyote in the Native American Church should be viewed as a religious sacrament akin to the use of wine in the Catholic Church or a violation of a state's criminal law against possession of a controlled substance cannot be adequately addressed without taking into account the practitioner's understanding as well as the will of the majority as manifest in the state's legisla-tion.[4] Assuming away this highly contextualized interpretive aspect of the legal conflict-resolution process not only risks doing violence to the lived reality of specific individuals and communities; it also risks doing injustice to shared norms differently understood. As the above example suggests, this includes shared notions regarding the funda-mental value of freely held religious beliefs as well as the important social objective of deterring the distribution and use of dangerous substances. Assessing the "factual truth" of the criminal violation in question as well as the propriety of its prosecution requires an ability to shift from a familiar to an unfamiliar perspective. Legislators and judges have not always managed to do this. As a result the legal stand-ing of local communities and their power to be heard have suffered from time to time at the hands of the majority.

Tragic wisdom expressly takes into account the contingencies, un-certainties, and limitations of human understanding and the imbal-ances that exist in particular linguistic interactions. In this way it in-vites us to take cognizance of the competing claims or warrants for belief that arise within a given conflict situation, including differences in discourse strategies, knowledge, and institutional or community-based power. In sum, tragic awareness acknowledges the diverse ways in which one may make sense of actions and events and the conse-quences of constructing truth, self, and reason in one way as opposed to another.

On this view, the task of evaluating discrete claims to truth and justice requires a variety of meaning-making skills and techniques. Familiarity with the use and effects of these cultural and cognitive tools, as chapters 3 through 5 point out, assists advocates, decision makers, and the public alike. It allows people to self-reflectively ask, what reality will my judgment preserve or call into being? What val-ues, beliefs and feelings do I authorize (or deny) in the course of for-mulating and communicating judgment in one way as opposed to an-other? Does my understanding rest upon the claims of factual truth or higher legal principle? Does it affirm the value of individual dignity or the punitive impulse of just retribution? Does it thrill to the de-tective's revelation concerning "whodunit" or to the mythic uplift of the hero's quest? Or is it entangled in the illusory and manipulative (authenticity-leaching) practices of advertising, public relations, and the hyperreal media event, discussed in chapter 6 under the rubric of the jurisprudence of appearances?

The affirmative postmodern synthesis of rhetorical and tragic perspectives that I refer to as "tragic constructivism" adopts this kind of multiplicity and dynamic disequilibrium as its point of departure. The default state of affairs on this view is one of tension and incessant oscillation. To reconceive our legal system along these lines requires that we rethink such core Enlightenment ideals as the universality of reason and truth and the stability of the autonomous self, as well as the presumption of progress that these ideals purportedly guarantee. The priority traditionally assigned to deductive and inductive logic, rationalist agency, and calculative reason must also undergo review so that notions of plurality, complexity, contingency, and uncertainty may be more fully and deliberately considered. In this way, the unduly repressive inclinations of modernist reason may be eased, and the non-rational forces that surge within and around us—fate, chance, fury, and desire—may be more readily assessed as co-constitutive of self, social, and legal reality.

Such a reconceptualization is now under way in a variety of fields, from the human and social sciences to the natural sciences themselves. For example, biologist Stuart Kauffman describes a science of complexity that views all manner of complex organisms as thriving in the transitional region between order and chaos. As Kauffman writes: "It is as though a position in the ordered regime near the transition to chaos affords the best mixture of stability and flexibility."[5] Kauffman has in mind here principles of self-organization, which he calls laws of complexity. Viewed in this light, the dynamic of pluralistic democratic society finds its impetus not in the Newtonian understanding of static equilibrium, but rather in the decidedly post-Newtonian notion of complexity and dynamic disequilibrium.[6]

I would like to suggest that this image of productive disequilibrium comports well with an affirmative postmodern understanding of our constitutional system of law. Here, then, is a compelling "frame-story" for the profusion of legal narratives that constitute and reconstitute law's domain. For what is the Constitution if not the legitimating source of multiple and conflicting forms of legal discourse, knowledge, and power? In this view, law is, to borrow Kauffman's term, a complex "ecosystem" made up of "a tangled bank of interwoven roles"[7] or, as I prefer to call them, *interwoven communicative practices and competencies*. It is precisely the proximity of disorder—deriving from constant contestation among conflicting discourse communities as well as from the various irrational forces that surround and suffuse them—that compels new forms of legal self-organization (or "emergent lawfulness"[8]). This is how law adapts to the contingencies and vicissitudes of shifting social, cultural, and technological (among other) developments.

This postmodern retelling of the Enlightenment story of constitutionally separated powers and institutional checks and balances offers no guarantees of total justice or absolute truth. Rather, emergent patterns of truth and justice form and reform as disparate legal discourse competencies compete for law's validation in the particular case. Perhaps it will be (1) the common sense of public opinion (*doxa*) based on the knowledge acquired in the course of our ordinary life experience (onscreen and off), or (2) the prudence of judicial interpretation based on specialized legal knowledge and skills of interpretation and persuasion regarding the applicability and meaning of particular legal rules, policies, and fundamental legal principles, or (3) the informed policy-making competencies of the legislative branch based on political prudence in conjunction with the technical knowledge of experts who are called upon to testify about the merits, drawbacks, and foreseeable consequences of endorsing one legislative policy as opposed to another. Out of the clash of these competing claims to knowledge, reason, and truth, the shifting mosaic of law's meanings takes shape.

Notably, each constitutionally institutionalized form of discourse-knowledge-power has its own unique set of strengths or virtues. Moreover, no single mode alone adequately reflects the range of knowledge and experience that may be brought to bear upon a specific legal conflict or social problem. The lasting genius of the republican constitutional system consists in the fructifying clash of diverse perspectives. This system is based on deep insights, steeped in the realities of history and human experience, regarding the need to respect multiple sources of knowledge and to keep fragmentary forms from attaining dominance over the entire political and legal field. Whether it is the lay public's ordinary common sense checking the unduly harsh or politically self-interested demands of a particular legal rule or policy, or the prudent restraint of the judiciary checking the excessive passions of an aroused public, the discrete virtues of one knowledge-discourse-power community counter the vices of another.

On this view, law, like culture generally, is constituted and maintained (or altered) by multiple forms of truth and reason. These forms are constructed by various communicative practices. Each practice has its own knowledge base and way of knowing, which determine what constitutes a legitimate warrant for belief. And each has its own special role in the legal system, on the strength of its special virtues and its ability to check the defects of other forms of knowledge-discourse.

This is what it means, for example, for factual truth at trial to be determined by the experiential (common-sense) knowledge of the community at large, while other issues, involving judgments of legal principle, such as that of limited police power and the inadmissibility of unlawfully obtained evidence, rest in the hands of legal experts.[9]

To be sure, the system is not immune to conflict, periodic crises, and even temporary breakdowns. A particular discourse competency may become corrupted from within, or it may seek to corrupt the competencies of other institutions in an effort to achieve system-wide dominance. We see examples of the former when courts sacrifice prudence for partisan politics, or when legislators sacrifice fundamental democratic principles or benefit-maximizing policy goals for the sake of financial gain or power for its own sake, or when ordinary citizens serving as jurors sacrifice the common sense of lived experience for the skewed information and artificially enhanced passions generated by commercial advertising, public relations, and hyperreal media events. As we have seen, the latter tactics are increasingly being relied upon inside the courtroom by lawyers savvy in the ways of visual representation, and in the court of public opinion by those who exploit the commercial mass media as an adjunct to litigation.

Distortions in the distribution of institutional competencies occur when a form of legal discourse more suitable to one sphere of influence seeks domination beyond its special area of competence. When this occurs the virtues of other forms of knowledge, reason, and truth may be lost and the special virtues of the dominant discourse turn into vices. This is what we see, for example, when popular passions or legislative policies appealing to irrational fears and prejudices override judicial prudence and constraint. Under such circumstances, the special virtue of the judiciary, which is to safeguard dignity, privacy, and property rights, fails to operate. One historic example of such a breakdown is the Supreme Court's refusal in *Korematsu v. United States* to condemn as unconstitutional an executive policy during World War II that compelled Americans of Japanese ancestry to leave behind their businesses and belongings in the course of being relocated to designated internment camps.

The convergence of law and popular culture I have described in this book provides an account of increasing distortions within the discourse competencies of both the public and the judiciary. It also suggests a growing imbalance in the distribution of various discourse competencies within the legal system as a whole. A synergistic convergence of skeptical postmodern theory, communications technol-

ogy, and the insistent gratification demands of the marketplace is leading to a flattening out of disparate discourse competencies. Common
sense and to an increasing extent legal discourse and knowledge are
showing signs of collapsing into the same gratification-based esthetic
that dominates contemporary popular culture. It is precisely this distortion that we have seen, for example, with the advent of the jurisprudence of appearances and the litigation public relations movement. As
a result, the discrete virtues of popular knowledge and discourse, like
those of the judiciary, which must at times operate as a brake upon
popular opinion, are being encumbered and diminished.

Kenneth Burke once wrote that "every way of seeing is a way of
not seeing." That is why multiple ways of seeing (and thinking and
speaking about) self and social reality are so valuable. Complemen-
tary perspectives minimize knowledge gaps and maximize alternative
ways of seeing and solving conflicts. The inherent limitations or "blind
spots" of specific forms of knowledge and discourse lack the capacity
for checks and balances alternative discourse communities would provide. The loss of a discrete point of view also deprives law of important contributions to knowledge and judgment, and of a discrete
community of contributors. When a particular knowledge-discourse
community is silenced, both the knowledge and the identity of the
suppressed community are at risk. Losing a voice in the legal process
quickens one's sense of having lost a stake in that process. This kind
of alienation is one of the chief precursors to law's delegitimation.

The main weapons of law are violence and enchantment. Enchantment legitimates the violence of law by persuading members of the
community to accept the terms under which law's violence may be
exercised. But when law's stories grow distorted, when the discrete
virtues of disparate discourse practices are lost or silenced or "flattened out," law's enchantment risks becoming illegitimate. When that
happens, law's violence becomes equivalent to naked power.[10] This is
but another way of describing the state of affairs when law goes *pop,*
a state in which tyranny rules.

To be sure, this may not be the form of tyranny George Orwell had
in mind when he wrote *1984* ("If you want a picture of the future,
imagine a boot stamping on a human face—forever"[11]). But tyranny
dons many faces, including the face of commodified desire and self-
love. In this respect, the image of "a boot on the neck" may give way
to one of more recent vintage, such as "booting up" for life on the
screen. After all, it is there, we are told, that the promise of reality
control and self-realization may be fulfilled. In this way, the self's con-

sumption of the object of desire (or is it the other way around?) becomes essential to "the good life." To paraphrase Jean-Paul Sartre's
existential credo, in such a world "commodification precedes essence." Here, then, is a new face for tyranny to wear. It describes the
tyranny of the machine that knows best not only what our desires and
preferences are, but also how best to fulfill them. Or so its producers
would have us believe. Their power of persuasion grows, however, to
the extent that law and its representations are captured by the same
image-driven esthetic that dominates mainstream culture. For then
our critical capacity to assess the object (or impetus) of desire weak-
ens. When popular images of reality control and untrammeled self-
gratification prevail it becomes increasingly difficult to find a basis
or means within the individual or collective imagination for critical
judgment to occur.

I have contended that a key moment in the advancement of this
danger arises when law seizes on the same putatively self-legitimating
images and forms of persuasion as the commercial mass media themselves. When that happens techniques of commercial advertising, public relations, and litigation-coordinated media events distort, by pre-
cluding more diversified forms of, common sense. This also has the
effect of suppressing the capacity for critical reflection. What we find
instead are artificially heightened and strategically manipulated urgencies of emotion—the disguised, and at times unconsciously displaced, compulsions and needs of irrational fury, retribution, fantasy,
and illicit desire. Here we enter the realm of the hyperreal, where image and story converge on gratification for its own sake. It is a realm
in which the good, the true, the real, and the right come to be known
on the basis of the feelings a particular story or image releases or the
impulses it gratifies.

A vivid example of the potency of this kind of hyperreal construction of reality is the media spectacle of the United States's war with
Iraq in 1991. The media's logic of visualization, its insatiable demand
for drama determined what we saw, or failed to see. For what was
most remarkable about the media's coverage of this war was how the
violent and tragic reality of war itself simply vanished. War as we
know it became a phantom: no suffering, no death, no sense of real
loss. What remained were electronic pyrotechnics, laser-guided missiles hitting their targets, as if we had all been swept up in a massive
video game. Nor can anyone confidently say that we weren't. As one
French journalist remarked, "During this war, nobody knows what
the truth [is], nobody knows what we saw. . . . [W]e have so many

things, so many pictures, we don't have the possibility to check, to be sure, of anything." [12] Whether the images we saw constituted disinformation (to demoralize the enemy) or were reality-based no longer seemed to matter. The media ran with the flash and drama of the images the military supplied. No commercial television producer could forgo the compelling ("you are there") visuals of laser-directed "smart bombs" and Patriot missiles hitting their marks—whether they did or not. [13] Veteran journalist Daniel Schorr addressed this issue when he remarked: "[I]mages now tend to replace reality, or create their own. . . . So we end up reacting to pictures that show you what pictures can show, and not knowing those things which pictures can't show, and that's a new reality. It is a reality of what is on television." [14]

This kind of esthetically driven imaging marks the triumph of illicit persuasion. It already dominates contemporary political communication and to an increasing extent it is now emerging inside the courtroom and in the court of public opinion as well. As a result, the virtues of judicial prudence and ordinary common sense are being corrupted. Artificially heightened passions and strategically manipulated representations of legal reality are converting the traditional virtues of common sense into defects. [15] Virtuality, fantasy, and the hyperreal inextricably intermingle with and unconsciously inform offscreen experience.

In this respect, Andy Warhol was surely prescient when he wrote: "Sex is more exciting on the screen and between the pages than between the sheets. . . . Fantasy love is much better than reality love." What Warhol compactly conveys here is the derealization effect of mass mediated hyperreality. In a similar vein, he aptly captures the sense of what I have referred to as hyper-catharsis when he says, "I think once you see ordinary emotions from a certain angle you can never see them as real again." [16] What Warhol is describing here is the collapse of lived reality (i.e., active, self-reflective experience) into imaged reality (i.e., passively experiencing life as an extension of on-screen reality). It is what happens when we make sense of real life with the internalized logic of mass media. Self and social reality suffer a loss of meaning. [17] For how can we have even a relatively critical understanding of the outside world, or of ourselves, or of the media for that matter, if our meaning-making capacity is based on eroticized archetypes that have been fabricated by the commodity makers who sponsor what we see on the air?

Absent a larger context of meaning into which these isolated information packages can be integrated, the temptations of skepticism grow strong.[18] "It's all absurd, incomprehensible; the world is full of frighteningly mysterious events and unsettling dangers," the voice of skepticism urges. Ironic detachment thus becomes a natural coping mechanism, as does the impulse simply to go along for the ride. And therein lie the power and self-perpetuating dynamic of radical disenchantment ("skeptical postmodernism").

This too is what we find when law goes *pop*. When constructivist (postmodern) theory, the media logic of new communication technologies, and the instant gratification demands of the marketplace converge, law's braking function, its ability to check popular passions and prejudices, breaks down. Indeed, it operates in reverse. In their emulation of media logic, savvy producers of legal representations today covet the same fuel for the same effect as the media themselves: namely, intensified, albeit fragmentary and disconnected, affect. The missile hits its target and we respond; the predatory other attacks, and we respond. Isolated images, decontextualized actions, foreknown responses, easily orchestrated, easily grasped.

To be sure, mass media journalists (the so-called fourth estate) have colluded in the information- and reflection-corrupting effects of this craving for quick, forceful impacts. As French sociologist Pierre Bourdieu has noted, "[J]ournalists point to the public's expectations. But in fact they are projecting onto the public their own inclinations and their own views." The result, Bourdieu observes, is an unwitting form of self-censorship: "They retain only the things capable of interesting them and 'keeping their attention,' which means things that fit their categories and mental grid; and they reject as insignificant or remain indifferent to symbolic expressions that ought to reach the popular as a whole."[19] The driving force behind this typically unconscious insistence on the inescapability of entertainment-driven journalism is clear. It is the market-based competition for ratings, audience share, and the sponsored support they assure.

In this respect, media journalists may be paying short shrift to their professional responsibilities as reliable purveyors of important public information. Yet we must also recall that what we are witnessing here is a process of mutually assured seduction between jurists and journalists alike. The impact of their combined efforts risks seriously compromising the discrete virtues of ordinary common sense. Put simply, members of the public cannot adequately fulfill their legal and political decision-making responsibilities, either as jurors or as voters, under conditions of sustained communicative distortion.

Prolonged public skepticism in response to these conditions risks law's delegitimation. Skepticism also invites the danger of alternative sources of lawmaking—whether in the form of increased jury nullification or the spread of antinomian social movements that lay claim to legal authorities of their own.[20] Distortions in the popular decision-making process also tend to give rise to a deepening distortion of judicial competencies. As courts struggle against a growing tide of popular disenchantment, the temptation to offer a "populist" jurisprudence grows stronger. But gratifying the public's passions in this way promises only to further undercut the court's vital braking function. Indeed, it is precisely the capacity to constrain popular passions in the name of higher legal principles or constitutional guarantees that is lost when law goes *pop*. For then the appeal of ("mass-mediated") truth and violent retribution arrests more sober reflection and judgment.

In a time of legitimation crisis courts may lack the institutional strength to risk becoming an even greater target of the public's aroused passions. This may also serve to increase existing pressures to privatize conflict resolution through out-of-court settlement. But this would only skew further the public's perception of law. As growing numbers of cases elude the courtroom (currently more than 90 percent of all civil and criminal cases end in negotiated settlements), it is the unrepresentative, highly symbolic notorious case that will increasingly bear the brunt of the public's frustrated craving for legal meaning. Once subject to the visual, commerce-driven logic of the mass media, however, these entertainingly staged, highly impassioned dramas—half human interest story, half celebrity talk show—end up breeding more skepticism within the community at large. The O. J. Simpson trial is a case in point. The net result is a deepened legitimation crisis for law.

There is no quick fix to the challenges we face when law goes *pop*. The problems are complex and multiple, and the strategies that we need to deal with them are similarly complex and multiple. They include the following:

As a threshold matter we must begin the process of recognition. This means that we must be clear about the nature and extent of the problem and the threat that it poses to law, and ultimately to democracy itself. We must also come to recognize that with the advent of postmodernism we have inherited a new agenda, with a new set of challenges and resources, different from those supplied in the age of modernity. It is fruitless to try to fit the modernist agenda and mindset to our current situation. Attempting to perfect the dichotomous categories of modern reason will no longer suffice.

The challenge before us is not to see if we can further refine the criteria of dispassionate rationality for the sake of universal standards of reason, truth, and the autonomous self. Nor is it to repress the irrational more effectively, to cleanse reason of desire or to sweep away the contingencies of chance and the necessity of fate in the world around us. Rather, it is to cultivate a more sophisticated appreciation of the extent to which the "antinomies" of modernity may be viewed as a complex mosaic of interpenetrating forces and constructs. We need to understand better the different ways in which reason and desire, logic and myth, suspicion and enchantment intermingle within and among diverse discourse practices. And we need to assess critically how these practices help to construct (or alter) our sense of self and social reality.

In short, what we are dealing with here is a fundamental epistemological shift. It is what happens when the rationalist ideals and repressive impulses of the Enlightenment admit the constructive and tragic insights of a mature rhetorical ("affirmative postmodern") culture. Law, culture, and media interpenetrate and co-constitute one another. They need to be studied from a broadly interdisciplinary perspective.

Moving beyond recognition, however, we must also begin to address constructively the new challenges postmodernity presents. For one thing, we must move to restore the discrete virtues of disparate modes of legal discourse and reasoning and redress imbalances in the way power is allocated among them. In a climate of media-enhanced passion and prejudice, the public's as well as the judiciary's discrete institutional competencies are especially prone to distortion. After all, it is the criminal accused, the alien facing deportation, the "oddball" whose unusual and ill-favored beliefs place him or her on the margins of society, who are most susceptible to the media's exploitation and derision. Yet, these same strangers and outcasts are a rich source of meaning in regard to our most precious constitutional rights and principles. It may be their actions or speech that define the scope of legitimate state power. For what the Constitution means with respect to them is what it means with respect to us all. In this sense, our fate and theirs are invariably linked. We define ourselves in part by the way we define the other. When we define away that link, we risk defining away our most cherished constitutional protections. There may be no greater safeguard for human rights than the one generated by our ability to identify, at least to some extent, with the hated, the feared, the Other.

In angry retribution against the "irrational predator" in our midst, we defend against the terror of criminal victimization. But at the same time we also defend against the possibility of tyranny or state oppression. For surely by increasing the power of those who enforce the law we also increase the risks associated with excessive police power. Rationalizing the need for externally directed repression helps make those fears go away. What need have we to fear? we tell ourselves. We could never share the Other's fate. But rationalizing in this way the need to repress the wholly Other accomplishes even more. It also helps to repress the fear (and illicit enjoyment) of powerful forces within. Externalized repression thus does double duty: it not only justifies enhancing the repressive power of law; it also masks forbidden impulses by displacing them onto predatory Others without. And it is here that the interests of the commercial mass media come in.

It is precisely this link between illicit enjoyment and externalized punishment of the predatory Other that commercial television has exploited with such success in its promulgation of police dramas, docudramas, and reality-based programming. Here is where the viewing public may vicariously enjoy forbidden sexual and aggressive impulses as well as the punishment that invariably follows. Indeed, it is precisely the guarantee of punishment that makes the illicit pleasure possible. And in this way, the predatory criminal also serves double duty. His "otherness" simultaneously disguises the source of illicit pleasure (within ourselves) and justifies its punishment.

When law adopts this kind of media logic it helps to legitimize the heightened passions and distorted prejudices that are embodied within this form of communication. As a result, the status of the other hardens within the popular legal imagination. Moreover, the court's vital function as constitutional guardian and countermajoritarian brake upon popular passions and prejudices grows proportionately weaker. This breakdown is the chief lesson of the jurisprudence of appearances.

Chief Justice Warren Burger feared a serious legitimation crisis in the aftermath of the Watergate break-in and cover-up and in the face of damaging public revelations about the inner workings of the Supreme Court itself. In response, he sought to enlist the visual logic of the mass media in a battle to control the flow of legal appearances. But his efforts only made matters worse. What Burger did not realize is that when law and the commercial mass media converge on the same images and stories in search of self-legitimation, it is the media who win. The net loss for law includes increased public skepticism regarding law's ability to seek truth and do justice.

This is what we have seen in connection with the media spectacle of the notorious case. As Justice Clark wrote in 1965 in *Estes v. Texas:*

> From the moment the trial judge announces that a case will be televised it becomes a cause celebre. The whole community, including prospective jurors, becomes interested in all the morbid details surrounding it. . . . And we must remember that realistically it is only the notorious trial which will be broadcast because of the necessity for paid sponsorship. . . . [This] invariably focuses the lens upon the unpopular or infamous accused.

For his part, though he may not have realized it at the time, Chief Justice Earl Warren's expression of concern in *Estes* regarding the reality-corroding effects of viewing trials on TV (between commercial interruptions, as Warren put it) reflects a prescient understanding of what we today call the hyperreal media spectacle. Warren's fear was that televising trials would cause the public to conflate "the trial process with the forms of entertainment regularly seen on television and with the commercial objectives of the television industry." He added: "Should the television industry become an integral part of our system of criminal justice, it would not be unnatural for the public to attribute the shortcomings of the industry to the trial process itself."[21]

Warren and Clark concluded that trials could not be broadcast on television without posing a serious threat to the constitutional guarantee of a fair trial. Subsequent experience has shown that their fears were warranted. However, it is Justice Harlan's more measured, pivotal fifth vote in *Estes* that may offer an even more compelling insight. Rather than impose a wholesale ban on cameras in the courtroom, Justice Harlan focused on keeping off the air only those notorious cases that are most likely to result in excessive prejudice. Harlan believed that the ordinary case, the representative case, was the type that could best fulfill television's edifying function.

As a practical matter, of course, drawing the line between the ordinary and the sensational case is no easy matter. But there is a way to square Harlan's point regarding the effects of commercial broadcasting on notorious cases with the opinions of Clark and Warren. All of them agree that the objectionable aspect of televising trials stems from the distorting effects of the medium's market-driven logic. How notorious trials are framed and how the public interprets them thus become the crux of the matter.

In chapter 4 I contended that the notorious case often serves as a site for deeper cultural anxieties and conflicts. I maintain that intensified public discontent with law is inevitable when the symbolic function of the notorious case is inadequately interpreted and worked through. Under such circumstances underlying urgencies in the way of belief go unmet. At the same time cultural anxieties that block the realization of underlying cultural beliefs and aspirations and in the process distort specific case outcomes are likely to continue to haunt the community. As Hamlet (and Freud) discovered, the ghost of unappeased anxiety always returns. In the meantime, unresolved conflicts cause law to be stigmatized even further within the collective imagination. We have seen as much in a number of notorious cases, from the murder trial of Harry Thaw to the double murder trial of O. J. Simpson.

I believe there is merit in allowing notorious trials to be publicly viewed and reflectively assessed. But Harlan is right. If in the process of broadcasting these trials the principle of fairness is lost and the possibility of public edification is drowned out by market-driven media distortions, then much is sacrificed for little return. The question thus becomes: how might we disentangle legal communication from the distorting effects of commercial broadcasting?[22]

When the commercial media alone decide how legal images and stories will be framed and disseminated, serious political questions arise concerning inappropriate and unchecked concentrations of power among the corporate entities that own the media or sponsor what they broadcast. Such a concentration of power in the hands of discrete corporate "factions" (the corporate "fifth estate" that controls the news-disseminating "fourth estate") poses the greatest threat to law and democracy that we face today. Their decisions not only help to shape and inform what most people know about law and politics, but they also produce the cultural and cognitive tools most people use to speak and think with.

In the justly famous Federalist Paper no. 10, James Madison argued that the tyranny of factions, whether a majority or a minority, could be avoided in two ways. In a constitutional republic (unlike direct democracies) the people rely on the "enlightened views" and "virtuous sentiments" of their representatives to articulate "the public good." In this respect, Madison believed that the Congress would stand as a buffer against "local prejudices" and the "confusion of the multitude." Madison also believed that the larger a society is—in terms of both the number of its citizens and the extent of its territory—the greater will be the number of factions and the differences that separate them. In Madison's view, the threat of tyranny dissipates so long as the danger of consolidated factional interests is held in check by diverse and multiple interests and viewpoints.[23]

When law goes *pop* both of these safeguards against the tyranny of faction break down. Madison could not have imagined how a nationwide (indeed, a global) electronic mass media could collapse the barriers of time and space. To the extent that mass communication today homogenizes popular culture it dissipates the braking force of diverse, countermajoritarian interests and views. What Madison also could not have anticipated is how the assimilation of media logic by the people's representatives and the citizens alike might homogenize popular interests, passions, and prejudices. This development flattens out discourse practices across the country in a way that is "adverse to the rights of other citizens, or to the permanent and aggregate interest of the community."[24] Indeed, the crucial role that mass media and money play in the election of state and federal representatives increasingly pressures politicians to operate on the basis of standard media logic.[25] As Ronald Dworkin notes:

> The power of money in our politics, long a scandal, has now become a disaster. Elections are fought mainly on television. . . . The national political "debate" is now directed by advertising executives and conducted mainly through thirty-second, "sound-bite" television and radio commercials that are negative, witless, and condescending. . . . Television newscasts, from which most Americans now learn most of what they know about candidates and issues, are more and more shaped by rating wars, in which networks and local news bureaus are pressed to provide entertainment rather than information or analysis.[26]

Today, the logic of mass media, particularly television, is not only a logic of quick and heightened visual and emotional gratification. It also entails a logic of finance: only those with the means of procuring access to air time may be heard. Dworkin addresses the issue dead on: "It seems perverse to suffer the clear unfairness of allowing rich candidates to drown out poor ones or powerful corporations to buy special access to politicians by making enormous gifts. . . ." Here the contemporary imbalance in the allocation of power among discrete economically advantaged factions is laid bare.

The means of "kindling a flame" that could spread from one state to another may not have existed in 1787, when Madison wrote in support of ratification of the federal Constitution. Today, however, the situation is different. The threat of tyranny by the corporate-media faction has become real in our lifetime. Addressing these problems compels a critical reevaluation of the Supreme Court's refusal to distinguish between commercial and other forms of public speech in its first amendment jurisprudence.[27]

Justice William Brennan once wrote: "[F]or a democracy to survive . . . [requires] solicitude not only for communication itself, but also for the indispensable conditions of meaningful communication."[28] When the conditions of meaningful communication are in jeopardy the very fabric of democracy is threatened. In this respect, Dworkin's sober warning about the corrupting effects of money applies with equal force whether it is to the inequalities associated with media access in the context of campaign financing or to those associated with the corporate media faction that produces popular legal knowledge and the cultural and cognitive constructs people use to make sense of the world around them.

To paraphrase Dworkin and Brennan, it is perverse in the television age to cloak with first amendment protection the power of wealthy factions to inform and shape effective legal and political speech via the commercial mass media when doing so erodes rather than advances the indispensable conditions of meaningful communication. On this view, regulating the media's presentation of public trials so as to disentangle this kind of legal communication from the effects of commerce-driven distortions should be constitutionally permissible. Alternatively, or perhaps concomitantly, creating more public or private nonprofit stations (on the model of C-SPAN) should also be pursued on the local level. If the discrete virtues of competing forms of discourse and knowledge are to be realized, a place within the mass media must be made for them.[29]

In addition to reconsidering how legal representations are framed and disseminated by the media, we also need to give renewed thought to how such representations are being received by members of the public at large. At issue here is the public's ability to discern the various ways in which the conventions of popular meaning making distort legal issues and conflicts. For example, does the public adequately appreciate how TV formats skew political and legal matters toward exaggerated and simplistic ("stereotypical") meanings for ease of assimilation and heightened emotional impact? Is the public able to discount the artificially enhanced contentiousness of TV law talk for what it is—namely, the byproduct of a ratings-driven need for drama? Is the public adequately sensitized to the effects of litigation public relations strategies that help to produce many of the talking heads and skewed story lines and images that appear on the screen?[30]

The public needs to be trained to decode the skewed meanings and distorted effects of mediatized legal representations. It is precisely this need for increased sophistication in media literacy skills that has spawned the worldwide media literacy movement. It is disconcerting to note, however, that the United States lags behind other countries in the development and implementation of education programs (from kindergarten through high school) designed to teach these skills.[31]

A concerted effort to cultivate critical thinking skills of this sort is essential to the continued flourishing of democracy in today's media-saturated world. Notably, it is precisely this ability to self-consciously deconstruct and reconstruct cultural meanings that rhetorical training has always aspired to cultivate. As Ruth Morse notes, "Rhetoric named a curriculum, a set of handbooks, tendencies of style which concentrated on the means of moving and persuading. . . ."[32] For similar training to occur in our time new rhetorical skills must be taught. The domain of rhetorical and interpretive construction and deconstruction must be expanded beyond the realm of print. A diverse range of electronic and computer-based communication technologies, along with other techniques and technologies, must also be taken into account.

With such training the posture of media users is likely to shift from mere passive receiver to active seeker, interpreter, and creator of information, in both narrative and visual forms. Regrettably, even in law schools today, despite the fact that the art and ethics of persuasion are central to the profession, this kind of education has hardly begun. Change is needed. New rhetorical handbooks must be written, new media laboratories must be created, to reflect current conventions of meaning making and to bring to bear new insights regarding how legal meanings are constructed, altered, or suppressed. Unconscious and symbolic forms of expression as well as popular cultural and cognitive constructs need to be included within a new interdisciplinary domain of law, media and cultural studies. The ability to discern the difference between licit and illicit forms of legal persuasion—in court and in the court of public opinion—requires no less.

At the same time, however, it must be admitted that improved critical skills alone will not suffice, not if the capacity for enchantment remains as problematic as it is today. Which is to say, not if the skeptical postmodern spirit goes unchallenged and uncountered. To be sure, cultural affirmation is not something that can simply be willed into being. And while deliberate strategies in its behalf may not be without merit—such as enhanced public and private financial support for increased creative activity and improved means (both virtual and actual) of public access[33]—who can say whether (or what kind of) cultural affirmation might ultimately emerge?

Yet, to concede the dubious efficacy of mandating cultural affirmation is not to say that we cannot cultivate heightened critical appreciation of the affirmations being made in the culture around us. The role of the cultural critic is precisely this: to open up a space for critical reflection in which underlying meanings, values, conflicts, and aspirations may be explored in a variety of cultural forms. This includes the works of popular, "high," and legal culture. We cannot forget that law is both a byproduct and a producer of mainstream culture. As a result, the fate of law is inextricably bound to the fate of culture in its various forms.

With a growing awareness of this deep interconnectedness, insights from legal, cultural, cognitive, and media studies should come to be viewed as mutually enriching. In this way, the highly symbolic (culturally overdetermined) notorious case may come to be seen as a rich source of knowledge and insight rather than as simply a bizarre media spectacle. These cases properly understood can help us to come to grips with the most pressing cultural and social conflicts of our time. The forms of disguise such conflicts assume in the collective consciousness, precisely in order to escape self-reflective confrontation, need to be studied in their own right. They have much to tell us about the way we constitute self and social reality in our own time. Insights here also alert us to the various ways in which we collude (by unconsciously participating) in the repression and disguise of meaning in the rituals and dramas of law. Armed with such insights we will be better able to assume responsibility for the conscious and unconscious meanings we share and for the realities they create. Enhanced responsibility in such matters brings into view two underemphasized aspects of the constructivist perspective: participation and choice regarding the creation of self and social reality.

These are fruits—bitter ones, perhaps—of the affirmative postmodern perspective. We all must accept responsibility for the legal and social meanings we affirm and, by extension, for the values and aspirations our affirmations help to actualize (or silence or deny). This broader responsibility implicates anew the underlying cultural *mythos* or constitutional frame story discussed earlier. For it may well describe the central normative task that our complex legal ecosystem of inter-related communicative practices and competencies must carry out. The question here becomes, what do we make of that *mythos* in our time? To be capable of such an inquiry conveys perhaps better than anything else what it means to speak of a "mature constructivism."

By now it must be clear that that inquiry constitutes a major theme of this book. It underlies my discussions of the various cultural narratives and images lawyers have deployed in notorious (mediatized) trials from John Brown on. It also informs my efforts to situate our understanding of law in cultural terms. By referring to a variety of contemporary films—from Errol Morris's alleged documentary about the frame-up of Randall Dale Adams to feature films and television productions—I have sought to demonstrate, as well as deepen our understanding of, the current cultural context for law. That understanding includes the possibility of making a cultural transition from public skepticism toward law, lawyers, and the legal process, and from the radical disenchantment of skeptical postmodernism, to an alternative position. I submit that a tragic constructivist take on affirmative postmodernism represents one such alternative. Adopting such a view, however, requires a renewed critical encounter with law's need for enchantment and the cultural resources from which that enchantment may come.

With this requirement in mind, I would like to close this chapter by evoking a contemporary film that in my view epitomizes the tragic constructivist perspective. In doing so, I aim to suggest that a mature constructivism is already taking shape in the culture around us. And with it a new understanding of reason, identity, truth, and justice is emerging.

The film I have chosen to bear the weight of this claim is the last work of the internationally renowned filmmaker Krzysztof Kieslowski. It is the third in a trilogy of films called *Blue, White,* and *Red.* Kieslowski co-wrote all three films with a lawyer named Krzysztof Piesiewicz. In titling the films after the colors of the French flag, Kieslowski signaled his intent to create a series of symbolic, intertwining tales about the mythic-foundational values they symbolize: liberty, equality, and fraternity. Let it be said at once, however, that these are by no means abstract studies. To the contrary, as Kieslowski himself put it, "Blue, white, red: liberty, equality, fraternity. . . . The West has implemented these three concepts on a political or social plane, but it's an entirely different matter on the personal plane. And that's why we thought of these films."[34]

How, then, does one provide a particularized account of the meaning of fraternity? That is the challenge Kieslowski sets himself in *Red*. And he succeeds brilliantly. Here is a complex tale of people apparently leading separate lives whose paths fatefully cross. It tells of the human struggle to connect with others and how that effort may be defeated or abetted by powerful irrational forces: fate and chance, rage and desire, perversity and suffering, compassion and redemption. We also come to see that these forces may be linked. There may even be a pattern, a law, an ethical code perhaps, to guide us amid the strange powers that surround us within and without.

It is in this sense, I maintain, that *Red* maps out what I shall call the metaphysics of tragic constructivism. Kieslowski offers no guarantees, no certainties. Tragic suffering seems inevitable. Yet, the film also shows us the manifold ways in which signs of affirmation may suddenly come into view: in an impulsive act of kindness, in the stray beauty of the setting sun, in a chance encounter from which mutual understanding and selfless love radiate like an act of grace. It is also no empty coincidence (if we can continue to speak of any coincidence as "empty") that Kieslowski's and Piesiewicz's tale centers on the lives of a retired judge and a young lawyer who by film's end will pass his exams to become a judge himself. Yes, this is also a film about the proper claims of law, truth, and justice in a postmodern world.

To be sure, the film says far more than I can tell here. What I hope to do, aside from inspiring others to attend more closely to Kieslowski's work, is suggest why I believe this film embodies the kind of affirmative postmodern response to skepticism and moral apathy I have been describing in this book. It is on this basis that we may begin to self-reflectively narrate a tragic constructivist jurisprudence, an account in which authenticity, tragic knowledge, and enchantment replace the deceptive manipulation of desire we find in the skeptical postmodern jurisprudence of appearances.

As the film opens its chief metaphor fills the screen. A man picks up the telephone and places an overseas call. With dizzying speed we at once rush into the telephone network. The camera becomes a bolt of light—shooting through cables over land and under water. A kaleidoscope of lights bursts into view. These are the calls people are making, from one instant, one place, one life, to another. The film's theme has been announced. What we are about to see is a story about the connections people everywhere seek to make with one another. We will soon see how those efforts may succeed and how they may go astray.

A telephone rings somewhere. It is the apartment of Valentine Dussaut, a university student and part-time fashion model. Valentine's anonymous, perpetually absent boyfriend, Michel, is on the line. We will hear his disembodied voice from time to time throughout the film, but we will never actually see him. His absence forebodes trouble in his relationship with Valentine. Nor is it simply the physical distance between them that is of concern—there is an emotional gap as well. Indeed, the precariousness of their connection is manifest from the start.

Their conversation immediately clues us in. Michel's opening words are emblematic of every conversation they will have. "First it was busy, now the machine. Are you alone?" Suspicion and jealousy are Michel's calling cards. But Valentine is quick to explain. The call that initially blocked his connection was a job offer. She's been invited to a photo shoot, a shoot that ultimately will result in a 25-by-65-foot advertising banner featuring Valentine's sorrowful face in profile. "A Breath of Fresh Air," the chewing gum commercial's logo will read. An ironic message, as we will soon discover. For Valentine *will* become a breath of fresh air, in the embittered life of the retired judge she is about to meet. But her own failing connection with Michel will only give way to another, more life-affirming encounter after a fierce storm forces her commodified image to come down. Coincidentally, it is the same force that will bring Valentine into the life of another man, Auguste Bruner, a young lawyer and judge-to-be. Valentine's false, commercial self—an easy target for the other's objectifying gaze—is about to recede, allowing a more authentic one to unfurl.

But Michel's and Valentine's connection is not the only one under way as the film opens. Even as they speak, another conversation is about to begin. We see this as the camera slips out of Valentine's window and travels across the street to a neighboring apartment. A man has just placed a call. It is Auguste Bruner. A woman's voice answers, "Personal weather reports," she announces. It is Auguste's girlfriend, Karin. Auguste says nothing, just the whisper of a kiss into the receiver, and he hangs up. His trust that Karin will immediately recognize that it is him, that there could in fact be no one else in Karin's life who would do such a thing, comes in stark contrast to Michel's unsavory suspicions. Auguste does not know it yet, but his trust is misplaced. Karin will soon betray him by sleeping with another man.

A network of relationships is settling into place, but invisible forces are waiting in the wings to alter them. These hidden forces will soon throw Auguste and Valentine together and break Auguste and Karin apart. The symbol of their invisible presence stands just beneath Valentine's window. It is a slot machine that Valentine ritualistically plays each morning after she buys her daily newspaper. If the three spinning icons line up, there's trouble ahead. Strange? Not at all. It's the logic of chance, in accordance with the law of the conservation of fate. A win now means a loss to come. As Kieslowski's film unfurls we witness separate strands in an invisible net of chance and fate being laid down. Invisible—and perhaps indivisible as well. For just as the separate lives of the characters we encounter fatefully connect and diverge, so too are our lives imperceptibly interconnected with the lives of others around us. The stray act of a stranger may irrevocably alter our fate, just as our acts may alter the lives of others around us. We see as much when Valentine Dussaut chances upon the life of retired judge Joseph Kern.

The agent of their encounter is Kern's dog, whom Valentine accidentally hits with her car. An address on the dog's collar leads her to Kern's home. Once a judge, Kern is now a full-time voyeur. He has placed himself outside the loop. Alone, unconnected to others, Kern no longer acts. He simply listens, furtively, electronically eavesdropping on the private sufferings of his neighbors—as their no longer private telephone conversations amply reveal. The truths Kern overhears confirm his profound disenchantment with humanity. The lies, the betrayals, the cruelty: here is human nature laid bare. That, at any rate, is how Kern explains his life as Valentine silently listens. To judge, he tells her, is pointless. Nothing changes. Besides, who knows when forgiveness is better than condemnation? He tells an anecdote to explain. Once, thirty-five years ago, when still a judge, Kern mistakenly acquitted a man. The man, he later learned, was guilty. But upon making his own investigation into the matter many years later, Kern also learned that the man subsequently married, had three children and a grandchild, and was, as Kern puts it, "living in peace."

"Deciding what is true and what isn't now seems to me a lack of modesty," Kern concludes. So he contents himself simply with listening. It is like when he was a judge except that now he knows the stories he hears are true. And the futile responsibility of judging has been lifted from his shoulders. "I'd do the same thing if I were in their place," Kern says. "Given their lives, I would steal, I'd kill, I'd lie. All that because I wasn't in their shoes, but mine." Then he recounts a story from his life. Three and a half decades ago a man seduced and ran off with Kern's one and, as it turned out, only love. Years later, the same man came before Kern in court. The roof of a closed market that Kern's rival had been building had collapsed. People were killed. Kern condemned him. "It was a legal sentence," he tells Valentine. But Kern's tone betrays his doubts. Indeed, it proved to be Kern's last judgment from the bench. After issuing it he asked for early retirement.

But the tale does not end there. Valentine does not share Kern's dismal view of life, and her fresh spirit now washes over Kern's deadened one. He stopped believing, he confesses to Valentine. Then he adds, "Maybe you're the woman I never met." If only their paths had crossed when he was still young, perhaps she could have changed his life. But perhaps she still can. Consider this exchange between them. Kern has been leading Valentine through the personal travails of his neighbors as their telephone conversations play one after the other on the air in Kern's living room. "Ah, next program, not very interesting," we hear Kern say. It is a distraught mother who incessantly telephones her daughter with complaints of ill health and lack of food. But she is lying and her daughter knows it. Lies that fall on deaf ears veil a mother's desperate need for her daughter to come, to ease the suffering of terrible loneliness. "Next program," Kern flatly intones, as if what we have just heard were no more than a TV soap opera. It's as Andy Warhol said, "once you see emotions from a certain angle you can never think of them as real again."

This is what it is like when compassion dies. It is what has become of Kern in the face of life's tragic disappointments. The suffering around (and within) him has destroyed his capacity to feel or care for anyone. But Valentine's response is different. She is repulsed both by Kern's actions and by his cynical philosophy, and she tells him so. When Kern says he cares for nothing, Valentine replies, "So stop breathing!" In her, the breath of life is strong. "You're wrong," she tells Kern. "People aren't bad. It's not true. . . . People may be weak sometimes." Valentine rushes in tears from his house. But not before having bestowed a great gift. Her breath of life revives Kern's spirit. After she departs he sits down at his desk to compose letters to each of his neighbors in turn. In them Kern confesses his immoral and illegal acts of spying. Recognition of loss and suffering precedes the change. Kern has come back to life. His first judgment concerns himself: guilty. Passive voyeurism, the reflection of his deadened spirit, has come to an end.

Kern's chance connection with Valentine has stirred memories of youthful love within him. But she has done more than that. She has inspired within him love of another sort, the kind of love that aspires to spiritual or fraternal rather than physical consummation. Rather than passively (and perversely) enjoying the spectacle of human suffering, Kern will now actively seek to untangle crossed connections and foster authentic ones. For as it turns out his years of listening to people's stories of suffering and conflict have given him insight into the mysterious ways of chance. Like Oedipus, whose long years of suffering culminated in divine sanctification, suffering also seems to have bestowed upon Kern a tragic wisdom. And something else besides, something akin to second sight, like the foresight of blind Teiresias, or perhaps we should say of an oracle of law. Kern will now set in motion ripples of fate that will change Valentine's life, and perhaps Auguste Bruner's as well. For it is through Kern's intervention that their paths will finally cross.

Separate lives, separate relationships: Valentine's faltering connection with the perverse Michel; Auguste's betrayed relationship with the fickle Karin; and Kern's transformative relationship with the vivifying Valentine. Yet, how easily each could become another. Like the way Auguste, a judge by film's end, also spurned in love, and in so many other ways Kern's double, seems primed to replicate Kern's disenchanted life. Just as Valentine, caught in another's gaze, an object of perverse desire, might never pierce the veil of inauthenticity—but for a chance event, a fateful encounter.

This is but one of the lessons that Kieslowski's characters, and we who follow their fate, may ultimately learn. There is another. "Character is fate," said the ancient philosopher Heraclitus. It is a claim that doubles back on itself. Who knows what fate will make of character? But we may also ask who knows what our character will make of our fate? For example, who knows if the one in need will recognize the form in which redemption or ruination may come? And even granting the power of recognition, still a choice must be made. There is a strict but invisible tradeoff between licit and illicit desire. The one must give way to enable the other. Only by resisting the perverse gaze of the voyeur, as Valentine may come to realize, or by choosing to abandon it, as Kern does, may we enable desire of a higher sort to take its place. Failing that our attempts to forge an authentic connection with another seem destined to falter or go astray.

In elucidating this crucial lesson, Kieslowski has put his finger on one of the key challenges postmodern disenchantment presents. Call it the leaching out of authenticity. What Andy Warhol describes as the substitution of virtual (electronically mass mediated, passively received) experience for real life—and the ensuing inability or unwillingness to tell one from the other. This danger in its quintessential form takes shape in the relationship between the consumer and the consumed. Here we see the illusory connection with things and others that advertisers and public relations experts conjure on the basis of hidden desire and the promise of quick and easy, responsibility-free gratification. In short, it demonstrates the perversion of authentic relationships. What Kieslowski seems to be saying is that in order for real relationships to flourish—which is to say, before fraternity may become a living reality within society—an alternative form of desire is needed. It is what Martin Luther King Jr. referred to as "understanding, [and] redeeming good will for all."

What, then, are we to make of truth and justice in a world of strange invisible forces like rage and desire, chance and fate? For one thing, contrary to the skeptic's view, acts of affirmative justice are possible. Realizing that possibility, however, will take more than passive voyeurism before the "spectacle" of human conflict and suffering. It begins with a sense of tragic affirmation, an awareness that our lives are mysteriously connected by hidden forces, and that our actions, however insignificant they seem, may suddenly transform our fate and the fate of others around us. In this vast entanglement of connections or misconnections waiting to happen, who knows but that the life of one, strangely other a moment before, may become ours, strange no more, but a moment hence? Here lies the tragic origin of fellow feeling, the feeling that gives birth to fraternity, compassion, and merciful justice. An affirmative postmodern principle of fraternity is at hand: invisible strands of chance and fate irrevocably tie us all to one another in a vast brotherhood of possible selves. Legal judgment in this view must take place against the backdrop of a complex network of human and impersonal forces and connections. Indeed, this acknowledgment humanizes law precisely to the extent that the inhuman has not been defensively discounted or repressed. On this account, then, "naked" factual truth and the demand for justice alone will not suffice, not if understanding and compassion are also to have a role within the legal system. Not if we are to come to grips with what it means to be an "Other" or how the Other is legally and culturally constructed. Or how the Other bears witness to law's lack, how it haunts the law with its ghostly presence, an anxiety-inducing reminder of a debt that must be paid.

Injustice impels reparation. The phantom of justice stalks the law when law falls short, or fails altogether. This is how justice seeks to become real. Law's limit thus demarcates a site of anxiety. In anxiety we hear the call for a reckoning. It announces that a debt to reality remains outstanding. To be sure, this is not "Reality" writ large in the modern Enlightenment sense of some objective, unchanging universal. Within the post-Enlightenment metaphysics of tragic constructivism, truth and justice are always provisional, which is to say their meaning is contingent upon the particular debt to be paid. This is why we study current and historic signs (or perhaps we should say "symptoms") of anxiety within mainstream and legal culture. They provide clues to the nature of the debt, and the kind of account that may be needed to meet its demands. In this sense, the anxiety that haunts the law may be justice's most palpable, perhaps its only sign. We encounter such a sign as law's "other" because it identifies a lack, or an excess: something law needs, or needs to work through, to complete the act of reparation.

The commodified self, steeped in fantasy and denial, like law's masked dalliance with the illicit in the jurisprudence of appearances, also gives rise to a ghostly "double." As we have seen in the case of Max Cady, the double seeks rectification in response to whatever transgressed norm has given rise to his spectral existence. Like the norms of authenticity and self-integration and the fraternal, life-affirming connection between self and others against which we measure the illicit desire and objectifying gaze of the voyeur. Or the norm of catharsis and compassion against which we measure the false (or hyper-)catharsis of masked titillation and the displacement of illicit desire upon the predatory other. Or the norms of chance and fate against which we measure the injustice of law's at times immoderately repressive, narrowly framed demands for order. To be sure, the anxiety that signals immoderate repression may be part of the price we pay for the rule of law. But we must not forget that disorder also has its truth. It, too, places demands upon justice: like the justice of reconciling legal condemnation with the repressed reality of strange irrational forces. There are times when we call this reconciliation mercy. It too has the power to rectify law's lack.

This analysis once again points up the vital disequilibrium that lies at the heart of things. It suggests that adjudication takes place within constantly shifting centers of localized and contingent reconciliations of order and discord. New tensions constantly arise calling forth new anxieties, new urgencies, and thus a constantly renewed need to reconfigure the balance of disequilibrium. Law is made, unmade, and

made anew within these shifting sites of provisional repair. Historically contingent debts to reality may falter before the rectifying call of
justice, or perhaps merely undergo heightened repression. New forms
of enchantment may arise to replace compromises that are no longer
tenable. Alternatively, heightened repression and the anxiety it produces may continue to stalk the law, sowing disenchantment so long
as law's power to redeem transgressed norms remains in doubt. In
short, there is no end to the rectifying work of justice. To heed its call,
however, we need to vigilantly deconstruct law's other. In this way
the critical *ethos* of suspicion (what symbolic meaning informs law's
lack?) may join with the potentially transformative—self-integrating
and community-building—power of legal enchantment (what aspira-
tional construct shall we affirm to hold self and social reality together?).

Today, opposing forces of reason and desire, logical proof and
mythical enchantment, free will and irrational seizure haunt the postmodern mind—particularly in its quest for truth and justice through
law. In *Red* Kieslowski explores the possibility of justice in a tragic
world. It is a world that offers no guarantees: not for truth, not for
self, and not for justice. Kieslowski's vision is no romance. But it does
envision a way of living with dignity, compassion, and merciful justice
amid the vicissitudes of chance and fate, rage and desire, loss and
redemption. Perhaps it is the very uncertainty of achieving this goal
wherein lies the chief source of law's humanity—an insight that is
rooted in the inescapable reality of tragic suffering.

Commodification of self and law in the service of disguised gratification is fueled by and in turn fuels further illicit desire. In this respect,
public relations, advertising, and the staging of hyperreal media events
are the opposite of myth. They offer a means by which cultural symbols may be converted into mere commodities, signs that exist to be
consumed for the pleasure such consumption allows. Their key function is to displace hidden desire and sustain the promise of continued
gratification in the future. When culture becomes decadent, pleasure
dominates meaning. As Warhol taught, turning emotions and beliefs
into commodities—consumable signs and images—leaches out meaning, authenticity, and finally reality itself. Feelings and beliefs ultimately become as derealized as the self that consumes them. Mythic
enchantment, by contrast, seeks the reverse. Its main purpose is to
animate cultural symbols and the norms they embody. Symbolic
meaning in this sense is irreducible to the pleasures it may yield. Myth
functions in the service of belief. In place of highly individualized acts
of self-gratifying consumption, myth produces shared rituals and so-

cial dramas. These are the means by which the values, beliefs, and aspirations of the community are self-reflectively made real.

Aided by the critical tools of suspicion and the anguish of tragic wisdom, we may be able to expose and perhaps even dispel by working through the appeal of illicit enchantments. In this way, law's emulation of commercial advertising's cynical manipulation of gratification and desire may be countered as denial and displacement yield to reflective affirmation of the frame story that best suits our psychological, cultural, and legal aspirations. I have endeavored to suggest that our constitutional *mythos* rhetorically and tragically construed, which is to say, understood as a dynamic disequilibirum among disparate communicative practices and truths, provides such a frame story for law. It is an affirmative postmodern account that encourages our coming to grips with the limits of modern rationality. Indeed, it traces the origin of compassion and mercy to our ability consciously to confront the irrational forces that course within and around us—forces like rage and desire, chance and fate.

In sum, it is through enchantment that law and culture converge. But to what extent will it be the commodified enchantment of voyeuristic desire and the displaced rage of retribution, or symbolic enchantment based on an affirmative (postmodern) construct that can counter the leaching out of authenticity and the ensuing erosion of meaningful ("fraternal") connections with others? And will we be able to distinguish the one form of enchantment from the other? When the time comes that that line can no longer be drawn, then law surely will have gone *pop*. Then justice and love of mercy will no longer direct the course of legal affairs. For justice without the possibility of authentic enchantment is but the will to power by another name. It is the reign of Sharyar's terror with no recourse to the humanizing cultural tales of Scheherazade, or Kieslowski. When law goes *pop* we are forced to consider anew the source and efficacy of doing justice through law. In so doing it is incumbent upon us to ask, who is it that suffers most from law's irrational violence amid the unforeseeable contingencies of chance and the uncontrollable mandate of fate? The ultimate measure of justice, on which law's legitimacy depends, lies in the response we make to that question.

So we ask, what have we made (are we making, will we make) of law's capacity for enchantment in response to or in behalf of the "Other"? Will the craving for quick and easy (responsibility-free) gratification and the will to power dominate law and popular culture alike? Will law go *pop* or will tragic wisdom and the critical tools of

de- and re-constructive reason in conjunction with the licit enchantments of postmodern affirmation prevail? The answer depends on the
kind of culture we accept, or help to construct, or refuse to affirm.

What images do we share? What stories do we tell ourselves and
others about truth and reason, about law and justice, and about the
masked rage of retribution and the hidden flow of illicit desire, or
about the contingencies of chance and the necessity of fate, or about
the civilizing force of compassion and mercy? Therein lies the fate of
truth, justice, and law in our time.

NOTES

Chapter One

1. Truman Capote pioneered the "nonfiction novel" with *In Cold Blood* (1965). Norman Mailer brilliantly followed suit with *The Executioner's Song* (1979). For a discussion of the blurred line between fact and fiction in documentary film, see Bill Nichols, *Representing Reality* (Bloomington: Indiana University Press, 1991).

2. According to Vico, "Once it was the glory of jurisprudence to apply fictions in order to square acts of equity with the law; today, it is that, through liberal interpretations, just laws measure up to the facts." Giambattista Vico, *On the Study Methods of Our Time,* trans. Donald Phillip Verene (Ithaca: Cornell University Press, 1990 [1709]), 59. However, as every beginning law student soon learns, legal fictions remain in abundance.

3. See Sir Philip Sidney, *An Apology for Poetry* or *The Defence of Poetry,* ed. Geoffrey Shepherd (London: Thomas Nelson and Sons Ltd., 1969 [1595]). See also Kathy Eden, *Poetic and Legal Fiction in the Aristotelian Tradition* (Princeton: Princeton University Press, 1986).

4. The more general cultural phenomenon at work here has been variously referred to as the emergence of "the society of the spectacle" (see Guy Debord, *The Society of Spectacle* [New York: Zone Books, 1995]), the dissolution of reality into the "simulacrum" (see Jean Baudrillard, *Fatal Strategies* [London: Pluto Press, 1990]), and the "television context of no context" [George W. S. Trow, *Within the Context of No Context* [New York: Atlantic Monthly Press, 1997]). See also Paul Virilio, *The Aesthetics of Disappearance* (New York: Semiotext(e), 1991).

5. See, for example, Alexis de Tocqueville, *Democracy in America,* ed. J. Mayer and M. Lerner (New York: Anchor, 1966), 254. According to Tocqueville, "The jury is both the most effective way of establishing the people's rule and the most efficient way of teaching them how to rule." See also Norman J. Finkel, *Commonsense Justice* (Cambridge: Harvard University Press, 1995), 337: "Rooted in a legal history far older than the U.S. Constitution, the jury, the conscience of the community speaks. . . . In calling the law to follow the path of the community, we are not urging it to heed majoritarian, transitory, ignorant, or unprincipled sentiment. We are asking it to acknowledge what it may have forgotten or lost sight of: the deeper roots of justice." See also Jeffrey Abramson, *We, The Jury* (New York: Basic Books, 1994), 250: "The direct and raw character of jury democracy makes it our most honest mirror, reflecting both the good and the bad that ordinary people are capable of when called upon to do justice."

6. Upon occasion the United States Supreme Court has noted the limits of common sense with respect to the lawful (albeit counterintuitive) demands

of constitutional principle. For example, in *Jackson v. Denno*, 378 U.S. 368, 382 (1964) the Court acknowledged the difficulty lay jurors face in choosing between a criminal defendant's *factual* guilt, based upon a trustworthy confession, and his *legal* guilt, which requires that the confession also be *voluntarily* made, which is to say, untainted by police coercion. As the majority states, "That a trustworthy confession must also be voluntary if it is to be used at all generates natural and potent pressure to find it voluntary. Otherwise the guilty defendant goes free."

7. In the words of novelist Richard Ford, it is as if the act of expressing an opinion has become "merely a spasmodic way to intensify a passing moment—a *now*—by making an act one performs seem to matter when in fact it doesn't." As we will see in chapter 2, what Ford is describing here is akin to Andy Warhol's prescient pop insight regarding the growing sense of *derealization,* or the inauthenticity of our being in the world. As I will contend further on, this degeneration of lived experience, this leaching out of self-authenticity, is a hallmark of postmodern *hyperreality,* a condition wherein "the real" is increasingly made up of media-constructed signs referring to other media-constructed signs. Ford describes the situation this way:

> What I'm talking about are the ways in which that series of present moments we describe collectively as our real lives is made insignificant, made ignoble or forgettable, made hellish or made in essence nonexistent by all sorts of forces outside our brains, yet forces whose existence we may have complicity with. . . . [T]he higher valuation placed on my immediate attention by others—vendors let's call them—is accompanied by or perhaps even causes a lower valuation to be placed on it by me.

Richard Ford, "Our moments have all been seized," *New York Times,* Week in Review, 27 December 1998, 9. One may discern a resonance here with Walter Benjamin's concern about our loss of the "unique aura" of the object and the person. See Walter Benjamin, "The work of art in the age of mechanical reproduction," in *Illuminations* (New York: Schocken Books, 1969). Anticipating what we recognize today as the culture of celebrity, Benjamin writes: "The film responds to the shriveling of the aura with an artificial build-up of the 'personality' outside the studio. The cult of the movie star, fostered by the money of the film industry, preserves not the unique aura of the person but the 'spell of the personality,' the phony spell of a commodity" (Benjamin, *Illuminations,* 231). Paul Auster's searing image of the detective trapped in the mystery of his own unraveling identity, where even the crime—much less its solution—seems to be missing, speaks to our uneasy familiarity with a smaller-than-life counterpart to the larger-than-life figure of the celebrity. See Paul Auster, *The New York Trilogy* (New York: Penguin, 1994).

8. See, for example, James Boyd White, *When Words Lose Their Meaning* (Chicago: University of Chicago Press, 1984), 267:

The law is best regarded not so much as a set of rules and doctrines or as a bureaucratic system or an instrument for social control but as a culture, for the most part a culture of argument. It is a way of making a world with a life and a value of its own.

See also Rosemary J. Coombe, *The Cultural Life of Intellectual Properties: Authorship, Appropriation, and the Law* (Durham, N.C.: Duke University Press, 1998); Carol J. Clover, *Our Trial: Movies and the Adversarial Imagination* (Princeton: Princeton University Press, forthcoming); and John Denvir, ed., *Legal Reelism: Movies as Legal Texts* (Urbana: University of Illinois Press, 1996).

9. Pioneering works on the role of culture in the production of legal meaning include: Clifford Geertz, *Local Knowledge* (New York: Basic Books, 1983) and Michel Foucault, *Discipline and Punish* (Harmondsworth: Penguin, 1977). See also Austin Sarat and Thomas R. Kearns, *Law in the Domains of Culture* (Ann Arbor: University of Michigan Press, 1998); Patricia Ewick and Susan S. Silbey, *The Common Place of Law: Stories from Everyday Life* (Chicago: University of Chicago Press, 1998); and Alison Young, *Imagining Crime* (London: Sage, 1996).

10. The conceptual history of the "image" is rich and varied. It ranges from the Platonic and neo-Platonic, Italian Renaissance concept of the visual image as a symbol of suprasensible luminosity (see E. H. Gombrich, *"Icones Symbolicae,* the visual image in neo-Platonic thought," *Journal of the Warburg and Courtauld Institutes* 11 [1948]: 163, 167–73; and Ivan Illich, *In the Vineyard of the Text* [Chicago: University of Chicago Press, 1993]) to the post-Newtonian concept of the image as that which is illuminated from without (see W. J .T. Mitchell, *Iconology: Image, Text, Ideology* [Chicago: University of Chicago Press, 1986], 16, 37–40), to the psychoanalytic concept of the "narcissistic image" and the death of the self (see Pierre Legendre, *Law and the Unconscious,* ed. Peter Goodrich [New York: St. Martin's Press, 1997], 215), to a plethora of filmic theorizations, including Barthes's evocation of the image's "flicker of illumination" in a "cave of myths" (see Roland Barthes, "On cinemascopes," *Jouvert* 3, no. 3 [1999]), Metz's psychoanalytic approach to film's invisible unconscious processes (see Christian Metz, *The Imaginary Signifier* [Bloomington: Indiana University Press, 1982]), and more recently Grodal's holistic analysis of the way prototypical film genres trigger the cognitive and affective models we use in everyday life (see Torben Grodal, *Moving Pictures: A New Theory of Film Genres, Feelings and Cognition* [Oxford: Clarendon Press, 1999]), to name only a few. See generally David Bordwell and Noel Carroll, *Post-Theory: Reconstructing Film Studies* (Madison: University of Wisconsin Press, 1996). For the sake of simplicity and convenience, in this book I use "image" to stand for any contrived visual production—including photography, film, and the electronically or digitally produced audiovisual constructs of television and computers.

11. See Richard Lanham, *The Electronic Word* (Chicago: University of

Chicago Press, 1993), 5: "Look THROUGH a text and you are in the familiar world of the Newtonian interlude, where facts were facts, the world was really 'out there,' folks had sincere central selves, and the best writing style dropped from the writer as 'simply and directly as a stone falls to the ground,' precisely as Thoreau counseled. Look AT a text, however, and we have deconstructed the Newtonian world into Pirandello's and yearn to 'act naturally.'"

12. On the general breakdown of the Enlightenment project, see Alasdair MacIntyre, *After Virtue* (Notre Dame, Ind.: University of Notre Dame Press, 1981), and Richard J. Bernstein, *Beyond Objectivism and Relativism* (Philadelphia: University of Pennsylvania Press, 1983). On the emergence of the "constructed" or "narrative" self, see Donald Spence, *Narrative Truth and Historical Truth* (New York: W. W. Norton & Co., 1982); Jerome Bruner, *Acts of Meaning* (Cambridge: Harvard University Press, 1990); and Jerome Bruner and David A. Kalmar, "Narrative and metanarrative in the construction of self," in *Self-Awareness: Its Nature and Development,* ed. Michael Ferrari and Robert J. Sternberg (New York: Guilford Press, 1998).

13. See Friedrich Nietzsche, *The Will To Power,* ed. Walter Kaufmann (New York: Vintage, 1968 [1887–88]), 9–82.

14. Pauline Marie Rosenau has also discerned a "skeptical" as well as an "affirmative" type of postmodernism in her excellent survey of a complex field, *Post-Modernism and the Social Services* (Princeton: Princeton University Press, 1992). For an example of the nostalgia for Enlightenment values within the legal culture, see Daniel A. Farber and Suzanna Sherry, *Beyond All Reason: The Radical Assault on Truth in American Law* (Oxford: Oxford University Press, 1997).

15. As Professor Linda Meyer notes,

> Our fear of the uncertainty inherent in our modern discovery that we do not live in a stable cosmos, but in time and in a "world," precipitates ever more desperate attempts to keep things ordered, to keep judges under control.... Prediction, rationalization, and control are also coming into vogue within areas of legal doctrine. Instead of defining due care in tort law as reasonableness, we define it as economic efficiency—as what sanctions are necessary in order to control behavior and organize energy effectively. Contracts is no longer about honor or promises, but about regulating or deregulating behavior to produce economically efficient distributions of capital. Tax law is not seen as determining what we owe for the common weal after accounting for any contributions to it we have already made (like giving to charity, or raising children), but as a collection of "incentives" to "cause" talk of "regulation." Evolution, biology, sociology, economics, and psychiatry are harnessed to provide better predictive models and achieve more effective regulation of human behavior.
>
> In criminal law, traditionally restricted to punishing responsible actors, the change is most striking of all. We are becoming less interested in *mens rea,* and more interested in controlling crime. For example,

when the news reports that a felon who has served his sentence commits yet another heinous crime, we direct our outrage not at the felon, but at the system that failed to protect us. "Crime" itself may come to be replaced by "dangerousness" as we concentrate more on incapacitation than on righting wrong, aiming our sights at predicting and controlling rather than chastening or reconciling or grieving. [Footnotes omitted.]

Linda Ross Meyer, "Is practical reason mindless?" *Georgetown Law Journal* 86 (1998): 647, 667, 672.

16. See Richard K. Sherwin, "What we talk about when we talk about law," *New York Law School Law Review* 37 (1992): 9–53. See generally the collection of essays in "Lawyering theory symposium: Thinking through the legal culture," *New York Law School Law Review* 37 (1992): 55–258.

17. The work of Anthony G. Amsterdam, Jerome Bruner, Neal Feigenson, Austin Sarat, Philip Bobbitt, and Dennis Patterson, among others, reflects this kind of localized, practice-oriented approach. See, for example, Anthony G. Amsterdam and Randy Hertz, "An analysis of closing arguments to a jury," *New York Law School Law Review* 37 (1992): 55; Jerome Bruner, *Acts of Meaning;* Neal Feigenson, *Legal Blame: How We Think and Talk About Accidents* (Washington, D.C.: American Psychological Association, 2000); Austin Sarat and William L. F. Felstiner, *Divorce Lawyers and Their Clients: Power and Meaning in the Legal Process* (New York: Oxford University Press, 1995); Philip Bobbitt, *Law's Fate* (Oxford: Oxford University Press, 1982); and Dennis Patterson, *Law & Truth* (Oxford: Oxford University Press, 1996). Law, in this more expansive view, extends beyond formal legal institutions. As Ewick and Silbey note, "Legality is constituted through everyday actions and practices." In this sense, legal consciousness may be understood as a dynamic cultural process in which individuals "draw from and contribute to legality." Ewick and Silbey, *The Common Place of Law,* 43, 247.

18. For a pathbreaking example of this kind of interdisciplinary analysis that focuses on appellate caselaw, see Anthony G. Amsterdam and Jerome Bruner, *Minding the Law* (Cambridge: Harvard University Press, 2000).

19. See, for example, Peter Goodrich, *Oedipus Lex* (Berkeley: University of California Press, 1995), and *Law in the Courts of Love* (London: Routledge, 1996).

Chapter Two

1. Elizabeth Kolbert, "Killing shown in TV prompts debate," *New York Times,* 22 January 1993, 10.

2. Josh Young, "Hung juries or no, It's Lyle & Erik I vs. Lyle & Erik II," *New York Times,* 20 February 1994, Section 2, 27.

3. Kevin Johnson, "Potential jurors have seen it before, on 'Law & Order,'" *New York Times,* 21 October 1997, 2A.

4. Caryn James, "The testing of a president: Clinton's role of a lifetime breaks cinema's rules," *New York Times,* 22 September 1998, 16.

5. Caryn James, "Testing of a president: A self-proclaimed Joe Friday just plays it straight," *New York Times,* 20 November 1998, 27.

6. *Beasley v. State,* 269 Ga. 620, 627 (1998).

7. Ibid., 627–28.

8. Robert A. Ferguson, "Story and transcription in the trial of John Brown," *Yale Journal of Law & the Humanities* 6, no. 1 (winter 1994): 37, 75.

9. Rorie Sherman, "And now, the power of tape; videos are being used to argue the case and not just demonstrate the 'facts'," *National Law Journal,* 8 February 1993, 1. In this particular case, Mr. Cotchett obtained the largest verdict ever against Mr. Keating, awarding bond holders $3.3 billion, a sum that was later reduced to the more modest figure of $1.75 billion.

10. Jerome Bruner, *Acts of Meaning* (Cambridge: Harvard University Press, 1990), 21 (citing George Miller's famous "seven plus or minus two" as the constraining biological limit on immediate memory). See also Roy D'Andrade, *The Development of Cognitive Anthropology* (Cambridge: Cambridge University Press, 1995), 43–45.

11. See, for example, Yvette Biro, *Profane Mythology: The Savage Mind of the Cinema,* trans. Imre Goldstein (Bloomington: Indiana University Press, 1982), 42–43, noting that consciousness contains "a whole gallery of visual images," and that even a fragment or tiny detail can evoke a whole experience, as when hearing a rattling wagon induces seeing the wagon, and vice versa.

12. D'Andrade, *Cognitive Anthropology,* 24.

13. Phillip Lopate, "It's not heroes who have bad grammar; it's film," *New York Times,* 18 June 1995, Section 2, 13.

14. Ibid.

15. Michael Riffaterre, *Fictional Truth* (Baltimore: Johns Hopkins University Press, 1990), 2–3.

16. See Joseph D. Anderson, *The Reality of Illusion: An Ecological Approach to Cognitive Film Theory* (Carbondale: Southern Illinois University Press, 1996); and Carl Plantinga and Greg M. Smith, *Passionate Views: Film, Cognition, and Emotion* (Baltimore: Johns Hopkins University Press, 1999). For a classic analysis of the use of cognitive scripts and schemas in everyday life, see Roger C. Schank and Robert P. Abelson, *Scripts, Plans, Goals and Understanding* (Mahwah, N.J.: Lawrence Erlbaum, 1977).

17. Deanna B. Marcum, "We can't save everything," *New York Times,* 6 July 1998, 11.

18. See Pierre Bourdieu, *On Television* (New York: New Press, 1998), 6, 44–45.

19. See Eugene Garver, *Aristotle's Rhetoric* (Chicago: University of Chicago Press, 1994), 123.

20. Mark Poster, *The Mode of Information* (Chicago: University of Chicago Press, 1990), 63.

21. For example, Columbia University developmental psychologist Deanna Kuhn and her colleagues Michael Weinstock and Robin Flaton have found that a significant number of jurors construct a single plausible story on the basis of which they form their verdict. These jurors give little or no

consideration to alternative possibilities, and when faced with "conflicting evidence" they disregard it for the sake of the story they have in mind. Frank D. Roylance, "Teaching jurors to think," *New York Times,* 26 February 1995, 6F.

22. Al Ries and Jack Trout, *Positioning: The Battle for Your Mind* (New York: McGraw-Hill, 1986).

23. Lawrence Savell and J. Ric Gass, "Day-in-the-life videos: The defense responds," *New York Law Journal,* 27 July 1992, S7. See also Cynthia Cooper, "Courtroom art: A tool of the trade," *New York Law Journal,* 9 August 1990, 1: "The best messages are simple and instantaneous. The jury doesn't have a lot of time to study the message—it has to be blatant."

24. Judith Williamson, *Decoding Advertisements* (London: Marion Boyars, 1978), 22.

25. See Alison Young, *Imagining Crime* (London: Sage, 1996), 19: "In its everyday nature, crime takes place as an axiomatic expression of one of the features of ultramodernity: the estheticization of the everyday, through which life is lived as an image or simulation of life. With life as an image, the subject lives as persona, or mask." See also Mike Crang, Phil Crang, and Jon May, eds., *Virtual Geographies: Bodies, Space & Relations* (New York: Routledge, 1999); and Kaja Silverman, *The Threshold of the Visible World* (New York: Routledge, 1996).

26. Appropriately enough, Buttafuoco makes a cameo appearance in Woody Allen's film, *Celebrity* (Miramax, 1998).

27. George Gerbner, "Trial by television: Are we at the point of no return?" *Judicature* 63, no. 9 (April 1980): 420. See also Mark Ehrman, "The not ready for prime time plaintiffs," *Los Angeles Times,* 19 November 1995, Magazine, 28: "People now are accustomed to hearing information put forth in a clear, concise manner. They are accustomed to hearing info-McNuggets."

28. Johannes H. Birringer, *Theatre, Theory, Postmodernism* (Bloomington: Indiana University Press, 1991), 117.

29. Andy Warhol, *The Philosophy of Andy Warhol* (Orlando: Harvest, 1975), 92.

30. Jean Baudrillard, *Fatal Strategies* (New York: Semiotext[e], 1990), 74.

31. Vicki Goldberg, "Photos that lie—and tell the truth," *New York Times,* 16 March 1997, Section 2, 1.

32. Diana Griego Erwin, "F. Lee Bailey's theatrics twist tragedy into farce," *Sacramento Bee,* 16 February 1995, A2 (quoting University of Southern California law professor Erwin Chemerinsky).

33. "Bugliosi for the prosecution: Interview," *Playboy* 41, no. 12 (December 1994): 152. See also Ann Sweeney, "'Only goal is to win,' consultant says of lawyers in Simpson case," *Detroit News,* 24 September 1994, describing jurors who are "so attuned to talk-show logic that they see the perpetrator as the victim" as the "Oprahization of juries." Dan Lungen, attorney general of California, described "Oprahization of the jury pool" this way: "It's the idea that people have become so set on viewing things from the [TV talk show hosts] Oprah [Winfrey] view, the Geraldo view or the Phil Donahue view

that they bring that into the jury box with them. And I think at base much of that tends to say, 'We don't hold people responsible for their actions because they've been the victim of some influence at some time in their life.'" Sophronia Scott Gregory, "Oprah! Oprah in the court," *Time,* 6 June 1994, 30.

34. Lawyers and judges have referred to numerous film and television characters both at trial and on appeal. Television character Perry Mason figures most prominently, but one also finds references to film vigilante characters Dirty Harry and Charlie Bronson, television detectives Kojak and Columbo, and television's family doctor Marcus Welby, among numerous others. See, for example, 252 N.J. Super. 356, 358; 599 A.2d 954, 955 ("The State's theory brings to mind a scene from the popular movie *Beverly Hills Cops, Two . . .*"); 668 S.W.2d 191, 194 (in which a defendant contended that he was qualified to represent himself in court because "he had watched *Perry Mason* on TV"); or 780 S.W.2d 600, 601 (in which the prosecution compared defendant to film character Dirty Harry).

35. *United States v. Bianco,* No. H-90-18 (AHN) (D. Conn. July 16, 1991).

36. Jeremiah Donovan, "Some off-the-cuff remarks about lawyers as storytellers," *Vermont Law Review* 18, no. 3 (spring 1994): 759.

37. See Philip N. Meyer, " 'Desperate for love': Cinematic influences upon a defendant's closing argument to a jury," *Vermont Law Review* 18, no. 3 (spring 1994): 721.

38. For example, consider the heavy reliance by defense lawyers in the first Rodney King assault trial on in-court digital reconstructions of the George Holliday videotape that showed Los Angeles police officers in the act of "subduing" Rodney King. The defense's re-orchestration of these images helped to persuade jurors that it was King's movements that "caused" the officers to strike King with their batons.

39. See *Standard Chartered PLC v. Price Waterhouse,* CV 88-34414 (Super. Ct., Maricopa Co., Ariz. 1989), in which the plaintiff used a summation video that included scenes from the 1957 British feature film *A Night to Remember* in order to make visually vivid its comparison of Price Waterhouse's negligence to that of the officers aboard the iceberg-bound *Titanic.*

40. The admission of such visual aids, while increasing, remains controversial. For example, while the trial judge who screened the *Titanic* video in the *Price Waterhouse* case found it appropriate for closing argument, the appeals court did not. *Standard Chartered PLC v. Price Waterhouse,* 945 P.2d 317, 359 (Ariz. Ct. App. 1996).

41. Sherry Turkle, *Life on the Screen* (New York: Simon and Schuster, 1995), 26, 46. In a similar vein, she notes: "We build our ideas about what is real and what is natural with the cultural materials available" (237). Donald Norman has similarly noted that

> Technology is not neutral. Each technology has properties—affordances—that make it easier to do some activities, harder to do others. . . . [E]ach technology poses a mind-set, a way of thinking about it and the

activities to which it is relevant, a mind-set that soon pervades those touched by it, often unwittingly, often unwillingly. The more successful and widespread the technology, the greater its impact upon the thought patterns of those who use it, and consequently, the greater its impact upon all of society.

See Ethan Katsh, "Rights, camera, action: Cyberspatial settings and the First Amendment," *Yale Law Journal* 104 (1995): 1688 n. 22.

42. Andie Tucher, *Froth & Scum: Truth, Beauty, Goodness, and the Ax Murder in America's First Mass Medium* (Chapel Hill: University of North Carolina Press, 1994), 62–63.

43. Ibid., 63.

44. Ibid., 56.

45. As journalism Professor Carole Gorney has said, "People don't remember where they saw something. They're flipping around with their remote control. It all gets kind of mishmashed." Pat Widder, "Fact and fantasy: Real world not nearly as simplistic as TV portrays it," *Chicago Tribune,* 21 February 1993, 1.

46. Alexis de Tocqueville, *Democracy in America* (New York: Doubleday/Anchor, 1969), 270.

47. Ibid., 268–69.

48. John Fiske, "Admissible postmodernity: Some remarks on Rodney King, O. J. Simpson, and contemporary culture," *University of San Francisco Law Review* 30, no. 4 (1996): 918.

Chapter Three

1. Austin Sarat, "Narrative strategy and death penalty advocacy," *Harvard Civil Rights–Civil Liberties Law Review* 31 (1966): 353, 367.

2. As Jerome Bruner has noted, each cognitive style provides its own distinct ways of "ordering experience" and "constructing reality." See Bruner on paradigmatic and narrative forms of reasoning in *Actual Minds, Possible Worlds* (Cambridge: Harvard University Press, 1986), 11.

3. Consider, for example, a personal injury lawsuit in 1992 against Dow Corning Corporation in which plaintiff sought damages for severe personal injuries stemming from ruptured silicon breast implants manufactured by the defendant corporation. In the course of the trial the jury would learn that plaintiff was a topless dancer, had had an abortion, and that she had put a child up for adoption. The legal relevance of this evidence is dubious, for it has little or no bearing on the question of whether defendant's product caused plaintiff's illness. Yet Dow's defense tactic was successful. As one juror admitted after the trial, the plaintiff's lifestyle choices influenced her decision to deny damages. See Kerith Cohen, "Truth & beauty, deception & disfigurement: A feminist analysis of breast implant litigation," *William & Mary Journal of Women & Law* 1 (1994): 149, 172.

4. O. J. Simpson Trial Transcript, 248. See <http://www.courttv.com/casefiles/simpson/transcripts>; pagination refers to the downloaded copy.

5. Ibid., 50.

6. Ibid., 68.

7. See Anthony Amsterdam and Randy Hertz, "An analysis of closing arguments to a jury," *New York Law School Law Review* 37 (1992): 55.

8. O. J. Simpson Trial Transcript, 68.

9. Ibid., 82.

10. Ibid.

11. See Richard Gerrig, *Experiencing Narrative Worlds* (New Haven: Yale University Press, 1993); Rom Harre and Grant Gillett, *The Discursive Mind* (Thousand Oaks, Calif.: Sage, 1994); Daniel T. Gilbert, "How mental systems believe," *American Psychologist* 46, no. 3 (February 1991): 107–19.

12. See Deborah Baldwin, "Is it fact? Or is it fiction?: From Hollywood to the 6 o'clock news, it's getting harder to tell," *Common Cause* (fall 1993).

13. Gerrig, *Experiencing Narrative Worlds,* 223. Gerrig goes on to note: "Fictions often have their effect because they call forth from memory real-world events and causal possibilities. Even when the impact of the original information is canceled out by virtue of its transparent fictionality, the rest of the accessed-belief structure remains intact" (230). Notably, rather than "suspend disbelief" at the outset, if Gerrig's view proves correct, it would seem that our more natural tendency is to automatically believe what we understand. On this view, it requires special effort to *suspend our belief* later on. See also Deborah A. Prentice and Richard J. Gerrig, "Exploring the boundary between fiction and reality," in *Dual-Process Theories in Social Psychology,* ed. Shelly Chaiken and Yaacov Trope (New York: Guilford Press, 1999).

14. See Vicki Smith, "Prototypes in the courtroom: Lay representations of legal concepts," *Journal of Personality and Social Psychology* 61, no. 6 (1991): 857–72.

15. Ibid., 863.

16. No. 87-15583-M (Tex. Dist. Ct. Dallas County 1992). See Avi J. Stachenfeld and Christopher M. Nicholson, "Blurred boundaries: An analysis of the close relationship between popular culture and the practice of law," *University of San Francisco Law Review* 30 (1996): 905.

17. Stachenfeld and Nicholson, "Blurred boundaries," 909.

18. See, for example, *Bruton v. United States,* 391 U.S. 123, 126 (1966): "Because of the substantial risk that the jury, despite instructions to the contrary, looked to the incriminating extrajudicial statements in determining petitioner's guilt, admission of [codefendant] Evans' confession in this joint trial violated petitioner's right of cross-examination."

19. William James, *The Varieties of Religious Experience* (New York: Modern Library, 1902), 373.

20. See Mircea Eliade, *Myth, Dreams and Mysteries* (New York: Harper & Row, 1975), 23.

21. Ibid.

22. See Victor Turner, *The Ritual Process: Structure and Anti-Structure* (Ithaca, N.Y.: Cornell University Press, 1977), 96. Turner describes the ritual process as presenting "a moment 'in and out of time,' and in and out of

secular social structure, which reveals, however fleetingly, some recognition (in symbol if not in language) of a generalized social bond that has ceased to be and has simultaneously yet to be fragmented into a multiplicity of structural ties." Turner calls that invisible bond "communitas."

23. Trial Transcript, 2–4. *United States v. Weaver,* No. CR 92-080-N-EJL (D. Idaho), 15 June 1993, before the Hon. Edward J. Lodge.

24. Ibid., 4.

25. Ibid.

26. Ibid., 5–6.

27. Ibid., 6–7.

28. Ibid., 28–29.

29. Ibid., 36, 66.

30. Ibid., 16–17.

31. "I had no idea my government was capable of this sort of thing," said jury foreman Jack Weaver (no relation to the defendant), speaking to a journalist after the trial. "If they can do that to Randy Weaver's wife, they can do that to my wife, and they can do that to my kids." *Washington Post,* 4 September 1995, A1.

32. Trial Transcript, 33–34.

33. See Aristotle, *The Rhetoric* (New York: Modern Library, 1954), 90–111.

34. Trial Transcript, 80–81.

35. See Christopher Vogler, *The Writer's Journey: Mythic Structures for Storytellers and Scriptwriters* (Studio City, Calif.: Michael Wiese Productions, 1992), 28.

36. Ibid., 29. Studies in "terror management" have suggested that when a jury's sense of mortality is made salient, their tendency is to respond positively toward those who uphold cultural values and negatively toward those who violate cultural values. In this way, the jurors' values and self-esteem protect against the anxiety produced by thoughts of human vulnerability. See Abram Rosenblatt et al., "Evidence for terror management theory: The effects of mortality salience on reactions to those who violate or uphold cultural values," *Journal of Personality and Social Psychology* 57, no. 4 (1989): 681–90.

37. Trial Transcript, 88–89.

38. "They're just playing games," Spence will tell a television interviewer years later regarding the federal government's handling of the Weaver case. CNN, *Burden of Proof,* 25 August 1997.

39. Upon the jury's return from deliberation the verdict was announced: Randy Weaver was acquitted of all the charges against him.

40. Bronislaw Malinowski, *Magic, Science, and Religion* (New York: Doubleday, 1948), 100.

41. Abraham Maslow, *The Farther Reaches of Human Nature* (New York: Viking, 1971), 269–70.

42. Ibid., 270.

43. Trial Transcript, 34.

44. James, *Varieties of Religious Experience,* 506.

45. Roland Barthes, *Mythologies* (New York: Noonday Press, 1992), 16–17.

46. Ibid., 18.

47. Ibid., 20–21.

48. Ibid., 22.

49. Ibid., 25.

Chapter Four

1. See Richard Wightman Fox, "Intimacy on trial," in *The Power of Culture,* ed. Richard Wightman Fox and T. J. Jackson Lears (Chicago: University of Chicago Press, 1993), 131.

2. Janna Malamud Smith, *Private Matters* (New York: Addison-Wesley, 1997), 92.

3. As William Bowdesley Best put it in his 1875 treatise, *The Principles of the Law of Evidence* (Albany, N.Y.: Weare C. Little, 1875), 17–18:

> Mutual confidence between man and man being indispensable to the acquisition of knowledge, the happiness of our race, and indeed to the very existence of society, the great Creator has planted the springs of truth very deep in the human breast. . . . [W]ere we to lose either our feeling of obligation to tell the truth, or our disposition to receive as truth whatever is told to us, there would be at once an end to all science and all knowledge, beyond that which every man had obtained by his own personal observation and experience. . . . Language would be useless, and we should be but little removed from the brutes.

See Laura Hanft Korobkin, "The maintenance of mutual confidence: Sentimental strategies at the adultery trial of Henry Ward Beecher," *Yale Journal of Law & the Humanities* 7 (1995): 26–27. For an excellent historical account of the Beecher-Tilton scandal, see Richard Wightman Fox, *Trials of Intimacy: Love and Loss in the Beecher-Tilton Scandal* (Chicago: University of Chicago Press, 1999).

4. See Robert Cover, "Nomos and narrative," *Harvard Law Review* 97 (1983): 68.

5. Slavoj Žižek, *Looking Awry* (Cambridge: MIT Press, 1995), 48.

6. Roger Cohen, "French church issues apology to Jews on war," *New York Times,* 1 October 1997, A1.

7. As Robert Ferguson notes, "Harper's Ferry, in the Blue Ridge Mountains of northern Virginia, had no large slave plantations nearby, and free whites outnumbered slaves in the surrounding six counties by a ratio of almost seven to one. None of the circumstances were propitious for a slave rebellion. The raiders neglected to bring so much as a day's rations to sustain their enterprise, and their first shots killed a black railroad worker who was already free." Robert Ferguson, "Story and transcription in the trial of John Brown," *Yale Journal of Law & the Humanities* 6 (1994): 40.

8. The nineteenth-century Romance style describes prose fiction "that is

conceived in terms of the fanciful and idealistic, rather than in terms of observation and faithful description of fact." Ibid., 38 n. 3 (quoting *The Oxford Companion to American Literature*).

9. Quoted by Ferguson, "Story and transcription," 37.

10. Ibid., 71, 53.

11. Ibid., 44.

12. See Stephen B. Oates, *To Purge This Land with Blood* (Amherst: University of Massachusetts Press, 1984), 361 (noting that "the man himself was all but forgotten") and 288 (recounting Osborn P. Anderson's description of Brown offering a prayer to God, prior to the raid on Harper's Ferry, "to assist in the liberation of the bondmen in that slaveholding state").

13. Korobkin, "Maintenance of mutual confidence," 10–11.

14. See Cover, "Nomos and narrative," 45: "The transformation of interpretation into legal meaning begins when someone accepts the demands of interpretation and, through personal acts of commitment, affirms the position taken."

15. Ferguson, "Story and transcription," 69. Contrast abolitionist Wendell Phillips's words: "Never until we welcome the Negro, the foreigner, all races as equal, and melted together in a common nationality hurl them all at despotism, will the North deserve triumph or earn it at the hands of a just God." C. L. R. James, *American Civilization* (Cambridge: Blackwell Publishers, 1993), 97.

16. Ferguson, "Story and transcription," 69.

17. See *Abraham Lincoln: Speeches and Writings 1859–1865* (New York: Library of America, 1989). Consider, for example, Lincoln's speech on July 12, 1862: "I do not speak of emancipation at once, but of a decision at once to emancipate gradually. Room in South America for colonization, can be obtained cheaply, and in abundance . . . the freed people will not be so reluctant to go" (*Speeches and Writings*, 341). As Ferguson notes, students of the raid on Harper's Ferry and its aftermath "agree that most antebellum Americans were not in sympathy with Brown's immediate goals. North as well as South feared a slave insurrection of the kind that Brown tried to instigate at Harpers Ferry." Ferguson, "Story and transcription," 42.

18. *Plessy v. Ferguson*, 163 U.S. 537 (1896).

19. *Walker v. City of Birmingham*, 388 U.S. 307 (1967), authorizing the exercise of state power in order to quell private disorder.

20. When twelve Simi Valley jurors voted on April 29, 1992, to acquit four Los Angeles police officers of assaulting Rodney King, the lid on race-based social division and moral unrest was once again blown free. Days of looting and violence followed the announcement of the officers' acquittal. The city of Los Angeles suffered a billion dollars in property damage and more than fifty deaths resulted.

21. See Malamud Smith, *Private Matters*, 98 (quoting Stevenson): "Henry Jekyll stood at times aghast before the acts of Edward Hyde; but the situation was apart from ordinary laws, and insidiously relaxed the grasp of conscience. It was Hyde after all, and Hyde alone, that was guilty."

22. See Korobkin, "Maintenance of mutual confidence," 26–33.

23. See Fox, *Trials of Intimacy,* 15, 28.

24. Elizabeth Tilton's post-trial confession in 1878, following her staunch denials throughout 1874 and 1875, remains controversial. For example, Fox suggests that "[b]y confessing to adultery, she may, ironically, have been *better* able to protect the children than she had been between 1875 and 1876." Ibid., 42 (italics in original). On the ultimate question of whether adultery occurred, Fox remains agnostic: "There is no way to know which story was true." Ibid., 4.

25. Korobkin, "Maintenance of mutual confidence," 132, 294–95.

26. Ibid., 23: "The socially successful hypocrite—the con man—became America's supreme criminal because he could 'sever the connection between inner character and outward appearances by consciously manipulating the impression he made on others.'"

27. Ibid.

28. Ibid., 39: "For Lionel Trilling, the awareness of the 'ambiguity of the personal life, the darkness of man's unknowable heart,' become the springboard into the modernist conception of the self. It divides modern man's often alienated self-consciousness from what now seems to have been a naive faith in appearances and in the easy availability of meanings."

29. Ibid., 35.

30. Ibid., 15.

31. Smith, *Private Matters,* 88.

32. Fox, "Intimacy on trial," 132.

33. See Stuart Ewen, *PR! A Social History of Spin* (New York: Basic Books, 1996).

34. Kate Chopin, *The Awakening and Selected Stories* (New York: Viking, 1984), 108.

35. Ibid., 74.

36. Henry Demarest Lloyd, *Lords of Industry* (New York: G. P. Putnam and Sons, 1910), 1.

37. Geoffrey Cowan, *The People v. Clarence Darrow* (New York: Times Books, 1994), 415.

38. As the defense put it in their opening statement to the jury: "[T]he defendant killed Stanford White under the delusion that it was an act of Providence; that he was the agent of Providence to kill Stanford White. . . . The defendant killed Stanford White because he did not know that that act was wrong, because he was suffering from a disease of the brain which induced that condition of mind, under the expansive operations of which he believed it was right to kill Stanford White, acting under the influence of his insanity." P. A. MacKenzie, *The Trial of Harry Thaw* (London: Geoffrey Bles, 1928), 37. The defense went on to say that from the time he learned from Nesbit of her affair with White, Thaw developed delusional thinking that "finally culminated in the final idea of imperious force that it was right to kill Stanford White and not wrong" (ibid., 40).

39. See Martha Merrill Umphrey, "The dialogics of legal meaning: Spec-

tacular trials, the unwritten law, and narratives of criminal responsibility," *Law & Society Review* 33 (1999): 393.

40. As Mazie Folette, Nesbit's fellow chorus girl, put it: "Harry Thaw cursed every time White's name was mentioned. Evelyn played on this from the first time she met Harry right up to the time of the shooting." Why? Nesbit provides the answer in her own words: "[W]hen I came across a little book in which [White] had recorded the birthday of every pretty girl he knew, I became violently jealous. . . . Like a silly child, I wanted to make [White] jealous of me." Gerald Langford, *The Murder of Stanford White* (Indianapolis: Bobbs-Merrill, 1962), 261–62, quoting Evelyn Nesbit's autobiography, *Prodigal Days: The Untold Stories* (New York: Julian Messner, 1934).

41. This notion is supported by accounts in which Nesbit responded to the shooting with the words, "My God Harry, you killed him. . . . Kiss me." See Suzannah Lessard, *The Architect of Desire* (New York: Delta, 1996), 301.

42. At the first trial Nesbit testified that a minute or two after she drank a glass of champagne at White's insistence, "a pounding began in my ear, a something and pounding, then the whole room seemed to go round. Everything got very black. When I awoke, I was lying in a room whose walls and ceiling were covered with many mirrors. As consciousness returned, I screamed repeatedly." In her memoir, Nesbit would admit that her testimony about her screams was a lie and that it was probably the quantity of champagne that went to her head. No mention of drugs is made.

43. Writing in 1901, historian F. J. Turner posed the penultimate question: "Under the forms of the American democracy is there in reality evolving such a concentration of economic and social power in the hands of a comparatively few men as may make political democracy an appearance rather than a reality?" (cited in C. L. R. James, *American Civilization*, 103). Looking back upon turn-of-the-century America, H. L. Mencken described the country as "just entering its most lurid phase of that vast, splendid, most lawless and most savage period in which the great financiers . . . were plotting and conniving the enslavement of the people and belaboring each other for power." Mencken, *Newspaper Days: 1899–1906* (Baltimore: Johns Hopkins University Press, [1920] 1996).

44. See, e.g., *Lochner v. New York*, 198 U.S. 45 (1905), holding that states could not regulate the working conditions or workday limits on bakers without violating the "liberty of contract."

45. Langford, *The Murder of Stanford White*, 252–53.

Chapter Five

1. See, e.g., Michael E. Tigar, *Examining Witnesses* (Chicago: American Bar Association, 1993), 5: "People, including judges and jurors, understand and restate events in terms of stories. They take the available evidence and weave it into a coherent whole. If pieces are missing, they will fill in the gaps based on intuition, probability, or prejudgment"; Albert J. Moore, "Trial by schema: Cognitive filters in the courtroom," *UCLA Law Review* 37 (1989):

273, 277: "In an actual case there will be many potential frames of references which could be recalled by jurors from their schematic databases and contribute to assessments of similarity. However . . . cognitive biases and limitations cause jurors to filter out many of these potential frames of reference."

2. *The Thin Blue Line* (Third Floor Productions, 1988), hereinafter Transcript.

3. Philip Gourevitch, "Interviewing the universe," *New York Times Magazine,* 9 August 1992, 18, identifying Errol Morris as the man "whose film *The Thin Blue Line* saved a man from death row." Movie critic Clarke Taylor opened his review with this hook: "Will a new movie succeed in getting convicted murderer Randall Dale Adams freed from prison? Director Errol Morris and Miramax, the distributor of *The Thin Blue Line,* frankly acknowledge that they hope the answer is yes." Clarke Taylor, "*Thin Blue Line:* Advocate for a killer," *Los Angeles Times,* 28 August 1988, 28.

4. I have assembled the following "facts" from a number of sources: Randall Adams, *Adams v. Texas* (New York: St. Martin's Press, 1990); the complete trial transcript; local newspaper articles about the case; and the entire corpus of legal papers connected with the case, including official statements made by Adams, Harris, and police officer Turko.

5. See Transcript, 67 (statement of David Harris).

6. Ibid., 22.

7. Adams recounts this part of the exchange in his book, but his description of these events in the film omits it. See Transcript, 13–14.

8. See Tex. Code Crim. Proc. Ann. art. 31(a)(1) (West Supp. 1994). See also *Herrera v. Collins,* 113 S. Ct. 853, 860 (1993), holding that a claim of factual innocence based on newly discovered evidence is not grounds for reversal on collateral review.

9. *Adams v. Texas,* 448 U.S. 38 (1980), reversing the imposition of the death penalty and remanding to the Texas Court of Criminal Appeals.

10. The sentencing procedure declared unconstitutional had required a prospective juror to state "under oath that the mandatory penalty of death or imprisonment for life [would] not affect his deliberations." Tex. Penal Code 12.31(b) (Vernon 1974). The statute was amended to eliminate this requirement. Tex. Penal Code 12.31(b) (Vernon Supp. 1994).

11. In 1988, the year of its release, *The Thin Blue Line* generated sufficient public interest to pressure Dallas authorities into investigating the need for a new trial. After a hearing on the matter, Judge Larry W. Baraka, who succeeded District Judge Don Metcalfe in 1984, recommended granting Adams's motion for a new trial. *State v. Adams,* No. W-77-1286-I (Tex. Crim. Dist. Ct. Nov. 30, 1988), ruling on motion. Following this recommendation, the Court of Criminal Appeals vacated Adams's conviction and ordered a new trial. *Ex parte Adams,* 768 S.W.2d 281 (Tex. Ct. Crim. App. 1989). The court found that: (1) the state illegally suppressed witness Emily Miller's prior inconsistent statement, (2) the prosecutor failed to correct Mrs. Miller's perjured testimony that she had identified Adams in a lineup, and (3) the im-

proper police coaching of Miller and failure to disclose problems with her testimony deprived Adams of a fair trial. Ibid., 291–92.

12. Errol Morris has said: "The scary part is . . . our desire to tell ourselves what we want to hear, perpetuates our own beliefs." Elsewhere, reflecting on what he calls "truth by convenience" and "the enormous gulf between belief and reality," Morris recalls the scene from the film "where a police officer is heard saying about Harris, 'I didn't want him to tell us what he thought; I wanted him to tell us what we knew.'" Alvin Klein, "Film dissects murder and justice," *New York Times,* 23 October 1988, 14. See Hayden White, *Tropics of Discourse: Essays in Cultural Criticism* (Baltimore: Johns Hopkins University Press, 1978), 1: "[W]e never say precisely what we wish to say or mean precisely what we say. Our discourse always tends to slip away from our data towards the structures of consciousness with which we are trying to grasp them."

13. Charles W. Nuckolls, "Culture and causal thinking: Diagnosis and prediction in a South Indian fishing village," *ETHOS* 19 (1991): 3–4, discussing theories of knowledge construction.

14. In this sense it emulates the crime novel rather than the classically linear detective story. Consider in this respect Hilfer: "[T]he central and defining feature of the crime novel is that in it self and world, guilt and innocence are problematic. The world of the crime novel is constituted by what is problematic in it." Tony Hilfer, *The Crime Novel: A Deviant Genre* (Austin: University of Texas Press, 1990), 2. A crime novel maneuvers its reader into various forms of complicity, managing to subvert the reassurances of the detective novel by "put[ting] the signification process into doubt or even exploit[ing] the gap between socially accepted signification and ultimate reality." Ibid., 3, 7.

15. See William Chase Greene, *Moira: Fate, Good and Evil in Greek Thought* (New York: Harper Torchbooks, 1944), 8, distinguishing fate, the due portion or moral share assigned to a person, from chance, the unforeseeable forces that affect life but have little or no moral quality.

16. See, for example, Samuel Beckett, *The Unnameable in Three Novels by Samuel Beckett* (New York: Grove Press, 1958), 414: "[P]erhaps they have carried me to the end of my story . . . I don't know, I'll never know, in the silence you don't know, you must go on, I can't go on, I'll go on." See also Katherine Dieckmann, "Private eye," *American Film,* January-February 1988, 38: "'Why did this happen? The answer is, I don't know. Maybe it happened for no good reason, except that evil things happen to people.'" (quoting Morris); Mark Singer, "Profiles: Predilections," *New Yorker,* 6 February 1989, 46: "'One of the things that have always fascinated me about abnormal behavior is that we can't really explain it to our satisfaction. . . . Almost everything I do now in my work is about epistemic concerns: how do we come by certain kinds of knowledge?'" (quoting Morris).

17. See Dorothy Holland and Naomi Quinn, *Cultural Models in Language and Thought* (Cambridge: Cambridge University Press, 1989). See

Nuckolls, "Culture and causal thinking," 9, citing Gordon H. Bower, John B. Black, and Terrence J. Turner, "Scripts in memory for text," *Cognitive Psychology* 11 (1979): 177.

18. As Odo Marquard notes: "Fateful accidents are the reality of our life, because as human beings we are always 'entangled in stories.'" Odo Marquard, *In Defense of the Accidental,* trans. Robert M. Wallace (New York: Oxford University Press, 1991), 120 (quoting William Schapp).

19. As Morris attests, "All my interviews are staged for the camera with the same lighting and poses." This compilation of visual and auditory data in Morris's film has been described as "an apt parallel to the randomness of evidence." Luc Sante, "Murder in the raw," *Interview,* September 1988, 152.

20. Nomination of Clarence Thomas to be Associate Justice of the Supreme Court: Hearings before the Senate Committee on the Judiciary, 102d Cong., 1st Sess., pt. 4, at 241 (1991) (statement of Senator Heflin).

21. Jean Baudrillard, *Fatal Strategies* (New York: Semiotext[e], 1990), 24.

22. Ibid., 9.

23. See Jean Baudrillard, "The evil demon of images," in *Baudrillard Live: Selected Interviews* (New York: Routledge, 1993), 141:

> [I]n the world which I evoke, the one where illusion or magic thought plays a key role, the signs evolve, they concatenate and produce themselves. . . . Thus they do not refer to any sort of 'reality' or 'referent' or 'signified' whatsoever. . . . [I]t is the pure strategy of the sign itself that governs the appearance of things. . . . [R]eality is the effect of the sign.

See Marcus A. Doel and David B. Clarke, "Virtual worlds: Simulation, suppletion, s(ed)uction and simulacra," in *Virtual Geographies: Bodies, Space and Relations,* ed. Mike Crang, Phil Crang, and Jon May (New York: Routledge, 1999), 275:

> If modernity is equated with "the immense process of the destruction of appearances . . . in the service of meaning . . . the disenchantment of the world and its abandonment to the violence of interpretation and history," then the postmodern amounts to "the immense process of the destruction of meaning, equal to the earlier destruction of appearances." (Quoting from Jean Baudrillard, *Simulacra and Simulation* [Ann Arbor: University of Michigan Press, 1994], 160–61)

See also James B. Twitchell, *Carnival Culture* (New York: Columbia University Press, 1992), 51: "What characterizes the condition of culture since World War II is . . . that now we have more signs that point nowhere. This is why it deceives and disappoints our demand for meaning, but does so enchantingly."

24. See Jean Baudrillard, *Fragments: Cool Memories III, 1991–1995* (London: Verso, 1997), 141: "There is no corpse of the real, and with good reason: the real is not dead, it has disappeared."

25. See, for example, Friedrich Nietzsche, *Twilight of the Idols, or, How One Philosophizes with a Hammer* [1889], in *The Portable Nietzsche* (Princeton: Princeton University Press, 1954), 463, 497: "First principle: any explanation is better than none."

26. The vitality and coherence of the affirmative postmodern meaning-making process need not be, and in fact have not been, undone by forces of chance, chaos, and complexity. To the contrary, as we will see in chapter 9, new insights into these forces are changing our understanding of how order emerges, stabilizes, or yields to new configurations. See, for example, Otto Imken, "The convergence of virtual and actual in the Global Matrix," in *Virtual Geographies,* ed. Crang, Crang, and May, 104–5:

> Learning to recognise near-random (or far from equilibrium) situations and nudging them in one direction or another at a crucial node, to help or to allow some new conglomeration to emerge, will become a highly-developed and sought-after skill: opening a temporary syncretic assemblage within the Matrix [i.e., the totality of our linked telecommunications and computer networks]. . . . With the proper build-up (either ritualised or spontaneous) to the edge of chaos, a skilled cartographer of the psychogeographical dynamics around a libidinal space of attractors can navigate amongst the pulls and pushes (like a bit of code running through the back streets of its motherboard, effortlessly recalling every nook and cranny of the circuit architecture) to reach singularities, crucial nodes of peak interaction and productivity per labour input. At these points (or spaces or curves), a seemingly minimal input (an incantation, a sacrifice, a dozen electrons, a kiss) can spontaneously alter the structure and even content of libidinal space, the input being hyper-magnified, in a butterfly-effect, because of the positioning of the fluxes right on the edge of chaos, at the point of self-criticality where complexity and innovation emerge.

27. See Anthony G. Amsterdam and Randy Hertz, "An analysis of closing arguments to a jury," *New York Law School Law Review* 37 (1992): 55, 64–75. See pages 45–47, 56–68 above.

28. Compare Joseph Campbell's Nigerian story of the trickster god Edshu who walks down a road in a hat that's red on one side and blue on the other. Fights ensue between people who traveled on opposite sides of the road about whether the man they passed had been wearing a red or a blue hat. The god takes credit for the trouble, saying "[s]preading strife is my greatest joy." See Christopher Vogler, *The Writer's Journey: Mythic Structures for Screenwriters and Storytellers* (Studio City: Michael Wiese Productions, 1992), 91. In this respect it may be added that upon viewing David Harris as the "trickster incarnate" we may not be able to dismiss him so easily as simply a pernicious force that must be suppressed. The importance of his role and his cultural power may turn out to be too great to allow that. Indeed, the trickster's de-

light in mischief and destruction have earned him in some cultures a godlike status—like the Hindu figure Kali, who is seen as the embodiment of an elementary (and indestructible) force in the universe. As pictured in Kali's erotic dance with the princely Shiva, it is the trickster who brings things into being and risks dashing them back into primordial chaos. In this sense, we are dealing here with a powerful creative as well as destructive force. And in this respect too we may say that Harris fits the bill. After all, while his tricks may have cost us dearly, they have also inspired new insights into our cultural and psychological makeup through Morris's and, in a preliminary sense, Randall Adams's fascination with him. The irrational power that courses through this "mythic" figure also alerts us to something vital and inescapable within our world, and perhaps within our own psyche. I return to this theme in chapter 7.

29. See Aeschylus, *Oresteia,* trans. Richmond Lattimore (New York: Washington Square Press, 1967), depicting necessary retribution as passing from one generation to the next by the messengers of fate, the Furies, until they are tamed by civil law.

30. Aristotle, *On Rhetoric* (Oxford: Oxford University Press, 1991), 244.

Chapter Six

1. See Jerome Bruner, *In Search of Mind* (New York: Harper & Row, 1983), 67–71.

2. Ivy L. Lee, "Publicity," address before the American Electric Railway Association (10 October 1916, Atlantic City), cited in Stuart Ewen, *PR! A History of Social Spin* (New York: Basic Books, 1996), 81.

3. Walter Lippmann, *Public Opinion* (New York: Free Press, 1985 [1922]), 81, cited in Ewen, *PR!,* 149. Ewen succinctly captures the prescience of Lippmann's insight: "Formulating a quintessentially twentieth-century vocabulary, Lippmann argued that mass-mediated words and pictures commingled in people's minds, constituting a credible—though often fallacious—'pseudo-environment,' a virtual reality informing ordinary thought and behavior" (148). In Ewen's view, "[t]he use of media images to stir emotions and circumvent thought is, today, a near universal feature of public discourse" (158).

4. Robert McNeal, "The flickering images that may drive presidents," *Media Studies Journal* 9, no. 1 (winter 1995): 123–24.

5. See Steve Brill's *Content* (July/August 1998): 23. Significant reductions in the number of violent crimes actually committed apparently have had no impact on television news's preference for these kinds of crime stories. For example, coverage of crime on the three major television network news shows tripled from 571 stories in 1991 to 1632 in 1993—notwithstanding a drop in the crime rate. Steven R. Denziger, *The Real War on Crime: The Report of the National Criminal Justice Commission* (New York: Harper Perennial, 1996), 69. According to one study, murder and robbery account for 80 percent of television crime news. While murder constituted 0.2 percent of the crimes known to police, it constituted 26.2 percent of the crime news stories

on television. According to another study, murder, robbery, kidnapping, and aggravated assault made up 87 percent of all television crimes. See Ray Surette, "Predator criminals as media icons," in *Media, Process and the Social Construction of Crime,* ed. Gregg Barak (New York: Garland Publishing, 1994), 134 nn. 11, 13.

6. According to one study, since 1958 nearly one-third of all entertainment shows have been about crime. See Steven Stark, "Perry Mason meets Sonny Crocker: The history of lawyers and the police as television heroes," *University of Miami Law Review* 42 (1987): 230–31.

7. The esthetic appeal of rapid image flow also carries over in the predominance on television of "episodic" as opposed to "thematic" narratives. Episodic story framing focuses on specific events—for example, a particular drug case, a particular homeless person. By contrast, thematic story framing focuses on broader social, political, or historical issues—for example, data linking drug crimes and employment statistics or homelessness and shifts in mental health policy. While the episodic frame enjoys the "advantage" of lending itself to good pictures and requiring only minimal journalistic expertise, this kind of storytelling carries a price. Studies have shown that episodic story framing "breeds individualistic as opposed to societal attributions of responsibility." As Iyengar notes:

National issues are traced to private actions and motives rather than deep-seated socioeconomic or political conditions. Given the public's sustained exposure to episodic framing, these results suggest that the ultimate effect of television news is to protect elected officials from policy failures or controversies and thus strengthen their legitimacy.

Shanto Iyengar, "Framing responsibility for political issues," *Annals of the American Academy of Political and Social Science* 546 (July 1996): 56. A similar effect has been noted in the field of tort litigation, where individualized findings of wrongdoing tend to obscure systemic causes of harm. See Neal Feigenson, "Accidents as melodrama," *New York Law School Law Review* 43 (1999), noting that "[m]elodramatized blaming typically leaves the systemic causes of accidents unscathed."

8. See Jonathan Rowe, "Gauging the impact of advertising," *Christian Science Monitor,* 28 January 1987, 14, quoting Jerry Mander, a former advertising executive who has written extensively on media and currently serves as senior fellow at the Public Media Center.

9. Ibid. See Tony Schwartz, *The Responsive Chord* (New York: Doubleday, 1974), 21–22:

For the advertiser, the issue of key concern should center on how the stimuli in a commercial interact with a viewer's real-life experiences and thus affect his behavior in a purchasing situation. Here the key is to connect products to the real lives of human beings. As long as the connection is made in a deep way, and as long as the experience evoked by the commercial is not in conflict with the experience of the product, purchase is possible, or probable.

10. Mark Crispin Miller, *Boxed In* (Evanston, Ill.: Northwestern University Press, 1988), 14.

11. See Herbert E. Krugman, "Impact of television advertising: Learning without involvement," *Public Opinion Quarterly* 29 (1965): 349–56.

12. Joe McGuinniss, *The Selling of the President* (New York: Trident Press, 1969). McGuinniss would subsequently produce a new kind of genre: the "interpretive biography." His study of Senator Edward Kennedy, a conflation of fiction and fact, led *Boston Globe* critic Gail Caldwell to observe: "Never has the truth seemed so anachronistic, or reality so manipulable." We might say that McGinniss too had fallen victim to the rule of thumb: whatever the mass media touch suffers from reality/fiction confusion. See Joe McGuinniss, *The Last Brother* (New York: Simon & Schuster, 1993).

13. The average political soundbite decreased from 42.3 seconds in 1968 to 9.8 seconds in 1988 and 8.4 seconds in 1992. See Kiku Adatto, *Picture Perfect: The Art and Artifice of Public Image-Making* (New York: Basic Books, 1993), 2, 170.

14. Ibid., 14. Notably, unmasking the image as "image" not only fails to curtail its impact, but the added exposure seems to enhance its appeal. This is the paradox of presenting backstage reality (i.e., the illusion-making process) as frontstage reality. As Daniel Boorstin presciently observed: "Information about the staging of a pseudo-event simply adds to its fascination." Daniel Boorstin, *The Image: A Guide to Pseudo-Events in America* (New York: Atheneum, 1961), 38, 44. Adatto describes the political ramifications of this phenomenon:

> Network reporters and producers thought that covering the construction of images for television would alert viewers to the contrivance of those images, and so expose the artifice of the campaigns. They thought that revealing the media advisers and handlers and spin-control artists manipulating the levers of illusion would dissolve that illusion and replace it with reality. But it did not work that way. Unlike *The Wizard of Oz*, revealing the man behind the curtain did not diminish the hold of the image. (Adatto, *Picture Perfect*, 93)

15. Consider, for example, veteran *New York Times* political correspondent Richard Berke's front-page coverage of Steve Forbes's announcement of his candidacy in the 2000 presidential election. The article's lead reads as follows:

> William Eisner, who heads an advertising agency in Milwaukee, is best known for his commercials about Mrs. Paul's fish sticks, including one that features a sloppy little boy lassoing his head with spaghetti. "Not impressed with pasta anymore?" the announcer asks. "Break the mo-

notony with fish sticks." Now Mr. Eisner is turning his handiwork to
another product that he says needs sprucing up: Steve Forbes.

Richard L. Berke, "Fitting Forbes for Oval Office is advertising man's assignment," *New York Times* (Sunday edition), 30 May 1999, 1.
   16. Richard Gerrig, *Experiencing Narrative Worlds* (New Haven, Conn.:
Yale University Press, 1993), 223.
   17. See Deborah Baldwin, "Is it fact? Or is it fiction?: From Hollywood
to the 6 o'clock news, it's getting harder to tell," *Common Cause* (winter
1993): 25, quoting Professor Timothy Murray of Cornell University.
   18. Specialists in litigation public relations attempt to counter, or preempt, negative publicity by disseminating the client's viewpoint in the court
of public opinion via the mass media. They also counsel clients on the public
implications of various legal strategies and help to package the client's message for public as well as jury consumption. As attorney Kathy Fitzpatrick
puts it:

> While it may take months—even years—before a case finds its way into
> a courtroom, the "public" trial begins with the first news report of the
> charges filed. People will assess the evidence as presented by the news
> media and quickly reach a decision about the allegations that have been
> made. If a reputation is destroyed by negative publicity, a later victory
> at the courthouse may not matter at all.

Kathy Fitzpatrick, "Practice management: The court of public opinion,"
Texas Lawyer, 30 September 1996, 30. See also Susanne A. Roschwalb and
Richard A. Stack, *Litigation Public Relations* (Littleton, Colo.: Rothman &
Co., 1995) and Dirk C. Gibson, "Litigation public relations: Fundamental
assumptions," *Public Relations Quarterly* 43 (22 March 1998): 19.
   As a historical matter, one may trace the art of litigation public relations
to the genius of two criminal defendants, Abbie Hoffman and Jerry Rubin,
who were members of the so-called "Chicago Seven." Rubin and Hoffman
were leaders in the antiwar ("Yippie") movement who had come to Chicago,
the site of the 1968 Democratic national convention, to protest the Vietnam
war. They were indicted under a federal law that made it a crime to cross
state lines with the intention of causing a riot. Hoffman and Rubin spent
much of their courtroom time analyzing trial coverage by the media: plotting
press conferences, arranging for Yippie witnesses to get on the stand in time
for news deadlines—what we recognize today as the art of spin control. As
codefendant Tom Hayden would later write: "[Hoffman and Rubin] wanted
to create the image of a courtroom in shambles. . . . Part of the Yippie genius
is to manipulate the fact that the media will always emphasize the bizarre.
Even the straightest reporter will communicate chaos because it sells. The
Yippies know this because their politics involve consciously marketing themselves as mythic personality models for kids." Tom Hayden, *Trial* (New York:
Holt, Rinehart & Winston, 1970), 69.

19. Ken Kunsman, "Panelists spar on 'litigation journalism,'" *Morning Call,* 6 May 1994, B7.

20. Even winning a lawsuit may not preserve a product's viability in the marketplace in the face of bad publicity. Thus, for example, in the course of litigation involving injuries allegedly caused by breast implants, Dow Corning, a maker of the silicone gel used in the implants, published full-page ads in five national newspapers contending that breast implants are safe. See J. Stratton Shartel, "Litigator offers range of suggestions for dealing with the media," *Inside Litigation* (April 1992), quoting Stuart W. Gold, a partner with the established New York law firm Cravath, Swaine, & Moore. Some law firms have hired individuals whose sole responsibility is to direct media relations. Ibid., 33.

21. Ken Kunsman, "Panelists spar on 'litigation journalism,'" B7.

22. Mary Lovitz Schmidt, "Communication counsel prepares attorneys for media exposure," *The Legal Intelligencer,* 16 April 1996, 7. Myles Martel, president of Martel & Associates, an international communication counseling service, offers similar advice: "Corporate attorneys aren't the only ones who need media training. . . . Criminal defense lawyers, too, face the media with its voracious appetite for news of crime. . . . With the help of a communication consultant, attorneys can learn to use the media to their clients' advantage instead of dreading exposure. . . . Just as lawyers hone their oral advocacy skills in law school moot court and their trial skills in advocacy workshops, they can learn to adapt those lawyering skills to the media. . . ." Ibid.

23. At one point in the O. J. Simpson criminal trial, defense lawyer Gerald Uelmen referred to witnesses who viewed their testimony as a "gig." *Larry King Live,* CNN, 23 May 1996 (Transcript #1755).

24. In the end, the prosecution of Altman and Clifford in Washington, D.C. petered out. A separate prosecution conducted by the Manhattan District Attorney's office resulted in an acquittal of Altman, after which the charges against Clifford were dropped. See Jonathan M. Moses, "Legal spin control: Ethics and advocacy in the court of public opinion," *Columbia Law Review* 95 (1995): 1837.

25. Daniel Cerone, "Menendez lawyers seek to halt TV films," *Los Angeles Times,* 11 April 1994, Part F, 1. While Abramson was unable to prevent the "bad vibes" that had been created concerning her client, she was able to provide her own counternarrative by appearing on such putative TV "news" shows as *Larry King Live.* From that venue Abramson could "report" to her national audience that the Menendez brothers "suffered from battered person syndrome, and that it was in that state of mind that they committed the homicides." *Larry King Live,* CNN, 23 August 1995 (Transcript #520); *Rivera Live,* CNBC, 13 November 1995.

26. Consider, for example, the made-for-television movie, *Love's Deadly Trial: The Texas Cadet Murder,* which was based on a highly publicized case involving U.S. Naval Academy and Air Force students Diane Zamora and David Graham. The docudrama shows the two Texas teenagers committing

murder notwithstanding the fact that they had not even been tried yet for the crime. Notably, the framing device for the story was David Graham's actual confession to police. As one critic observed, "'The Texas Cadet Murder,' far beyond hinting at guilt, delivers a flat-out indictment via two separate, detailed depictions of the murder. . . ." Howard Rosenberg, "NBC playing judge and jury in airing 'Texas Cadet,'" *Los Angeles Times,* 10 February 1997, Part F, 1. Zamora's lawyers attempted to prevent local television affiliates from airing the film before the trial, but they were unsuccessful based on the network's First Amendment right to broadcast it. See David Zurawik, "Docudrama becomes a rush to on-air judgment," *Baltimore Sun,* 10 February 1997, 1D.

27. It has been reported that Canadian citizens have insisted upon receiving "Miranda" warnings after being arrest by Canadian police. Of course the United States Supreme Court's pronouncements have no authority in Canada, even if their televised representations frequently do cross the border. See Steven Stark, "Perry Mason meets Sonny Crockett: The history of lawyers and police as television heroes," *University of Miami Law Review* 42 (1987): 231.

28. J. Stratton Shartel, "Litigator offers range of suggestions," 34. See also Carole Gorney, "The case against litigation journalism," *USA Today* (Magazine), March 1994, 72: "Litigation journalism is a trend which represents a symbiotic relationship that meets both the needs of the media and those of trial lawyers and their clients. As cable channels have proliferated . . . competition for topics and guests has become fierce."

29. See *Gentile v. Nevada,* 501 U.S. 1030, 1070 (1991). There are qualifications to the general prohibition. For example, so-called "safe harbor" exceptions may permit extrajudicial statements that are limited to stating "the general nature of the claim or defense" or that "an investigation is in progress," or that represent an effort to protect a client by responding to a barrage of prejudicial publicity.

30. ABA Model Rule 3.6, Trial Publicity, Comment [7].

31. See *Offut v. United States,* 348 U.S. 11 (1954).

32. The standard reference to *Estes,* and there are scores of examples to choose from, incorrectly characterizes it as a case that was conducted in a "circus-like atmosphere." On the federal level, see, for example, *Murphy v. Florida,* 421 U.S. 794 (1975) and *DeLisle v. Rivers,* 161 F.3d 370 (1998). At the state level, see *State v. Harris,* 716 A.2d 458 (N.J. 1998) and *State v. Billings,* 500 S.E.2d 423 (N.C. 1998). The scholarly literature also reflects this factual misreading of the case. See, for example, Leonard Pertnoy, "The juror's need to know vs. the Constitutional right to a fair trial," *Dickinson Law Review* 97 (1993): 627—"A media circus surrounded the trial."

33. Ewen, *PR!,* 153.

34. Roland Barthes, "Myth today," in *Mythologies* (New York: Noonday Press, 1972), 143. See Vivian Sobchack, "The insistent fringe: Moving images and historical consciousness," in *The Persistence of History: Cinema, Television, and the Modern Event* (New York: Routledge, 1996).

35. S. Paige Baty, *American Monroe: The Making of a Body Politic*

(Berkeley: University of California Press, 1995), 60, cited in Sobchack, "Insistent fringe," 11–12.

36. For Warren this represents a throwback to "the early days of this country's development," when the criminal trial was regarded by many as a source of entertainment, a combination of theater and public spectacle. Warren associates this perception of law with "frontier justice," a corrupt form of justice in which entertainment values predominate. In a startlingly prescient anticipation of media spectacles such as the O. J. Simpson double murder trial, Warren noted the "natural tendency on the part of broadcasters to develop the personalities of the trial participants, so as to give the proceedings more of an element of drama." Warren was equally prescient in observing that "the television industry might decide that the bare-boned trial itself does not contain sufficient drama to sustain an audience. It might provide expert commentary on the proceedings and hire persons with legal backgrounds to anticipate possible trial strategy, as the football expert anticipates plays for his audience." That is precisely the format that Steve Brill's Courtroom Television Network adopted a score and six years later. As Brill himself would say, Court TV was conceived as a combination of C-SPAN and soap operas. See Peter Pringle, "The channel where the stars are behind bars," *The Independent,* 11 October 1994, 27. Brill's new commercial network would have to compete with both in order to succeed. This ratings-driven environment is precisely what the *Estes* Court anticipated and feared. Indeed, the network has gone on to blur the reality/fiction divide even further by broadcasting fictional law dramas such as *Homicide: Life on the Streets.*

37. Bob Woodward and Scott Armstrong, *The Brethren: Inside the Supreme Court* (New York: Simon and Schuster, 1979), 74.

38. For example, in the aftermath of the O. J. Simpson criminal trial, a case in which the appearance of justice was more often eclipsed than evoked, courtrooms around the country moved to bar TV cameras. The list of blacked-out trials includes: the California trial of Richard Allen Davis, the killer of Polly Klaas; the South Carolina trial of Susan Smith, who drowned her two young sons; and the Colorado trial of Timothy McVeigh, who was convicted of multiple murders in the Oklahoma City bombing case.

39. Charles R. Nesson and Andrew D. Koblenz, "The image of justice: *Chandler v. Florida,*" *Harvard Civil Rights–Civil Liberties Law Review* 16, no. 2 (1981): 413. Nesson's insight is of particular interest in light of the fact that he was Justice Harlan's law clerk at the time *Estes* was decided.

40. Writing for a plurality of four justices, Justice Clark expressly states that with respect to television, "one cannot put his finger on its specific mischief and prove with particularity wherein [the appellant] was prejudiced." *Estes v. Texas,* 381 U.S. 532, 542 (1965). Similarly, in his concurring opinion, Chief Justice Warren describes in general terms the adverse effects of television on trial participants and the judicial process as a whole. Ibid., 569–78.

41. In Harlan's view, in notorious cases jurors face the danger of being drawn into a variety of heated popular controversies surrounding the trial and becoming subject to a variety of pressures from family, friends, neigh-

bors, and colleagues to whom even sequestered jurors must return. Similarly, in notorious trials defense lawyers are drawn to grandstanding tactics for the sake of their reputations and the potential to attract clients in the future. Prosecutors similarly feel the tug of their own personal ambitions, whether it is the ambition for advancement in their present office or the ambition for future public office. And even judges, particularly elected judges, Harlan contends, cannot be expected to remain unaffected by trial publicity. They too watch the news and read the papers, as do trial witnesses who will be similarly gripped by the glare of publicity. Ibid., 590–92.

42. *Richmond Newspapers, Inc. v. Virginia,* 448 U.S. 554, 570 (1980), emphasis added.

43. As George Gerbner writes, "Arbitrary power wants no public witness to its private deliberations, but needs all the hoopla it can get to legitimize its actions." Gerbner, "Trial by television: Are we at the point of no return?" *Judicature* 63, no. 9 (April 1980): 420.

44. Peter Arenella, "Explaining the unexplainable: Analyzing the Simpson verdict," *New Mexico Law Review* 26 (1996): 349, 356.

45. Ray Surette, "Predator criminals as media icons," 131–32. See also Elayne Rapping, "Aliens, nomads, mad dogs and road warriors: The new face of criminal violence on tabloid TV," in *Mythologies of Violence in Postmodern Media,* ed. Christopher Sharett (Detroit: Wayne State University Press, 1999), 249–73; Linda Ross Meyer, "Is practical reason mindless?" *Georgetown Law Journal* 86 (1998): 647, 668–70.

46. See Gerbner, "Trial by television," 419–20.

47. See Michael J. Sandel, *Democracy's Discontent: America in Search of a Public Philosophy* (Cambridge: Harvard University Press, 1996).

48. See *Kansas v. Hendricks,* 117 S. Ct. 2072 (1996). In *Hendricks,* the Court upheld a state statute providing for the civil commitment of "sexually violent predators" who are found to be "mentally abnormal," a condition that makes them "likely to engage in the predatory acts of sexual violence." According to the statute, involuntary commitment may continue "until such time as the person's mental abnormality or personality disorder has so changed that the person is safe to be at large."

Chapter Seven

1. Richard Kuhns, *Tragedy: Contradiction and Repression* (Chicago: University of Chicago Press, 1991), 7.

2. For example, even as the number of violent crimes committed goes down, the number of mandatory minimum sentencing schemes, bringing even nonviolent felons within the range of mandatory life sentences, increases—as does the number of people incarcerated and the number of prisons built. See Stephen J. Schulhofer, "The trouble with trials; the trouble with us," *Yale Law Journal* 105 (1995): 825, 853. At the same time, on the civil side, even statistically marginal harms have prompted legal claims for damages. Consider, for example, medical malpractice cases in which physicians are sued for failing to conduct a diagnostic test that might have detected cancer earlier,

and thus allowed treatment to begin sooner, even though the chances of survival remained less than 50 percent. The legal claim stems from a statistical probability of shortened life expectancy for which damages are sought. See, e.g., *Herskovits v. Group Health Cooperative,* 664 P.2d 474 (Wash. 1983).

3. See note 7 below.

4. Rikke Schubart, "From desire to deconstruction: Horror films and audience reactions," in *Crime and the Media,* ed. David Kidd-Hewitt and Richard Osborne (London: Pluto Press, 1995), 227–28.

5. For example, according to Earl Dunlap, president of the National Juvenile Detention Association, which represents the heads of the nation's juvenile jails, "The issues of violence against offenders, lack of adequate education, and mental health, of crowding and of poorly trained staff are the norm rather than the exception." Fox Butterfield, "Profits at a juvenile prison come with a chilling cost," *New York Times,* 15 July 1998, 1.

6. As the goddess Athena appeasingly tells the ancient Furies at the end of Aeschylus' *Eumenides:*

> Here are my actions. In all good will
>   toward these citizens I establish in power
> spirits who are large, difficult to soften.
> To them is given the handling entire
> of men's lives . . .
> Fury is high queen
> of strength even among the mortal gods
> and the undergods, and for humankind
> their work is accomplished, absolute, clear:
> for some, singing; for some, life dimmed
> in tears; theirs the disposition.

Aeschylus, *Oresteia,* trans. Richmond Lattimore (New York: Washington Square Press, 1967), 182.

7. Danny's Prologue goes as follows: "My Reminiscence. I always thought that for such a lovely river the name was mystifying. Cape Fear. The only thing to fear on those enchanted summer nights was that the magic would end, and real life would come crashing in."

8. Kuhns, *Tragedy,* 2. See also Martha C. Nussbaum, *Poetic Justice* (Boston: Beacon Press, 1995) and *Love's Knowledge* (Oxford: Oxford University Press, 1990).

9. In this way, the riddle of Cady's contradictions also embodies the purest spirit of Greek tragedy:

> [I]t could be said that tragedy rests on a double reading of Heraclitus' famous dictum, *ethos anthropo daimon* [character is fate]. . . . For there to be tragedy it must be possible for the text simultaneously to imply two things: It is his character, in man, that one calls *daimon* and, conversely, what one calls character, in man, is in reality a *daimon.* . . .

In a tragic perspective man and human action are seen, not as things that can be defined or described, but as problems. They are presented as riddles whose double meanings can never be pinned down or exhausted.

See Jean-Pierre Vernant and Pierre Vidal-Naquet, *Myth and Tragedy in Ancient Greece* (New York: Zone Books, 1996), 37–38.

10. See Schulhofer, "The trouble with trials," 853:

As our fears drive us toward ever harsher sentencing policies, capital punishment and life sentences proliferate; mandatory minimums become more common, and those that exist are pegged at ever higher levels; prison programs such as weightlifting and college studies are replaced by hard labor on chain gangs; "three-strikes-and-you're-out" legislation brings lesser felons, including non-violent felons, within the ambit of mandatory life sentences; and "two strikes" proposals loom as the inevitable next step. Increasingly, the ground rules for our "war" on crime are set not by the Geneva Convention but by a scorched earth, take-no-prisoners philosophy (literally, for advocates of capital punishment).

11. René Girard, cited in Vernant and Vidal-Naquet, Myth and Tragedy, 17.

12. See Kuhns, *Tragedy,* 68.

13. See Slavoj Žižek, "Ideology between fiction and fantasy," *Cardozo Law Review* 16 (1995): 1525, 1529–30: "It is the way we picture the wholly Other that gives us insight into the nature of the repressed trauma, the fantasy, that makes the Other what he is. For example, in the hated Jew lies the split-off, uncanny double of the Nazi's repressed unconscious fantasy, the destabilizing taint that haunts him. This 'conceptual Jew' symbolizes the perennial threat to an opposite fantasy, a fantasy of undisturbed desire. Only the (fantasized) Other's extermination allows (fantasized) desire to be fulfilled." The urge to rectify tragic wrongs through the various instrumentalities of law at times eclipses, even as it channels, our rage and fear of impotence in the face of senseless death and suffering. The draconian "three-strikes-and-you're-out" mandatory sentencing law, which Californians enacted in 1994 following the highly publicized kidnapping and murder of twelve-year-old Polly Klaas, fueled in significant part by the rage and grief of her distraught father, is an example of this urge in action. For a rare look at how societies cope with decisions they regard as tragic, see Guido Calabresi and Philip Bobbitt, *Tragic Choices* (New York: W. W. Norton, 1978).

14. Richard Kuhns, *Tragedy,* 76.

15. Ibid., 146.

16. Sophocles, *Oedipus the King,* trans. Richmond Lattimore (New York: Washington Square Press, 1970), 49.

17. Consider, for example, the founding organizing principles of order

among pre-Socratic philosophers: Anaximenes' air, Heraclitus' fire, Thales' water. See G. S. Kirk and J. E. Raven, *The Presocratic Philosophers* (Cambridge: Cambridge University Press, 1957), and John Burnet, *Early Greek Philosophy* (New York: Meridian Books, 1969).

18. Absurd as this seems, in the context of a reversion to primitive ("premodern") thinking such a character may not be so surprising. The projection of human qualities onto the natural world, a process in which the subjective and objective fuse, is not unusual for a number of tribal cultures. Consider, for example, the pygmies of the Ituri forest who sing to cheer up the forest when it falls into a bad mood. As Mary Douglas notes: "So here is another way in which the primitive, undifferentiated universe is personal. It is expected to behave as if it was intelligent, responsive to signs, symbols, gestures, gifts, and as if it could discern between social relationships." Mary Douglas, *Purity and Danger* (New York: Routledge, 1991), 87.

19. See Vernant and Vidal-Naquet, *Myth and Tragedy,* 49 (noting that it is precisely the inability to make reasoned decisions about how to act or to anticipate how things will come out in the face of mysterious divine forces that defines the tragic consciousness of the Greeks). A similar breakdown in modern psychology can be observed today, with conflicting responses. For example, contemporary psychologists Sherry Turkle (in *Life on the Screen* [New York: Simon & Schuster, 1995]) and Robert Jay Lifton (in *The Protean Self* [New York: Basic Books, 1996]) have written about the emancipatory and enriching aspects of the mutable postmodern self. However, others, like James M. Glass (in *Shattered Selves* [Ithaca, N.Y.: Cornell University Press, 1993]), are far less sanguine about the much touted virtues of living with multiple personalities. As for law, the discontinuity of the self, whereby the actor of today may not be responsible for the actor of yesterday, cuts directly at the root of individual accountability.

20. Marina Warner suggests that the male characters in *Lost Highway* seem to possess "dream selves" who take up multiple occupancy in their bodies. See Marina Warner, "Voodoo Road," *Sight and Sound* 8 (August 1997): 6. In the same essay, Warner also makes the intriguing observation that "the model of personality presented in Lynch's film resembles far more closely the beliefs of spirit religions as practiced in Haiti, or elsewhere, among the Buissi people in Southern Congo. . . . In such schema of identity, the dream self can wander and perform independent acts or become possessed by the spirit and identity of a local stranger over whom the self has no authority."

21. Consider the god Dionysus of ancient Greek myth:

> Like wine, Dionysus is double: most terrible yet infinitely sweet. His presence, which is a bewildering intrusion of otherness into the human world, may take two forms, be manifested in two different ways. On the one hand it may bring blessed union with the god, in the heart of nature, with every constraint lifted—an escape from the limitations of the everyday world and oneself. . . . On the other hand, it may precipi-

tate one into chaos in the confusion of a bloodthirsty, murderous madness in which the "same" and the "other" merge and one mistakes one's
nearest and dearest, one's own child, one's second self for a wild beast
that one tears apart with one's bare hands: ghastly impurity, inexpiable
crime, misfortune without end, without relief.

Vernant and Vidal-Naquet, *Myth and Tragedy*, 400.

22. See Robert Bartlett, *Trial by Fire and Water* (Oxford: Clarendon
Press, 1988).

23. See Burnet, *Early Greek Philosophers*, 52; Kirk and Raven, *The Pre-
Socratic Philosophers*, 106. The ancient Greek philosopher Heraclitus expressed a similar thought: "The sun will not over step his measures; if he
were to do so, the Erinyes, handmaids of Justice, would seek him out." Philip
Wheelwright, *Heraclitus* (New York: Atheneum Press, 1968), 102.

24. See Edward S. Herman and Robert W. McChesney, *Global Media*
(London: Cassell, 1997), on the uncontrollability of market forces by governments and industry alike.

25. The catalogue of names for such forces throughout history is far too
great to list here. But to give an idea of the role they have played in one historic context, that of Greece in the age of Pericles, Jean-Pierre Vernant has
probably said it best:

> *Mania, lussa, ate, ara, miasma, Erinyis*—all these nouns refer in the
> last analysis to one and the same mythical factor, a sinister numen that
> manifests itself in many guises, at different moments, both within a
> man's soul and outside him. It is a power of misfortune that encom-
> passes not only the criminal but the crime itself, its most distant ante-
> cedents, its psychological motivations. . . . In Greek there is a word for
> this type of divine power, which is not usually individualized and which
> takes action at the very heart of men's lives, usually to ill-fated effect
> and in a wide variety of forms: It is *daimon*.

Vernant and Vidal-Naquet, *Myth and Tragedy*, 35–36. For another rich
source of names one may also consult the growing list of Gothic archetypes in
contemporary pop culture. See Mark Edmundson, *Nightmare on Mainstreet*
(Cambridge: Harvard University Press, 1997).

26. In one recent account, the Gothic genre was described this way:

> Gothic combines the sexual theme of the sentimental novel—the "in-
> verted" love story of a young virgin/daughter pursued by an older vil-
> lain/father—with supernatural horror. . . . With its fascination for
> middle-age architecture Gothic set the now classic scene for horror: a
> female victim tortured in the claustrophobic space of deserted and de-
> cayed castles, a space linked with the dark, the night, the dream, and
> the unconscious. . . . The subconscious functions as a nightmarish point

of view, a "distorting lens". . . . The distortion lets fantasies of sexuality and sadism spring into full bloom with violence, sadism, masochism. . . .

Schubart, "From desire to deconstruction," 225.

27. I do not believe that it is simply a coincidence that the first words uttered by the Mystery Man in David Lynch's *Lost Highway* are the same as those first spoken by Count Dracula in Bram Stoker's original work of that title: "It is not my custom to go where I am not wanted." These words signal the kinship that exists between the mysterious other and his alleged victims. Indeed, it offers support for the notion that what we are dealing with here is the victim's dark double within, the repressed impulse or forbidden fantasy that calls the mysterious other into being, to do the bidding of the victim's unconscious rage and desire.

28. As Rikki Schubart notes, the essence of horror lies in the "monster"— a word deriving from Latin, meaning "a freak announcing the wrath of the gods." Schubart, "From desire to deconstruction," 226.

29. Edmundson, *Nightmare on Mainstreet,* 127–28.

30. Ibid., 178–79.

31. Ibid., 130–31.

32. Ibid., 145.

Chapter Eight

1. John Barth, *Chimera* (New York: Fawcett Crest, 1972), 15.

2. See Jacqueline de Romilly, *Magic and Rhetoric in Ancient Greece* (Cambridge: Harvard University Press, 1975).

3. See Richard K. Sherwin, "Dialects & dominance: A study of rhetorical fields in the law of confessions," *University of Pennsylvania Law Review* 136 (1988): 731 n.4.

4. Ibid.

5. Jonathan Lear, *Opened Minded: Working Out the Logic of the Soul* (Cambridge: Harvard University Press, 1998), 55. I believe Lear is equally astute when he adds: "Tragedy begins with the recognition that neither [the return to premodern fundamentalism nor the deconstructive playfulness one finds in much of postmodern literature, art and philosophy] will work for long: that flight is not possible, that breaking up of past orthodoxy is itself a defense which will eventually collapse."

6. See Jerome Bruner, *Acts of Meaning* (Cambridge: Harvard University Press, 1990), 106. Compare Gorgias' originary insight along similarly constructivist lines: "For that by which we impart information is *logos,* but *logos* is not the things that are or that exist." Segal comments:

Gorgias, in other words, is aware of the peculiar nature of the communicatory medium qua medium. Communication itself, therefore, is a special area of human activity, an invention of society based upon prearranged conventions, and must inevitably involve distortions and rearrangements of the message. There is no such thing as a purely objective transmission of reality.

Charles P. Segal, "Gorgias and the psychology of the *logos*," in *Harvard Studies in Classical Philology*, vol. 66 (Cambridge: Harvard University Press, 1962), 109.

7. John Stuart Mill, *The Autobiography* (Boston: Houghton Mifflin, 1969), 81.

8. Kathy Eden, *Poetic and Legal Fiction in the Aristotelian Tradition* (Princeton: Princeton University Press, 1986), 7.

9. Ibid., 53.

10. See *Courvoisier v. Raymond,* 47 P. 284 (Colo. 1896).

11. See Sherwin, "Dialects & dominance," 762 n. 120 (quoting George E. Dix).

12. See *Jackson v. Denno,* 378 U.S. 368, 391 (1964).

13. Ibid., 386.

14. See Sherwin, "Dialects & dominance," 749–95; *Bruton v. United States,* 391 U.S. 123, 126 (1968).

15. Eden, *Poetic and Legal Fiction,* 39.

16. See, for example, Pierre Schlag, "Normative and nowhere to go," *Stanford Law Review* 43 (1990): 167.

17. It is no less misleading than the choice between skeptical postmodernism and the felt need to return to the naive realism of the Enlightenment. See, for example, Daniel A. Farber and Suzanna Sherry, *Beyond All Reason: The Radical Assault on Truth in American Law* (Oxford: Oxford University Press, 1997), 16, describing the pitted struggle between Enlightenment scholars, like Farber and Sherry, on the one hand, and "radical multiculturalists" on the other.

18. Ernst Cassirer, *Language and Myth* (New York: Dover, 1946).

19. Note that this also distinguishes postmodern constructivism from its classical and medieval rhetorical antecedents. See Cassirer, *Language and Myth,* and Ruth Morse, *Truth and Convention in the Middle Ages: Rhetoric, Representation, and Reality* (Cambridge: Cambridge University Press, 1991).

20. Pietro Pucci, *Hesiod and the Language of Poetry* (Ithaca, N.Y.: Cornell University Press, 1997), 2–3.

21. See Richard K. Sherwin, "A matter of voice and plot," *Michigan Law Review* 87 (1988): 543–612.

22. See Segal, "Gorgias and the psychology of the *logos*," 105: "The force of the *logoi* thus works upon the psyche; they have an immediate, almost physical impact on it. . . . All persuasion is thus action upon and manipulation of the psyche of the audience; and the *dynamis* of the *logos* acts like a real drug in affecting the state of the psyche."

23. Bram Stoker, *Dracula* (New York: Modern Library, 1996), 232.

24. de Romilly, *Magic and Rhetoric in Ancient Greece,* 5; John Kerrigan, *Revenge Tragedy* (Oxford: Oxford University Press, 1997), 36; Segal, "Gorgias and the psychology of the *logos*," 112.

25. Kerrigan, *Revenge Tragedy,* 37.

26. Ibid.

27. Simonetta Falasca-Zamponi, *Fascist Spectacle: The Aesthetics of Power in Mussolini's Italy* (Berkeley: University of California Press, 1997), 4.

28. Ibid., 9.

29. One is reminded here of the radical stimulation in such rock phenomena as the Marilyn Manson "Anti-Christ" Tour of 1997, which Manson described as a desperate attempt to feel something, an effort that at times involved acts of self-mutilation.

30. Falasca-Zamponi, *Fascist Spectacle,* 20.

31. Stuart Ewen, *PR! A Social History of Spin* (New York: Basic Books, 1996), 154.

32. Victoria Harbord, "*Natural Born Killers:* Violence, film, and anxiety," in Colin Summer, *Violence, Culture and Censure* (London: Taylor & Francis, 1996), 154.

33. Ibid., 156.

34. In this respect, skeptical postmodern filmmakers like Quentin Tarantino and others depend upon their audience's natural semiotic sophistication, which is to say, the film viewer's ability to deconstruct a film genre and respond to content in a self-reflective state of genre-awareness. See Rikki Schubart, "From desire to deconstruction: Horror films and audience reactions," in David Kidd-Hewitt and Richard Osborne, *Crime and the Media: The Post-Modern Spectacle* (London: Pluto Press, 1995), 234, describing a source of postmodern pleasure in the audience's ability to "make meaning out of the bits and pieces." As Schubart notes: "[T]he textuality of psychotic horror shares traits with films like *Pretty Woman, Last Action Hero* and other meta- and self-reflective genre films."

35. See Segal, "Gorgias and the psychology of the *logos,*" 110.

36. Ibid., 108, referring to Gorgias' awareness of the power to manipulate collective emotions for the sake of creating what Segal refers to as "a mob effect." The connection with twentieth-century propaganda techniques and the American public relations movement is readily discernible. For example, commenting on Gorgias' assessment of public opinion (or *doxa*) Segal notes: "Because the majority have no adequate knowledge of past, present, or future, they are dependent on *doxa,* and they must receive it as the 'counselor for their psyche.' It is admitted that *doxa* is deceptive and unstable, but the human psyche has no better guide." In short, having forsaken any hope of attaining absolute knowledge, rhetoricians like Gorgias are concerned simply with "creating impressions upon the psyche" of their audience and thus "somehow directing their actions." The art of persuasion is therefore an art of enchantment: its "magic spell" joins together with opinion and thereby charms and changes it. Ibid., 111.

37. Ibid., 131.

38. In this respect, the classical rhetorical challenge to wed eloquence with ethical wisdom remains very much a part of contemporary life. As the Italian humanist Poggio Bracciolini observed, deception and hypocrisy are

the greatest of social ills, "for Cicero testifies this to be more against nature than death, than pain, than the other ills that can befall the body or our possessions externally." In Poggio's view, the growth of tyranny and cultural decadence is inextricably tied to the loss of faith in communication. See Nancy S. Struever, *The Language of History in the Renaissance* (Princeton: Princeton University Press, 1970), 165–66. Paraphrasing the opening affirmation of Cicero's great rhetorical text, *De inventione*, Seigel succinctly captures the key insight that is at work here: "Wisdom without eloquence was of little use to civic life, eloquence separate from wisdom was often of great harm; only the man who joined the two could bring true benefit to himself and to his fellow men." Jerrold E. Seigel, *Rhetoric and Philosophy in Renaissance Humanism* (Princeton: Princeton University Press, 1968), 6.

39. See Victor Turner, *Dramas, Fields, and Metaphors* (Ithaca, N.Y.: Cornell University Press, 1974), 17: "Paradigm conflicts arise over exclusion rules. 'Arenas' are the concrete settings in which paradigms become transformed into metaphors and symbols with reference to which political power is mobilized and in which there is a trial of strength between influential paradigm-bearers. 'Social dramas' represent the phased process of their contestation." See also Victor Turner, *The Ritual Process* (Ithaca, N.Y.: Cornell University Press, 1977), 128–29:

> *Communitas* breaks in through the interstices of structure, in liminality; at the edges of structure, in marginality. . . . Liminality, margin ality, and structural inferiority are conditions in which are frequently generated myths, symbols, rituals, philosophical systems, and works of art. These cultural forms provide men with a set of templates or models which are, at one level, periodical reclassifications of reality and man's relationship to society, nature, and culture. But they are more than classifications, since they incite men to action as well as to thought.

40. See Victor Turner, *Revelation and Divination in Ndembu Ritual* (Ithaca, N.Y.: Cornell University Press, 1975), 23: "*Communitas* is the primal ground, the *urgrund* of social structure." According to Turner, it is through social rituals and dramas that members of a community "transmit the inherited wisdom of their culture about this primal ground of experience, thought, and social action and about its fitful intrusions into the ordered cosmos which native models portray and explain."

41. de Romilly, *Magic and Rhetoric in Ancient Greece*, 79.

42. Ibid., 70.

Chapter Nine

1. John Kerrigan, *Revenge Tragedy* (Oxford: Oxford University Press, 1997), 354 (citing J.-F. Lyotard, *The Differend: Phrases in Dispute* [1988], 110–11).

2. Jürgen Habermas, *Communication and the Evolution of Society* (Boston: Beacon Press, 1979), 2. Habermas also finds it useful to endorse Law-

rence Kohlberg's allegedly "transcultural" or transcendental "stages" of human development in support of his own universal ethics of speech (90). Claims to universal norms of this type, however, have been challenged by cultural anthropologists and developmental psychologists alike. See, for example, D.C. Phillips and Jennie Nicolayev, "Kohlbergian moral development: A progressing or degenerating research program?" *Educational Theory* 28, no. 4 (fall 1978); James W. Stigler, Richard A. Shweder, and Gilbert Herdt, *Cultural Psychology* (Cambridge: Cambridge University Press, 1992), 130–51: "We believe that so few people around the world meet Kohlberg's criteria for postconventional thinking because they reject his particular rationalization of morality."

3. Richard A. Schweder, *Thinking Through Cultures* (Cambridge: Harvard University Press, 1991), 22–23.

4. In *Smith v. Employment Division, Department of Human Services,* 485 U.S. 660 (1988), a majority of the United States Supreme Court concluded that the First Amendment's free exercise clause does not protect religious practices that are in violation of "an otherwise valid law prohibiting conduct that the State is free to regulate." Under this interpretation, so long as the legislative goal of prohibiting the use or distribution of peyote is manifestly "neutral," the law's incidental effect of delegitimating the Native American Church is not constitutionally objectionable. See Richard K. Sherwin, "Rhetorical pluralism and the discourse ideal," *Northwestern University Law Review* 85 (1991): 399

5. Stuart Kauffman, *At Home in the Universe* (Oxford: Oxford University Press, 1995), 91.

6. Ibid., 299, 304. Richard Lanham has proposed a similar perspective except that the oscillation he describes reflects the classic alternation between the polarities of rhetoric and philosophy. See Richard Lanham, *The Electronic Word* (Chicago: University of Chicago Press, 1993), 71, 73.

7. Kauffman, *At Home in the Universe,* 207.

8. Ibid.

9. For example, while the law generally frames questions of criminal accountability in terms of factual guilt, thus privileging the common sense of the jury, it also allows experts to trump common-sense expectations. We see this when higher legal principles exclude even reliable evidence (in the form of coerced confessions, say) or when medical experts offer opinions regarding an accused's competence to stand trial.

10. See Sherwin, "Rhetorical pluralism," 412, 416, discussing the complex theory of human nature embodied in the federal Constitution's division of power into disparate sources of knowledge and discourse.

11. George Orwell, *1984* (New York: Harcourt, Brace & Co., 1949), 220: "Progress in our world will be progress toward more pain. The old civilizations claimed that they were founded on love and justice. Ours is founded on hatred. In our world there will be no emotions except fear, rage, triumph, and self-abasement. Everything else we shall destroy—everything."

12. David L. Altheide, *An Ecology of Communication* (New York: Walter de Guyter, 1995), 186.

13. Following the Gulf War, Israeli intelligence revealed that not a single Patriot missile brought down an Iraqi Scud missile. See Tim Weiner, "Pentagon loses bid to keep report on Gulf War secret," *New York Times,* 29 June 1997, 20.

14. Cited in Altheide, *An Ecology of Communication,* 217.

15. See C. Edwin Baker, *Advertising and a Democratic Press* (Princeton: Princeton University Press, 1994), 45: "As a central symbolic structure, advertising may shape our sense of values even under conditions where it does not greatly corrupt our buying habits" [quotation marks omitted].

16. Andy Warhol, *The Philosophy of Andy Warhol* (San Diego: Harvest, 1975), 44. Warhol demonstrated early on a highly sophisticated grasp of the implications of hyperreality. For example, commenting on the sense of derealization that accompanies the blurring of reality and fiction, he wrote:

> When I got my first TV set, I stopped caring so much about having close relationships with other people. . . . I started an affair with my television which has continued to the present. . . . But I didn't get married until 1964 when I got my first tape recorder. . . . Nothing was ever a problem again. . . . An interesting problem was an interesting tape. Everybody knew that and performed for the tape. You couldn't tell which problems were real and which problems were exaggerated for the tape. Better yet, the people telling you the problems couldn't decide any more if they were really having problems or if they were just performing. . . . (26–27)

17. See Pierre Bourdieu, *On Television* (New York: New Press, 1998), 45.

18. See George W. S. Trow, *Within the Context of No Context* (New York: Atlantic Monthly, 1997).

19. Bourdieu, *On Television,* 3, 47.

20. See, for example, Susan P. Koniak, "The chosen people in our wilderness," *Michigan Law Review* 95 (1997): 1761, and David Papke, *Heretics in the Temple* (New York: New York University Press, 1998).

21. Justice Warren specifically had in mind the scandal created by the disclosure that a popular quiz show had been "fixed" in order to "heighten their dramatic appeal" and thus generate higher ratings. *Estes v. Texas,* 381 U.S. 532, 570 (1965).

22. Bourdieu, *On Television,* 47.

23. Clinton Rossiter, *The Federalist Papers* (New York: New American Library, 1961), 82–83.

24. Ibid., 78.

25. See, for example, Caryn James, "It was all too familiar, like a *Nightline* rerun," *New York Times,* 6 October 1998, A21:

Who needs Congress when there's *Crossfire*? During the House Judiciary Committee's televised debate about an impeachment inquiry yesterday, Representative Robert Wexler of Florida, a vehement opponent of impeaching the President, said he was scheduled to appear on *Crossfire* late that night with Representative Bob Barr of Georgia, one of the President's fiercest critics. "In an effort not to ruin the show tonight, I'm going to wait to respond to Mr. Barr's comments earlier until we get on the show," Mr. Wexler said. It was a joke and it wasn't. Television has clearly superseded Congress as the primary site of political debate.

26. Ronald Dworkin, "The curse of American politics," *New York Review of Books,* 17 October 1996, 20–21.

27. In *Virginia Board of Pharmacy v. Virginia Citizens Consumer Council,* 425 U.S. 748 (1976), the United States Supreme Court extended full first amendment protection to commercial advertising, declaring that "[a]s to the particular consumer's interest in the free flow of commercial information, that interest may be as keen, if not keener by far, than his interest in the day's most urgent political debate" (763). As one commentator archly noted, "[I]f free speech was defended with the metaphor of the market, it was only a matter of time . . . before the market was defended with the metaphor and substance of free speech." Mark Tushnet, "Corporations and free speech," in *The Politics of Law,* ed. David Kairys (New York: Pantheon, 1982), 260.

The Court's controversial decision that same year in *Buckley v. Valeo,* 424 U.S. 1 (1976), striking down regulation of campaign expenditures, drew intense and wide-ranging criticism from the outset—and continues to do so today. See, for example, C. Edwin Baker, "Campaign expenditures and free speech," *Harvard Civil Rights–Civil Liberties Law Review* 33, no. 1 (1998): 1, 50, in which the author asserts that "*Buckley* was out of line with precedent and appropriate First Amendment theory in not seeing that elections are instrumentally designed, institutionally bound realms where appropriate regulations of speech have been and should be permitted." In Baker's view, the goal of such regulation is to maintain "a vibrant, unregulated public sphere" (49). Increasing the fairness and openness of the electoral process (e.g., by regulating contributors' use of the airwaves or by requiring broadcasters to give candidates or political parties free time) might also improve the quality of public discourse. In this sense, regulating political campaign expenditures seeks to correct distortions—such as using corporate wealth to gain an unfair advantage—in the political process the same way that state interventions in the market seek to correct economic distortions created by "market failure." See *Austin v. Michigan Chamber of Commerce,* 494 U.S. 652, 658 (1990), in which the Court noted that "state law grants corporations special advantages [which] . . . not only allow corporations to play a dominant role in the Nation's economy, but also permit them to use 'resources amassed in the economic marketplace' to obtain an unfair advantage in the political marketplace" (quoting *Federal Election Commission v. Massachusetts Citizens for Life, Inc.,* 479 U.S. 238, 258 [1986]).

28. *Richmond Newspapers, Inc. v. Virginia,* 448 U.S. 555, 587 (1980).

29. A number of private, nonprofit television stations (local "C-SPANS") have emerged on the state level. See, for example, the "Planning Report" of the Washington State Public Affairs Network at <http://www.tvw.org>. Similar stations have emerged in Rhode Island (1984), Massachusetts (1984), Nebraska (1984), Minnesota (1988), California (1990), Hawaii (1993), and Washington State (1993). Some form of televising state government takes place in approximately 46 states. Internet possibilities may also represent a vast untapped potential in this regard.

30. As O. J. Simpson defense attorney Barry Scheck has observed:

> The producers pick people who they know are going to disagree, they don't provide an atmosphere, frankly, where thoughtful debate can take place, and so it doesn't. . . . The problem is the shows we're talking about are designed to accentuate conflict, to sound bite people in like seconds, the producers are picking people so they'll fight with each other to make good television, to create a certain kind of ratings vehicle, and basically we're not getting context, we're not getting a sense of proportion, we're not really getting educated.

The NewsHour with Jim Lehrer, 19 October 1998 (Transcript #6279). An additional problem is that TV producers also typically fail to identify the political agenda or paid sponsor for a particular "talking head's" "expertise" and point of view on the matter in question. As legal analyst Ann Coulter understatedly notes: "If you're being paid by the tobacco industry and you're on TV discussing tobacco legislation, or tobacco laws, or the tobacco lawsuit, I think it would be a relevant piece of information." Ibid.

31. The literature on the global media literacy movement is rich and diverse. The aims of the movement are not free from controversy. However, an excellent outline of the history and goals of the movement has been provided by Gary Ferrington of the University of Oregon:

> With so much information being generated in various electronic forms, it has become essential that children and adults be able to access, analyze, evaluate, and make effective choices about the audio, visual, and print material they encounter each day. . . . A media literate society will be brought about by the integration of media studies across the curriculum. Reading, writing, and communicating using the symbolic visual and aural languages of film, photography, radio, computers, television, and other media, is at the heart of media education in grades K-16, and beyond.

<http://interact.uoregon.edu/medialit/fa/mlarticlefolder/whatisml.html>.
See generally W. James Potter, *Media Literacy* (Beverly Hills, Calif.: Sage, 1998); Peter McLaren et al., *Rethinking Media Literacy* (New York: Peter Lang Publishing, 1995).

32. Ruth Morse, *Truth and Convention in the Middle Ages: Rhetoric, Representation, and Reality* (Cambridge: Cambridge University Press, 1991), 83.

33. See, e.g., Peter Applebome, "The Medici behind Disney's high art," *New York Times,* 4 October 1998, Section 2, 1 (discussing Walt Disney Company's CEO, Michael Eisner, among other transnational corporate heads, as sponsors of culture analogous to the Medici family during the European Renaissance).

34. *Kieslowski on Kieslowski,* ed. Danusia Stok (London: Faber and Faber, 1995), 212.

INDEX

Abramson, Jeffrey, 265n. 5

Abramson, Leslie: on *Larry King Live,* 288n. 25; litigation public relations and, 150–51; on media's shortcomings, 143; on Menendez docudramas, 15–16

acausality: arguments based in, 127; in *Lost Highway,* 190–91; rejection of, 130–31; in storytelling, 122, 123–26, 133. *See also* nonlinearity; *The Thin Blue Line* (film)

accountability. *See* responsibility/ accountability

Adams, John, 57, 66–67

Adams, Randall Dale (case): circumstances of, 109–11; details and disorder in, 108–9, 121–22; fate in, 123–24; framing frame-up in, 114–17; Goetz defense applied to, 134–35; new trial for, 280–81n. 11; sentence in, 113–14, 280nn. 9–10; skeptical postmodernism's impact on, 12–13; sources on, 280n. 4; trial events of, 111–14; verdict in, 107–8, 113. See also *The Thin Blue Line* (film)

Adams v. Texas, 280n. 4, 280n. 9. *See also* Adams, Randall Dale (case)

Adatto, Kiku, 146, 286n. 13, 286n. 14

adultery case. *See* Beecher, Henry Ward (case)

advertising: actors in, 48; emergence of, 26–27, 224, 227; emotional associations in, 33; familiarity in, 144, 285–86n. 9; first amendment protection for, 302n. 27; function of, 262–63; irony in, 144–46; values shaped by, 301n. 15. *See also* public relations

Aeschylus: on fate/chance, 284n. 29; irrationality and, 116; on law and vengeance, 181, 213, 292n. 6; rituals and, 52

affirmative postmodernism: chance and complexity in, 131–32, 235, 283n. 26; components of, 237–38; concept of, 9–10, 13, 131–33, 194–95, 221, 233; on interpenetration of law and culture, 230–31; in *Music of Chance,* 172, 195–203; obstacles to, 235; pre-Platonic perspective and, 229; in *Red,* 255; skeptical postmodernism vs., 126–28, 231–32; storyline needed in, 136; strategies in fostering, 245–54; task of, 202–3; in *The Thin Blue Line,* 133–39; truth/justice in, 131, 136, 229–33, 260–64; values of, 166. *See also* enchantment; myth; tragic constructivism

Ailes, Roger, 145

Allen, Woody, 33, 271n. 26

Altman, Robert, 150, 288n. 24

Amsterdam, Anthony G., 269n. 17

Anaximander, 200

Anderson, Osborn P., 277n. 12

Anderson, Pamela, 163

Annie Hall (film), 33

"Anti-Christ" Tour (Marilyn Manson), 298n. 29

anxiety: about criminals, 165–66; about information, 186–87; about postmodern irrationality, 220; countering Enlightenment's cause of, 232–33; as cultural barometer, 75–78; epistemological type of, 85–93; moral type of, 80–85; as response to disequilibrium, 261–62; socioeconomic type of, 93–94, 95–96, 98–104; in unresolved conflict, 231. *See also* notorious legal cases

Appleborne, Peter, 304n. 33

archetypes: order reinforced through, 34–36; in public spectacles, 68–69

Arenella, Peter, 162

argumentation: storytelling vs., 42–44; use of term, 42

Aristotle: on enthymeme, 217–19; on meaning making, 139; on persuasion, 206, 213

Armstrong, Scott, 156–57

art: affirmative postmodernism nourished in, 194–95; consumption and, 28–29; function of, 229–30; mass production of, 28–29; rationality pitted against, 207–8; social context reflected in, 95; uncertainty in, 186–87

Artaud, Antonin, 209

Aryan Nations, 52–53, 60

associative logic, concept of, 20, 193. *See also* nonlinearity; visual images

attorneys. *See* lawyers

audience: for crime novel, 281n. 14; as detective/juror in linear mystery story, 115–17, 127; expectations of, 25–26, 30–31, 298n. 34; narrative resolution by, 43–44; passive state of, 143–44; responsive state of, 45–46, 56–63, 132–34; televising trials and, 162–63. *See also* genres; jurors

Auster, Paul, 195, 209, 266n. 7. See also *The Music of Chance* (film)

Austin v. Michigan Chamber of Commerce, 302n. 27

authenticity, degeneration of, 13, 27, 259–60, 266n. 7. *See also* derealization; Warhol, Andy

The Awakening (Chopin), 94–95, 96

Bailey, F. Lee, 30

Baker, C. Edwin, 301n. 15, 302n. 27

Baraka, Larry W. (judge), 280–81n. 11

Barr, Bob, 301–2n. 25

Barth, John, 206

Barthes, Roland, 68–69, 155, 267n. 10

BATF (Bureau of Alcohol, Tobacco, and Firearms), 52–53, 54, 62

Baty, S. Paige, 155

Baudrillard, Jean: on disappearance of the real, 282n. 24; on hyperreality, 29, 68; on simulacrum, 128–29, 265n. 4, 282n. 23

Baywatch (television program), 163

Beasley, Ronnie Jack (case), 16–17

Beckett, Samuel, 117, 281n. 16

Beecher, Henry Ward (case): circumstances of, 85–87; epistemological anxiety in, 76, 86–92; triumph of denial in, 92–93; verdict in, 86, 92

beliefs: clarification of, 67–68, 77; common sense and, 47–48; comprehensability and, 129; construction of, 221; instability in, 186–87; myth's role in, 63–65, 262–63; questioning of, 77, 91, 116; revelation of values in, 60–61, 228; social reality shaped by, 73, 96, 99–100, 102, 123, 212. See also *communitas*

Benjamin, Walter, 266n. 7

Bentham Jeremy, 211

Berke, Richard, 286–87n. 15

Bernays, Edward L., 144, 224, 226

Berranger, Olivier de, 77

Best, William Bowdesley, 276n. 3

Beverly Hills Cop, Two (film), 272n. 34

biography, interpretive type of, 286n. 12

Biro, Yvette, 270n. 11

Birringer, Johannes H., 14, 28

Blake, William, 202, 208

Blue (film), 254

Blum, Harold P., 72

Bobbitt, Philip, 269n. 17

Boesky, Ivan, 149

Boorstin, Daniel, 286n. 14

Bourdieu, Pierre, 244

Bracciolini, Poggio, 298–99n. 38

Braindead (film), 225

Brando, Marlon, 30

breast implants, lawsuit regarding, 273n. 3, 288n. 20

Brennan, William J. (justice), 126, 251

The Brethren (Woodward and Armstrong), 156–57

Breton, André, 208–9
"bricoleur," use of term, 192, 193
Brill, Steve, 163, 284–85n. 5, 290n. 36.
   See also Courtroom Television
   Network
Bronson, Charles, 272n. 34
Brown, John (case): details ignored in,
   79–80, 82; fear of, 277n. 17; moral
   anxiety in, 75–76, 80–85; as Romance
   narrative, 76, 78–84
Brown v. Board of Education, 78
Bruner, Jerome: approach of, 269n. 17;
   on cognitive styles, 273n. 2; on com-
   munal tool kit, 40; on public meaning
   making, 18–19; on understanding self,
   209
Bruton v. United States, 274n. 18
Buckley v. Valeo, 302n. 27
Budd, John, 148
Bugliosi, Vincent, 30
Buñuel, Luis, 170
Bureau of Alcohol, Tobacco, and Firearms (BATF), 52–53, 54, 62
Burger, Warren (justice): on community
   catharsis, 162–63, 166; jurisprudence
   of appearances and, 157–58; socio-
   historical context of, 156–57; on televising trials, 153–61, 167–68, 226,
   247–48
Burke, Kenneth, 241
Burroughs, William, 209
Buttafuoco, Joey, 27, 271n. 26

Cage, John, 208–9
Caldwell, Gail, 286n. 12
Campbell, Joseph, 283–84n. 28
Camus, Albert, 208
Canada, Miranda warnings and, 289n.
   27
Cape Fear (film, 1962): context of, 171;
   reading of, 174–75, 182; remake com-
   pared to, 176–77, 180, 181, 182;
   storyline of, 173–74
Cape Fear (film, 1991): context of,

171–72; reading of, 181–85; storyline
   of, 175–82
Capote, Truman, 3, 265n. 1
Cassirer, Ernst, 221
catharsis: assimilation and transcendence of terror in, 223; distortion of,
   166; notorious legal cases as, 162–63,
   243; possibilities for, 182–85
causality: arguments based in, 126–27;
   deconstruction of, 127–28; effects of,
   117–22; reinforced by uncertainty,
   130–31. See also linearity
CBS, Menendez case miniseries on, 15–
   16, 150–51
celebrities, televised trials of, 163
Celebrity (film), 271n. 26
certainty. See closure/certainty
chance. See fate/chance
Chandler v. Florida, 152–62
character types: common-sense motivation for, 118–22; critical approach to
   stereotypes in, 138–39; fate and, 168,
   259; "fetish power" and, 192–93; mutability of, 188–91, 294n. 20; transformation of, 30–31; trickster as,
   133–34, 189–90, 283–84n. 28; understanding differences in, 43. See also archetypes; double; hero
checks and balances: concept of,
   239–40; as constitutional theory, 238.
   See also popular culture; Tocqueville,
   Alexis de
Chicago Seven, 156, 287n. 18
Chopin, Kate, 94–95, 96
Cicero, 298–99n. 38
civil disobedience, 84
Civilization and Its Discontents (Freud),
   181
Civil War, 84–85, 87
Clark, Marcia, 44–45, 219
Clark, Tom C. (justice), 248, 290n. 40
Clarke, David B., 282n. 23
Clifford, Clark, 150, 288n. 24
Clifford, Robert, 147–48
Clinton, Bill, 16, 301–2n. 25

closure/certainty: absence of, 116–17; break from, 187; denial of, 104, 122, 249; embrace of, 130–31; fate vs., 124; need for, 135–39; self-deception in, 121; truth/justice and, 11, 47, 108–9

Cochran, Johnnie, 24, 45–47, 219

cognition: film/video viewing and, 21–22; print culture vs. visual images and, 6; styles and habits in, 23–26, 273n. 2

Columbine High School (Littleton, Colo.), student shootings in, ix

commodification: in art, 28–29; in law, 148, 151, 166, 242, 262; in popular culture, 23–24

common law, virtual caselaw divorced from, 193

common sense: beliefs contained in, 47–48; as check on abstract principles, 239–41; creating framework for, 118–22; enthymeme and, 218–19; limitations of, 50; logic vs., 42; manipulation of, 217, 241–42; principled resistance to, 215–16, 265–66n. 6

communal tool kit: concept of, 18–22; function of, 22–23, 136–39, 141, 205; knowledge constructed in, 211; lawyers' knowledge of, 25–26, 38; meaning lost outside of, 81. *See also* Bruner, Jerome

communication: in democracy, 251; manipulation of, 220, 296–97n. 6; simulation vs., 128

communication practices (law): expanded understanding of, 10–11; implications of, 8; limits of, 240–41; models for, 26–27; multiplicity of, 238–40, 246–47; political discourse tactics in, 7. *See also* checks and balances; litigation public relations; storytelling; visual images

communitas, use of term, 52, 231, 274–75n. 22, 299nn. 39–40

The Confidence Man (Melville), 85–86

conflict: competing claims in understanding, 237–38; cultural, 39, 73–78, 249,
253; function of, 230–31; as narrative framework, 26; symbolic, 69–71, 73–75

con man, implications of, 278n. 26

consistency/contradiction, cognitive implications of, 118–22

constructivist approach. *See* affirmative postmodernism; skeptical postmodernism; tragedy

consumption: art's disappearance into, 28–29; components of, 260; familiarity in, 144, 285–86n. 9; of image, 225–26; of law, 27–30, 150–52, 167–68, 242; postmodern self and, 186; reality tied to, 142–44

contradiction/consistency, cognitive implications of, 118–22

Cooper, Cynthia, 271n. 23

Coppola, Francis Ford, 30

corporations, public relations of, 148

Cotchett, Joseph, 18, 270n. 9

Coulter, Ann, 302–3n. 30

Courtroom Television Network, 163, 165, 226, 290n. 36

Cover, Robert, 36, 77, 277n. 14

creativity, affirmative postmodernism nourished in, 194–95. *See also* art

crime story genre, 114, 281n. 14. *See also* genres

criminal justice system: expansion of, 168, 184, 293n. 10; law and, 268–69n. 15; paradox of, 291–92n. 2; police fantasies and, 164; social healing and, 184–85

criminals: anxieties about, 165–66; coerced confessions of, 215, 265–66n. 6; definition of, 183–84, 246–47; forcible confinement of sexual, 168, 291n. 48; as "Other," 164, 168, 247, 260–63; predator stereotype of, 140, 164–66, 218; prison conditions for, 292n. 5; television programs on, 164–65, 247. *See also* double

critical legal studies movement, 209

Crossfire (television program), 301–2n. 25

C-SPAN, 251
cult of personality (Mussolini's), 224
cultural convergence: concept of, 4,
    17–19; as condition for pop law, 5,
    24
cultural critic, role of, 253
culture: affirmative postmodernism nour-
    ished in, 194–95; alternatives in,
    9–10; anxieties in, 165–66, 186–87,
    202; conflicts in, 39, 73–78, 249, 253;
    enchantment and, 212, 230; interdisci-
    plinary legal studies and, 10–11, 138;
    law's influence on, 5–6, 8, 36, 266–
    67n. 8; media's role in, 171, 304n. 33;
    norms and, 69, 194; rationality/irratio-
    nality in, 206–8; as source of law,
    ix–x, 33, 37, 48–49, 74, 193; story-
    telling practices in, 205; as symbolic
    order, 5. *See also* communal tool kit;
    language

Darden, Christopher, 44–45, 219
Darrow, Clarence, 25, 95
Davis, Richard Allen, 290n. 38
Dean, John, 156
Debord, Guy, 265n. 4
deceit: fears of, 221–22, 226–28; irratio-
    nality linked to, 207–8. *See also*
    fiction
Declaration of Independence, 78, 83
DeLillo, Don, 44, 109
DeLisle v. Rivers, 289n. 32
Demjanjuk, John, 149–50
democracy: communication needs of,
    251; cultural change and, 39; threats
    to, 245–46, 249–51; wealth in, 279n.
    43
De Niro, Robert, 175
Denny, Reginald, 78, 193
Denziger, Steven R., 284–85n. 5
derealization: concept of, 27–28, 266n.
    7; implications of, 8, 262–63; process
    of, 23–24, 32–33; of sexuality, 243.
    See also commodification
Derrida, Jacques, 209
Descartes, René, 51, 207, 208, 221

desire: alternative form of, 260; aware-
    ness of, 235; in *Cape Fear* (1991),
    175–76, 178–84; commoditization of,
    23–24, 262–63; condemnation of
    other in, 104–5; enchantment and,
    221–22; horror genre and, 202; identi-
    fication with, 92–93, 98–99; in *Lost
    Highway*, 189–91; media's exploita-
    tion of, 167–69; modernity's repres-
    sion of, 208; postmoderns' infatuation
    with, 186; power of, 219–20; preda-
    tor criminal and, 166; in *Red*, 255,
    259–60
Dieckmann, Katherine, 281n. 16
Dillinger, John, 120
Dilthey, Wilhelm, 211
Dionysus, 191, 222–23, 294–95n. 21
"Dirty Harry" (character), allusions to,
    272n. 34
disenchantment: with law, 171–72,
    176–77; with marriage, 171–72,
    177–79; in popular culture, 171–72,
    227. *See also* skeptical postmodernism
disorder: in case details, 108–9, 121–22;
    laws of complexity and, 238–39; rejec-
    tion of, 130–31; truth of, 261–62. *See
    also* fate/chance; science; uncertainty
"Dr. Death" (Grigson, James), 113, 114
docudramas: aired before trials, 150–51,
    288–89n. 26; allusions to, 24; on
    Amy Fisher, 27; antidocumentary
    frame in, 122, 123–26; impact of,
    107–9, 247; perspective of, 15–16; as
    reality, 141. See also *The Thin Blue
    Line* (film)
Doel, Marcus A., 282n. 23
Doke, Tim, 148
Donovan, Jeremiah, 30, 31–33
The Doors (film), 19
Dostoevsky, Fyodor, 86, 208
Do the Right Thing (film), 24
double: creation of, 293n. 13; Dionysus
    as, 294–95n. 21; function of, 261;
    identity breakdown and, 189–90; in
    pop culture, 179, 184; social healing
    of, 184–85

Douglas, Mary, 192–93
Douglass, Frederick, 46, 81–82
Dow Corning Corporation, 273n. 3,
    288n. 20
Doyle, Arthur Conan, 188
Dracula (Stoker), 222, 296n. 27
Dragnet (program), 19
Dred Scott case, 78
Drexel Burnham Lambert (firm), 149
Dunlap, Earl, 292n. 5
Dworkin, Ronald, 250, 251

Eco, Umberto, 146
economy: diminished faith in control of,
    201, 295n. 24; uncurbed market
    forces in, 95, 102, 279n. 44
"ecstasy of the real," use of term, 128
Eden, Kathy, 212, 214
Edmundson, Mark, 202–3
Edshu (trickster), 283–84n. 28. *See also*
    Harris, David; Kali; *Lost Highway*
    (film)
Egoyan, Atom, 25
Ehrman, Mark, 271n. 27
Eisner, Michael, 304n. 33
Eisner, William, 286–87n. 15
Eliade, Mircea, 51–52, 67–68
Emancipation Proclamation, 84
Emerson, Ralph Waldo, 79, 81–82
emotions: about notorious legal cases,
    74; in argumentation vs. storytelling,
    45–47; commodification of, 258, 262;
    hyper-catharsis and, 166; in litigation
    public relations, 147, 167; manipula-
    tion of, 242, 298n. 36; in mythic real-
    ity, 60–65; perception influenced by,
    33; rejection of, 44–45
enchantment: affirmative dimension of,
    13, 232–33; capacity for, 230–31,
    252–53; craving for, 206–7, 212,
    227–28; of esthetics, 230; forms of,
    231–32; function of, 262–63; law's
    need for, 241–42, 254; power of,
    222–24; suspicion of vs. belief in,
    221–22
engineering of consent, 142–43

Enlightenment: reconsideration of,
    238–39; rhetoric and, 136. *See also*
    modernity
entertainment: journalism driven by, 35–
    36, 244; law conflated with, 155, 248,
    290n. 36
enthymeme, concept of, 217–19
epistemological anxiety. *See* anxiety
equality, filmic symbolization of, 254
Estes, Billie Sol. See *Estes v. Texas*
Estes v. Texas: jurisprudence of appear-
    ances and, 152–61, 290n. 40; refer-
    ences to, 289n. 32; on televising noto-
    rious legal cases, 140, 155, 248
estheticization of the real: concept of,
    26–27, 29–30; life as image and,
    271n. 25. *See also* commodification
esthetics: of deliberate normative con-
    struction, 231–32; disorder vs.,
    130–31; enchantment of, 230; of
    skeptical postmodernism, 224–26
Eumenides (Aeschylus), 181, 213,
    292n. 6
Euripides, 52
Evarts, William, 91
evidence: common-sense vs. expert,
    300n. 9; critical approach to, 138–39;
    logic of Romance as, 90–91; as pieces
    of jigsaw puzzle, 45; social status and,
    123; storytelling via, 41; visual vs.
    print, 154–55. *See also* expert opin-
    ion; judicial expertise; visual images
Ewen, Stuart, 226, 284n. 3
Ewick, Patricia, 269n. 17
The Executioner's Song (Mailer),
    265n. 1
exemplar, as mythic truth, 67–69
expert opinion: expression of, 266n. 7;
    reliance on, 227. *See also* judicial ex-
    pertise
Eyes on the Prize (documentary), 24

Failla, Louis, 31–33
Falasca-Zamponi, Simonetta, 224
familiarity: desire for, 144, 285–86n. 9;

trial stories and, 167–68. *See also* common sense
family: as dysfunctional, 178–80; redemption for, 182–83
fantasy: cost of, 76, 79–83, 93; denials in, 86–87; function of, 83–84; in notorious legal cases, 76–77; as response to anxiety, 75; transformation of, 88–90; violence condoned in, 99–104
Farber, Daniel A., 297n. 17
fate/chance: Aeschylus on, 284n. 29; affirmative postmodernism and, 195–200, 263–64; awareness of, 235, 260; concepts of, 281n. 15; hero and, 58; legal system and, 137; modernity's repression of, 208; in *Music of Chance*, 195–200; as reality, 282n. 18; in *Red*, 255–59; rejection of, 130–31; in *The Thin Blue Line*, 123–24
FBI (Federal Bureau of Investigation), 53–54, 55, 61, 62
Federal Election Commission v. Massachusetts Citizens for Life, Inc., 302n. 27
federal government: as antagonist, 55–56, 58–63; in antitrust action, 148; distrust of, 156; litigation public relations of, 148–49
federalism, jurisprudence of appearances and, 159
Federalist Paper no. 10, 249–51
Feigenson, Neal, 269n. 17, 285n. 7
Ferguson, Robert, 18, 79, 81, 276n. 7, 277n. 17
Ferrington, Gary, 303n. 31
"fetish power," use of term, 192–93
fiction: manipulation of, 220; method of, 3–4, 6–7, 12, 212–20, 229–30, 232–33; as protective fantasy, 75; reality commingled with, 128–29; Romance style of, 276–77n. 8; truth's linkage with, 36–37, 47–48, 274n. 13; validation of, 47–48, 146. *See also* enchantment; fantasy; narratives; storytelling
Fifth Amendment, 215

film: about storytelling, 125–26, 133; affirmative postmodernism in, 133–39, 172, 195–203, 255; allusions to, 24, 120, 125, 129, 272n. 34; audience expectations and, 30–31; cognitive tools in, 21–22, 272n. 38; irrationality in, 172, 255–59; law and fiction mingled in, 3–4; law's transformation into, 17–18; as legal persuasion, 270n. 9; reality construction and, 34, 37–38; skeptical postmodernism in, 171–72, 176–85, 187–93; as social reality, 15–17; style in, 19–20; tragic constructivism in, 13, 254–60; "unique aura" lost in, 266n. 7. *See also* specific films
Finkel, Norman J., 265n. 5
First Amendment, 251, 300n. 4, 302n. 27
Fisher, Amy, 27, 34–35
Fiske, John, 14, 37
Fitzpatrick, Kathy, 287n. 18
Flaton, Robin, 270–71n. 21
Fleischner, Cheryl, 147
Folette, Mazie, 279n. 40
Ford, John, 19, 79
Ford, Richard, 266n. 7
Fox, Richard Wightman, 74, 93, 278n. 24
Fox Network, Menendez case docudrama on, 15–16, 150–51
fraternity, 254–57, 260, 263. See also *Red* (film)
Freeman, Robert, 149
Freud, Sigmund: on civilization, 181; irrationality and, 209; on punishment, 190; on return of repressed, 70; on self-estrangement, 86; symbolic truth and, 51
The Fugitive (film), 33
Fuhrman, Mark, 46–47, 162
futurism (Italian), 224

Gavin, William, 145
Geertz, Clifford, 267n. 9

gender relations: in notorious cases,
    93–96; Romantic ideal and, 93–94
genres: audience expectations based in,
    30–31; melodramatic, 96–97, 102–5;
    modernity's impact on, 94–95; post-
    modern, 123–33; understanding differ-
    ences in, 43; utilizing different, 219.
    See also crime story genre; Gothic
    genre; myth; Romantic era; Victorian
    ethos
Gentile v. Nevada, 289n. 29
Gerbner, George, 27, 140, 291n. 43
Gerrig, Richard, 48, 146, 274n. 13
Girard, René, 184
Giuliani, Rudolph, 149
Glass, James M., 294n. 19
Glass, Philip, 3, 125
global media literacy movement, 19,
    210, 251–52, 303n. 31
The Godfather (film), 30, 31
Goethe, Johann Wolfgang von, 208
Goetz, Bernhard (case): as archetype,
    35; defense strategy of, 134–35, 218;
    fantasized facts in, 73; as part of ver-
    nacular of society, 5–6
Gold, Stuart W., 288n. 20
Goldberg, Vicki, 29
Goldman, Ronald, 16, 47
Goldman, Sachs (firm), 149
Goodrich, Peter, 267n. 10
Gorgias: communication and, 296–97n.
    6; irrational enchantments of, 206–7;
    knowledge and, 225; on persuasion,
    220, 227, 232, 298n. 36
Gorney, Carole, 273n. 45, 289n. 28
Gothic genre: essence of horror in, 296n.
    28; in Lost Highway, 296n. 27; re-
    vival of, 201–2, 295n. 25, 295–96n. 26
Gourevitch, Philip, 280n. 3
Graham, David, 288–89n. 26
Grand Canyon (film), 20–21
Greek drama: contradictions in tragic,
    292–93n. 9; inability to rationalize
    and, 294n. 19; law's link to, 181, 212,
    292n. 6; logos/mythos in, 222–23. See
    also specific characters

Greene, William Chase, 281n. 15
Grigson, James ("Dr. Death"), 113, 114
Grodal, Torben, 267n. 10
guilt: denial of Brown's, 83–84; factual
    vs. legal, 265–66n. 6; making sense
    of, 115, 127. See also verdict
Gulf War, hyperreality and, 242–43,
    301n. 13

Haas, Philip, 172, 195. See also The Mu-
    sic of Chance (film)
Habermas, Jürgen, 236, 299–300n. 2
Haldeman, H. R. "Bob," 145
Hamlet (Shakespeare), 41, 44, 74, 249
Harlan, John M. (justice): jurisprudence
    of appearances and, 156, 160–61,
    162, 290–91n. 41; law clerk of, 290n.
    39; on notorious cases, 248, 249
Harper's Ferry (Va.), Brown's raid on,
    75, 78, 276n. 7, 277n. 17
Harris, David: actions of, 110–11; on
    fate, 124; film's portrayal of, 118–20;
    Goetz defense applied to, 134–35; on
    guilt/innocence, 127; testimony of,
    112, 121–22; as trickster, 133–34,
    283–84n. 28
Harris, Kevin, 53, 54, 64
Hawks, Howard, 19
Hayden, Tom, 287n. 18
Heidegger, Martin, 209, 223–24
Heine, Heinrich, 208
Heraclitus, 191, 259, 295n. 23
Herdt, Gilbert, 299–300n. 2
Herman, Edward S., 295n. 24
hero: act of resistance by, 62–63; in
    Brown trial, 76, 78–80; call to adven-
    ture for, 56–58; construction of, 76,
    219; fate of, 58; juror identification
    with, 73; mythic reality for, 60–62;
    as narrative genre in Beecher trial,
    90–91; resurrection stage for, 65; re-
    turn to ordinary by, 65–66; supreme
    ordeal for, 63–65; task of, 58–60,
    132–33; Thaw as, 99–100, 102–3. See
    also Amsterdam, Anthony G.; Coch-
    ran, Johnnie; Spence, Gerry

Herrera v. Collins, 280n. 8
*Herskovits v. Group Health Coopera-
tive,* 291–92n. 2
Hesiod, 204
Hesse, Hermann, 208
Hilfer, Tony, 114, 281n. 14
Hill & Knowlton (firm), 150
historians, methods of, 213
Hoffman, Abbie, 287n. 18
Holbrook, John, 113
Hölderlin, Friedrich, 208
Holliday, George, 212–13, 272n. 38
Holocaust, 77
Homer, 201, 221–22
Homicide: Life on the Streets (television
program), 290n. 36
Horiuchi, Lon, 54
Horton, Willie, 155
human experience: affirmative dimension of, 194, 199; in *Red,* 255–59. *See
also* derealization; lived experience
humor, as storytelling tool, 32–33
hyper-catharsis, 166, 243. *See also* jurisprudence of appearances
hyperreality: appearances in, 141, 193;
authenticity and, 266n. 7; definition
of, 68, 242; emergence of, 29–31,
128; example of, 242–43, 301n. 13;
function of, 262–63; implications of,
247, 301n. 16; informational excess
and, 23–24; transformation into, 31–
33, 38. *See also* derealization; jurisprudence of appearances; simulacrum

icons, function of, 155
Imken, Otto, 283n. 26
impeachment proceedings, 16, 301–2n.
25
In Cold Blood (Capote), 265n. 1
information: cultural anxieties about,
186–87; excess in hyperreality, 23–24;
onscreen packaging and, 26; for public entertainment, 244
insanity standard, 98–101
insider trader cases, 49, 149
interpenetration: of law/fiction, 4, 31,

33; of pop culture/legal culture, 15–
17, 24, 34; of rhetoric/knowledge, 229
irony: advertising and, 144–46; of contemporary criminal justice, 173; danger of, 226, 230; in skeptical postmodernism, 220–21, 243–44
irrationality: attempt to come to grips
with, 172, 200–201; influence of, 7–8;
law in service of, 193–94; as law's
tool, 188, 192–93; names for, 201,
295n. 25; patterns of, 231–32; rationality vs., 206–8; reconceptualization
of, 238, 263–64; in *Red,* 255–59; repression of, 211–12; resurgence of,
188, 190–93, 208–9, 220, 235. *See
also* Lynch, David; magic; skeptical
postmodernism
Isocrates, 229, 232
Iyengar, Shanto, 285n. 7

Jackson v. Denno, 215, 265–66n. 6
James, Caryn, 16, 301–2n. 25
James, William, 51, 67
Jaws (film), 47, 146
Jefferson, Thomas, 57, 65, 66–67, 223
Jewett, Helen, 35
JFK (film), 19
Johnson, Lyndon B., 153
Jones, Paula, 16
Joyces, James, 208
Judeo-Christian tradition, 137
judges: directions for jury from, 48; jurisprudence of appearances and, 290–
91n. 41; litigation public relations
and, 150, 151
judicial expertise: as check on popular
passions, 239–41, 245, 247; virtues
of, 5
judicial system: avoiding antinomian impulse, 245; condemnation of, 80; destabilization in, 4–5; public confidence
in, 156–64, 167–68. *See also* criminal
justice system; law
Jung, Carl Gustav, 106
jurisprudence of appearances: concept
of, 10; cultural anxieties and, 165–66;

jurisprudence of appearances (*continued*)
development of, 152–62, 241, 247;
emotions in, 167; estheticization and,
226; federalism and, 159; Gothic revival in, 202; legal process in, 167–69;
magical appearances and, 193; skeptical postmodernism and, 12–13; Supreme Court and, 141, 152–61

jurors: attention span of, 25; certainty
needed by, 117; common sense and,
265–66n. 6; deliberations of, 48–49;
expectations of, 30, 215–16, 271n.
27; folk knowledge of, 18–19; frames
of reference of, 279–80n. 1; function
of, 265n. 5; media's manipulation of,
217; mythic experience for, 51–52,
56–57, 132–33; Oprahization of, 271–
72n. 33; as passive vs. protagonists,
45–47; in Ruby Ridge trial, 54–66; sentencing procedure and, 280n. 10; television and film viewing by, 16–17; terror management and, 275n. 36; trial
as test of, 91; TV audiences vs., 163;
verdict formation by, 24, 270–71n.
21, 271n. 23; virtues of, 5. *See also*
checks and balances; common sense

Kaelin, Brian "Kato," 16, 162–63
Kafka, Franz, 86, 208
Kali, 191, 222, 283–84n. 28
Kansas v. Hendricks, 291n. 48
Kant, Immanuel, 236
Kasdan, Lawrence, 20–21
Katsh, Ethan, 272–73n. 41
Kauffman, Stuart, 238
Kazantzakis, Nikos, 208
Keating, Charles H., Jr., 18, 270n. 9
Kennedy, Edward, 286n. 12
Kennedy, John F., 145
Kermode, Frank, 76
Kerrigan, John, 222, 235
Kieslowski, Krzysztof, 254–55. *See also*
Red (film)
King, Martin Luther, Jr., 84, 156, 260
King, Rodney (case): digital reconstruc-
tions and, 272n. 38; legacy of, 78,

193, 277n. 20; as "mediapheme,"
155; naive realism vs. storytelling in,
212–13; as part of vernacular of society, 5–6; verdict in, 277n. 20

Klaas, Polly, 290n. 38, 293n. 13. *See
also* "Three-strikes-and-you're-out"
law

Klein, Alvin, 281n. 12

knowledge: construction of, 138, 211,
221; enthymeme and, 218–19; lay and
expert, 5; learning without involvement, 144–45; multiple forms of,
216–17, 239–41, 251. *See also* checks
and balances

Kohlberg, Lawrence, 299–300n. 2

Korematsu v. United States, 240

Korobkin, Laura Hanft, 81, 90–91,
278nn. 26–28

Kronman, Anthony T., 2

Krugman, Herbert E., 144–45

Kuhn, Deanna, 270–71n. 21

Kuhns, Richard, 172, 183, 184, 185

Lacan, Jacques, 209

language: function of, 27–28; idealized
norms of, 236, 299–300n. 2; raising
spirits and, 222–24; reconceptualization of, 209–11; uncertainties and imbalances in, 235–38, 240–41

Lanham, Richard, 6, 267–68n. 11,
300n. 6

Larry King Live (television program),
288n. 25

law: autonomy of, 17, 39; as check on
popular passions, 36–37, 171, 244,
247; commodification of, 139,
262–63; culture's contribution to, 6,
18–19, 37; destabilization of, 192–93;
disenchantment with, 171–72,
176–77; expanded understanding of,
10–11; in face of fate/chance, 195–96;
legitimation of, 167–69; postmodernization of, 7, 37–39; postmodern-
primitive phase of, 192; rule of police
vs., 164–65; weapons of, 241–42. *See
also* culture; legitimation

law cases. *See* trials
Law & Order (program), 16
lawyers: function of, 205–6; primary strategies of, 126–28; professional conduct rules for, 151–52; as storytellers, 4, 25, 206; training for, 138, 252–53, 288n. 22. *See also* jurisprudence of appearances; legal persuasion; litigation public relations
Lear, Jonathan, 208, 296n. 5
Leary, Timothy, 88
Le Bon, Gustave, 224, 226
Lee, Ivy L., 142
Lee, Spike, 24
legal fictions, evaluation of, 38
legal meaning making: changing due to historic/cultural demands, 4–5, 81; enchantment and, 206; process of, 277n. 14; visual media's impact on, 12, 18–19
legal persuasion: adaptations in, 6–7; fictional method in, 4, 6, 212–20, 232–33; magic of, 206; objectives of, 213, 231–32; popular culture's impact on, 241; tactics of, 25–26. *See also* persuasion; rhetoric
legal reasoning, types of, 42–43
legitimation: conditions for, 216, 238–39; crisis of, 5, 163, 240–41, 245. *See also* cultural convergence; law
Lesser, Wendy, 72
Levine, Dennis, 149
Lévi-Strauss, Claude, 192, 193
liberty, filmic symbolization of, 254
Lifton, Robert Jay, 294n. 19
Lincoln, Abraham, 84, 277n. 17
Lincoln Savings and Loan, 18, 270n. 9
linearity: arguments based in, 126–27; associative reasoning vs., 37; common-sense framework and, 118–22; deconstruction of, 127–28; effects of, 115–17, 137–38; nonlinearity's reinforcement of, 129–31; reconceptualization of, 13; truth's link to, 136. *See also* causality

Lippmann, Walter, 142, 155
litigation public relations: concept of, 7; danger of, 242; development of, 241, 287n. 18, 289n. 28; motivation for, 148–50, 244; rules for lawyers' conduct and, 151–52; tactics of, 146–49, 167; training in, 288n. 22. *See also* jurisprudence of appearances
lived experience: cognitive styles and, 273n. 2; concept of, 211; eclipsed by mass media, 217, 260; law's evasion of, 38, 269n. 17; tragic knowledge and catharsis in, 183. *See also* common sense; derealization; reality; uncertainty; Warhol, Andy
Lochner v. New York, 279n. 44
logic: appeal to, 44–45; common sense vs., 42; emotions and, 45–47; of visual mass media, 171–72, 242–43, 250
Long Island Lolita (Fisher, Amy), 27, 34–35
Lopate, Phillip, 19–20
Lost Highway (film): cultural context of, 171; desire in, 222; Gothic genre's influence on, 296n. 27; male characters in, 294n. 20; reading of, 190–91; storyline of, 188–90
Love's Deadly Trial: The Texas Cadet Murder (film), 288–89n. 26
Lungen, Dan, 271–72n. 33
Lynch, David, 172, 187. See also *Lost Highway* (film); *Twin Peaks* (film and series)
Lyotard, Jean-François, 235

MacNeil, Robert, 142–43
Madison, James, 23, 249–51
Madison Square Roof Gardens, 98
mafia: as symbol, 30–31; trial of members of, 31–33
magic, as form of law, 192–93. *See also* enchantment; irrationality
Mailer, Norman, 265n. 1
Malinowski, Bronislaw, 66
Mallarmé, Stéphane, 208–9
Malle, Louis, 16

Mander, Jerry, 285n. 8
Manson, Marilyn, 298n. 29
The Man Who Shot Liberty Valance
    (film), 79
Marcum, Deanna, 23
Marinetti, Filipo Tommaso, 224
Marquard, Oto, 282n. 18
Martel, Myles, 288n. 22
Maslow, Abraham, 66–67
Mason, Perry (character), 272n. 34
mass media: agendas in, 302–3n. 30; on
    Beecher trial, 85–93; on Brown trial,
    78–80; desire exploited in, 167–69;
    disenchantment with, 171–72; enter-
    tainment-driven journalism in, 35–36,
    244; logic of, 171–72, 242–43, 250;
    power of, 249–51; responsibility of,
    244; on Thaw trial, 96–97, 98–99. *See
    also* litigation public relations; televi-
    sion; visual mass media
mature constructivism, concept of, 221
Maxis Corp. v. Kidder, Peabody Co., 49
McChesney, Robert W., 295n. 24
McGuinniss, Joe, 145, 286n. 12
McLuhan, Marshall, 145
McVeigh, Timothy, 16, 290n. 38
meaning making: in affirmative postmod-
    ernism, 131–33, 233; alternatives in,
    107–8; challenge for, 136; compo-
    nents in, 211–12; critical thinking
    about, 251–53; disorder in, 108–9; of
    guilt/innocence, 115, 127; irrational-
    ity and, 172, 200–201; judgment of,
    220; in linear vs. nonlinear storytell-
    ing, 115–17, 125–26; multiple ways
    of, 210–11, 236, 239–41; psychologi-
    cal need for, 130–31; by public,
    18–19; responsibility for, 138–39; so-
    cial scripts for, 22; tools for, 237; un-
    certainty in, 186–87. *See also* legal
    meaning making
media literacy movement, 19, 210, 251–
    52, 303n. 31
"mediapheme," use of term, 155
medical malpractice suits, 291–92n. 2
Melville, Herman, 85–86

Mencken, H. L., 279n. 43
Menendez, Erik, 15–16
Menendez, Jose, 150
Menendez, Lyle, 15–16
Menendez case: films about, 15–16; liti-
    gation public relations and, 150–51,
    288n. 25
metaphors: knowledge production and,
    139; in *Red,* 255–56; of reversions,
    124–26
Metcalfe, Don, 119–20, 129, 280–81n.
    11
Metz, Christian, 267n. 10
Meyer, Linda Ross, 268–69n. 15
Milken, Michael, 149
Mill, John Stuart, 211–12
Miller, Emily, 119, 125, 129, 280–81n.
    11
Miller, Henry, 179, 208
Miller, Mark Crispin, 144
Milton, John, 222
Miranda, Ernesto, 219
Miranda warnings, 289n. 27
Mitchell, John, 156
modernity: alternatives to, 9–10; correc-
    tives for, 7–8; dichotomies in, 51,
    108–9, 210, 228, 235; diminished
    faith in, 200–201; end of monopoly
    of, 38–39; epistemological anxiety
    about, 76, 85–93; "lite" version of,
    104–5; rationalist mindset in, 192,
    207–8; rhetoric rejected in, 136; shift-
    ing understanding of, 233, 246; skepti-
    cism and uncertainty in, 103–4; wom-
    en's roles in, 94–95. *See also*
    reactionary rationalism
Moore, Albert J., 279–80n. 1
moral anxiety. *See* anxiety
moral righteousness, in Thaw trial, 98–
    104, 278n. 38
Morris, Errol: on abnormal behavior,
    281n. 16; on interview setting, 282n.
    19; modern and postmodern storytell-
    ing by, 12, 117, 128; revisions of, 3,
    133–39; on truth, 11, 281n. 12. See
    also *The Thin Blue Line* (film)

Morse, Ruth, 252

murder: cases of, 76, 96–105, 147; filming of actual, 15; in *Lost Highway*, 188–91; in television news stories, 284–85n. 5; television programs on, 163, 165; in *Twin Peaks*, 187–88. *See also* Adams, Randall Dale (case)

Murphy v. Florida, 289n. 32

Murray, Timothy, 47

The Muses, 221–22

The Music of Chance (film): affirmative postmodernism in, 172; message of, 195; storyline of, 196–99

Mussolini, Benito, 224

mutual confidence, use of term, 276n. 3

mutually assured seduction, concept of, 27, 167–68, 217, 244. *See also* jurisprudence of appearances

My Dinner with Andre (film), 16

myth: affirmative postmodernism and, 200–203; articulating law's, 233; beliefs influenced by, 63–65, 262–63; emotions in, 60–65; function of, 66–68, 212, 262–63; interpenetrating reason, 186; *Music of Chance* as, 197–200; order reinforced through, 34–36; power of, 172, 223–24; as response to anxiety, 75; Ruby Ridge trial and, 54–66; symbolic truth enacted in, 45–47, 50–52, 132–33; as tool, 13; trickster in, 283–84n. 28

narratives: components of, 42–44, 218–19; episodic vs. thematic, 285n. 7; framework for, 26–27; identification of, 19, 41; jurors' need for, 24; multiplicity of, 137, 229–30; symbolic conflicts among, 69–71, 73–75; truth constructed in, 219–20. *See also* common sense; genres; storytelling

Native American Church, 236–37, 300n. 4

Natural Born Killers (film), 16–17, 19

Nazism, 181, 223–24, 293n. 13

Nazi war criminals, 149–50

Nelson, Alvin "Hooty," 112

Nelson, Charles, 112

Nelson, Frank, 112

Nesbit, Evelyn: characterization of, 99–102, 279n. 41; testimony of, 279n. 42; Thaw's relation with, 97–98, 279n. 40; in trial, 96; White's relation with, 97

Nesson, Charles, 158, 290n. 39

Nestor, 221–22

The NewsHour with Jim Lehrer (television program), 302–3n. 30

Nichols, Terry, 16

Nietzsche, Friedrich, 8, 191, 283n. 25

A Night to Remember (film), 272nn. 39–40

1984 (Orwell), 241, 300n. 11

Nixon, Richard M., 89, 145, 156

nonlinearity: approach to, 122; arguments based in, 127; concept of, 20–21; deceit's traditional link to, 136; fate and, 123–24; linearity reinforced by, 129–31; metaphors of reversions and, 124–26

normalization: clarification of, 77; of consumption, 143–44; source of, 69

Norman, Donald, 272–73n. 41

notorious legal cases: of adultery, 76, 85–93; anxiety in, 12, 75, 249; as community catharsis, 162–63, 166, 243; definition of, 248–49; as double trials, 77, 102–3; of murder, 76, 96–105; related to slavery, 75–76, 78–85; social/cultural conflicts in, 73–78, 231, 249, 253; televised, 153–56, 160–61, 162, 166, 248, 290–91n. 41; types of anxiety in, 75–76, 249; unrepresentativeness of, 245

novels: crime, 130, 281n. 14; nonfiction, 265n. 1

Nuckolls, Charles W., 281n. 13

Oates, Stephen, 79, 277n. 12

objectivity: appeal to, 44–45; reconceptualization of, 13, 209; rejection of possibility of, 296–97n. 6. *See also* truth/justice

Oedipus, 186, 259. *See also* tragedy

Offut v. United States, 289n. 31
opening/closing statements: affirmative
  postmodernism applied in, 132–33; in
  Beecher trial, 90–92; length of, 25; in
  Ruby Ridge trial, 12, 52, 54–66; in
  Simpson trial, 44–47; in Thaw trial,
  100–101, 278n. 38; video as replace-
  ment of, 34, 272nn. 39–40
order: effort to obtain, 43–44; in face of
  fate/chance, 195–96, 199–200; harmony in, 199–200; mythicizing to create, 186, 201–2; mythic organizing
  principles of, 293–94n. 17; need for,
  126, 137–39; reinforced through myth,
  34–36; revelation and, 137; in social reality, 8; symbolic restoration of, 69
Orwell, George, 241, 300n. 11
Ovid, 201

Paradise Lost (Milton), 222
particularization, increase of, 37
Patterson, Dennis, 269n. 17
penny press, 35
Perelman, Chaim, 232
Pericles, age of, 295n. 25
Persephone, 222
persuasion: in affirmative postmodernism, 131; art of, 205–6; controlling reality in, 37–38; critical approach to,
  138–39; as drug, 297n. 22; as enchantment, 298n. 36; look of reality as, 34;
  manipulation through, 227; means of,
  25–26; raising spirits and, 222–24; as
  science, 232; suspicion of, 221–22; triumph of illicit, 243. *See also* enchantment; legal persuasion; rhetoric
pcyote, legal perspective on, 236–37,
  300n. 4
Phillips, Wendell, 82, 277n. 15
Piesiewicz, Krzysztof, 254–55. See also
  Red (film)
Pirandello, Luigi, 40
Plato, 206–7, 221, 227, 228–29
Plessy v. Ferguson, 84
pluralization, 37, 210
poetry: inspiring truth/judgment via,

214, 221–22; as source of affirmation,
  211–12
police: constitutional limits on, 215,
  247, 265–66n. 6; fantasies about,
  164–65; television programs on, 163–
  65, 193, 247
politics: campaign expenditures and,
  302n. 27; cognitive habits and, 23–24;
  competing discourses and, 239–40;
  controlling reality in, 37–39; corruption in, 156; disenchantment with,
  171–72; media's influence on, 250; retribution and, 165–66; soundbites in,
  286n. 13; spin control and, 145–46
Pollock, Jackson, 209
Pop Art, 28–29
popular culture: affirmative postmodernism in, 194–95; control over, 142; disenchantment in, 171–72, 227; Gothic
  archetypes in, 201–2, 295n. 25, 295–
  96n. 26; image-based logic of, 5, 28;
  law's convergence with, 7, 168–69,
  171–72, 226, 240–41, 244–45; order
  reinforced through, 34–36; proliferation of, 39; as source of law, 17–19,
  24; "use value" in law, 146–47. *See
  also* postmodernism; visual images;
  visual mass media
Poster, Mark, 23
postmodernism: challenges of, 245–47;
  characteristics of, 186–87; dangers in,
  220, 226; as fatal to law, 9; Gothic
  genre in, 201–2, 295n. 25, 295–96n.
  26, 296n. 27; increasing skepticism in,
  200–201; opposing forces in, 262; possibilities in, 209–11, 294n. 19. *See
  also* affirmative postmodernism; skeptical postmodernism
Pottawatomi massacre, 79
premodernity: postmodernity's use of,
  210; primitive law in, 192–94
print culture, 6, 154–55
productive disequilibrium, 238–40
Protagoras, 232
psuchagogein, use of term, 222
public: cognitive habits and, 23–26;

information for, 244; meaning making by, 18–19; media literacy skills of, 19, 210, 251–52, 303n. 31; skepticism of, 245, 248

public opinion: cases tried in, 146–49, 216–17, 287n. 18; on judicial system, 156–64, 167–68; on justice, 152–55. *See also* litigation public relations

public relations: engineering of consent in, 142–43; function of, 262–63; origins of, 224, 227; reality constructed in, 142; skeptical postmodernism and, 12–13; tactics of, 146–48. *See also* advertising; litigation public relations

public spectacles, 68–70. *See also* rituals; trials

Pulp Fiction (film), 30–31, 33, 224–25

Pythagoras, 207

quiz show, scandal of, 301n. 21

race, in Adams case, 113

race relations, divisions over, 84, 156

racism, symbolic battle against, 45–47

radical disenchantment/skepticism. *See* skeptical postmodernism

rape, 147, 165, 177

Rapping, Elayne, 291n. 45

rationality: diminished faith in, 200–201; failure of, 187–93; folk knowledge vs., 294n. 18; irrationality repressed by, 211–12, 228; limits of, 230, 235–36, 238, 263–64; oscillations with magic and logic, 206–8; patterns of, 47, 231–32; rebellion against, 208–9; science's impact on, 136; skeptical postmodernism vs., 193–94

Rawls, John, 236

reactionary rationalism, 9, 11, 268–69n. 15

reality: cognitive styles and, 273n. 2; conforming to beliefs, 73; construction of, 24–25, 30–31, 34, 41, 137, 141–42, 212–13; consumption tied to, 29, 142–44; control of, 37–38; denial of,

76, 83–84; disappearance of, 282n. 24; fantasy's blurring with, 185; fiction commingled with, 128–29; fragmentation of, 125–26; framework for, 27–28; internal and external, 191–92; myth and, 50–52, 60–62, 66–69. *See also* estheticization of the real; hyperreality; social reality

reality effect: cultural anxieties and, 165–66; source of, 47–48, 146

reason. *See* rationality

Red (film): lessons from, 259–60, 262; storyline of, 255–59; tragic constructivism in, 13, 254–55

repression: anxiety as symptom of, 261–62; externalized, 247; Other conceived via, 293n. 13; through unconscious displacement, 9–10, 11. *See also* return of the repressed

responsibility/accountability: affirmation of, 229; in affirmative postmodernism, 200, 253–54; criminal, 300n. 9; mutability of self vs., 294n. 19; in skeptical postmodernism, 129

return of the repressed: after unresolved trial, 70–71, 76–78, 249; signs of, 208; skeptical postmodernism and, 194; strength of, 228; in unresolved conflict, 231

rhetoric: affirmative dimension of, 13, 232–33; critical thinking in, 252–53; fear of, 226–27; function of, 229–30; philosophy and, 300n. 6; rejection of, 136, 207–8; truth vs., 51; understanding culture through, 209–11; wisdom and eloquence in, 298–99n. 38. *See also* legal persuasion; meaning making; persuasion

Richardson, Gary, 151

Richmond, Rev. George Chalmers, 103

Richmond Newspapers, Inc. v. Virginia: Brennan on, 251; Burger on, 161–62

Ries, Al, 24

Riffaterre, Michael, 20

rituals: absence of, 228; function of, 51–52; legalistic devices in, 192–93;

rituals (*continued*)
 process in, 274–75n. 22; stale vs. dy-
 namic, 230–31. See also *communitas;*
 trials
robbery: jury deliberations and, 48–49;
 in television news stories, 284–85n. 5
Rogers, Earl, 95–96
Rogers, Richard, 53
Romance: modern melodrama vs.,
 103–5; sentimental genre of, 76, 78–
 84, 95, 276–77n. 8
Romantic era: Civil War and, 84–85;
 gender relations and, 93–94; rebellion
 of, 208–9
Romilly, Jacqueline de, 233, 234
Rosenau, Pauline Marie, 268n. 14
Rosenberg, Howard, 288–89n. 26
Rosenblatt, Abram, 275n. 36
Rowe, Jonathan, 285n. 8
Rubin, Jerry, 287n. 18
Ruby Ridge (Idaho). See Spence, Gerry;
 Weaver, Randy (case)

sadomasochism, rise in preoccupation
 with, 202
Sandel, Michael, 165
Sarat, Austin, 269n. 17
Sartre, Jean-Paul, 117, 242
Scheck, Barry, 30, 302–3n. 30
Scheherazade, 205
Schiller, Johann Christoph Friedrich
 von, 208
Schorr, Daniel, 243
Schubart, Rikki, 179, 295–96n. 26,
 296n. 28, 298n. 34
Schulhofer, Stephen J., 291–92n. 2,
 293n. 10
Schwartz, Tony, 144, 285–86n. 9
science: complexity and disequilibrium
 in, 238; rationality linked to, 207–8
Scorsese, Martin, 171–72. See also *Cape
 Fear* (film, 1991)
Segal, Charles P., 229, 296–97n. 6,
 297n. 22, 298n. 36
segregation, 84
Seigel, Jerrold E., 298–99n. 38

self: autonomous, 13; commodification
 of, 261, 262–63; concepts of, 17, 129,
 131, 278n. 28; construction of, 19,
 23–24, 236, 246; as distributed and
 situated, 209–11; emancipatory aspect
 of postmodern, 294n. 19; enchantment needed by, 212; estrangement of,
 86; mutability of, 188–91, 241, 294n.
 19; reconceptualization of, 238; in
 spirit religions, 294n. 20; transcendence of, 66–67; transcendentalists'
 focus on, 81–83
self-mutilation, 298n. 29
The Selling of the President (McGuinniss), 145
sensationalism, 35, 38
sentimentality, use of term, 23. *See also*
 genres
Seward, William, 196
sex crimes: film's depiction of, 177; Supreme Court on, 168, 291n. 48; television programs on, 163, 165. *See also*
 rape
Shakespeare, William: on discord, 123;
 Hamlet, 41, 44, 74, 249
Shelley, Percy Bysshe, 202
Sherman, Rorie, 270n. 9
Sherry, Suzanna, 297n. 17
Shiva, 191, 283–84n. 28
Shweder, Richard, 236, 299–300n. 2
Sidney, Philip: on enchantment, 232; on
 the fictional method, 212, 214, 229;
 on law and poetry, 4, 13; on persuasion, 206; on testing truth claims,
 213; on truth, 204
signs: in public spectacles, 68; reality as
 effect of, 37–38, 282n. 23
Silbey, Susan S., 269n. 17
Simpson, Nicole Brown, 16, 47
Simpson, O. J. (case): Beecher trial compared to, 85, 88–89; closing arguments in, 44–47; fictional method in,
 12, 29, 219; film allusions and, 24;
 Kaelin video and, 16; legacy of, 245,
 249; merging with television and film
 reality, 29–30; as part of vernacular of

society, 5–6; televising of, 162–63; verdict in, 163; witnesses' "gigs" in,
288n. 23
simulacrum: concept of, 128–29, 265n.
4, 282n. 23; law as, 139. *See also*
hyperreality
simulation, 29, 128
Singer, Mark, 281n. 16
skeptical postmodernism: affirmative
postmodernism vs., 126–28, 231–32;
alternatives to, 9–10, 13; authenticity's degeneration in, 13, 27, 259–60,
266n. 7; in *Cape Fear* (1991), 171–72,
176–85; choice offered by, 221, 297n.
17; components of, 7–8, 23–24, 37–
38, 104–5, 166; countersigns to, 195–
203; cultural manifestations of, 13,
168–69; dangers of, 11, 12–13, 235,
245; emergence of, 26–28; esthetics
of, 224–27; evaluation of, 194–95; explanation of, 128–31; failure of, 129,
202–3; irony in, 220–21, 243–44; law
and, 172–85, 186–95, 200–203; in
Lost Highway, 188–91; trend toward,
171–72; in *Twin Peaks,* 187–88,
192–93
slavery, cases related to, 75–76, 78–85
Slotnick, Barry, 134–35, 218
Smith, Janna Malamud, 74, 277n. 21
Smith, Susan, 290n. 38
Smith, Vicki, 49
*Smith v. Employment Division, Depart-
ment of Human Services,* 300n. 4
social class: cases related to, 76, 95, 98–
102. *See also* wealth
social reality: acausal construction of,
125–26; beliefs for understanding,
123, 212; breakdown of, 13; conceptions of, 17, 21–22; construction of,
19, 23–25, 141–42, 236, 246; film as,
15–17; media-constructed signs of,
266n. 7; multiple approaches to, 241;
"order" in, 8; situational nature of,
210
social system: destabilization in, 4–5;
diminished faith in, 201; postbellum

changes in, 87–88; values under-
girding, 52
"society of the spectacle," use of term,
265n. 4
socioeconomic anxiety. *See* anxiety
Socrates, 4, 232, 233
Sophists, 206–7, 213, 227, 229
Sophocles, 52, 116
Spence, Gerry: closing argument by, 12,
52, 54–66; mythic reality created by,
56–68; reminiscence by, 275n. 38; tac-
tics of, 69, 218, 219
Stachenfeld, Avi J., 274n. 16
*Standard Chartered PLC v. Price Water-
house,* 272nn. 39–40
Starr, Kenneth, 16
Star Wars (films), allusions to, 55, 57,
61
states' rights, jurisprudence of appearances and, 159
State v. Adams, 280–81n. 11
State v. Billings, 289n. 32
State v. Harris, 289n. 32
Stevenson, Robert Louis, 86, 277n. 21
Stewart, Potter (justice), 159
Stigler, James W., 299–300n. 2
Stoker, Bram, 222, 296n. 27
Stone, Oliver, 16–17, 19–20, 225
storytelling: acausal-nonlinear frame in,
122, 123–26, 133; alternatives suppressed in, 107–8, 111; believability
of, 136–39; causal-linear frame in,
117–22; details and disorder in, 44,
107–9, 121–22; emotions and, 45–47;
expectations in, 19, 107; film about,
125–26; function of, 4, 34–36, 81,
105; hyperreality in, 31–33; opposing
plot lines in, 115–17; order internal
to, 43–44; proving truth via, 41–43;
structure of in courtroom, 25–26,
41–42; televisual type of, 19; trial sum-
mations and, 44–47; truth/justice produced in, 12; understanding use of,
10–11, 212–13. *See also* fiction; meaning making; narratives
Struever, Nancy S., 298–99n. 38

subway vigilante. *See* Goetz, Bernhard (case)
suffrage movement, 94
Surette, Ray, 140, 164–65, 284–85n. 5
Sweeney, Ann, 271–72n. 33

talk shows: litigation public relations and, 150–51, 288n. 25; ratings drive of, 302–3n. 30
Tarantino, Quentin: audience expectations of, 298n. 34; on estheticized violence, 225; *Pulp Fiction* and, 30–31, 33, 224–25
Tarde, Gabriel, 224, 226
Taylor, Clarke, 280n. 3
technology, 6–7, 25, 33–34, 272–73n. 41. *See also* mass media
television: allusions to, 24, 272n. 34; cognitive tools in, 21–22; "context of no context" in, 265n. 4; courtrooms affected by, 155–61; crime shows on, 285n. 6; episodic vs. thematic narratives in, 285n. 7; esthetic of, 225–26; fiction/truth confused in, 167, 290n. 36; image control in, 142–43; law's transformation into, 17–18; Nixon on, 145; nonprofit stations and, 251, 303n. 29; packaging messages for, 147–48; program models in, 19; reality's construction and, 34, 301n. 16; trials on, 153–64, 167–68, 226, 247–48, 290n. 36, 290n. 40. *See also* docudramas
terpsis, use of term, 230
terror: assimilation and transcendence of, 223; defense against, 247; studies in management of, 275n. 36
Texas: death penalty statute in, 113, 120, 280n. 10; Texas cadet murder case in, 288–89n. 26. *See also* Adams, Randall Dale (case); *The Thin Blue Line* (film)
Thaw, Harry (case): circumstances of, 96–99; legacy of, 249; as melodrama, 96–97, 102–3; socioeconomic anxiety

in, 76, 93–94, 95–96, 98–104; verdict in, 98; wealth issue in, 101–2, 104
The Thin Blue Line (film): acausal-nonlinear frame in, 122, 123–26, 133; achievement of, 126; causal-linear frame in, 117–22; failures in, 3, 123, 127–31, 133, 139; images in, 129–30; impact of, 107–8, 114–15, 280–81n. 11; interview setting in, 282n. 19; legal meaning making and, 11, 109; motivation for making, 114; opposing plot lines in, 115–17, 137–39, 187; order vs. revelation in, 137; portrayal of defendant in, 120; revisions in, 133–39; skeptical postmodernism and, 12; veracity of, 107–8, 135–36, 141. *See also* Adams, Randall Dale (case)
Thompson, J. Lee, 173. See also *Cape Fear* (film, 1962)
Thompson, J. Walter, 145
Thoreau, Henry David, 79, 81–83
"Three-strikes-and-you're-out" law, ix, 293n. 13
Tigar, Michael E., 26, 149–50, 279–80n. 1
Tilton, Elizabeth, 85, 89, 278n. 24
Tilton, Theodore, 85, 87, 91–92
Tilton v. Beecher, 85–93
time: in *Lost Highway,* 190–91; sacred type of, 51, 68–69; transcendence of, 66–67
Titanic (ship), in trial summation, 272nn. 39–40
Tocqueville, Alexis de, 36–37, 171, 265n. 5
Toffler, Alvin, 170
tragedy: origin of, 222–23; as source of wisdom, 184, 237, 259–60
tragic constructivism: catharsis and, 184–85; function of, 229–30; multiplicity acknowledged in, 237–41; in *Red,* 13, 254–60; truth and justice in, 260–64. *See also* affirmative postmodernism
transcendentalists, John Brown trial and, 79, 81–83

trials: dangers of televised, 13, 248–49; function of, 213–14; Greek drama as source of, 181, 292n. 6; language in, 18–19; multiple forms of knowledge in, 216; narratives/counternarratives in, 35; out-of-court alternatives to, 245; principal strategies in, 126–28; purification via, 69; reality constructed in, 24, 41; reliving things through, 44; right to fair, 151–61; storytelling's function in, 4; as symbols of conflicting cultural forces, 69–71, 73–75; televised, 153–64, 167–68, 226, 247–48, 290n. 36, 290n. 40; television barred from, 290n. 38; truth and fiction confused in, 48–49, 150–51. *See also* notorious legal cases; *specific individuals and cases*

Trilling, Lionel, 278n. 28

Trout, Jack, 24

Trow, George W. S., 265n. 4

truth/justice: in affirmative postmodernism, 131, 136, 229–33, 260–64; affirming law's construction of, 39; beliefs in relation to, 85–87, 281n. 12; closure/certainty and, 11, 47, 108–9; construction of, 47, 114, 187, 209, 216; deception and, 36; evaluating claims of, 213–14, 217–20, 232–33, 237–38; factual type of, 49–50; fate and, 124; fictional method and, 47–48, 214–15, 229–30; indeterminacy of, 12, 116–17; legal ("higher") type of, 50; local vs. universal, 37, 137–38, 236–37; magical vs. legal, 193; multiplicity of, 217–18, 229–30, 239–41; mutual confidence in, 276n. 3; popular perceptions of, 152–55; productive disequilibrium applied to, 238–39; rational vs. rhetorical, 207–8; skepticism about, 171–72, 181–83; symbolic type of, 45–47, 50–52, 74, 80, 91

Tucher, Andie, 35–36

Turkle, Sherry, 34, 272–73n. 41, 294n. 19

Turko (officer), 121

Turner, F. J., 279n. 43

Turner, Victor: on *communitas*, 52, 274–75n. 22, 299nn. 39–40; on social dramas, 230, 299n. 39

Tushnet, Mark, 302n. 27

Twining, William, 111

Twin Peaks (film and series): context of, 171; reading of, 192–93; storyline of, 187–88

Twitchell, James B., 126, 282n. 23

tyranny: defense against, 247, 250; mass media's, 251; multiple faces of, 241–42

Uelmen, Gerald, 288n. 23

uncertainty: cultural changes and, 186; effects of, 130–31, 268–69n. 15; implications of, 121–22, 125–26; irony of, 173; meaning making in, 186–87; in modernity, 103–4

unconscious: denial of, 226; emergence of belief in, 85–86; function of, 212

United States Supreme Court: on civil disobedience, 84; on coerced confessions, 215, 265–66n. 6; fallibility of, 240; on First Amendment, 251, 300n. 4, 302n. 27; images of, 156–57; jurisprudence of appearances and, 141, 152–61; laissez-faire philosophy of, 102, 279n. 44; on lawyers' out-of-court statements, 151–52; on sexual offenders, 168, 291n. 48; on slavery, 78; on televising trials, 13, 153–61, 167–68, 226, 247–48, 290n. 36, 290n. 40; on Texas death penalty statute, 113, 120, 280n. 10

United States v. Bianco, 30, 31–33

universal reason: limits of, 236; reconceptualization of, 13, 238. *See also* rationality

values: advertising's influence on, 301n. 15; social system undergirded by, 52; threats to, 70–71; in transition to modernity, 87–88. *See also* beliefs; *communitas*

Vattimo, Gianni, 37
verdict: in Adams trial, 107–8, 113; in Beecher trial, 86, 92; in Brown trial, 79, 80; as journey's completion, 65–66; in King trial, 277n. 20; matching story to desired, 42–43; pretrial publicity and, 288n. 20; in Simpson trial, 163; in Thaw trial, 98; in Weaver trial, 275n. 39
verisimilitude: establishment of, 20, 219–20; legal reality and, 167; truth/fiction in, 146
Vernant, Jean-Pierre, 292–93n. 9, 294n. 19, 295n. 25
Vico, Giambattista, 232, 265n. 2
Victorian ethos, 75, 85, 93–94. See also genres
Vidal-Naquet, Pierre, 292–93n. 9, 294n. 19, 295n. 25
video. See film
Vietnam war, 156
violence: in Cape Fear (1962), 174–75, 182; in Cape Fear (1991), 178–84; condoned in fantasy, 99–104; estheticization of, 224–26; of law, 183–84; as law's weapon, 241–42; television programs on, 163–65
Virginia Board of Pharmacy v. Virginia Citizens Consumer Council, 302n. 27
virtual reality, x, 7, 24–28, 33–34
visual images: authority of, 154–55; as commodity, 225–26; in consciousness, 270n. 11; context of, 31; emotional associations of, 33; history of, 267n. 10; hyper-catharsis and, 166, 243; impact of, 6, 25; increased use of, 25–26; lack of control of, 162–63; number per minute, 143–44, 285n. 7; preferences in, 142–43, 284–85n. 5; simulacrum and, 128–29; in Supreme Court decisions, 154–56; truth/fiction of, 146; understanding differences in, 43; use of term, 267n. 10. See also hyperreality; technology
visual mass media: backstage and frontstage reality in, 286n. 14; con-

sumption tied to, 142–44; format of, 143–44, 285n. 7; Gulf War in, 242–43, 301n. 13; hyper-catharsis through, 166, 243; literacy in, 19, 252, 303n. 31; meaning making in, 5, 22–24; model of truth/justice in, 17; overstimulation in, 23–24; pervasiveness of, 37–38, 284n. 3; political manipulation of, 145–46; proliferation of mass culture through, 39; reality constructed by, 24–25; as source of communal tool kit, 21–22; storytelling's function in, 4; surface images in, 19–20; thought processes shaped by, 18–19; truth/fiction confused in, 141, 152, 167–69. See also communication practices (law); hyperreality; public relations
Vogler, Christopher, 65
Voltaren (drug), 147

Wachtler, Sol (judge), 151
Walker v. City of Birmingham, 277n. 19
Walt Disney Company, 304n. 33
war, estheticization of, 224, 242–43, 301n. 13
Warhol, Andy: on art/culture as commodity system, 28–29; on derealization and hyperreality, 14, 243, 259–60, 266n. 7, 301n. 16; on emotions, 258, 262; on enchantment, 227. See also commodification; consumption; interpenetration
Warner, Marina, 294n. 20
Warren, Earl (justice): hyperreality and, 157–61; public opinion on, 156; quiz show scandal and, 301n. 21; on televising trials, 154–59, 248, 290n. 36, 290n. 40
Washington, George, 57, 66–67, 223
Watergate crisis, 156, 247
wealth: in democracy, 279n. 43; power of, 250; in Thaw case, 101–2, 104
Weaver, Elisheba, 53, 54
Weaver, Jack, 275n. 31
Weaver, Rachel, 53

Weaver, Randy (case): closing arguments in, 12, 52, 54–66; factual background of, 52–54; fictional methods in, 219; verdict in, 275n. 39. *See also* Spence, Gerry

Weaver, Sammy, 53, 64

Weaver, Sara, 53, 54

Weaver, Vicki, 53, 54

Weber, Max, 192, 193

Webster, Daniel, 84

Weinstock, Michael, 270–71n. 21

Welby, Marcus (character), allusions to, 272n. 34

Wellington, Ralph, 148

Wexler, Robert, 301–2n. 25

White, Byron S. (justice), 126, 159–61, 215

White, James Boyd, 232, 266–67n. 8

White, Stanford: accusations against, 101–4; characteristics of, 96–98, 99, 100; murder of, 76, 98; as symbol of wealth, 101–2

White, Terry, 212. *See also* King, Rodney (case)

White (film), 254

Whitman, Walt, 67

Wigton, Richard, 149

Wilde, Oscar, 23

Williams, Damian, 193

Williams, Francis, 92

Williamson, Judith, 26

Winfrey, Oprah, 271–72n. 33

Wittgenstein, Ludwig, 117

The Wizard of Oz (film), allusions to, 57, 61

Wood, Robert, 107–13. *See also* Adams, Randall Dale (case)

Woodhull, Victoria, 89

Woodward, Bob, 156–57

Wordsworth, William, 208, 212

World War II, Japanese Americans in, 240

Yippies, litigation public relations and, 287n. 18

Young, Alison, 271n. 25

Zamora, Diane, 288–89n. 26

Žižek, Slavoj, 77, 234, 293n. 13